XML: A Primer

Third Edition

XML: A Primer

Third Edition

Simon St.Laurent

M&T Books

An imprint of Hungry Minds, Inc.

New York, NY ♦ Cleveland, OH ♦ Indianapolis, IN

XML: A Primer, Third Edition

Published by
M&T Books
An imprint of Hungry Minds, Inc.
909 Third Avenue
New York, NY 10022
www.hungryminds.com

Library of Congress Control Number: 2001089112

ISBN: 0-7645-4777-1

Printed in the United States of America

10 9 8 7 6 5 4 3 2 1

3O/SX/QU/QR/IN

Distributed in the United States by Hungry Minds, Inc.

Distributed by CDG Books Canada Inc. for Canada; by Transworld Publishers Limited in the United Kingdom; by IDG Norge Books for Norway; by IDG Sweden Books for Sweden; by IDG Books Australia Publishing Corporation Pty. Ltd. for Australia and New Zealand; by TransQuest Publishers Pte Ltd. for Singapore, Malaysia, Thailand, Indonesia, and Hong Kong; by Gotop Information Inc. for Taiwan; by ICG Muse, Inc. for Japan; by Intersoft for South Africa; by Eyrolles for France; by International Thomson Publishing for Germany, Austria, and Switzerland; by Distribuidora Cuspide for Argentina; by LR International for Brazil; by Galileo Libros for Chile; by Ediciones ZETA S.C.R. Ltda. for Peru; by WS Computer Publishing Corporation, Inc., for the Philippines; by Contemporanea de Ediciones for Venezuela; by Express Computer Distributors for the Caribbean and West Indies; by Micronesia Media Distributor, Inc. for Micronesia; by Chips Computadoras S.A. de C.V. for Mexico; by Editorial Norma de Panama S.A. for Panama; by American Bookshops for Finland.

For general information on Hungry Minds' products and services please contact our Customer Care department within the U.S. at 800-762-2974, outside the U.S. at 317-572-3993 or fax 317-572-4002.

For sales inquiries and reseller information, including discounts, premium and bulk quantity sales, and foreign-language translations, please contact our Customer Care department at 800-434-3422, fax 317-572-4002 or write to Hungry Minds, Inc., Attn: Customer Care Department, 10475 Crosspoint Boulevard, Indianapolis, IN 46256.

For information on licensing foreign or domestic rights, please contact our Sub-Rights Customer Care department at 212-884-5000.

For information on using Hungry Minds' products and services in the classroom or for ordering examination copies, please contact our Educational Sales department at 800-434-2086 or fax 317-572-4005.

For press review copies, author interviews, or other publicity information, please contact our Public Relations department at 317-572-3168 or fax 317-572-4168.

For authorization to photocopy items for corporate, personal, or educational use, please contact Copyright Clearance Center, 222 Rosewood Drive, Danvers, MA 01923, or fax 978-750-4470.

 is a trademark of
Hungry Minds, Inc.

 is a trademark of
Hungry Minds, Inc.

Credits

Acquisitions Editor
Grace Buechlein

Project Editor
Susan Christophersen

Technical Editor
Ethan Cerami

Copy Editor
S. B. Kleinman

Project Coordinator
Jennifer Bingham

Graphics and Production Specialists
Amy Adrian, Joe Bucki,
Brian Torwelle

Quality Control Technicians
Dwight Ramsey, Marianne Santy,
Charles Spencer

Book Designer
Kurt Krames

Proofreading and Indexing
York Production Services, Inc.

Cover Image
© Noma/Images.com

About the Author

Simon St.Laurent is a Web developer, network administrator, computer-book author, and XML troublemaker living in Ithaca, N.Y. His books include *XML Elements of Style, Programming Web Services with XML-RPC, Building XML Applications,* and *Cookies.* He is a contributing editor to xmlhack.com and an occasional contributor to XML.com.

For Tracey, who sparkles

Preface

Extensible Markup Language (XML) has been hyped and hyped and hyped in the press. With this third edition of *XML: A Primer*, I hope to show you the reality of XML, exploring its current situation as well as several possible future directions.

XML has roared from specification to buzzword to implementation. Thousands, perhaps even millions, of developers and users are using services built on XML without necessarily knowing it. E-commerce developers, systems integrators, Web developers, document managers, and a wide variety of programmers are using XML as a common glue for connecting information to an enormous number of different systems. Microsoft has used "He doesn't know what XML is" as a catchphrase in a television advertisement, and XML is on list after list of technologies worth watching.

XML has changed dramatically since I began writing the first edition of this primer three years ago. At that time, it seemed possible to describe all of the possibilities of XML 1.0 and its related specification in detail in one slim volume, providing a concise but comprehensive introduction. The first edition had many times as many pages as the XML specifications of the day, and while the specifications could be difficult reading, the structures they described weren't especially complex. Now the specifications vastly outweigh this book, but more and more developers need an introduction to the technology. One of those specifications, *W3C XML Schemas*, even has its own 92-page primer!

The XML community has also diversified substantially since XML 1.0 first appeared. Initially, XML's reputation as "SGML for the Web," its home at the World Wide Web Consortium (W3C), and its focus on hypertext and integration with existing Web technologies made it seem as if XML would be the next tool of choice for Web developers. The SGML community provided the initial XML core community, bringing experience, tools, and an understanding of document-centric information modeling. While these groups have made, and continue to make, a substantial contribution to XML, developers building channels of communications among computers make up much of the community actually building XML-based applications.

XML: A Primer, Third Edition remains focused on users and developers using XML for the first time, but the approach has had to change. Readers will find detailed coverage of the core of XML — XML 1.0, Namespaces, and DTDs — but coverage of the supplemental technologies is necessarily introductory, with pointers to other resources. This edition covers XML processing styles, while leaving the details to other tutorials more sharply focused on particular approaches.

Most developers working with XML struggle to find a set of tools they're comfortable with and then work inside that set for a while before branching out. In this book I focus on the core set of tools developers need to understand to get started and then discuss the rest of the ever-growing and often contentious toolbox. The examples should get you started thinking through the process of creating your own documents.

XML got its start as a small and relatively simple technology, for which we have a small crew of visionaries and bold pioneers to thank. Its continuing development has sometimes been arduous, but developers can reap the benefits of a large toolset created by a variety of developers. Many of those developers have effectively given away their work, either as open-source software or as helpful words in community forums, giving XML a rich foundation of tools and practices in addition to a set of specifications. I hope that this new edition of *XML: A Primer* will introduce a few more members to that community and the toolset it shares and builds.

Whom This Book Is For

This book should help anyone who's just getting started with XML. Its biases lean toward the document side of information processing, but those interested in using XML to exchange raw data should find useful information as well. HTML developers will have a head start, coming to XML with an understanding of basic markup, but I hope that anyone with a basic understanding of the Web will be able to understand it. This book is definitely a primer — you won't find extended explanations of some of XML's odder corners or code samples for programmers — but you should get a thorough grounding in XML markup.

Conventions Used in This Book

Throughout the book, XML and HTML content is presented in monospace type. If you encounter monospace type in the middle of a regular sentence, it refers to an XML or HTML structure or content.

Icons Used in This Book

Most of this book is the usual mix of text and pictures, but every now and then some important information stands out, useful as an aside, a tip, a reference, or, most important of all, a warning.

Note

Notes provide extra details about the topic being discussed, which not everyone may find as exciting as I do. Notes provide extra information that may be useful but shouldn't be critical.

Tip

Tips are the kind of information that often doesn't make it into traditional documentation but are learned through hard experience. Tips are appropriate to every situation but can be real time-savers when they appear.

Caution

Caution icons are important. You may not think there's a problem, but ordinary-seeming actions can have dire consequences. Read the Caution to avoid potential problems.

Acknowledgments

Tracey Cranston has seen three editions of this book go by, and this edition is much better thanks to her comments and her support. Ann Lush saw the potential in this book when it was first getting started, and Grace Buechlein kept this edition rolling. Thanks to Susan Christophersen and Eric Newman for their work in developing the book, and S. B. Kleinman for cleaning up my language. Thanks to Ethan Cerami for his hard work at technical review, though all mistakes, as always, are mine.

Contents

Part II: Describing Documents

Part III: Supporting Specifications

Part IV: Building Your Own Markup

Part I

Getting Started

Chapter 1

Structured Labeled Information

XML, the Extensible Markup Language, promises to transform the basic structure of the Web, moving beyond HTML and replacing it with a stronger, more extensible architecture. XML provides developers with a way to create their own tightly structured and clearly labeled formats for documents and data. XML could free the Web from format-based structures, creating a Web where data has parity with documents. The developers of the dominant Web browsers are losing their stranglehold on Web vocabulary development and implementation as XML opens the gates to a much larger community. XML also promises application developers, whether or not they work on the Web, an extremely convenient format for storing many different kinds of information.

XML makes it possible — even easy — for developers to create their own interoperable dialects of markup languages, including but no longer limited to HTML. XML enables developers to create markup structures based on logical content rather than on formatting. This intelligent markup will make it easier for humans and computers to search for specific content-based information within a document rather than just search the entire text of a page.

XML's origins lie in document processing, but much of its current application lies in data exchange. The "document-data divide," the continuing argument about different needs, is a persistent feature of the XML user community, but XML has an enormous amount to offer both sides. XML may even have the potential to abolish that division once and for all. XML, in concert with style technologies, will enable authors to create attractive pages that are also easy to manage. At the same time, it gives all kinds of developers a new level of control over their information, as well as enormous flexibility.

The Document Side

XML's foundations are thoroughly document-oriented. XML enables us to picture documents that are unconstrained by proprietary formats while also supporting the ability to integrate a wide variety of data structures. Although the current state of XML applications for document creation and management isn't entirely encouraging, XML at least offers possibilities for a brighter future. XML makes it possible to create documents free of the limitations of what-you-see-is-what-you-get (WYSIWYG) approaches and the one-size-fits-all vocabulary HTML provides.

The WYSIWYG disaster

The first word processor I used was a very simple text editor. I thought it was really amazing how the screen could move around my cursor point to make my 40-column screen display most of an 80-column page, but for the most part the editor was good only for doing homework and writing other similarly boring documents that I printed on my lovely dot-matrix printer.

After working with computers for a few years, programming them and cursing them, I gave up and bought an electric typewriter. It let me do some pretty fancy things, such as underline text without having to enter bizarre escape codes. A good way to type boldface text wasn't available, but I didn't have to worry about wasting acres of paper because of a typo in a strange code. The typewriter gave me WYSIWYG in a classic ink-on-paper kind of way.

I stuck with my typewriter for a couple of years until I discovered the Macintosh. I hated the Mac when it first came out, because every magazine I got covered an expensive machine I didn't own. The Mac didn't even have a decent programming package. But when I encountered the Mac again about four years later, I was thrilled. Writing papers was actually fun (sort of) because I could toggle all the style information, write in multiple columns, and even use 72-point type once in a while. It didn't look very good on my ImageWriter, but it was pretty amazing compared to my old dot-matrix computer text. I turned in papers with headlines, bibliographies that used proper italics, multiple columns, and even a picture or two. Writing wasn't just about spewing out sentences anymore. I could create subheads, tables, and footnotes, and use all kinds of other formatting to give even a short paper a structure that made it look deceptively smart. Using styles made applying a set of formatting tools just once, and then calling those tools up as a named set, even easier. It seemed like magic.

Ten years later, I still format my documents with headings and subheads. Fortunately, I'm not as concerned about footnotes, but I've developed a new problem: reusing my old documents is hard. When I was writing papers for a grade, the ability to reuse documents didn't matter very much—I wrote the paper, turned it in, and never thought about it again. Now I spend my days working with piles of information written years ago by people thousands of miles away; converting all the files into the same word-processing format is the least of my worries. Instead of editing material, I frequently find myself spending hours reformatting it, and not because I love doing so. A whole generation that grew up abusing tabs and spaces (typewriter habits die hard) has created documents that can't be cut and pasted into other documents because everything breaks. Line breaks come out totally wrong, text gets shoved to the left or right, tables collapse, and even simple things such as line spacing cause problems. The same magic formatting that made creating documents that looked exactly the way they should so easy is now creating massive problems.

Other, more subtle problems exist as well. All those years when I thought I was creating headlines and subheads, I wasn't really. I was creating text that was formatted like a headline. I might even have called the style "headline," but to the computer, "headline" didn't mean anything except font size. WYSIWYG changed people, too. People who probably shouldn't have been allowed to graduate from a fifth-grade art class started using 30 fonts on a page. After the novelty wore off, many of them adopted a more conservative approach to formatting, but always with the declared intention of making their documents look precisely the way they wanted them. Designers became accustomed to specifying placement to thousandths of an inch — as if anyone can see differences measured in such a small increment.

Before WYSIWYG, documents were undoubtedly ugly, but they had virtues that went unnoticed. There were moves afoot to create document-management and document-markup systems that would enable computers to efficiently manage large libraries of documents. Plain text, dull though it may be, is much easier to manage than the output of the average word processor or desktop publishing program. There's no formatting to remove, no characters that won't translate, none of the weird stuff that appears when you transfer text from one application to another. Document-management tools were very new in the early days of WYSIWYG, and they didn't become affordable or readily available until long after users had become accustomed to systems that used paper-based, and therefore WYSIWYG, media. The final printout of a document always remained the ultimate goal of most of the design programs on the market.

The HTML explosion

When the World Wide Web first received widespread attention in 1994, a small army of amateur and professional designers set out to create the most exciting pages they could. Many left quickly; accustomed to full WYSIWYG environments, they were disappointed by the dearth of HTML formatting tools. Further, the strange differences among browsers made predicting what any page would look like difficult, and corporate users demanded a level of layout control over their electronic documents that was similar to the control they had over paper documents. For a while, these limitations nearly throttled HTML development.

Like many Internet technologies before it, HTML was used by enthusiasts who were working for fun and because HTML was interesting. HTML was simple enough to learn in a day or two, and it offered a whole new reading and authoring experience. The momentum generated by these early enthusiasts and the press coverage they received gave HTML the potential to become the next big thing.

For the Web to become an economically viable marketplace, however, HTML had to change to meet user demands. Designers and their employers wanted to be able to create pages that looked precisely the way they wanted them, and they wanted to have a level of control comparable to that provided by the average desktop publishing system. An often explosive browser war (in which the designers were frequent casualties) led to more powerful, though hazardously incompatible, dialects of HTML, which the W3C (World Wide Web Consortium, a group organized to manage standards on the Web) has more or less cobbled together into HTML 4.0. HTML still isn't exactly a simple page-layout system for the average user, but the tools have become a lot more convenient. Web design has become a specialty of designers and communications specialists the world over, making it possible for companies and individuals to create sophisticated, if not always visually pleasing, sites.

Tables were a huge step forward for HTML design, though their widespread usage subverted many strongly held opinions about the proper application of tables. Designers applied tables to create documents that bore some resemblance to the traditional grid systems used in many print designs, using them in many situations that required much more than the normal tabular display of information in rows and columns. Continuing improvements in image-map technology made it easy for frustrated designers to create their own point-and-click interfaces when HTML just couldn't produce what they needed. Frames and pop-up windows enabled developers to focus on pieces of information and overall presentation rather than have to rebuild entire screens of information every time something changed. The <FONT> tag made it possible to specify text presentation much more precisely than the old structure-based formatting had allowed. Escalating competition between Microsoft and Netscape added all kinds of tools to the workbench as the companies fought for market share and mind share. Netscape created <BLINK>; Microsoft countered with <MARQUEE>. Both companies created extensions to the elements and the attributes of HTML, yet they did not implement tags in exactly the same way. Spacing varied, colors could change, and carefully aligned elements would scatter across a page. Checking site layout in multiple browsers was, and is, confusing for developers and requires enormous expenditures of time and money.

Note

If the constant bickering over standards, and vendors' apparent lack of interest in complying with them, bothers you, explore the Web Standards Project (http://www.webstandards.org). HTML's semi-standard nature and vendors' partial implementations of other standards, including CSS and XML itself, has driven a significant group of Web developers to take up arms in defense of standards.

The number of pages on large Web sites exploded. Sites routinely grew to include 10,000 pages or more, vaguely organized into hierarchical schemes concocted by developers who knew little about hypertext and apparently even less about organization. Many sites were organized according to cluttered directory structures built by developers who were originally conditioned by the structures of FTP archives and gopher sites, the predecessors of the Web.

The combination of volume and increasingly complex formatting led developers to wonder whether a better way might exist to mark up a document. HTML has come a long way quickly, but the constraints of a markup language designed for formatting are beginning to cause developers to chafe. As the browser wars move into a new phase, designers are beginning to demand an alternative to letting the browser determine the presentation of individual tags. The limitations of search engines become more apparent every time the Web doubles in size. Finally, as the Web grows more toward omnipresence, the limitations of HTML for presenting information that doesn't easily fit the standard text and graphics model are becoming more pressing. For example, we are now seeing a whole new array of devices for browsing the Web, including handheld computers, Web phones, and video-game consoles. Developers need to be able to create their own tag vocabularies, and they need to be able to do so in a way that will work with their customers' browsers.

Navigating HTML debris

Large sites presented continual difficulties to the managers who had to keep up with them and the users who attempted to read them. Navigating hypertext is a strange art form all its own, a blend of memory on your part, good design on its part, and sheer luck. Designing it is even more difficult. Search engines arrived to help users find their way, but it quickly became clear that librarians, even those with massive computing power available, could never keep up with the explosive growth of this new medium.

Automated tools appeared as crawlers and robots began searching the enormous swamp of Web documents. Some merely indexed titles, whereas more sophisticated ones began to index the entire contents of a page. AltaVista (`http://www.altavista.com`), a search engine originally created by Digital to demonstrate and promote its Alpha processor, used brute force to index the Web, applying multiple processors that shared gigabytes of memory and enormous bandwidth. Although AltaVista, like many other search engines, can and does provide a service, it's a blunt instrument that provides imprecise results by searching the complete contents of a document.

We've managed to confer a lot of intelligence on search engines, even letting them identify languages and handle word forms, but we're still a very long way from teaching them to read, categorize, and organize documents without our having to specify which part is which. For the most part, the formatting information that humans use to recognize key parts of a document is discarded by the search engines.

Back to the origins: Structure and SGML

When Tim Berners-Lee created HTML in 1991, he based it in part on a more powerful but vastly more complex markup language called SGML, the Standard Generalized Markup Language. SGML had been around in various forms for 20 years, but its complexity had hobbled its adoption by organizations outside of publishing, government, and large-scale information processing. SGML markup, management, and processing were specialized skills mastered by a small group of government, corporate, and academic users.

Developers who complain that the XML and HTML standards are developing too slowly may want to look back at the tortured pace of SGML's development for comparison. First conceived in the late 1960s, the Generalized Markup Language (GML) was created at IBM in 1969 by researchers coincidentally named Goldfarb, Mosher, and Lorris. Charles Goldfarb went on to chair the American National Standards Institute (ANSI) committee on Computer Languages for the Processing of Text in 1978, after GML had become an important standard in publishing. In 1980, the committee released its first working draft, and by 1983 the sixth working draft was adopted by users such as the Internal Revenue Service and the Department of Defense, which mandated that its largest contractors use SGML as well. In 1984, the committee expanded into a group of collaborating committees developing standards for the International Organization for Standardization (ISO) as well as ANSI. In 1986, eight years into the standards process and seventeen years into its development, SGML became ISO 8879:1986. Work on SGML continues, of course. A group of committees regularly evaluates changes such as projects on scripted style sheets, multimedia, link extensions, and a variety of document-management issues.

Note

To see the SGML specification as a complete and open book (almost – some modifications have been made over the years), take a look at what amounts to the SGML Bible: Charles F. Goldfarb's *The SGML Handbook* (Oxford University Press, 1992).

Unlike HTML, SGML doesn't specify how text should be presented. SGML is not a formatting language; it's not even a markup language as Web developers would recognize one. SGML is a specification that enables people to create their own markup languages. It specifies content identifiers that make it easy to format text consistently and enable document-management systems to locate information quickly. The `<headline>` tag would actually mean "headline" in SGML, not just point size and font information. SGML is well suited to projects that involve large quantities of similarly structured data, such as catalogs, manuals, lists, transcripts, and statistical abstracts. SGML is a favorite of the federal government, as well as IBM and other large companies. It makes it easy for a centralized team to develop specifications, its own markup language for data structures, by creating a Document Type Definition (DTD) that can then be applied to any document throughout the organization.

More important, documents created with SGML are theoretically easy to port to different formats. Because SGML uses content-based markup, it's easy to change the formatting rules to suit the purpose of the output: Is it going to a dot-matrix line printer, a laser printer, a four-color press, a CD-ROM, a Web site, or even audio speakers? Design teams can determine formatting that works with the original DTD to present information in different styles that are appropriate; they can do this even if the output medium is completely different from the one the DTD designers had imagined. Computerized storage systems can also treat the documents as small databases, querying them with searches based on names provided in the markup, such as "headline," and index information. Companies that use the same information repeatedly — for proposals, for instance — can benefit greatly from having prefabricated text ready to be slightly altered for a new document. It doesn't make the writing any better, but it does make managing and reusing it easier.

HTML's roots

Most of what SGML contributed to HTML was syntax: a markup language that used the now familiar `<TAG ATTRIBUTE="VALUE">` *Content here* `</TAG>` style. Some of SGML's intent to separate content from formatting survived as well, as evidenced by the wildly divergent interpretations of common tags by different browsers. By describing elements with terms such as `<EM>` for emphasis and `<ADDRESS>` for address information, Berners-Lee created a simple formatting language that was flexible enough to handle many different kinds of information. The `<H1>` through `<H6>` tags indicated levels of headings, providing a somewhat natural structure to documents. The `<HEAD>` and `<BODY>` tags separated meta-information describing the document (initially just the `<TITLE>`) from the visible text of a document. Most important, the `<A    HREF="` `destination.html">` anchor tags provided a simple yet powerful structure for hypertext links.

HTML did a wonderful job of simplifying SGML and putting markup directly into the hands of amateurs, a necessary move for broadening markup's appeal. Ironically, Tim Berners-Lee never really intended for users to have to deal with markup directly as text. The initial experiments at CERN used a simple markup processor that managed the codes invisibly. While HTML remained a small collection of tags with only a few attributes, this friendly tool made it easy for authors to get started using the Web to exchange papers and share information.

As we've seen, however, HTML was ill-suited to a world that had been pampered by the control WYSIWYG tools had already given designers. Although hyperlinks and the Web's incredible ease of use were clearly good things, rumblings took place from the start about what these academics had done to create a useless formatting language. At the beginning of the browser wars, people knew that HTML's extremely simple formatting tools were not going to be accepted in the long run by designers and developers who wanted to create documents on the Web that were as detailed (allowing for screen resolution) as documents on paper. The inherent flexibility of the very simple tags from the original standard lacked appeal. Tags whose sole duty was formatting sprawled across the HTML land-scape, with `<B>` and `<I>` and eventually `<FONT>` receiving much more use than `<EM>` or `<ADDRESS>`. Designers hand-crafted HTML, mixing and matching tags to achieve the precise appearance they wanted without regard to document structure. Because the HTML tags were used only to specify appearance formatting, with very little attention paid to content structuring, HTML was doomed to life as a formatting language rather than a structured framework for documents. These problems grew as the Web expanded, springing from fundamental flaws in the originally brilliant and simple nature of HTML.

The emergence of XML: 20% of SGML's complexity, 80% of its capacity

The creators of the original Web standards and their successor organization, the W3C, scrambled to catch up to the commercial browser developers for a while. "Netscape extensions" provided designers with controls that the early versions of HTML had lacked, and these extensions fueled the phenomenal growth of

Netscape. Only recently has the W3C caught up to the browser developers and cut them off at the pass with the next set of standards. Cascading Style Sheets (CSS) was the first step ahead. CSS makes it possible for designers to declare their formatting intentions for a document without having to cook up a tortured mix of tags and graphics. CSS frees tags (such as <font> or <b>) from the burden of carrying formatting information, and permits them to carry content information once again (<headline> or <em> for example). By providing a complete vocabulary for describing formatting (more complete, in fact, than was possible with HTML 4.0), CSS provides a styling tool that can work with HTML or any other markup language.

After a formatting standard was available that didn't interfere with content-conscious markup, the W3C was able to create a markup standard that took advantage of the flexibility of SGML. This brings us to XML. XML emphasizes the importance of content information by making it possible for designers to create and manage their own sets of elements without necessarily stumbling into "tag soup." Designers can apply these sets with CSS in the background to create tags that manage content, including hypertext links, while still being able to create an aesthetically appealing page. XML arose from the concerns of the SGML Editorial Review Board at the W3C, which felt that HTML was heading in the wrong direction. To improve the situation, the board proposed a markup language that could work with existing Web technologies, using tools developed for use with HTML, while still adding flexibility for data- and document-management techniques. XML provides a subset of SGML functionality rather than just a set of tags using SGML syntax. It is a significant simplification (and there is some grumbling from SGML users about how gross a simplification it may be), but it promises to restore the initial promise of the Web. It adds a little of SGML's complexity in an attempt to simplify the complicated mess that is the current state of Web pages. One measure of how well this attempt has succeeded is the W3C's plans for the next generation of HTML (available at `http://www.w3.org/MarkUp/Activity.html`), which should result in the breakdown of the currently enormous HTML project into a number of smaller modules defined using XML.

XML implementations have taken a while to appear. Although the W3C Recommendation for XML 1.0 syntax appeared in February 1998, and most of the support for XML is still at the level where programmers can use it, regular HTML developers can't do much with it because little browser support exists. This situation is changing slowly, as Microsoft, Mozilla, Netscape, and Opera are providing significant (though not necessarily complete) support in their latest builds. Because people don't always upgrade their browsers, it may be a while before everyone has access to XML-enabled viewers, XML editors, and other XML applications.

The Data Side

Although XML's origins lie in documents, and most of the tools provided by XML 1.0 are aimed at document description rather than data description, XML has made more of an immediate impact on the data-processing side of computing than on the document-management side. Although text formats have long served as a lowest-common-denominator approach to storing and exchanging information, the long-held advantages of binary formats may be crumbling in the face of greater and greater needs to manage and distribute information across networks.

XML's provision of structured labeled information addresses real needs for developers who need to exchange information across organizational boundaries, and the ready availability of XML parsers has proven extremely useful to application developers in need of an easy way to read and store information.

Binary formats

Binary formats offer developers convenience and control. Binary-format convenience comes from more efficient data storage, more flexible structures, and a typically tight match between internal program structures and the contents of the binary file. On the control side, programmers get both the ability to organize and manipulate the file any way they like, and the ability to make the data format obscure and proprietary. By tightly binding the data structures to the file format, developers can create formats that are difficult for competitors to interpret and that make conversions far more difficult.

Binary formats open a wide range of possibilities to developers, from integrated compression and expansion to "quick save" functionality, in which changes are appended to the end of a file rather than integrated with the body of the contents. Binary files can be treated as lists of instructions rather than as data structures — how the files are loaded and processed is up to the programmers to decide. Developers can choose how to store their information at very low levels, packing information tightly for efficient transmission when space is limited, or packing them loosely to make moving around or expanding chunks of information without collisions easy.

Although convenience and efficiency for programmers made binary formats popular across a wide range of applications, binary formats had another significant effect. Their complexity and opacity made them useful tools in the battles for customers between software vendors. Customers who wanted to change from one application to another often faced daunting choices. Users could save documents in basic formats (typically text formats) to move them from one application to another; however, moving them to easily convertible formats often cost critical information and required additional cleanup work. Even when developers created conversion tools, competitors weren't exactly excited about sharing the details of their format. Users often found conversions less than perfect. For software vendors, this meant customers would stick with their original programs rather than battle the double challenge of new interfaces plus new file formats. This lock-in also let vendors sell new versions of software that could read the old format while saving information in a format that the old version couldn't read.

XML: Verbose, but structured, labeled, easily exchanged

XML offers developers a different kind of convenience while offering users control over their data. This combination of features promises a much more open world than binary formats allowed, making it more difficult for vendors to lock users into a particular product by making format conversion difficult. Instead, XML encourages vendors to create tools that are maximally interoperable, building their business models on open information flows rather than proprietary files that can be used only in limited environments.

Rather than the convenience of control, XML offers developers the convenience of standardized tools for loading and saving information. Developers need to define formats, but they don't need to read and write files directly — XML parsers handle that work and can provide different levels of integrity-checking along the way. For developers who want or need direct control over every byte their programs create this change can be jolting, but for others it means significantly less work in a field that was rarely considered exciting. Some developers will likely stick with binary formats for some kinds of data that require more efficiency or flexibility than XML can provide — large databases, images, and multimedia — but other developers are rapidly migrating to XML as an exchange format or as a native format.

XML files, like most text file formats, are generally larger than binary files storing the same information, and XML's redundant markup adds more volume. Although XML files can be much larger than their binary equivalents, they compress very well. What XML offers developers isn't *efficient* transfer, however, but *open* transfer. XML documents can carry information with structures and labels, making it possible for computers to pass information without losing content or structure. Programs on both sides of a communication need to understand the meanings of those structures and labels, but loss-free transmission no longer requires users to have the same program or even programs from the same vendor.

Despite XML's origins in document-centric technologies, it has plenty to offer developers and users who need to communicate between programs. Although the data side of XML has more limitations than the document side, largely because data-oriented programs often carry more efficiency-sensitive information (such as video files), it has opened even more possibilities than the document side of XML. Vendors are building tools for sending and processing XML, while companies and organizations band together to discuss formats.

Who Controls XML?

XML is under the control of the XML Working Group at the W3C, the descendant of the SGML Editorial Review Board. The XML Working Group controls most of the specifications directly relating to XML: XML syntax, extended linking for XML, and XML fragment use. At the same time, other Working Groups at the W3C control support standards such as the Document Object Model (DOM), Cascading Style Sheets (CSS), Extensible Style Language (XSL), and standards that complement or apply XML in a Web context, such as Mathematical Markup Language (MathML), Synchronized Multimedia Integration Language (SMIL), Scalable Vector Graphics (SVG), and Resource Description Framework (RDF). The implementation of XML, as is typical of the W3C, is up to vendors, though we can hope that they will stick closely to the standards.

Although this part of this alphabet soup is under the control of the W3C, many other applications of XML — with their own acronyms, of course — are under the control of other organizations, corporations, and individuals. You can create your own XML vocabulary to meet your needs, or you can explore standards being created by a wide variety of organizations and individuals. XML provides only a syntactical foundation — you have to choose how to use it.

Note

To keep up with the latest XML developments from the W3C, visit its Web site at `http://www.w3.org/XML/`. Information about current developments is available in the XML Working Group's Activity Statement at `http://www.w3.org/XML/Activity`. For news stories about the W3C's latest XML-related activities, see `http://xmlhack.com/list.php?cat=4`.

Moving Forward

This book takes a close look at the tools XML provides and how developers can apply them to common tasks. HTML developers should find much of the information familiar, although much of the content (creating DTDs, for instance) may be fairly alien. Programmers and database developers may be more familiar with data modeling, but they'll have to learn an unfamiliar syntax in a new document framework. This book isn't targeted at SGML developers, but readers familiar with SGML should find many familiar concepts integrated with the concepts from the wilder world of the Web.

Although this book focuses on creating documents with XML, it also covers techniques for managing XML and integrating it with other Web technologies. Software developers have also been a key market for XML, and many of the projects discussed here may supplement the toolbox for software developers as well. XML may seem abstract at first, but its practical implications should become more evident as you proceed through the book and try the examples. You'll see how sets of XML documents can be treated like databases even though they are very unlike the previous generations of strictly hierarchical or tabular structures, and you'll explore the new architectures for documents and data that XML makes possible.

Chapter 2

Building on a Markup Foundation

XML 1.0 stripped SGML down to a relatively small core set of functions, enabling developers to work with a tiny set of tools to create documents containing structured information. Because this tool set can be shared, and because the basics of XML aren't very hard to learn, developers can create a wider variety of tools than with the previous version with that same small set. XML was originally created for use with documents, but many developers use it with data sets that can only loosely be called documents. XML's small but solid core answers a few key questions about how to describe information but leaves the rest to developers to determine.

Note

All the tools described in this chapter are discussed in much greater detail later in the book. The purpose of this chapter is to give you a basic idea of what XML is capable of and to provide you with a high-level guide to the many additional standards that have become part of the XML family.

Examining the core: Marked-up text

XML documents are fundamentally streams of characters that follow a particular format. Some of the characters represent the document's content, whereas others constitute *markup*, which is information that tells applications about the structure and nature of the content. You can strip XML documents down to plain text by removing all the markup, but you lose a lot of information about the contents that way.

This chapter starts by examining some plain text without markup, looking for the kinds of cues that human readers often use to sort out information. Next you'll see how to represent those cues so that computers can use them easily. The following text represents a list of products with specifications and prices:

```
S127.29 Maple - 1"x1"x2'    $4.25
S128.29 Oak - 1"x1"x2'      $5.75
S130.29 Pine - 1"x1"x2'     $2.00
```

This list contains a set of three items, each represented by a line of text. Line breaks can be critical cues for human readers, making jumbles of characters into lists. The first piece of information in each line appears to be an item number. Its contents don't seem as though they're really intended for direct human interpretation, except perhaps for copying onto an order form. The next piece of information identifies a type of wood. (At this point, it isn't entirely clear whether the names Maple, Oak, and Pine refer to trees or lumber, but the measurements that follow suggest that this list is about cut lumber, not live trees.) The last piece of information in each item, neatly aligned at the rightmost edge of the list, is the price. The dollar sign ($) identifies the numbers in the price as a currency value.

Developers could write code that reads text files containing information like the items above, presents them to humans in a Web-based catalog that sells the goods, and uses the same information to help the warehouse find the items that customers had requested and bill them for it. However, developers would need to create a new tool for reading the information every time the document format changed.

Rather than write code that understands this text format, XML offers developers an approach that gives them more flexibility and the opportunity to use generic tools to solve specific problems. By inserting labels into the text, humans (or eventually computers) can create documents that are much easier for computers to process, present to humans, and share with other computers. Some programs may still need to know what the product number is, but they can ask an XML parser to hand them the information identified as product_number rather than have to read the text file and make a guess.

XML markup lets you insert textual information that labels content and identifies structures within that content. Labeled information may contain other labeled information, which may then contain yet more labeled information, and the contents and structures can stack on each other. In the case of this document, you have a label called product_list that contains all the list items. You start by identifying that this is a list containing products:

```
<product_list>
<product>S127.29 Maple - 1"x1"x2'    $4.25</product>
<product>S128.29 Oak - 1"x1"x2'      $5.75</product>
<product>S130.29 Pine - 1"x1"x2'     $2.00</product>
</product_list>
```

The text I've added to this list is called *markup* and is separated from the regular content by "angle brackets," the less-than (<) and greater-than (>) signs around the labels. The text items inside those brackets are commonly referred to as *tags*. Tags are used in pairs to identify the beginning and end of a run of labeled content, which are called XML elements. Start tags begin with < and the element name, whereas end tags begin with </ and the element name. The element product_list includes the entire document, whereas each product element includes one product in the list.

Cross-Reference

Detailed rules for choosing element names and creating element structures are covered in Chapter 3.

Although you now have a `product_list` element with three product elements in it, the content of those product elements could use more labeling. You start by identifying the product number, description, and price:

```
<product_list>
<product><product_number>S127.29</product_number>
<description>Maple - 1"x1"x2'</description>
<price>$4.25</price></product>
<product><product_number>S128.29</product_number>
<description>Oak - 1"x1"x2'</description>
<price>$5.75</price></product>
<product><product_number>S130.29</product_number>
<description>Pine - 1"x1"x2'</description>
<price>$2.00</price></product>
</product_list>
```

Now programs can ask for product numbers, descriptions, and prices on an item-by-item basis because the markup provides a road map through the document. This might be an adequate stopping point for a catalog, and to celebrate, I rearrange the document a little so that you can see the contrast between the structures that humans see and the structures that computers see:

```
<product_list>
  <product>
    <product_number>S127.29</product_number>
    <description>Maple - 1"x1"x2'</description>
    <price>$4.25</price>
  </product>
  <product>
    <product_number>S128.29</product_number>
    <description>Oak - 1"x1"x2'</description>
    <price>$5.75</price>
  </product>
  <product>
```

```
        <product_number>S130.29</product_number>
        <description>Pine - 1"x1"x2'</description>
        <price>$2.00</price>
      </product>
    </product_list>
```

Whitespace — spaces, line breaks, carriage returns, and tabs — is preserved by XML processors, so this document is slightly different from the original version. However, the tools for processing and presenting XML can generally work around particular whitespace formats quite easily. Depending on the level of structure in the document, you should be able to choose how best to format your marked-up documents.

Some applications of this information might want to be able to explore the description more precisely. Although a program sent out to locate lumber for particular projects could probably be trained to recognize Oak, Maple, and Pine as identifiers inside a description, adding an extra layer of markup might make it easier for those programs to say things such as "send me a list of all your pine lumber" or "send me a list of all your lumber whose longest dimension is at least two feet." You can start by breaking down the description into smaller components. For example,

```
<description>Maple - 1"x1"x2'</description>
might become:<description><species>Maple</species> -
<height>1"</height>x<width>1"</width>x<length>2'</length>
</description>
```

Potential for refinement still exists here, though. Height, width, and length are using inch and foot marks to identify their units. These marks work well with human readers, but are commonly used for other things (such as for quotation marks) in computing environments. Specifying what kind of units are being used for each dimension would be nice. Doing so would simplify conversions between feet and inches as well as between imperial units and metric units. Surrounding the measurements with units might be one solution:

```
<description><species>Maple</species> -
<height><inches>1"</inches></height>x
<width><inches>1"</inches></width>x
<length><feet>2'</feet></length>
</description>
```

Even for the markup-crazed, this code is starting to look verbose. XML offers another kind of markup, called *attributes*, that can clarify element types rather than just create more elements. The same content, marked up using attributes to indicate units, might look like this:

```
<description><species>Maple</species> -
<height unit="inches">1"</height>x
<width unit="inches">1"</width>x
<length unit="feet">2'</length>
</description>
```

The height, width, and length elements now have attributes, which provide a little more information about their contents without requiring additional layers of markup. As you see later in the book, attributes are very useful for adding extra information and can be used to store content as well.

Putting this all together, and indicating the structure with white-space, you get a result like this:

```
<product_list>
  <product>
    <product_number>S127.29</product_number>
    <description>
      <species>Maple</species> -
      <height unit="inches">1"</height>x
      <width unit="inches">1"</width>x
      <length unit="feet">2'</length>
```

```
      </description>
      <price>$4.25</price>
    </product>
    <product>
      <product_number>S128.29</product_number>
      <description>
        <species>Oak</species> -
        <height unit="inches">1"</height>x
        <width unit="inches">1"</width>x
        <length unit="feet">2'</length>
      </description>
      <price>$5.75</price>
    </product>
    <product>
      <product_number>S130.29</product_number>
      <description>
        <species>Pine</species> -
        <height unit="inches">1"</height>x
        <width unit="inches">1"</width>x
        <length unit="feet">2'</length>
      </description>
      <price>$2.00</price>
    </product>
</product_list>
```

We now have some cases where the markup duplicates the textual content, like the dash used to divide the species from the measurements, and the ', ", and x inside of the measurements, and those could be eliminated if the developer saw it as appropriate. XML itself doesn't make those demands, however—you can maintain this format however best suits your needs.

You've come a long way from the original:

```
S127.29 Maple - 1"x1"x2'     $4.25
S128.29 Oak - 1"x1"x2'       $5.75
S130.29 Pine - 1"x1"x2'      $2.00
```

The original 100 characters (including whitespace) have become 849 characters in the fully marked-up version. XML doesn't do very much to encourage developers to keep their documents concise, but the marked-up version may prove to be far more efficient than the original text because it is far easier to process, reference, and present. Rather than assume that human readers can figure out the contents of a document through context and formatting, the new XML document provides explicit labels that both humans and computers can use to find information easily in large collections of structured and labeled information.

The many things you can do with XML

When XML first appeared, it seemed a relatively simple way to create documents that described their contents and structures. Although the core of XML remains fairly simple and small, the infrastructures built on top of XML have grown larger and far more complex. You can do more with XML than ever before, but those opportunities require you to choose among different options and plan for an uncertain future. The rest of this chapter takes a brief look at many of the different options and approaches available to developers who want to use XML for various projects.

Describe and share data and document formats

Although adding markup to documents can make them much easier to work with, it doesn't do much good if everyone uses completely different formats that don't correspond to each other very well. Marked-up information provides more clues about its contents than information without markup, but processing information is generally much simpler if all participants in the communication have a shared understanding of the markup they're using. Common formats simplify writing programs and style sheets for processing and presenting information.

Although textual descriptions of formats are definitely useful as documentation, computer-readable formal descriptions give computers the capability to check documents as they arrive and determine whether they conform to a given structure. This "validation" process enables developers to hand over some responsibility for checking incoming information to a parser, potentially sparing programmers a lot of work. Because XML 1.0 validation has been implemented on nearly as many different computing platforms as XML itself, these formal descriptions make exchanging information reliably easier, even when you're sending information between very different environments.

XML 1.0 includes a set of tools, called Document Type Definitions, for describing document structures. XML DTDs are a subset of SGML DTDs and provide structural-level descriptions of documents — XML 1.0 doesn't provide any way to describe data types for content, for instance. DTDs do an excellent job for many document-oriented applications, but don't provide enough functionality for some applications, leading the W3C and others to create new tools for describing document structures with more power — Microsoft's XML-Data, the W3C's XML Schema Description Language, and REgular Language Description for XML (RELAX), which is being submitted to the International Organization for Standardization (ISO).

A supplementary standard, *Namespaces in XML*, also provides developers with a way to indicate which vocabulary is being used in a given document or part of a document. Namespaces enable developers to mix different vocabularies in the same document without leaving users and programs hopelessly confused about the many possible interpretations of a given label.

Cross-Reference

DTDs, XML Schema Description Language, and RELAX are all covered in greater detail in Part II of this book.

Create, present, and manage documents

XML provides a powerful set of tools for representing the chaotic style of information that is common inside human-created and human-readable documents. XML provides a unique collection of capabilities — structure balanced with flexibility, and an open approach that enables any application to read and write any XML format — that offer an opportunity to move beyond both the limited capabilities of HTML and the more powerful but proprietary approaches of most word-processing and page-layout tools. XML's clean internal structures also open possibilities for in-depth content management, where revision tracking, document sharing, and versioning are not only possible but relatively easy.

You can create XML documents by hand in a text editor or by using tools that provide varying degrees of flexibility. Some XML editors look like word processors; others provide tree-based views that present the structure of a document as well as its content; and a few are custom-built to create documents in specific vocabularies through forms or other interfaces. The word processor–like editors are generally easiest for document-oriented applications, but the other types may also be very useful depending on how complex a structure you have to deal with.

The structures and labels inside XML documents make presenting their information using sets of rules easy. In some XML vocabularies — such as Scalable Vector Graphics (SVG) and Extensible Stylesheet Language Formatting Objects (XSL-FO) — the structures and labels themselves explicitly describe how the content of the document should be presented. These formats are entirely about presentation. However, most developers using XML tend to separate presentation from the content of their documents, storing information about how to present their document structures in separate files.

Cascading Style Sheets (CSS) provides a set of tools for describing how to present information stored in XML documents, whereas Extensible Stylesheet Language Transformations (XSLT) provides a template-based mechanism that describes how to convert XML documents to XSL-FO, which is then presented to the user. CSS is simpler and less invasive, whereas XSLT is more complex and more powerful. XSLT enables developers to reorganize documents during the presentation phase, for instance. Both style-sheet approaches are moving slowly into browsers and other presentation applications.

On the management side, XML's insistence on clean structures within documents means that you can create tools for managing documents and document fragments that aren't tightly bound to a particular vocabulary. Although the labels may change, the structures are enough of a foundation on which to build a storage system or processing tools. Content management systems can treat XML files as nested collections of smaller pieces instead of having to keep track of large and opaque binary files. Having access to the inside of the document makes it easier for these systems to keep track of revisions inside of documents, store multiple versions of documents, and give multiple users read-write access to different portions of documents at the same time. It also makes providing a single search-and-reference approach to collections of diverse types of documents easier. The W3C is currently developing XLink and XPointer, technologies for creating hypertext links between XML documents that build on this clean structure.

Cross-Reference

Cascading Style Sheets, XSLT, XLink, and other technologies supporting XML are explored in greater detail in Part III of this book.

XML hasn't exactly taken the document field by storm, because it faces well entrenched competition from word processors and HTML. XML is starting to move into situations in which large-scale document management or exchange is critical, and into some applications in which information must be presented in more than one form — a Web browser, a cell phone, a slide show, and a book, for instance.

Build applications that read and write XML

Although XML processing is designed to be fairly easy and generic, it hasn't appeared instantly in all kinds of software. Companies that have long depended on opaque proprietary formats aren't likely to give them up overnight in favor of a newcomer that exposes them to competition, and even companies excited about XML have had to figure out how best (if at all) to integrate XML with their existing structures.

As a result, a lot of developers are building their own XML interfaces, using generic XML tools as a foundation and connecting XML to their internal program structures as they find appropriate. XML parsers are generic tools that read XML documents and report the contents of those documents to applications. They may also check the structure or contents of the documents against rules in W3C XML Schemas, RELAX schemas, or a DTD, but doing so is optional.

Parsers typically use one of two approaches to present the document content to the application. Some parsers build a model of the entire document in memory and then present the application with that model. Because XML documents have tree-like structures inside them, this approach is typically referred to as *tree-based parsing*. Other parsers report the contents of the document to the application as they read it, announcing the beginnings and ends of elements along with their content. This approach is referred to as *event-based parsing* because it presents the documents as a series of events.

Each approach has its advantages and disadvantages. The event-based model is designed to have a minimal impact on memory usage, and is great for programs that need to rapidly map XML directly to their internal structures. This model requires developers to work with the XML as it runs through the parser, which can be a problem if an error appears late in the document and it's suddenly necessary to roll back all the information that was just loaded. The event-based approach is also difficult to use in cases in which processing of the beginning of the document might rely on information at the end of the document. The tree-based model, on the other hand, presents all the information at one time, after the parse is complete, and lets programs explore the document structure. This is the model typically used in Web browsers, but it comes at a significant cost: The memory required to store the document tree is typically many times larger than the document itself, inflicting a performance cost.

XML parsers typically implement one or both of these approaches. The most common event-based model is the Simple API for XML (SAX); the most common tree-based model is the W3C's Document Object Model (DOM). Application builders can use either of these approaches to let their programs read XML, and can either use these models or rely on simple text-generation to write XML documents.

Cross-Reference

The SAX and DOM APIs are explored in greater detail in Chapter 9.

Create, manage, and present data

Developers focusing on data have taken better advantage of many of the tools XML created with documents in mind than have developers and authors focusing on documents. In some ways, developers working with data have it easier — the structures involved are usually far more predictable, the documents often reflect internal structures already built into applications, and many data-oriented applications use XML only for transmitting information, not for storing it. In the process of creating, transmitting, and reading data, however, developers have used technologies such as the HyperText Transfer Protocol (HTTP), Document Object Model (DOM), and Extensible Stylesheet Language Transformations (XSLT) — all originally created for documents — as frameworks for data processing and exchange.

Although markup isn't (as noted previously) the most efficient way to encode data, HTTP isn't an especially efficient way to transfer data, the DOM isn't the most efficient way to process it, and XSLT is an entirely new technology for developers to learn, all these technologies are readily available in free implementations. HTTP is widely supported by Web servers, Web browsers, and all kinds of intermediate tools on the network, including proxy servers and firewalls. Developers can reuse existing frameworks to get their work done immediately, without having to wait for the major infrastructure upgrades that frequently hold back the growth of new technologies.

These possibilities have touched off a gold rush in companies seeking to capitalize on XML's ability to carry so many different kinds of information among so many different kinds of systems. Large companies, small companies, and open-source projects all offer their own combinations of tools for transmitting and processing XML. Various frameworks, vocabularies, and protocols are appearing, though which of these approaches will work for which groups of customers isn't yet clear. Some approaches use fixed XML vocabularies whereas others use fixed vocabularies as wrappers around content that may have any vocabulary, and still others use a messaging approach that supports the interchange of any vocabulary.

Developers are using XML to address data interchange both inside organizations and among organizations. Although a lot of attention is currently focused on business-to-business (B2B) exchanges, many companies and other groups are using XML to exchange information between their own internal systems. Because XML is so flexible, it can deal with a wide variety of different vocabularies, structures, and developer needs. XML enables developers to use commodity protocols and components to build custom solutions to particular problems.

XML is even spurring the development of new protocols for communications between systems — approaches including XML-RPC, SOAP, Blocks, Extensible Protocol, and many more. Some of these approaches ride on top of existing protocols, notably HTTP; others are beginning to find HTTP too limiting and are moving to custom protocols with more of an XML-specific foundation.

 Cross-Reference

Using XML to exchange business-oriented information is explored in greater detail in Chapter 18, and using XML in lower-level data-oriented applications is covered in Chapter 20.

Moving forward into the XML jungle

All these possibilities are exciting, but making them happen requires a lot of work, often custom work. XML provides a solid foundation on which to build communications pathways, but it doesn't wave a magic wand and make communications happen. Putting XML to work requires creating (or choosing) a vocabulary and structures, and building an infrastructure around them. Off-the-shelf solutions and vocabularies will work for many applications, but others will require some mixture of custom development and pre-built components.

The next few chapters show you how to read and write XML documents, and the later chapters show you how to describe those documents so that you can easily share your XML documents and the processing expectations surrounding them. After you've learned to create and describe documents, you take a brief look at processing tools that support XML, and then explore data modeling with XML. Markup is a simple concept but one that requires you to understand lot of supporting concepts, features, and tools.

Chapter 3

Core XML: Elements, Attributes, Text, and Namespaces

Although XML and the XML family of specifications offer a seemingly endless number of features that developers can use, all those features rely on a small core of markup tools. All XML documents contain elements, nearly all contain textual content, and most contain attributes. A relative newcomer to the scene, namespaces, reinforces these core features, making them a more solid base on which to build applications. Everything else in XML is built on or supplements this core, which every XML processing tool must understand.

Note

The documents created in this chapter will work well in non-validating parsers, which don't check the overall document structure. Chapter 6 explains the additional tools – Document Type Definitions, or DTDs – you need to work in a validating parser environment. Lightweight applications and experimental development projects are more likely to use non-validating parsers, whereas heavier-duty document-management and other standards development activities will rely heavily on validation.

Building Blocks: Element Structures

Elements form the backbone of XML documents, identifying information and building labeled structures that can contain other structures. Every XML document must contain one top-level element, called the *root element*, which contains all the other elements and textual content of the document. Applications that process XML expect to see a single container holding other containers, making it easy to begin processing from the top and work down through the elements inside.

All XML elements have names. Element names must begin with a letter, underscore, or colon, and may contain letters, digits, hyphens, underscores, colons, and periods. Colons are reserved for use with namespaces, described later, but the remaining choices leave developers with plenty of options. Appendix B of the XML specification lists the Unicode ranges of characters that XML parsers consider to be letters and digits, giving developers a wide range of choices outside the usual ASCII text. XML vocabularies may use any language; English has no special privileges. Element names may use upper- or lowercase, and case will be preserved. Element names may be as long as necessary or as short as a single character.

Elements are indicated using tags. Tags always begin with < and end with >. There are three kinds of tags: *start tags*, *end tags*, and *empty tags*. Start tags indicate the beginning of an element and identify the name of the element. They may also contain attributes, discussed later in this chapter. The syntax for an element start tag without elements looks like the following:

```
<ElementName>
```

For example, the start tag of an element named `paragraph` might look like this:

```
<paragraph>
```

End tags simply mark the end of an element and can't contain any attributes. The syntax for end tags looks like the following:

```
</ElementName>
```

For example, the end tag of an element named `paragraph` might look like this:

```
</paragraph>
```

The last kind of tag, used to indicate elements without any textual content, is the empty tag. The empty tag may optionally contain attributes because it is effectively a stand-in for a start tag immediately followed by an end tag. The syntax for an empty tag without attributes looks like the following:

```
<ElementName />
```

An empty tag for an element named `paragraph` (perhaps a placeholder for a paragraph that will be filled in later) might look like this:

```
<paragraph />
```

Note

The space between the element name and the `/>` in the empty tag is optional. Developers working to integrate XML and HTML have found that the space circumvents compatibility conflicts, but developers working exclusively with XML often leave out the space.

An element must be marked as either an empty tag or a start tag followed by an end tag. Elements that contain text or other elements must use the start tag-end tag sequence, whereas empty elements may use either an empty tag or a start tag immediately followed by an end tag. Elements must not overlap. The end tag of an element must appear inside the same element in which the start tag appeared.

Building clean structures: An HTML example

XML uses structures that are very similar to those in HTML, which isn't surprising given their shared roots in SGML. Underneath XML's syntactical structures, however, is a language for defining document structures that gives it the power HTML lacks. This chapter starts by examining some simple structures from HTML and then digs down until you've uncovered enough to begin building a foundation with some simple XML documents.

HTML developers frequently talk about tags: <P>, <B>, or <LI>, for example. XML developers tend to talk about elements instead, which represent fully formed applications of those same tags. A paragraph element might look like this:

```
<P>This is a <EM>sample</EM> paragraph element. It
includes several other elements, including an emphasis
(EM) element that includes the word 'sample' and a
<B>bold</B> element that includes the word 'bold.'</P>
```

This text includes six tags (three opening, three closing) but only three elements. The paragraph element includes two other elements. XML's nesting rules rely on this distinction between tags and elements, which was long ignored by Web browsers. The following code is illegal HTML, even though some browsers will render it properly anyway:

```
<B>This is bold. <I>This is bold italic.</B> This is
italic.</I>
```

In my word processor, I get away with this every day. I don't need to convert text back to normal before I'm allowed to add additional formatting; formats are understood to be additive and can layer on top of each other. If the <B> and <I> tags were simply for formatting, this code would work the same way. It doesn't work that way in HTML (or XML or SGML), however. That kind of code attempts to create elements whose beginning and end tags overlap, as shown in Figure 3-1.

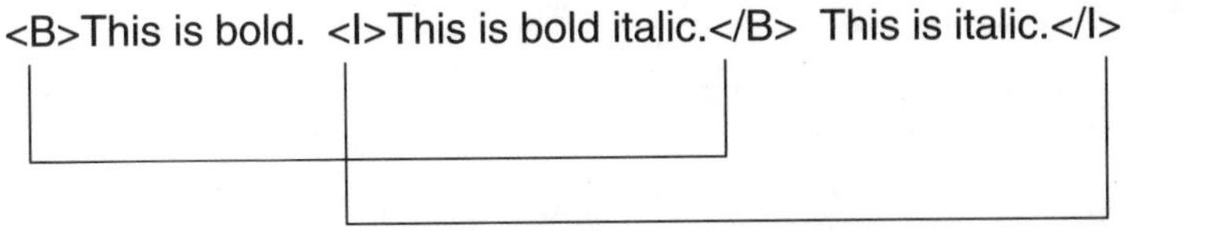

<B>This is bold. <I>This is bold italic.</B> This is italic.</I>

Figure 3-1 *Overlapping elements are prohibited.*

Overlapping elements produce all kinds of ambiguity, especially when content (and formatting) gets more complicated. In HTML, the proper way to produce the result shown in Figure 3-2 is to use the following code:

```
<B>This is bold.</B> <I><B>This is bold italic.</B></I>
<I>This is italic.</I>
```

or

```
<B>This is bold.</B> <I><B>This is bold italic.</B> This
is italic.</I>
```

or

```
<B>This is bold. <I>This is bold italic.</I></B> <I>This
is italic.</I>
```

These three ways take more tags, but the beginning and end tags do not overlap. The first sample variation uses the most markup but is probably the safest way to create this text, especially if you anticipate cutting and pasting or otherwise moving it around. The other two variations use fewer markup tags and take advantage of HTML's ability to nest tags and allow elements to absorb the formatting of the elements surrounding them. The only change is in whether the bold italic element is an italic element nested in the bold element preceding it or a bold element nested in the italic element that follows it. Figure 3-3 shows these three variations on nesting.

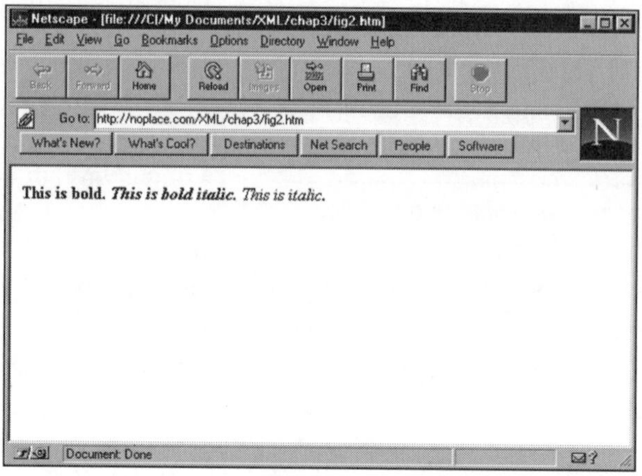

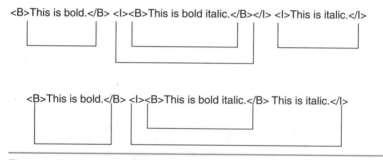

Figure 3-2 *Bold, bold italic, and italic*

```
<B>This is bold.</B> <I><B>This is bold italic.</B></I> <I>This is italic.</I>
```

```
<B>This is bold.</B> <I><B>This is bold italic.</B> This is italic.</I>
```

Figure 3-3 *Acceptable element creations*

I always recommend creating the most containerized solution (like the first variation here), so that you can pick up elements and move them around without worrying about losing half your structures.

Note

The very fact that three different XML interpretations of the "correct" meaning of a set of broken HTML tags are possible illustrates the problems that malformed syntax can cause developers who need to be able to refer to document structures in their scripting and styling. Developers who apply style sheets or try to reference elements through the document object model will get unpredictable results when they work with broken code. XML solves this problem by prohibiting broken code.

Creating element markup

To demonstrate how elements work, I mark up a simple recipe document with multiple (and somewhat unpredictable) layers of structure. Although many developers are used to working with orderly data (such as the wood-catalog example in the previous chapter), documents often contain more of a mix than simple lists and tables.

The recipe is fairly simple: title, author, ingredients, and instructions. Still, a few layers of structure must be organized if this document is to work. The ingredients and the instructions are both lists, although the instructions could be presented as a paragraph if that is more convenient. Ingredients often have alternates. Even the instructions can vary: Most instructions are about preparation, but some are serving suggestions. Marking up this recipe is a little more complicated than formatting it for a browser, but most of the work comes from choosing labels and applying them consistently.

```
<RECIPE>
<AUTHOR>Simon St.Laurent</AUTHOR>
<RECIPENAME>Super-Duper Grilled Cheese</RECIPENAME>
<DESCRIPTION>Succulent grilled cheese sandwiches that
go beautifully with soup but are still delightful on
their own.
```

Continued

```
</DESCRIPTION>
<INGREDIENTLIST>
<INGREDIENT>
<REALINGREDIENT>
2 Tablespoons butter
</REALINGREDIENT>
(or
<ALTERNATEINGREDIENT>
non-stick spray</ALTERNATEINGREDIENT>
if preferred)
</INGREDIENT>
<INGREDIENT>
<REALINGREDIENT>
8 slices wheat bread
</REALINGREDIENT>
(or
<ALTERNATEINGREDIENT>
other bread
</ALTERNATEINGREDIENT>)
     </INGREDIENT>
     <INGREDIENT>
<REALINGREDIENT>
1/4 pound jalapeño Monterey Jack
     </REALINGREDIENT>
     (or
     <ALTERNATEINGREDIENT>
     other cheese
     </ALTERNATEINGREDIENT>)
     </INGREDIENT>
     <INGREDIENT>
         <REALINGREDIENT>
         2 bottles beer
         </REALINGREDIENT>
     </INGREDIENT>
</INGREDIENTLIST>
```

```
<INSTRUCTIONS>
    <STEP>
Melt butter in frying pan over low to medium heat.
</STEP>
    <STEP>Slice cheese into thin slices.</STEP>
    <STEP>Place cheese slices evenly on 4 slices bread;
    cover with other slices.</STEP>
    <STEP>Fry sandwich carefully in butter, flipping
    repeatedly to avoid burning.</STEP>
<STEP>Cut sandwiches into quarters diagonally.</STEP>
    <STEP>Serve hot with beer.</STEP>
</INSTRUCTIONS>
</RECIPE>
```

Although uppercase markup seems to be falling out of style, it does make the markup stand out visually from the content. The RECIPE element here contains an AUTHOR element, RECIPENAME element, DESCRIPTION element, INGREDIENTLIST element, and INSTRUCTIONS element. The AUTHOR, RECIPENAME, and DESCRIPTION elements contain textual content directly, whereas the INGREDIENTLIST and INSTRUCTIONS elements contain only child elements (and some whitespace). The INGREDIENTLIST element contains INGREDIENT elements, each of which can hold a REALINGREDIENT element, some text, and possibly an ALTERNATEINGREDIENT element. The INSTRUCTIONS element holds STEP elements, each of which contains the text describing a single step in the cooking process.

All the containment is clean — the code has no overlapping elements. Everything nests smoothly and all the start and end tags match up properly. You don't have to do the markup this way precisely — you see how to refine it a little in the next section — but it is well-formed XML. You may have tag names that you prefer — REALINGREDIENT and ALTERNATEINGREDIENT are a bit clunky, after all — or an industry standard for cookbooks may appear, in which case you should probably follow the standard. The key thing to notice about this markup is that all elements have opening and closing tags that nest cleanly. A real cookbook could be considerably more detailed and would certainly have more sophisticated recipes.

Supplementing Elements with Attributes

Although some elements are just simple labels or containers (for example, B or BR in HTML), others need more information to do their work. Including an IMG element in an HTML document without specifying a SRC attribute produces nothing in the page, because an IMG tag needs an SRC attribute for the browser to figure out what image it's supposed to display. Most elements, even the simplest ones, now have attributes in the latest HTML standard, 4.01 (and the XML version, XHTML 1.0) and additional attributes often appear as document structures mature. Attributes enable designers to provide additional information about elements without having to add extra layers of element structure or modify the content of the document directly. This feature makes it easy to give elements unique identifiers, identify hypertext links, or provide hooks for application-specific behavior without changing the content, and some developers use attributes to store content as well.

Attributes can appear in the start tag of an element or in an empty tag; they cannot appear in the end tag. Like elements, all attributes must have names that conform to XML's rules. Attribute names must begin with a letter, underscore, or colon and may contain letters, digits, hyphens, underscores, colons, and periods. Colons are reserved for use with namespaces, described later in this chapter. Attribute names may be as long as necessary or as short as a single character. After the attribute name, an equals sign and an attribute value must appear. Attribute values, which must be contained in quotation marks, contain text, but they cannot contain element markup—no tags are permitted. An element may have only one attribute with a given name; duplicate names should cause the parser to report an error.

The syntax for attributes appearing in a start tag looks like this:

```
<ElementName attName1="attValue1" attName2="attValue2">
```

For example, the start tag of an element named `paragraph` with attributes named `author` and `modifiedDate` might look like this:

```
<paragraph author="Simon" modifiedDate="01/31/01">
```

or

```
<paragraph modifiedDate="01/31/01" author="Simon">
```

Developers consider the order in which attributes appear in an element unimportant, and applications shouldn't count on parsers reporting attributes in the order in which they originally appeared in the document. Whitespace in attribute values is also normalized so that spaces, line breaks, tabs, and carriage returns are all reported as single spaces, even if multiple spaces appeared in the original document. Extra whitespace can also appear between attributes and will be ignored.

XML requires that all attributes have values and that attribute values appear inside quotation marks. Single and double quotation marks are both acceptable, though they have to match. Even though double quotation marks are more common, single quotation marks are handy if an attribute must include a double quotation mark. (If you need to include both kinds of quotation marks within an attribute value, see the section on built-in entities later in this chapter.)

It's not always clear when information belongs in an attribute and when it deserves an element of its own, especially with the formatting of information. Although the W3C tends to favor putting formatting information inside elements as attributes over creating new elements, this hasn't always been the dominant approach. Compare, for example, the following two pieces of HTML code:

```
<p><font face="Arial">This paragraph is in Arial, except
for <b><font face="Times New Roman">this
piece,</font></b> which is in Times New Roman
bold.</font></p>
```

and

```
<p style="font-face:Arial">This paragraph is in Arial,
except for <span style="font-face:Times New Roman; font-
weight: bold">this piece,</span> which is in Times New
Roman bold.</p>
```

The second style is the newer standard, applying formatting information through the `style` attribute rather than `font` elements. It requires the creation of many fewer elements, which (as you'll see later) is a tremendous aid when you begin to apply style sheets and manipulate elements dynamically through scripting. The `font` element has been officially "deprecated" in HTML 4.0 and XHTML 1.0; it is no longer recommended. Although it's still a part of the standard and will probably be available for many browser versions to come, the next version of the XHTML standard will not support it in its core version.

The logic behind what defines an attribute and what defines an element isn't always clear. Lists could have been defined in such a way that the list items were attributes of the main list element, but this approach would have created gigantic opening tags with multiple repetitive parts sprawling across pages. Because it doesn't make much sense to build pages that way, the creators of HTML opted to define certain types of elements, lists, that contain child elements, the list items. On the other hand, the `input` element creates several different kinds of interface pieces — fields, check boxes, radio buttons, and so on — using the same element name and a different set of attributes for each item. Defining the `input` element is complex and messy, requiring several pages to explain the possible combinations of relevant attributes needed to create different types of input. The `input` element is an example of overextending one element with attributes to accomplish a task that would probably be easier to manage with separate elements.

Finding the right balance of attributes and elements is difficult for beginning document designers. Attributes enable XML tags to pass more information to dedicated programs about the way their information should be handled, possibly about the way it should be presented, and even whether it should be presented at all. However, HTML doesn't always provide the best examples, and there are still fairly few other widely used formatting languages. Consequently, developers should create some sample documents and then try to mark them up. When you think you've reached a decent balance, show someone else your document and see whether he or she can understand the markup and describe how the document is composed. If that person can describe it to you in familiar terms, you've probably done well.

Professional designers team with others on a regular basis for this type of consultation, but individual designers who need to build their own document structures often don't have those resources available. Designers working with HTML are concerned about whether the document looks right when it appears on a reader's screen; designers working with XML are more concerned about whether the document is easy to create on the author's screen. Using elements and attributes inappropriately is the fastest way to snarl what might seem like a reasonable representation of document structure.

Note

For a comprehensive discussion of document structure design issues, see Rick Jelliffe's *The XML and SGML Cookbook* (Prentice-Hall, 1998) and David Megginson's *Structuring XML Documents* (Prentice-Hall, 1998). Holy wars about when to use elements and when to use attributes have snarled discussions for years, but these two books provide many balanced examples as well as theories.

To demonstrate appropriate use of attributes, I've revised the recipe example, moving some content to attributes, using attributes to identify different subcategories within an element type (instead of using the clunky REALINGREDIENT and ALTERNATEINGREDIENT), and adding extra information to some of the steps.

```
<RECIPE AUTHOR="Simon St.Laurent">
<RECIPENAME>Super-Duper Grilled Cheese</RECIPENAME>
<DESCRIPTION>Succulent grilled cheese sandwiches that go
beautifully with soup but are still delightful on their
own.</DESCRIPTION>
<INGREDIENTLIST>
<INGREDIENT><ITEM>2 Tablespoons butter</ITEM> (or <ITEM
TYPE="ALT">non-stick spray</ITEM> if preferred)
</INGREDIENT>
<INGREDIENT><ITEM>8 slices wheat bread</ITEM> (or <ITEM
TYPE="ALT">other bread </ITEM>)</INGREDIENT>
<INGREDIENT><ITEM>1/4 pound jalapeño Monterey Jack</ITEM>
(or <ITEM TYPE="ALT">other cheese</ITEM>)</INGREDIENT>
<INGREDIENT><ITEM TYPE="OPTIONAL">2 bottles
beer</ITEM></INGREDIENT>
</INGREDIENTLIST>
<INSTRUCTIONS>
<STEP TYPE="COOKING">Melt butter in frying pan over low
to medium heat.</STEP>
<STEP TYPE="COOKING">Slice cheese into thin
slices.</STEP>
<STEP TYPE="COOKING">Place cheese slices evenly on 4
slices bread; cover with other slices.</STEP>
<STEP TYPE="COOKING">Fry sandwich carefully in butter,
flipping repeatedly to avoid burning.</STEP>
<STEP TYPE="SERVING">Cut sandwiches into quarters
diagonally.</STEP>
<STEP TYPE="SERVING">Serve hot with beer.</STEP>
</INSTRUCTIONS>
</RECIPE>
```

Again, the markup doesn't need to be done this way precisely, but this example demonstrates a few possibilities for using attributes to annotate element structures.

Namespaces: Identifying Elements and Attributes

Namespaces, which in practice look quite simple, have generated enormous debate over the responsibilities of parsers and applications, the weaknesses of DTDs, the importance of XML's compatibility with SGML, and distinctions between markup and semantics. Although XML's flexibility in allowing developers to choose their own structures and labels for content opens up incredible new possibilities, it also creates enormous potential for chaos. Developers are supposed to create their own vocabularies, and they are certainly doing so, but keeping all those vocabularies straight can rapidly become difficult, especially if multiple vocabularies need to be combined in a single document. Because a key part of the W3C's plans for using XML — with HTML — was intended to make HTML itself extensible with additional vocabularies, these issues were addressed quickly after XML 1.0 itself became a recommendation.

Namespaces are an add-on to XML 1.0, which has caused some incompatibilities with DTDs, as discussed in Chapter 6. Namespaces rely on attributes for their declarations but apply mostly to element names, using a prefixing strategy that associates element names with particular Uniform Resource Identifiers (URIs). By using URIs (a superset of the familiar Uniform Resource Locators, or URLs) as identifiers, the W3C avoided the need to run its own registry for XML namespaces, because anyone with access to a domain name or even control of a URL can use that as an identifier for his or her namespace.

Although some developers argue that every XML document should use namespaces to identify its vocabulary, the *Namespaces in XML* Recommendation isn't so insistent. Namespaces are an optional feature, a useful tool that you can but don't have to use. They're certainly at the core of the W3C's plans for XML moving forward, but you can use them as you see appropriate. All the documents shown thus far in the chapter haven't had namespaces, and that's perfectly fine. If these documents were going to be exchanged with systems looking for particular vocabularies or integrated with documents written in other vocabularies, however, using namespaces would probably be wise.

Namespaces use attributes to define mappings between prefixes (including no prefix) and URIs. All namespace declarations take place in attributes beginning with `xmlns` and apply to all the contents of the element in which they appear, unless another element overrides the declaration with its own declaration. (If one does, its new declaration holds for that element and all the elements it contains.) This means that if your entire document uses a single vocabulary, you can make a namespace declaration once, in the root element, and never have to think about it again.

To associate a namespace URI to a namespace prefix, you use an attribute whose name starts with `xmlns:` and ends with the prefix, and assign as its value the namespace URI:

```
<elementName xmlns:prefix="namespaceURI">
```

That URI will then be associated with that prefix. For example, to create a `myDoc` prefix associated with the URI `"http://www.example.com/mydoc"`, you might use:

```
<myDoc:document
    xmlns:myDoc="http://www.example.com/mydoc">
...more elements prefixed with myDoc: to which
declaration applies...
</myDoc:document>
```

The namespace URI `"http://www.example.com/mydoc"` will now apply to any element whose name (called the "local name") is prefixed with `myDoc:`. Prefixes can quickly make documents verbose, however, and it's often convenient to define a namespace for all elements *without* prefixes.

To associate a namespace URI with all elements that don't have a specific prefix on their name, you simply use an `xmlns` attribute whose value is the URI:

```
<document xmlns="http://www.example.com/mydoc">
...more elements to which declaration applies...
</document>
```

One minor point worth noting is that the default namespace, the namespace without a prefix, doesn't apply to attributes. Attributes may have explicit prefixes, an approach discussed in Chapter 16 on XLink, but attributes without prefixes exist in a kind of limbo. Generally, processors assume that unprefixed attributes belong to the namespace of the element that includes them.

The namespaces mechanism provides a lot of flexibility and can accommodate many different namespaces. In well-formed documents, adding a namespace is as easy as adding an attribute; in valid documents, it requires creating an attribute with a name appropriate to the prefix to be used. This mechanism makes it easy to mix and match namespaces within a document, and can support unlimited (until your parser or application breaks) numbers of namespaces without conflict.

Because you can override namespace declarations, it's possible to use the same prefix to refer to different URIs in the same document. It's also possible to define multiple prefixes for the same URI. In general, however, it's usually easiest to define prefixes once and remain consistent throughout the document. Developers often make namespace declarations in the root elements of documents or other times when a new prefix first appears. Although assigning multiple URIs to the same prefix or multiple prefixes to the same URI is possible, it's definitely confusing to human readers. Namespace-aware XML parsers can handle these intricacies, but trying to figure out what's happening as a document is processed can become strangely difficult.

If you create new XML vocabularies, it's probably a good idea to create namespaces for them. It isn't always clear where the dividing lines between different vocabularies are, but generally you should apply the same namespace URI to elements that can be processed together. You should assign URIs that are under your control, and you may put documents at those URIs that describe or document the contents of your namespaces, but you should avoid writing code that relies on particular kinds of documents being available at that URI. If your application ever needs to process documents whose creators expected something else (or nothing) to be available at the namespace URI, or which use a URI that can't be resolved, your application may not be able to do the work you expected.

Textual Content

Text is used to store all the information in an XML document. As you saw in the previous chapter, XML documents include markup that identifies, structures, and sometimes annotates the content of a document. All that content, whatever it represents, is stored inside the document as text. Although this makes it difficult to use XML for some applications where binary formats are needed for their greater efficiency, it makes it very easy for both programs and humans to read XML documents, and makes it possible to work with XML using standard text-creation and processing tools.

Although ASCII text, commonly used for text files, is adequate for most documents in English, the limitations of a 128-member character set rapidly became clear (even when expanded to 256 members) as computers began to spread to areas using other languages. Even Latin-based European alphabets have enough accented and other special characters to fill up the 256 spaces rapidly. Adding Cyrillic, Greek, Turkish, Hebrew, or Arabic characters to that moves well beyond the available space. Character and glyph sets for Asian languages have tens of thousands of ideographs. Creating standards that will work for all these languages is a complex task, demanding political and technical compromise.

Although most English-speaking developers have grown used to the standard character sets available for that language, developers elsewhere have strained to use their languages in computers that weren't really designed to accommodate them. After several years of development, the Unicode standard is finally gaining some use, chipping away at the 8-bit character sets that have dominated com-puting since the arrival of the (later extended) 7-bit ASCII charac-ter set. Unicode offers 16 bits, for 65,536 possible characters.

Note

Developers who want to know more about Unicode may want to start with Tony Graham's *Unicode: A Primer* (IDG Books, 2000). If you need even more technical information, including a listing of all of the Unicode characters, try *The Unicode Standard, Version 3.0* (Addison-Wesley, 2000). Additional information and updates are available from the Unicode Consortium at http://www.unicode.org.

To make certain that XML can support languages all over the world, its creators decided to use Unicode as a base, giving docu-ment authors access to more than 50,000 character possibilities, though XML limits the use of some kinds of characters in Appendix B, which categorizes Unicode characters and leaves a few ranges of characters (mainly compatibility characters) out of the picture. XML documents don't have to use a Unicode character encoding, but UTF-8 and UTF-16, the two primary encodings for Unicode, are the only encodings that all proper XML parsers *must* support.

Cross-Reference

Developers who need or want to encode their XML docu-ments using character encodings other than UTF-8 or UTF-16 should read about the XML Declaration, in particular the Encoding Declaration, in Chapter 4.

XML's support for a wide range of characters and the use of markup inside documents raise a number of issues for developers who want to make full use of the character set. Most computers pro-vide direct input for only a limited range of characters, while the potential for collisions with the characters used to separate markup from content means that developers need a means of differentiating those characters in text from those characters in markup. XML pro-vides a set of similar mechanisms for handling both of these cases.

When developers want to include content in an XML document without typing it in directly, they use identifiers that begin with an ampersand (&) and end with a semicolon (;). If the first character after the ampersand is a pound sign (#), the content will be interpreted as a numeric character reference. If the first character is a letter, the content will be interpreted as an entity reference.

Character references comes in two versions, allowing document authors to identify characters using either decimal or hexadecimal values. Character references refer to characters by the numeric value assigned them in the Unicode standard, *not* any other encoding that might be used by the document. Although this might seem inconvenient to developers working only in local encodings, it makes it much easier for XML processors to handle these characters reliably.

To produce a character reference using the decimal value identifying the character, the syntax looks like:

```
&#Value;
```

The syntax for character references using hexadecimal values is similar, but adds an x between the # and the value:

```
&#xValue;
```

(The hexadecimal value is allowed to use either lowercase or capital letters within its value for the digits A–F.)

For example, either

```
&#222;
```

or

```
&#xDE;
```

will produce a capitalized Icelandic Thorn, a character not frequently seen on American keyboards. Character references have also proven useful in handling the Euro character, a new addition to the world's currencies. The Euro character is defined in Unicode 3.0 as 8364 decimal or 20AC in hexadecimal. To include a Euro character in an XML document when direct entry is unavailable, use either `&#8364;` or `&#x20AC;` in your document.

Note

You can use character references anywhere in element or attribute content. Although they are typically used only when it's difficult to enter a character directly, the specification itself lets you use them anywhere and for any acceptable character when they represent the textual content of an element or attribute.

Although document authors can use numerical references to represent markup characters, the XML 1.0 specification provides an alternative approach that's a bit shorter and easier to remember. Rather than try to remember that `&#38;` is the ampersand, you can use `&amp;` instead. XML provides five built-in entities, shown in Table 3-1.

Table 3-1 *Entities Built into the XML Standard*

Entity	Character Represented
`&amp;`	ampersand (&)
`&lt;`	less-than sign (<)
`&gt;`	greater-than sign (>)
`&apos;`	apostrophe (')
`&quot;`	quotation mark (")

Whereas `&apos;` and `&quot;` are primarily for use in attribute values, you should use `&amp;`, `&lt;` and `&gt;` anywhere those characters appear in either element or attribute content.

Cross-Reference

XML also provides another mechanism for "escaping" element content that includes markup characters, called CDATA sections. If your documents contain large sections that use markup characters throughout, you might want to explore this feature, covered in Chapter 4.

Testing Documents with Parsers and Browsers

Although it's a lot of fun to hand-code documents when you're developing the tags yourself, most XML probably will be coded using programs similar to the ones developers currently use for HTML. (Much XML will be generated directly out of databases, cutting individual coders even further out of the process.) XML has much stricter standards to meet and is considerably less forgiving of missing tags than HTML. Figuring out where you forgot a tag can be frustrating under the best of circumstances, and the tools at present are fairly primitive.

One of the best of the early tools for checking your work is Lark, a non-validating parser for XML documents. Validating parsers check the XML markup against a Document Type Definition that describes the document structure, whereas non-validating parsers check only to make sure that the document is well-formed. Lark isn't exactly beautiful, but it does a very good job of presenting the structure of documents and exposing the parts in the way that a parser or browser will interpret them. (If you want to frighten yourself, apply it to some HTML documents and see how many errors it finds.) Lark is a Java application developed by Tim Bray, one of the editors of the XML specification, and is available with much (though not all) of its source code at http://www.textuality. com/Lark/. Although Lark is getting a bit old, it continues to do a thorough job of reporting well-formedness errors.

Tip

A Web-based implementation of Lark, called RUWF (Are you well-formed?), is available at http://www.xml.com/ pub/tools/ruwf/check.html. It accepts URLs and returns either a congratulatory message that the document is well-formed, or a list of error messages returned by the parser. Badly formed documents can sometimes return an enormous list of errors.

Lark is a command-line utility at this point (Version 1.0 final beta), with no graphical user interface. To run it, you'll need a Java virtual machine that can run outside a browser. To run this example, you'll need a Java Runtime Environment (JRE) or Java Development Kit (JDK). Most people have seen Java only through an applet window in a browser, but Java is quite capable of working in text-only command-line environments as well. The `java` application takes as parameters the name of the Java application (which is the same as the name of its class file, without the `.class` extension) and any parameters the application may need. Running a Java application without any parameters usually produces a message outlining what parameters are available.

Tip

In case you don't need to develop Java applications, Sun offers a slimmer Java Runtime Environment (JRE) at `http://java.sun.com/`. It's still large, but much smaller than the full development environment.

Lark is useful for reading document structures only. Even though it does a wonderful job of matching up tags and building document trees, Lark doesn't compare the structures in your document to the structures in a DTD. I examine tools that handle that comparison in later chapters. Lark is definitely a tool worth keeping around, however, especially if you plan to be creating your own document structures or must convert legacy HTML to XML.

Note

Lark does have problems with certain parameters and XML entities. Check the Lark documentation for the full details.

This Lark example begins with a simple XML document. This document is a weather report, with only basic information encoded.

```
<WEATHERREPORT>
<DATE>7/14/97</DATE>
<CITY>NORTH PLACE</CITY>, <STATE>NX</STATE>
```

Continued

```
<COUNTRY>USA</COUNTRY>
High Temp:<HIGH SCALE="F">103</HIGH>
Low Temp:<LOW SCALE="F">70</LOW>
Morning:<MORNING>Partly Cloudy, Hazy</MORNING>
Afternoon:<AFTERNOON>Sunny and Hot</AFTERNOON>
Evening:<EVENING>Clear and Cooler</EVENING>
</WEATHERREPORT>
```

To have Lark parse this document, you need to tell the Driver class to analyze your XML file. In Windows 95 (if you have the Sun JDK installed, and the Lark files are in C:\lark), the command and its results look like the following output. Users of Microsoft's Visual J++ environment will use the command jview rather than java.

```
C:\My Documents\xmlaprim2\lark>java Driver weather.xml
Hello Tim
Lark V1.0 final beta Copyright (c) 1997-98 Tim Bray.
 All rights reserved; the right to use these class files
for any purpose
 is hereby granted to everyone.
Parsing...
Done.
```

If all goes well and Lark doesn't announce errors, your code is well-formed. Fortunately, Lark provides comprehensible error messages that can help you find any errors that creep into your code. For example, leaving off the final </WEATHERREPORT> yields the following session:

```
C:\My Documents\xmlaprim2\lark>java Driver weather.xml
Hello Tim
Lark V1.0 final beta Copyright (c) 1997-98 Tim Bray.
 All rights reserved; the right to use these class files
for any purpose is hereby granted to everyone.
Parsing...
Lark:weather.xml:9:43:E:Fatal: End of document entity
before end of root element.
Done.
```

Lark presents a meaningful message (that the end of the document happened before the root element was closed), as well as the
line number (9) and character number on that line (43) where the
error occurred.

An easier tool for some users is Internet Explorer 5, which will
check documents for well-formedness as well. Loading the preceding Weather Report Document (without any style information)
produces the screen shown in Figure 3-4.

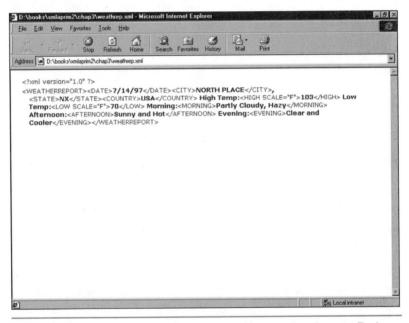

Figure 3-4 *When given an XML document with no styling, Internet Explorer
5 parses the document and displays it, including markup.*

It isn't lovely, but it's a good way to check your code. If you make
a mistake, Internet Explorer 5 notifies you of that as well, as shown
in Figure 3-5.

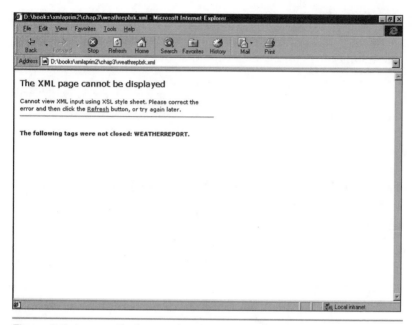

Figure 3-5 *Internet Explorer 5 also displays error messages generated by poorly formed documents.*

Internet Explorer 5's error messages aren't as comprehensive as those produced by Lark, but the two products serve different niches. Lark is really a developer's parser, designed for use in testing and processing XML documents. As a command-line tool, it reports only the problems it finds. (The RUWF tool built on top of Lark, mentioned previously, behaves similarly.) The parser built into Internet Explorer 5 is more of a production parser, optimized for speed and built into a friendly multi-purpose interface. Both models may prove useful for different projects.

Note

For some perspective on the usefulness of these core structures, read the Common XML specification (http:// simonstl.com/articles/cxmlspec.txt), which outlines an always-interoperable subset of XML and explains why more advanced features may not work in all XML processing environments.

Chapter 4

Adding a Few More Parts

Although the basic structures described in the previous chapter carry most of the information in XML documents, XML also provides some additional features that give document authors and developers more flexibility. Some of these tools enable document authors to add information outside the XML document element structures for human or machine processing, whereas others give parsers or applications extra information about the contents of the document. These supplemental tools can help you create documents that meet your particular needs, though their contents can be (and often are) ignored by applications.

<?xml?>: A Very Special Declaration

Although XML documents can be well-formed without an XML declaration, XML documents should begin with one. In particular, all documents that use encodings other than UTF-8 or UTF-16 should use the XML declaration to tell the parser which encoding the document is using. If all your documents use one of those Unicode encodings (or the US-ASCII set, which is a subset of UTF-8) the XML declaration can be omitted, but you lose an opportunity to explicitly state that your documents use Version 1.0 of XML. The XML declaration contains version information, encoding information, and information about which (if any) DTDs the document will use. Even though the contents of the XML declaration give only a very broad idea of the kind of XML document that follows, they provide critical basic information to the parsers that interpret the document.

The XML declaration looks like a processing instruction, another XML feature described later in the chapter, but it isn't one. The XML declaration includes several parts: the opening `<?xml`, the version information, the encoding declaration, the standalone declaration, and the closing `?>`. All XML declarations must include version information, but the encoding and standalone declarations are optional.

Caution

Unlike the HTML element, the XML declaration has no closing tag. `</?xml>` should *never* appear in a document. The XML declaration is an opening statement and nothing more.

Version number

An XML declaration that includes only version information is quite simple:

```
<?xml version="1.0" ?>
```

All XML declarations must at least contain a version number, despite the popularity of `<?xml?>` logos on various Web sites about XML. Unlike HTML, which arrived as Version 0.9 when it became publicly available, XML has been at Version 1.0 since the working drafts first appeared.

Encoding declaration

The encoding declaration addresses complex issues related to internationalization. It enables developers to specify which of several different character encoding schemes should be applied to a document.

All XML parsers are required to support and automatically detect UTF-8 and UTF-16 character encodings, even when the document has no encoding declaration. UTF-8 includes direct representations of most of the characters used in English, using values of 0–127 for the ASCII set of characters, and provides multi-byte encodings for Unicode characters with higher values. UTF-16 applies the Unicode/ISO/IEC 10646 standards, which extend the character space to 16 bits, enabling values from 0 to 65,535, a very significant expansion that includes most modern languages. Significant problems still exist with Chinese characters and several other character and glyph sets.

Although they aren't required to, XML parsers can support several other encodings, including ISO 8859-1 through ISO 8859-9, which represent most European languages, and EUC-JP, Shift_JIS, and ISO-2022-JP, which represent Japanese. The encoding scheme's name must always be enclosed in single or double quotation marks and described with the Latin character set. For example, to declare that a document uses XML version 1.0 and the ISO-8859-1 encoding, the following XML declaration is appropriate:

```
<?xml version="1.0" encoding="ISO-8859-1"?>
```

Although using an encoding declaration is not required when you're using a UTF-8 or UTF-16, doing so is still good practice. The following example shows an XML declaration for XML version 1.0 and the UTF-8 encoding:

```
<?xml version="1.0" encoding="UTF-8"?>
```

Table 4-1 lists the encodings required or recommended for support in the standard. Some parsers support many more encodings than these, whereas others stick exclusively to the two core requirements, UTF-8 and UTF-16. (Some parsers don't support UTF-8 or UTF-16 and therefore aren't in compliance with the XML specification.)

Table 4-1 *Common XML Encoding Schemes*

Encoding Scheme	# of Bits	Notes
UCS-2	16	Canonical Unicode character set
UCS-4	32	Canonical Unicode character set, using 32 bits
UTF-8	8	Unicode Transformation – 8 bit
UTF-7	7	Unicode Transformation – 7 bit (for mail and news)
UTF-16	16, 32	Unicode format that escapes 32-bit characters
ISO-8859-1	8	Latin alphabet No. 1 (Western Europe, Latin America)
ISO-8859-2	8	Latin alphabet No. 2 (Central/Eastern European)
ISO-8859-3	8	Latin alphabet No. 3 (SE Europe/miscellaneous)
ISO-8859-4	8	Latin alphabet No. 4 (Scandinavia/Baltic)
ISO-8859-5	8	Latin/Cyrillic
ISO-8859-6	8	Latin/Arabic
ISO-8859-7	8	Latin/Greek
ISO-8859-8	8	Latin/Hebrew
ISO-8859-9	8	Latin/Turkish
ISO-8859-10	8	Latin/Lappish/Nordic/Eskimo
ISO 10646	32	32-bit extended set; includes Unicode as subset
EUC-JP	8	Japanese (uses multibyte encoding)
Shift_JIS	8	Japanese (uses multibyte encoding)
ISO-2022-JP	7	Japanese (uses multibyte encoding; for mail and news)

Developers used to working exclusively with the ASCII set of characters (typically Americans) shouldn't have too much difficulty because most of the standards include that set as a base. Because the UTF-8 encoding is detected automatically, developers can expect most pages in English to display without difficulty. The Unicode UTF-16 encoding begins with a code sequence that identifies it, and parsers should be able to auto-detect it. A well written parser will be able to protect users to some extent from the seemingly random characters that currently fill screens when users visit pages written in encodings that differ from the default.

Unfortunately, displaying all these character sets still requires additional operating-system support. Windows NT and 2000 and Solaris 2.6 and 7 both offer native Unicode support, but developers on other platforms will need additional language kits that enable the conversion between formats. Collecting an adequate set of fonts to represent multiple languages remains a problem, but support for doing so is rapidly increasing. Programming languages present similar problems: most use an 8-bit space for character data rather than a 16-bit space. Java already uses Unicode as its default format for character information, giving developers a ready-made language for Unicode text processing. Unicode support is growing, and XML's use of it as a standard should widen its acceptance.

Cross-Reference

See the subsection on `xml:lang` in the section "Predefined Attributes" for another tool that makes XML more useful in multilingual situations.

Standalone declaration

The standalone declaration announces whether a document contains references to external document-type declarations. The value may be either yes or no. If no standalone declaration appears, the default is no. Because the no value has no effect on parsing, this declaration only matters when a document provides a value of yes but then goes ahead and references external DTDs (covered in the Chapter 6) anyway.

Valid documents must provide an honest answer for this declaration, if in fact they use the standalone declaration. Documents may make references to external entities and still claim yes, but may not refer to external DTDs. The XML 1.0 Recommendation suggests that any XML document can be converted into a standalone document for processing if necessary, and some simple applications may well choose to reject all documents that are not standalone documents. In general, however, document developers building sets of valid documents will most likely answer no or leave out this declaration entirely.

If it appears, the standalone declaration must appear at the end of the XML declaration:

```
<?xml version="1.0" encoding="UTF-8" standalone="yes"?>
```

or:

```
<?xml version="1.0" encoding="UTF-8" standalone="no"?>
```

If the encoding declaration is left out but the standalone declaration is used, the XML declaration might look like this:

```
<?xml version="1.0" standalone="yes"?>
```

or this:

```
<?xml version="1.0" standalone="no"?>
```

Caution

The standalone declaration is better at creating confusion than solving problems for most people. You should use it only when you are completely certain that a document doesn't rely on any external sources of DTD or entity information, but the declaration actually doesn't need to be present in those cases. The W3C is developing a standard for canonical XML documents that must be standalone, which may make this feature more useful. Normally, however, you probably don't need to use the standalone declaration.

Cross-Reference

See Chapter 5's discussion of parser behavior for more information on the standalone declaration.

CDATA Sections

By default, XML assumes that all the <, >, and & characters it encounters are markup. Sometimes you need to use these characters a lot within documents, and not just for markup. Anyone who has written an XML tutorial in XML knows that working with <, >, and & gets to be very tiring after a while, especially when you're marking up large sections of content. Similarly, scripting languages often use markup characters for other purposes. XML provides a convenient tool called CDATA sections that makes these problems less vexing. All the content inside a CDATA section is assumed to be "character data" — no markup is allowed.

To declare a section as CDATA, mark its beginning with `<![CDATA[` and its end with `]]>`. For example:

```
<![CDATA[ AT&T  ]]>
```

This will fail if the data includes any `]]>` sequences, which is an unusual and generally avoidable circumstance.) For example, the CDATA section in

```
<DOCUMENT><![CDATA[@#X! <<<<   >> & <<<<<
>>>]]></DOCUMENT>
```

will be interpreted as the characters "@#X! <<<< >> & <<<<< >>>" and will not generate a parsing error. When queried for the text in this document, a parser will return the information contained in the CDATA section:

```
@#X! <<<<   >> & <<<<< >>>
```

If this text weren't "escaped" with the CDATA declaration, parsers would stop at the first < sign because it appears to open a tag with no proper closing. CDATA sections may be used only in element contents and don't have a strong connection with the CDATA attribute type.

Cross-Reference

The CDATA attribute type is discussed in Chapter 6.

Even though using CDATA prohibits developers from using markup in a section of text, the tradeoff may be worthwhile if the section doesn't require markup anyway. If you need to use markup, either shrink the CDATA section to enclose only the offending text or replace the offending characters with their entity equivalents, as discussed in the previous chapter.

Note

The use of CDATA sections to escape text is actually a specific example of a more general SGML technique – *marked sections*. Marked sections follow a <![keyword[data...]]> syntax. Even though developers may use this syntax for CDATA, the SGML RCDATA, TEMP, IGNORE, and INCLUDE keywords are not available in XML documents. IGNORE and INCLUDE marked sections, however, are available within DTDs and are covered in Chapter 6.

Comments

Comments provide a means by which developers can add information meant strictly for human consumption to documents (and DTDs). Although some applications, typically editors, preserve and support comments, many applications discard them, and parsers aren't required to report their contents to the application. Because of the throwaway nature of comments, humans can put nearly anything they want inside them without affecting the applications processing the document.

Comments begin with <!-- and end with -->. XML comments cannot have two consecutive dashes (--) in their content because the dashes may confuse older parsers that interpret two dashes as the end of an SGML comment. XML comments can appear in both documents and DTDs. XML comments can't appear inside tags or in declarations and will not work in CDATA sections. (In CDATA sections, the comment symbols are treated as regular characters and will appear as part of the document.) Comments may appear in the prolog of a document, after the XML declaration but before the root element's start tag. They may also appear in element content — not in attributes — or after the end of the root element.

The parser will always ignore the contents of comments, though it may pass them on to the application. The following is a sample comment:

```
<!--This is a comment. Please ignore me if you are
parsing.-->
```

You may use XML comments in both DTDs and documents, but they are critically important in DTDs. Comments provide signposts that future editors will need to understand the structures you have created. Comments can explain otherwise mysterious entity references and are useful for labeling declarations, especially if element names are abbreviated. Comments may seem like wasted space to developers with perfect memories, but a DTD without comments is truly wasted space to the next developer who must work with it.

Processing Instructions

Processing instructions don't directly affect the document structure, except in that the application receives notice of their existence. Like comments, processing instructions may appear in the prolog of a document, after the XML declaration but before the root element's start tag. They may also appear in element content — not in attributes — or after the end of the root element. Unlike comments, processing instructions are generally used to include information inside documents that is meant for the application processing the document, not for human consumption.

Processing instructions begin with <? and end with ?>, and the sequence ?> can't appear anywhere inside the processing instruction. Although strict rules exist for the first word appearing in the processing instruction (the *target*), the rest of the contents of the processing instruction may use any syntax their creators find useful.

The target must be composed of letters, digits, periods, dashes, underscores, or colons, and must begin with a letter or an underscore. The *Namespaces in XML* recommendation strongly suggests — essentially for the sake of avoiding confusion — that developers not use colons in processing instruction targets. Like elements and attributes, names beginning with XML, xml, or any other case-variation on XML are reserved for use by the W3C.

The remainder of the processing instruction, after a space, may be composed of any characters, including equals signs and quotation marks. Although many processing instructions use "pseudo-attributes" that look like regular XML markup, doing so isn't required. Processing instructions can use any syntax their creators deem appropriate after the target. Although it would be unusual, the following:

```
<?Jimmy - use the burnt umber crayon for this. ?>
```

would be an acceptable processing instruction if the receiving application (perhaps a child named Jimmy?) understood its meaning. A more typical processing instruction might be:

```
<?xml-stylesheet type="text/css" href="mystyle.css"?>
```

The use of xml at the beginning of the target is acceptable in this case because the W3C created this processing instruction in *Associating XML Documents with Stylesheets* (http://www.w3.org/TR/xml-stylesheet/). This processing instruction, which I use later in Chapters 10 and 12, uses the more conventional pseudo-attribute syntax. The type pseudo-attribute identifies the style sheet as Cascading Style Sheets, and the href pseudo-attribute gives the application a URL where the style sheet can be found.

Processing instructions have an important role to play in specifying processing for documents. Though processing instructions (or PIs, as they're known) can't be standardized through the use of DTDs, standards are key to enabling programmers to create functionality that works across multiple document types. Processing instructions have been condemned as a diabolical means of creating unnecessarily complicated markup that doesn't transfer well between different parsers, but they remain very convenient for certain uses.

Predefined Attributes

XML 1.0 reserved all element and attribute names beginning with "XML," "xml," and similar variations, but it also created two attributes in that reserved space. Developers can use these two attributes in their own documents and DTDs.

xml:space

As you see in Chapter 2, whitespace is sometimes used to make the markup structure of a document explicit rather than function as content. Whitespace characters — spaces, tabs, line breaks, and carriage returns — occupy an uncertain place in markup languages. Developers like to use them to make their structures easier to read, so some markup languages (including HTML) either discard whitespace or "normalize" it to single spaces. In other cases, whitespace matters, and removing it may change the meaning of the document. To address this disparity, Section 2.10 of the XML Recommendation defines a new attribute, xml:space, that allows elements to declare to an application whether their whitespace is significant, using one of two values: default or preserve.

The xml:space attribute provides a hook that style sheets can use to display documents correctly and may also affect processing documents that aren't necessarily meant for display. XML parsers already must pass all non-markup characters to the application and inform the application of the element in which they appeared. The xml:space attribute acts as a flag, telling the application whether it should pay attention to whitespace characters. It remains up to the application whether it actually does anything with the whitespace characters. While browsers and some other XML display applications may take heed of xml:space, many other applications will find it irrelevant.

The xml:space behavior is inherited from parent elements; if an element containing an xml:space value contains other elements, they too will handle whitespace as specified by the parent element. You can override this behavior by creating a new xml:space attribute in the child elements.

I demonstrate `xml:space` with a poetry example in which the line breaks are considered significant. For the rest of the document, however, whitespace isn't important.

```
<poem xml:space="default">
<author>Simon St.Laurent</author>
<comments>This is a pretty poor poem, but you never
know!</comments>
<contents xml:space="preserve">Roses are red,
Violets are blue.
XML is a dream
and so are you!
</contents>
</poem>
```

The root element, poem, sets `xml:space` to `"default"`. This value applies to the author and comments elements, telling applications they can handle whitespace as they see fit. The contents element, however, overrides the value from the root element and suggests that applications preserve the whitespace between the lines of the poem. As bad as the poem may be, its creator considers its whitespace significant.

Note

If you want to use the `xml:space` element in a validating XML environment you need to declare it in your DTD or schema. You can also use DTDs and schemas to provide default values for `xml:space`, making it easy to set the value once and not have to include it in every document explicitly.

Caution

Microsoft's MSXML parser discards whitespace by default, even when the `xml:space` attribute is used. To make this parser preserve whitespace when `xml:space` is set to `true`, your applications need to set the `preserveWhiteSpace` property of the parser to `true`. MSXML also treats whitespace contained in CDATA sections as significant.

xml:lang

The `xml:lang` attribute gives XML authors a consistent way to identify the language contained within a particular element. Combined with XML's support for Unicode, the use of `xml:lang` should make it easier to present internationalized versions of information. Developers can create documents with built-in translations, or make it easier for applications to know when to provide a translation.

The `xml:lang` attribute takes as its value a code defined in ISO 639 or registered with the Internet Assigned Numbers Authority (IANA). You can use an ISO 639 code directly and follow it with a country code to more precisely define the language: `en-GB`, for instance, as opposed to `en-US`. IANA codes must be prefixed with `i-` or `I-`; you can use other codes, but you must prefix them with `x-` or `X-`. Unlike most of the rest of XML, none of these codes are case sensitive. (This usage is explained in greater detail in IETF RFC 1766.)

For example, suppose that someone is trying to present quotes in Latin, with an English description:

```
<SECTION>
<DESCRIPTION xml:lang="en">
Caesar begins by describing the geography of Gaul.
</DESCRIPTION>
<QUOTE xml:lang="la">
Gallia est omnis divisa in partes tres, quarum unam
incolunt Belgae, aliam Aquitani, tertiam qui ipsorum
lingua Celtae, nostra Galli appellantur.
</QUOTE>
<EXPLANATION xml:lang="en">It isn't the most thrilling
opening to a great work on war, but it does explain some
key issues to Romans who probably have never been
anywhere near Rome.</EXPLANATION>
</SECTION>
```

In this case, I use "en" to indicate English and "la" to indicate Latin. An application equipped with a Latin translator might be able to convert the Latin section, when prompted (or not), into something resembling:

```
All of Gaul is divided into three parts, one of which is
inhabited by the Belgae, another by the Aquitani, and the
third by those who are called Celts in their own
language, and Gauls in ours.
```

A translation program would probably produce something more literal, but you get the idea. The xml:lang attribute works much like the xml:space attribute and namespace declarations, applying to the content of child elements as well as the element in which it is actually used. Because the majority of the content is in English and only the quote is in Latin, you could achieve the same results with:

```
<SECTION xml:lang="en">
<DESCRIPTION>
Caesar begins by describing the geography of Gaul.
</DESCRIPTION>
<QUOTE xml:lang="la">
Gallia est omnis divisa in partes tres, quarum unam
incolunt Belgae, aliam Aquitani, tertiam qui ipsorum
lingua Celtae, nostra Galli appellantur.
</QUOTE>
<EXPLANATION>It isn't the most thrilling opening to a
great work on war, but it does explain some key issues to
Romans who probably have never been anywhere near
Rome.</EXPLANATION>
</SECTION>
```

This way, the DESCRIPTION and EXPLANATION elements inherit the xml:lang value of en, whereas the QUOTE element overrides it with la, indicating that its contents are in Latin.

The xml:lang attribute provides applications with more language information than the bare Unicode data, and may save applications a lot of time that would otherwise be spent determining which language is being used for a particular element. It isn't a cure-all, though; effective use of this element requires consistent application support and probably some fairly complex style usage. The browser developers will, I hope, seize this opportunity to sort out some of the language confusion currently pervading the Web. Combined with Unicode, this attribute makes it possible to deliver on many of XML's promises of easier internationalization.

Note

If you want to use the xml:lang element in a validating XML environment, you need to declare it in your DTD or schema. You can also use DTDs and schemas to provide default values for xml:lang, making it easy to set the value once and not have to include it in every document explicitly.

Part II

Describing Documents

Chapter 5

Types of XML Processing

XML documents and XML document processing are tightly bound together, so much so that the XML 1.0 specification reads more like a set of rules for processing documents than a set of rules for writing documents. Whether you're planning to create XML documents or to build applications for processing them, a basic understanding of different kinds of XML processing can help keep you from encountering mysterious problems when the same document is processed by different parsers. XML gives application developers an opportunity to use generic tools to read and write information, but it also requires them to make choices about which tools to use.

Parsers and Programs

XML parsers are useful to developers for two critical reasons. First, they provide an easy way for document creators to check their work. Create a document, run it through a parser, and watch for any errors. More important, however, parsers are the components that programs use to read and write XML, freeing the developers from having to understand the XML 1.0 specification in depth. Software developers can pick a parser that meets their needs and wire it into their code without having to focus on XML's syntactic details. Although developers still need to write integration code, the parser hides an enormous amount of detail.

Note

The word *application* is a bit tricky in XML. Although software programs are still referred to as applications, XML vocabularies are also referred to as XML applications. They provide specific applications of generic XML syntax. In general, this book uses the word *application* to refer to software, not to XML vocabularies.

Basically, parsing is just the interpretation of text. Computers can't really read, but they can interpret text files. Markup languages simply aid them in this interpretation, specifying explicitly to computers (or occasionally to humans) the nature of chunks of text. XML parsers transform XML documents into application data structures, and sometimes back again. There's more to this than just reading and writing, however; XML parsers have to check document structures, often add information to the document, and sometimes choose to ignore content as well. All this work is encapsulated in the parser, and parsers have grown to support additional features as well, such as checking documents against XML schemas, processing namespace information, and providing applications with an interface for managing and manipulating XML documents in memory.

Cross-Reference

For more information about the interfaces that XML parsers use to connect to applications, see Chapter 9.

Depending on the environment in which developers are working, they may have a choice of multiple parsers. Because many parsers use standard interfaces, it's even possible in some cases to switch out one parser in favor of a different one, and to layer tools between the parser and the application. Separating parsing logic from application logic gives developers new options and capabilities at a fraction of the cost of building new input and output for applications. Developers can switch between validating and non-validating, namespace-aware or not, schema-aware or not, and external-resource-loading or not by changing a few lines of code. Some parsers provide switches for different feature sets, making switching even easier.

Validating and Non-Validating Parsers

XML parsers must always check the document's markup to make sure it fits a set of rules. All conforming XML parsers check at least that a document is *well-formed* — that is, that it satisfies a minimal set of rules about the grammar used to create a document. By definition, to be an XML document, the document *must* be well-formed. Validating XML parsers also check that documents conform to a complex set of specifications outlined in document type definitions (DTDs). A document that conforms to a DTD is said to be *valid*; parsers that can interpret DTDs and check document structures against their strictures are called validating parsers.

Note

XML 1.0's definition of validating parsers doesn't take into account schema-based (rather than DTD-based) validation of documents. In general, whenever you see the term "validating parser" you should assume that the discussion involves validation against DTDs unless schemas are explicitly mentioned.

Creating DTDs is often considered a necessary step in building robust applications. DTDs provide critical information that enables XML processors to parse the code and make certain that it contains all the information the application needs, in a form the application will accept. The DTD provides a critical link between the data files given to the XML processor and the data transmitted from the XML processor to the application. DTDs help computers understand structures that may seem obvious to humans; they also force humans to consider the structure of the information that they are modeling.

Note

Although the W3C's XML Schema Description Language and its competitor RELAX may eventually replace DTDs, XML 1.0 defines validating and non-validating parsers through their relationships to DTDs, not schemas or other alternatives. Schemas do introduce new complications, however, as discussed later in the chapter.

Unfortunately, a few complications lurk under the distinction between validating and non-validating parsers, some of which have the potential to cause serious irritation. XML provides a few critical exemptions for non-validating parsers despite XML 1.0's goal: "the number of optional features in XML is to be kept to the absolute minimum, ideally zero."

The basic problem comes from a separation between the types of documents and the types of parsers interpreting them. XML documents must be well-formed and may be valid. Parsers may be validating or non-validating. Validating parsers check to make certain that documents are valid, whereas non-validating parsers check only to make certain that they are well-formed. Non-validating parsers do, however, process any DTD information they encounter, assigning default values for attributes and expanding entities based on the information in the DTD. To take advantage of these features, it's often useful to create a DTD even for documents you don't plan to process with a validating parser.

This approach creates some large problems, however, because non-validating parsers, unlike validating parsers, aren't required to load pieces (typically DTDs or entities) external to the document. Because those external pieces may contribute to the content of the document, that content may disappear when the document is processed by a non-validating parser. The document will parse — it is, after all, well-formed — but it may be missing information, with no warning from the parser.

This creates the potential for some fairly disastrous situations. Non-validating parsers vary in their behavior because they are, after all, allowed to load the external resources at their discretion. For example, the AElfred parser will read external DTDs and apply the default values, whereas James Clark's Expat does not, at least by default. Because Expat is probably the most widely used C-language parser, used in both the Netscape and Mozilla browsers and the XML::Parser module for Perl, external resources may disappear in a wide variety of environments. Applications, such as Xlink processors, that depend heavily on default values might find those values missing when a non-validating parser is used in place of a validating parser. This could happen for a number of reasons, including:

- A user changed the settings in his or her browser to a fast-load mode, turning off the optional loading of external resources.

- A developer decided to change the parser used in an application (thanks to the SAX and DOM standards, it isn't that hard).

- Documents that were designed for use in one application must now be reused in a different application.

If users open XML documents and find unexpanded entities ("What's this &sunset; in the middle of the paragraph?") or some functionality disappears (probably because of lost default values for attributes), they've probably encountered some flavor of this problem.

Note

For an excellent summary of what non-validating parsers are required to do, see John Cowan's "Non-Validating XML Parsers: Requirements" list at http://www.lists.ic.ac.uk/hypermail/xml-dev/9808/0019.html. For more on Expat's behavior, see http://www.jclark.com/xml/expat.html.

The ways to avoid the problem are reasonably clear, though not always workable. One way is to include all DTD information in the internal subset, described in the next chapter. Putting every declaration into every file will ensure that even parsers that won't fetch external resources have a complete set of declarations on which to operate. This may require you to create gateways that gather all declarations and pile them into the main file at key interfaces between applications that will use external resources and those that won't. It's not exactly an efficient solution, but it does fix the problem.

The W3C and IETF's XML Signatures Working Group is developing a Canonical XML format (http://www.w3.org/TR/xml-c14n). Canonical XML documents are well-formed and don't rely on any DTD information, though the original document on which they were based might have had a DTD that contributed to its content. Creating a Canonical XML document is mostly a matter of parsing a document to create a fully processed version that includes all the information from the DTD, and then re-serializing that information into an XML document. Developers working with digital signatures need a stable base like this in order to build signature algorithms that work consistently, but the same tools can be used by developers who simply need a more reliable interchange format.

Another popular alternative, available only to those with total control over an environment (typically developers who expect their documents to be used in only one application context), is to use external resources and simply accept that other tools may be incapable of using those files correctly. If you use this approach, indicating that your documents need external resources may be wise. A standalone declaration set to no won't stop a parser from processing a document and ignoring its external resources without a warning, but it could tip off a human reader trying to figure out what's going on.

Tip

If you use DTDs to assign default values to attributes or process entities, it's usually worth the trouble to create a DTD that genuinely describes your document structure. Doing so ensures that you don't create documents that look as though they *should* work in a validating parser but that are missing too many declarations. Going halfway means creating documents that will lose information in some non-validating parsers, but that still can't get through a validating parser – the worst of both worlds.

Namespace and Schema-Aware Parsers

XML 1.0 was published as a W3C Recommendation in February 1998 (with errata incorporated as revisions in October 2000), and several key XML features have appeared since XML first arrived. Namespaces in XML, a critical part of the W3C's plans for using XML to build a *Semantic Web*, arrived only in January 1999. As of this writing, XML Schema Description Language is still in Candidate Recommendation and may undergo some revision before proceeding to Recommendation. As a result, different parsers provide different levels of support for these late arrivals. Developers choosing parsers need to examine their needs closely when picking a parser, perhaps even looking to future prospects for development.

Namespace support is available in most recent XML parsers and can be implemented with some additional processing on the results from parsers that don't natively understand namespaces. Most parsers implement proprietary interfaces for that information, however. Neither DOM Level 1 nor the original version of SAX provided interfaces supporting namespaces, leaving parser developers to create their own approaches. Although SAX2, now available, and DOM Level 2, in Candidate Recommendation status, both provide direct support for namespaces in a parser-independent API, developers should check parser support for namespaces carefully. Developers who want to be able to choose among parsers should be especially careful because of the potential for API lock-in.

Schema support has been slower in coming and is often implemented as processing after the initial XML parsing process is complete. Whereas XML 1.0 rolled DTD processing directly into the parser, schema processing is more clearly an additional option. Even when schema processing is built directly into a parser you can usually switch it off entirely, and many schema processors — such as the Relaxer package for checking XML documents against RELAX descriptions — are actually built as separate modules.

Schemas face another potential problem: several different schema languages are in use, and it isn't clear as of this writing which (if any) will triumph. It's not easy to choose among the W3C's XML Schemas, Microsoft's XML-Data Reduced, RELAX, and even XML 1.0's DTDs. DTDs are widely supported but don't provide data typing. XML-Data is widely distributed in Microsoft's Internet Explorer and MSXML parser, but Microsoft has announced plans to support W3C XML Schemas when they arrive. RELAX is still emerging, with a small core of software only getting started. The W3C's XML Schemas are also still in development, with a small core of software. Although they will probably have the benefit of W3C endorsement, they're also far more complex than any of their competitors.

You may have to choose among these options on a case-by-case basis, at least until the dust settles further and XML becomes a more stable set of tools. Some companies are providing tools for converting among these different information descriptions (Extensibility's XML Authority, for example), but software developers are still going to have to choose which of these features to build into their software.

Tip

Although it isn't an official standard, a new initiative called Resource Directory Description Language (RDDL) describes a human- and machine-readable format for connecting namespace URIs to appropriate schema processing. See `http://www.rddl.org` for details.

Parser Choices

Many XML parsers are available, often (even usually) for free. A large and relatively comprehensive list is available at `http://www.xmlsoftware.com/parsers/`. If you're an author or a reader of XML documents, you're more likely to work with a friendlier editor, browser, or other application, but to programmers and those who need to check XML at the command line, these free parsers are valuable tools. Picking one can be difficult, however. Your criteria may include:

- *Environment*—Java developers have an embarrassingly rich selection of parsers to choose from, whereas developers working in other languages and platforms may have fewer choices. Obviously, you need an XML tool that works well with the other parts you're using.

- *Code size*—Some parsers are tiny, suitable for use in embedded applications and applets, whereas others occupy megabytes of hard-drive space.

- *Memory footprint*—Different parsers may use very different amounts of memory to process the same documents, even when they both return SAX events or DOM trees.

- *Efficiency*—Some parsers, notably Expat, are highly optimized speed demons. Other parsers have focused on features or size and paid less attention to sheer speed.

- *Features*—Validation, loading external resources, namespaces, schema processing, additional APIs, and a wide variety of additional options differentiate parsers.

- *Cost*—Some parsers cost money to use and redistribute. Depending on the environment in which you operate, spending some money may make more sense than writing your own parser.

- *License*—Some parsers are open-source whereas others are proprietary, even when free. If you want to be able to extend or fix a parser, this may be a significant issue.

- *Stability*—Not all parsers are completely finished, and many of them have remained in various states of beta testing for most of their existence.

One last warning about XML parsers is in order: Some parsers conform to the W3C Recommendation better than others. Some parsers, such as AElfred's initial versions, have been built for maximum efficiency and minimum file size. As a result, AElfred, for example, deliberately omitted some relatively obscure well-formedness checks. AElfred will therefore accept some documents that stricter parsers would ignore. Parsers built for embedded systems often have even fewer features, making them not-quite-XML parsers. Even parsers designed for compliance sometimes have problems. OASIS (http://www.oasis-open.org) has developed a test suite for XML 1.0, and XML.com has run a number of articles exploring parser conformance to that test suite, so details about these parser problems shouldn't be difficult to find.

So far, mixing parsers seems to be okay in most situations. The XML specification, though difficult to read, is fairly precise. If, however, you find an odd glitch or two in your work, be sure to check your work using multiple parsers (or multiple applications that use different parsers) and notify the developers of the parser or application.

Note

Although the XML community is aware of interoperability problems, there hasn't exactly been an outpouring of effort to fix them. XML Processing Description Language (XPDL – http://purl.oclc.org/NET/xpdl), a project of the author's, is one attempt to identify the options needed to process documents as intended, but it hasn't found much use. Developers generally seem willing to take their chances, if and when they rely on DTDs and namespaces.

Chapter 6

Document Type Definitions

Although the tools for creating valid XML documents may look a little strange, the logic behind them is not really that complicated. Creating a document type definition is not easy, but a well-written DTD is well worth the effort. DTDs provide you with a useful set of strictures that can make application development and authoring easier and provide many useful features for reducing the size of your XML documents. Even if you don't plan to write your own DTDs, knowing how to read them may be useful during a late night of work on documents created with a poorly documented DTD. Even developers planning to use schemas should probably at least be familiar with DTDs because they will probably encounter them at some point.

Starting Simple

The details involved in building DTDs can be daunting, even to experienced HTML coders, SQL developers, and C++ and Java programmers. XML has lessened SGML's reputation for complexity, but it still has some strange detours and odd passageways. The various parts of the XML standard refer to each other constantly, requiring page flipping on an enormous scale. To avoid marching forward into quicksand, I start with lightweight documents that demonstrate some of XML's tools. In this first section I use many parts of XML without explaining them in depth; the detailed explanations are in the following sections. Unfortunately, the explanations aren't likely to make too much sense until you've seen some XML in action. The purpose of this brief section is to present a general idea of the appearance of a valid XML document, not to explain the details.

Note

Although you can work with these examples and try to validate them, this first section is here mostly to give you a picture of what XML documents and DTDs look like in their raw form. All of the examples in this chapter are available for download at http://www.simonstl.com/xmlprim/.

Initially, my examples use only the internal DTD subset, keeping the declarations that describe the document in the same file as the document content. DTDs can appear inside the document they describe, in separate files, or split across both. Most large-scale projects will use external DTDs stored in centralized file structures, but the simple document I present here probably wouldn't be managed in any large-scale system.

Caution

Some of the features described in this chapter work only in the external DTD subset. I flag those features, but remember that the internal subset is somewhat more limited than the external subset.

The document begins with the XML declaration, followed by a document type declaration that includes one element type declaration and a general entity declaration. The element type declaration defines the simple structure that will follow, whereas the entity declaration defines some content referenced in the document. After the declarations appear, they are followed by a document that conforms to the structure they describe:

```
<?xml version="1.0" encoding="UTF-8"?>
<!DOCTYPE DOCUMENT [
<!ELEMENT DOCUMENT (#PCDATA)>
<!ENTITY Description "This is entity content.">
]>
<DOCUMENT>This is element text and an entity follows:
&Description; </DOCUMENT>
```

Internet Explorer 5.0 enables you to validate this document, though making it happen takes a little work. By default, Internet Explorer 5.0 checks only for well-formedness, and you must set an obscure JavaScript switch to turn on validation. As a result, you still have to take a few steps in order to validate your documents against a DTD. (Generally, validation in IE 5.0 is still easier than validation on the command line with a raw validating parser.)

First, you need to get the code that performs the validation. If your XML pages are on an HTTP server you can do your validation directly from Microsoft's Web page. If not, you need to save a copy of the page to your system, open it as a file in Internet Explorer 5.0, and then validate it. The validator is available from Microsoft at `http://msdn.microsoft.com/downloads/samples/internet/x ml/xml_validator/default.asp`.

Tip

Put a copy of the validation page into the same directory as your XML files. That way, you need only open the validation page there and use the relative paths to the files – just the file name.

Tip

If you prefer to use Netscape Navigator, try the XML Validator service available from Brown University: `http://www.stg.brown.edu/service/xmlvalid/`. This service performs server-side validation and therefore works with any Web browser.

The validator, shown in Figure 6-1, enables you to enter a URL or paste in some raw XML code for validation. Results appear at the bottom of the page.

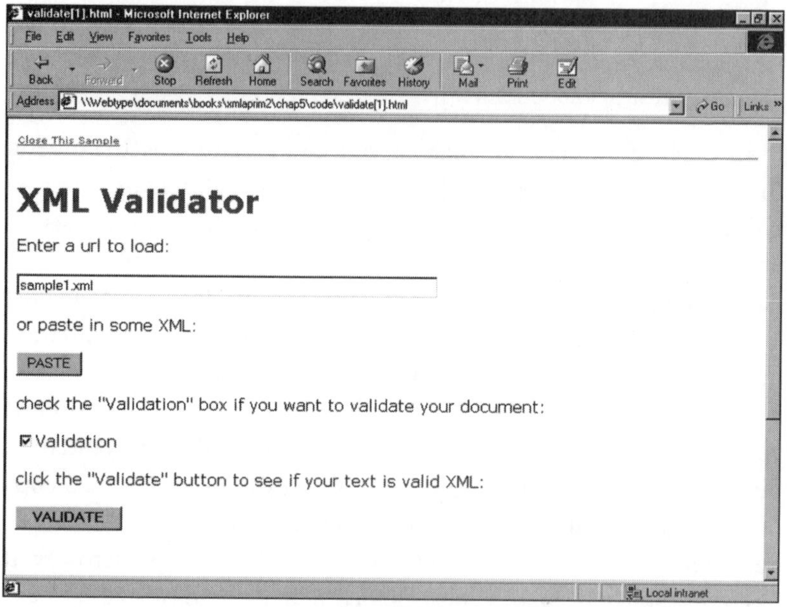

Figure 6-1 *You must access Internet Explorer's validation tools through a Web page.*

Loading the test document into the validator produces the results shown at the bottom of the Web page in Figure 6-2.

Internet Explorer (technically, the parser inside Internet Explorer) interprets the declarations, enabling the creation of the DOCUMENT elements and expanding the &Description; entity. This code doesn't do much yet, but it provides a basic framework upon which a structure can grow. The XML declaration on the first line of the document tells the parser the version of XML being used, and that the document encoding is compatible with the UTF-8 standard, which includes the standard Latin-1 set of characters for most European languages. The document type declaration on the next line (`<!DOCTYPE name [...]>`) creates a DOCUMENT definition, which includes two key pieces — an element and an entity. (You need to choose Source from the View menu to see the full DTD, which is hidden by the browser so that it can display more content.) The element declaration on the third line (`<!ELEMENT name data`) announces a DOCUMENT element that can contain parsed character data (`#PCDATA`), and the entity declaration on the fourth line (`<!ENTITY name EntityDefinition>`) provides a particular value to go with the name Description. The actual markup includes only a single DOCUMENT element. This element contains some text and an entity reference, which is the entity name (from the declaration) preceded by an ampersand and followed by a semicolon. By the time IE 5 displays the document, it has expanded the entity. From these humble beginnings, you can create more complex types that begin to define a sample document.

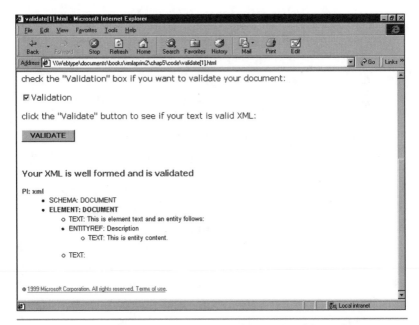

Figure 6-2 *Internet Explorer will expand entities as it validates documents.*

The next example adds several attributes to the DOCUMENT element, providing some information that a document management system can use for tracking. The <!ATTLIST name data...> declaration enables the DOCUMENT element to carry a tracking number and a security level.

```
<?xml version="1.0" encoding="UTF-8"?>
<!DOCTYPE DOCUMENT [
<!ELEMENT DOCUMENT (#PCDATA)>
<!ATTLIST DOCUMENT
    trackNum CDATA #REQUIRED
    secLevel (unclassified|classified) "unclassified">
<!ENTITY Description "This is a very simple sample
document.">
]>
<DOCUMENT trackNum="1234">This is element text and an
entity follows: &Description; </DOCUMENT>
```

The attribute list declaration (<!ATTLIST name values>) should go under the element to which it refers, although it technically doesn't have to because it names the element. The two attributes are of different types. The trackNum attribute can have any value of type CDATA. CDATA (as you'll see in much more detail later) as character data. Most attributes will be of type CDATA. The attribute declaration also announces that it is required (#REQUIRED). Attributes may also be optional (indicated by #IMPLIED, or a default value) or have fixed values assigned to them by default (#FIXED followed by the default value). The second attribute, secLevel, can accept only one of two values: unclassified or classified. (The | symbol always indicates an OR statement in XML markup.) The default value (see Figure 6-3), which is specified after the listing, is unclassified. The actual document element contains the required trackNum attribute but not the secLevel attribute, so the default value of unclassified will apply.

Internet Explorer 5.0 has hidden the DTD, but its impact is clear: the secLevel attribute is shown with a value of unclassified, the default value declared in the DTD, even though it wasn't in the document. If you add a secLevel attribute with a value of NONE to the DOCUMENT element, Internet Explorer reports the errors shown in Figure 6-4.

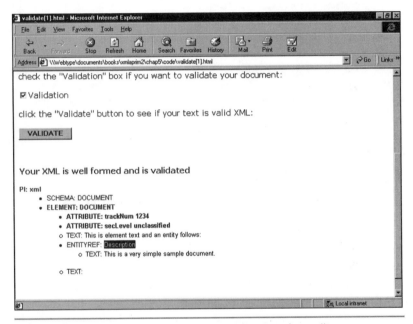

Figure 6-3 *Internet Explorer will apply default values for attributes to documents.*

Now that the example element has attributes, you can give it some additional elements to oversee. XML enables developers to identify what content elements may hold, of what type, in what order, and how often. This example acquires a title, an author, and a description. The title must appear one time only, the author field must appear at least once, summary elements are optional, and a special note element may appear either once or not at all. All these elements must appear in the order in which they are listed.

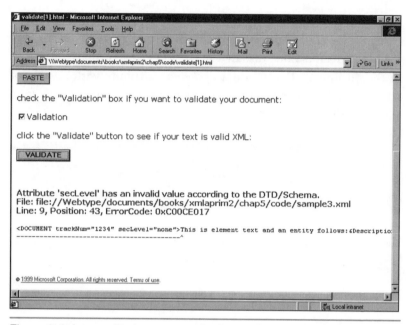

Figure 6-4 *Internet Explorer reports the first validation error in a file.*

```
<?xml version="1.0" encoding="UTF-8"?>
<!DOCTYPE DOCUMENT [
<!ELEMENT DOCUMENT (TITLE,AUTHOR+,SUMMARY*,NOTE?)>
<!ATTLIST DOCUMENT
     trackNum CDATA #REQUIRED
     secLevel (unclassified|classified) "unclassified">
<!ELEMENT TITLE (#PCDATA)>
<!ELEMENT AUTHOR (#PCDATA)>
<!ELEMENT SUMMARY (#PCDATA)>
<!ENTITY Description "This is a very simple sample
document.">
]>
<DOCUMENT trackNum="1234">
<TITLE>Sample Document</TITLE>
<AUTHOR>Simon St.Laurent</AUTHOR>
<SUMMARY>This is element text and an entity
follows:&Description; </SUMMARY></DOCUMENT>
```

This code produces a fairly rigid document structure, built by the (TITLE,AUTHOR+,SUMMARY*,NOTE?) part of the DOCUMENT element declaration. Because all the entries are separated by commas, they must appear in the order in which they are listed. TITLE, because it has no suffix, must appear once and only once. The plus sign following AUTHOR means that it must appear at least one time and possibly many more. The asterisk following SUMMARY enables any number (including zero) of SUMMARY elements to appear at this point. The question mark after NOTE makes it an optional element, but it can appear only once. Internet Explorer 5.0 returns the document structure shown in Figure 6-5.

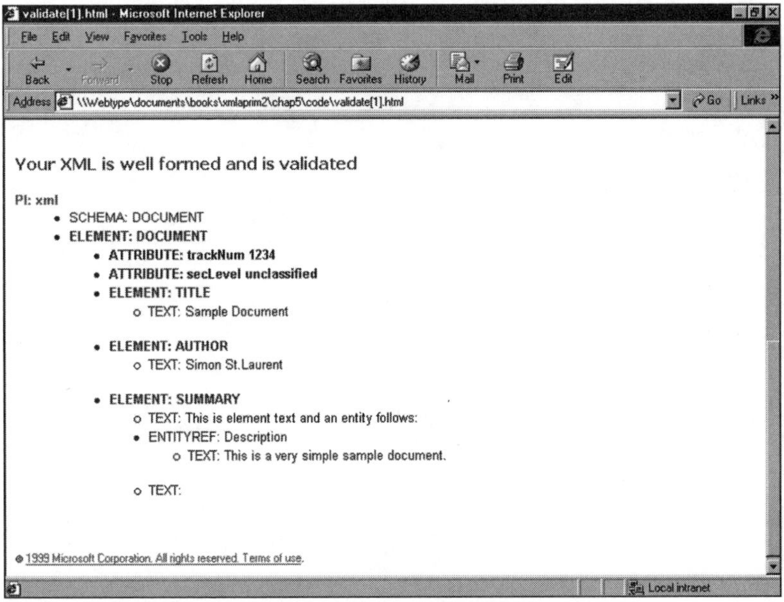

Figure 6-5 *Internet Explorer validates nested structures.*

Changing the sequence of the elements in this document will make the parser fail because the document will no longer conform to the structure specified in the DTD: it will no longer be valid. For example, moving the SUMMARY element above the TITLE element produces the error shown in Figure 6-6.

The next example extends the DTD one level deeper, providing more information under the AUTHOR element. In this case, the author can identify both an organization (company or university) and a name.

```
<?xml version="1.0" encoding="UTF-8"?>
<!DOCTYPE DOCUMENT [
<!ELEMENT DOCUMENT (TITLE,AUTHOR+,SUMMARY*,NOTE?)>
<!ATTLIST DOCUMENT
     trackNum CDATA #REQUIRED
     secLevel (unclassified|classified) "unclassified">
<!ELEMENT TITLE (#PCDATA)>
```

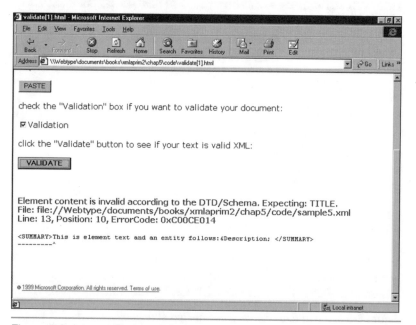

Figure 6-6 *Internet Explorer 5.0 reports document-structure errors in documents it validates.*

```
<!ELEMENT AUTHOR (FIRSTNAME, LASTNAME, (UNIVERSITY |
COMPANY)?)>
<!ELEMENT FIRSTNAME (#PCDATA)>
<!ELEMENT LASTNAME (#PCDATA)>
<!ELEMENT UNIVERSITY (#PCDATA)>
<!ELEMENT COMPANY (#PCDATA)>
<!ELEMENT SUMMARY (#PCDATA)>
<!ENTITY Description "This is a very simple sample
document.">
]>
<DOCUMENT trackNum="1234">
<TITLE>Sample Document</TITLE>
<AUTHOR><FIRSTNAME>Simon</FIRSTNAME>
<LASTNAME>St.Laurent</LASTNAME>
<COMPANY>XML Mania</COMPANY></AUTHOR>
<SUMMARY>This is element text and an entity
follows:&Description; </SUMMARY></DOCUMENT>
```

The main change, apart from the addition of a few elements, is in the AUTHOR element declaration: `<!ELEMENT AUTHOR (FIRSTNAME, LASTNAME, (UNIVERSITY | COMPANY)?)>`. This declaration enables developers to create somewhat more flexible structures. In this case the AUTHOR element must include (in this order) a FIRST-NAME element, a LASTNAME element, and either a UNIVERSITY element or a COMPANY element. (Using both elements produces a parsing error.) Internet Explorer 5.0 seems happy enough with this arrangement (see Figure 6-7).

At this point, the document is getting somewhat long, and most of it is just defining the document type. For the last example I separate the DTD file from the actual document. The document becomes considerably shorter:

```
<?xml version="1.0" encoding="UTF-8"?>
<!DOCTYPE DOCUMENT SYSTEM " simple.dtd">
<DOCUMENT trackNum="1234">
```

Continued

```
<TITLE>Sample Document</TITLE>
<AUTHOR><FIRSTNAME>Simon</FIRSTNAME>
<LASTNAME>St.Laurent</LASTNAME>
<COMPANY>XML Mania</COMPANY></AUTHOR>
<SUMMARY>This is element text and an entity
follows:&Description;
</SUMMARY></DOCUMENT>
```

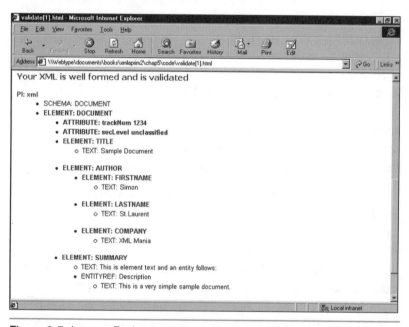

Figure 6-7 *Internet Explorer can parse structures that are many layers deep.*

The `<!DOCTYPE>` declaration now points to a relative URL, simple.dtd, which must be in the same directory as the file. The simple.dtd file contains all the declarations that used to be in the document itself:

```
<!ELEMENT DOCUMENT (TITLE,AUTHOR+,SUMMARY*,NOTE?)>
<!ATTLIST DOCUMENT
     trackNum CDATA #REQUIRED
     secLevel (unclassified|classified) "unclassified">
```

```
<!ELEMENT TITLE (#PCDATA)>
<!ELEMENT AUTHOR (FIRSTNAME,LASTNAME, (UNIVERSITY |
COMPANY)?)>
<!ELEMENT FIRSTNAME (#PCDATA)>
<!ELEMENT LASTNAME (#PCDATA)>
<!ELEMENT UNIVERSITY (#PCDATA)>
<!ELEMENT COMPANY (#PCDATA)>
<!ELEMENT SUMMARY (#PCDATA)>
<!ENTITY Description "This is a very simple sample
document.">
```

To see the results, load the document into Internet Explorer 5.0 as usual. As Figure 6-8 shows, you can see by the expanded entity and default value for the secLevel attribute, it did find the DTD.

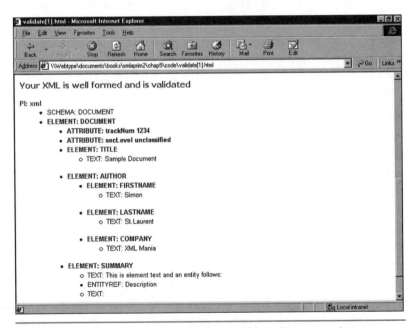

Figure 6-8 *Internet Explorer can load and validate documents that use external document type definitions.*

Now that you've seen what a DTD might look like, you can explore all its possible parts in greater detail.

Document Type Declarations

Document type declarations glue the DTDs to the actual document or may even provide their own declarations about the structure of the document. From the prolog, after the XML declaration has announced that this is an XML document, the document type declaration announces what kind of XML document it is to be. It identifies the root element name, provides one or two pointers to external information describing the document, and may include a set of declarations describing the document directly.

> **Note**
>
> Whenever the acronym DTD appears in this book or in other XML documentation, always assume that it stands for document type definition, not document type declaration. Document type declaration is sometimes abbreviated *DOCTYPE declaration*.

A document type declaration always begins with <!DOCTYPE, followed by the name of the DTD, followed by a declaration of the DTD or a link that points to where the DTD can be found, and finally a > to close the declaration. The name of the DTD doesn't need to correspond to the file name of the DTD file specified, but it should convey some sort of intelligible description of what the DTD is for and (most important) match the name of the root element used by the document. After the name, the declaration can provide a link to a file containing the DTD, provide a DTD within the declaration itself — enclosed in brackets ([ ]) — or both.

Two ways exist to identify external XML DTDs. The more Web-like approach uses URLs, whereas the more SGML-like approach uses public identifiers. The public identifier structure uses the same format as SGML public identifiers. If the entity or DTD described is an ISO standard, the identifier starts with *ISO*. Otherwise, the first character is a plus sign (+) if the standard is officially approved by a standards body, or a minus sign (-) if it is not, followed by two forward slashes (//), and then an identifier of the owner of the DTD. After two more slashes, the type of the document (DTD, for example, or TEXT) appears, followed by whitespace, and then the name of the document. After yet another two slashes, the language identifier appears, using the codes specified in ISO 639. EN, for example, is English.

The PUBLIC keyword first provides a public identifier (in quotation marks) that the parser can use to locate the standard if the parser is connected to a library of standards. Following the public identifier is a URL (also in quotation marks) that can lead a parser directly to a copy of the DTD. If you want to use only a URL, the SYSTEM keyword appears, followed only by the URL. Large document-management systems may well have libraries of DTDs identified by public identifiers available to parsers, but developers of other types of projects may not have such resources. The following two document type declarations link the document to the same DTD, but the first also provides a public identifier for the DTD:

```
<!DOCTYPE manual PUBLIC "-//simonstlcom//DTD manual//EN"
"http://www.simonstl.com/dtds/manual.dtd">


<!DOCTYPE manual SYSTEM
"http://www.simonstl.com/dtds/manual.dtd">
```

Some document type declarations supplement the externally referenced DTD with an internal subset. These document type declarations put the additional declarations inside square brackets after the PUBLIC or SYSTEM information:

```
<!DOCTYPE manual PUBLIC "-//simonstlcom//DTD manual//EN"
"http://www.simonstl.com/dtds/manual.dtd"
[
<!ELEMENT extraElement (#PCDATA)>
]>
```

Continued

```
<!DOCTYPE manual SYSTEM
"http://www.simonstl.com/dtds/manual.dtd"
[

<!ELEMENT extraElement (#PCDATA)>
]>
```

Other documents, like some of the initial examples, forgo external resources entirely and just use the square brackets:

```
<!DOCTYPE manual [
<!ELEMENT manual ANY >
<!ELEMENT extraElement (#PCDATA)>
]>
```

Although internal DTD subsets (which are declared in the document they apply to) can be used and may be appropriate for certain situations, using external DTDs is often preferable. Keeping DTDs separate makes them considerably more reusable across multiple documents and assures document managers that developers and authors aren't creating incompatible document types by taking liberties with the DTD to suit their own purposes. I mention some drawbacks to using external DTDs at the end of the chapter, but most large document systems (and even Web sites) will want to refer to a single library of DTDs that applies to multiple documents in the system.

DTDs can also be nested: One DTD file may include another through parameter entities, described in the later section, "Entities." DTDs are cumulative, combining all the referenced parts, although elements and notations may be declared only once, and the first declaration for a given attribute or entity will be given precedence. The internal subset is always considered to come first, which enables document authors to override some kinds of declarations.

Element Type Declarations

Every element in a valid XML document must correspond to an element type declaration in the DTD, and its contents must meet the criteria specified in that declaration. Only one element type declaration is permitted within a DTD for elements with a given name: no duplication or overriding is permitted. (Attributes are defined in separate declarations described in the next section.)

XML DTDs define element structures in terms of containment. When you declare that a certain element type may be used in a document, you must also define the content it may hold, called the *content model*. Elements define contexts for their children, but there is no way for an element to insist that it may be used only in a certain context. Understanding context is a prerequisite of building a DTD that works efficiently. In XML, the context provider is the parent element, and the child element may provide context to elements nested inside it. For example, in the structure:

```
<SECTION >
     <PARAGRAPH>
          <SENTENCE>
          </SENTENCE>
     </PARAGRAPH>
</SECTION >
```

the SECTION element is the parent element of the PARAGRAPH element, which in turn is the parent element of the SENTENCE element. Similarly, the SENTENCE element is the child element of the PARA-GRAPH element, which itself is the child of the SECTION element. XML also describes a document entity, which provides a root from which the markup tree structures (including the root element) can grow. If SECTION were the first element in a document, it would be a child of the document entity. (There isn't any special way to define a document entity — it just provides parsers with a place to start.)

As you saw earlier in the chapter, creating elements is very simple. The element declaration syntax is the following:

```
<!ELEMENT name contentModel>
```

The name of an element must be composed only of letters, digits, periods, dashes, underscores, or colons. The name must begin with a letter or underscore and cannot begin with XML, xml, or any other case variation unless the name is officially sanctioned by the W3C. Colons should be reserved for use with namespaces only.

> **Tip**
>
> You may define the name of an element, or its content, with a parameter entity. (Remember, if the declaration is in the internal DTD subset, the parameter entity must include the entire declaration, not just parts.)

The content of an element can be of four types: a mixed-content declaration; a list of elements; the keyword EMPTY; or the keyword ANY. ANY is the simplest declaration, announcing that this element can contain all kinds of data and markup:

```
<!ELEMENT BOXOSTUFF ANY>
```

Using this declaration, all BOXOSTUFF elements will allow any kind of element or data to be included in their content. A document that uses the BOXOSTUFF element could look like the following:

```
<BOXOSTUFF><DARKSPACE>emptiness</DARKSPACE>more
junk</BOXOSTUFF>
```

The DARKSPACE element would need to be declared elsewhere, but otherwise, ANY doesn't impose rules on its contents.

Caution

Although using ANY is perfectly acceptable XML, I strongly recommend that developers try to be more specific about document structure. XML parsers can provide error-checking when given a fully developed DTD, complete with rules that define which elements can go where. Try to restrict the use of ANY to the early stages of DTD development, replacing it with a more complete content specification as quickly as possible. It may remain necessary to use ANY to support future extensions, but use it as infrequently as possible.

The EMPTY keyword is ANY's polar opposite. Rather than allow any content, it allows no content. Elements defined with EMPTY content may have attributes but do not permit information to be stored between their beginning and end tags. The element declaration for an empty element is concise:

```
<!ELEMENT EMPTYSPACE EMPTY>
```

Using this empty tag in a document requires even less room:

```
<EMPTYSPACE />
```

Most of the time an EMPTY element will be written as only an empty element tag ending with a /> (
, for example). Typical beginning and end tags are permitted, but no elements or data may come between the tags.

Most element declarations will contain lists of elements, setting rules for which elements are required, and how often and in what order they can appear. (Remember that all elements in the list must always be defined separately in their own declarations.) Parameter entities may also appear in the list, making it easier for developers to create multiple similar structures. Table 6-1 lists a few symbols to provide rules for using elements.

Table 6-1 *Symbols for Specifying Element Structure*

Symbol	Symbol Type	Description	Example	Example Notes
|	Vertical bar (also called pipe)	Any element named may appear.	thisone | thatone	Either thisone or thatone must appear.
,	Comma	Requires appearance in specified sequence.	thisone, thatone	thisone must appear, followed by thatone.
?	Question mark	Makes optional, but only one may appear.	thisone?	thisone may appear once or not at all.
	No symbol	Requires one, and only one, to appear.	thisone	thisone must appear once.
*	Asterisk	Allows any number to appear in sequence, even zero.	thisone*	thisone may be present; multiple appearances (or zero appearances) of thisone are acceptable.
+	Plus sign	Requires at least one to appear; more may appear in sequence.	thisone+	thisone must be present; multiple thisone elements may appear.
( )	Parentheses	Groups elements.	(thisone | thatone), whichone	Either thisone or thatone may appear, followed by whichone.

Note

SGML developers may wonder what happened to the ampersand (&). XML, at least in version 1.0, does not support that content model group. Mixed declarations and creative use of OR statements can provide some similar capabilities in XML.

These options create a tremendous number of possibilities, as well as a dangerous temptation to create complex structures to cover every possible use of child elements that seems sensible. The following examples provide some simple examples and descriptions of acceptable declarations.

The simplest element content is the rare circumstance in which an element may contain only one other element. This might happen in cases in which a frustrated developer needs to create a "wrapper" element for an element in an outside DTD that can't be modified. The declaration for WRAPPER would read:

```
<!ELEMENT WRAPPER (UNTOUCHABLE)>
```

In this case, the only acceptable use of the WRAPPER element would be as follows:

```
<WRAPPER><UNTOUCHABLE>untouchable
content</UNTOUCHABLE></WRAPPER>
```

A more likely declaration would include two elements in sequence. A briefing, for example, might include a title and some content. The declarations would be as follows:

```
<!ELEMENT TITLE (#PCDATA)>
<!ELEMENT CONTENT (#PCDATA)>
<!ELEMENT BRIEFING (TITLE, CONTENT)>
```

This enables more sophisticated markup:

```
<BRIEFING>
<TITLE>Another dull briefing</TITLE>
<CONTENT>Today, too much happened for me to adequately
discuss it.</CONTENT>
</BRIEFING>
```

If the boss grows weary of such despondent headlines, the DTD can be modified to make the TITLE optional:

```
<!ELEMENT BRIEFING (TITLE?, CONTENT)>
```

In extreme cases, the CONTENT can also be made optional with the addition of a question mark. If briefings grow longer, the developer can enable writers to include multiple CONTENT elements under a single briefing element by adding a plus sign:

```
<!ELEMENT BRIEFING (TITLE?, CONTENT+)>
```

Substituting an asterisk for the plus sign would enable briefings to be shorter as well as longer, which would enable writers to create briefings with no CONTENT elements or thousands of CONTENT elements.

Although most simple documents, and some larger documents, contain single elements in reasonably obvious sequences, more complex documents need more combinations to enable greater flexibility. Paragraphs and lists can often substitute for each other. A recipe, for instance, might include a list of ingredients or a story of a trip to the grocery store. The following declarations would make either approach valid:

```
<!ELEMENT STORY (#PCDATA)>
<!ELEMENT ITEM (#PCDATA)>
<!ELEMENT INGREDIENTLIST (ITEM+)>
<!ELEMENT INGREDIENTS (STORY | INGREDIENTLIST)>
```

The XML code for an ingredient section could then look like this for a more traditional recipe:

```
<INGREDIENTS><INGREDIENTLIST>
<ITEM>Butter, enough to coat frying pan</ITEM>
<ITEM>Hot dogs, as many as needed</ITEM>
</INGREDIENTLIST></INGREDIENTS>
```

Authors who preferred to tell tales of their ingredients could use this format instead, and XML parsers would accept it:

```
<INGREDIENTS><STORY>
```

No one wants to talk about where hot dogs come from, but I know their origin. They come from trucks that unload them regularly into the backs of grocery stores. Clerks open the boxes and put the hot dogs on the shelf. It's really not that complicated, and at least it's plastic-wrapped. Butter works the same way, but it comes in boxes and waxed paper.
</STORY></INGREDIENTS>

The OR structure also makes it possible to create spaces where a limited number of elements may be used freely in combination. A discussion of poetry, for instance, might consist of quotation marks interspersed with commentary. The sequence wouldn't be especially predictable, but it would clearly fit within the structure of a chapter. The following declaration creates a CHAPTER element that comes complete with a title and allows multiple quotation marks and comments.

```
<!ELEMENT TITLE (#PCDATA)>
<!ELEMENT QUOTE (#PCDATA)>
<!ELEMENT COMMENT (#PCDATA)>
<!ELEMENT CHAPTER (TITLE, (QUOTE | COMMENT)*)>
```

The following XML document would parse properly, interpreting the (QUOTE | COMMENT)* as an invitation to use multiple QUOTE and COMMENT elements in any sequence.

```
<CHAPTER><TITLE>Bad Poetry Rocks</TITLE>
<QUOTE>I'm a poet and I didn't know it</QUOTE>
<COMMENT>This is the classic bad poem. Some might claim
that its natural rhythm makes it a fine found poem, but I
must disagree.</COMMENT>
<QUOTE>Jack and Jill went up the hill</QUOTE>
<COMMENT>Who let the nursery rhymes in?</COMMENT>
</CHAPTER>
```

QUOTE elements and COMMENT elements can appear in any sequence. Two quotation marks followed by a comment are acceptable, as are 10 comments with no quotation marks at all.

XML enables developers to create very elaborate sets of rules using the parentheses and the |, *, and + operators. It is possible to define entire documents so that all the child elements appear in the root parent element; it just takes an extremely twisted declaration and frequently results in markup that isn't useful for very much. If a markup declaration becomes too complicated, it's usually a sign that it's time to break up the declaration and create some subelements. For example:

```
<!ELEMENT CRAZY((TITLE | ART)+, (HEADLINE | PARAGRAPH |
SUBHEAD | PICTURE | TABLE | POP-UP)*, CONCLUSION)>
```

The CRAZY element is perfectly legal, if complex. It begins with at least one of a TITLE element or an ART element. The next section, which is probably the body of the article, can include HEADLINE, PARAGRAPH, SUBHEAD, PICTURE, TABLE, and POP-UP elements in any sequence and any order. After that mess is complete, a CONCLUSION element must appear to finish the article. This declaration might be better broken up into multiple elements with more structure:

```
<!ELEMENT CRAZY (HEADER, ARTICLE+,CONCLUSION)>
<!ELEMENT HEADER (TITLE?, ART?)>
<!ELEMENT ARTICLE (HEADLINE, CONTENT)>
<!ELEMENT CONTENT (PARAGRAPH | SUBHEAD | PICTURE | TABLE
| POP-UP)*>
<!ELEMENT CONCLUSION (#PCDATA)>
```

The CONTENT element can stay mixed up because every article is bound to vary, but the rest of the document has considerably more structure.

Mixed-content declarations are the final option. Technically, the (#PCDATA) content used in most of the examples in this chapter is a mixed-content declaration all by itself. Mixed-content declarations can enable multiple elements to appear as child elements without requiring them to appear or making any specific demands on the sequence in which they appear. The simplest mixed-content declaration is one of the most frequent. Declaring content to be PCDATA so that text and entities (but no other elements) may appear is common in DTDs:

```
<!ELEMENT ORDINARY (#PCDATA)>
```

The ORDINARY element can now contain text or entity markup in any combination. XML offers only PCDATA for elements that need to contain text (and not only other elements). Consequently, you use this basic declaration for nearly any leaf element. (Leaf elements have parent elements but no child elements; figuratively, they're the branches farthest out on the tree, where the action actually takes place.) In some situations, however, developers may want to allow other elements to appear in a leaf element. Not all leaf data are appropriate to every element. An ingredient, for instance, shouldn't contain a table of contents, but it might contain a note. The declaration creating an element that could hold an ingredient description and/or a note would look like this:

```
<!ELEMENT INGREDIENT (#PCDATA | NOTE)*>
```

This declaration would permit INGREDIENT elements to contain the textual information they need to present ingredients, as well as NOTE elements to explain ingredients that are strange or difficult to find.

With parameter entities listing the elements, you can simplify DTDs that include a significant set of child elements that can be used in multiple parent elements. The parser parses the parameter entity and adds its markup to the element content declaration.

```
<!ENTITY % parts "prologue | detail | moral | punchline |
joke">
<!ELEMENT STORY (#PCDATA | %parts;)*>
<!ELEMENT TALE (#PCDATA | %parts;)*>
<!ELEMENT FABLE (#PCDATA | %parts;)*>
```

In this case, STORY, TALE, and FABLE elements can contain text and any of the PROLOGUE, DETAIL, MORAL, PUNCHLINE, or JOKE elements. Any number of these subelements may appear in any order. All other elements are prohibited from appearing in a STORY, TALE, or FABLE element. The parameter entity could also include the parentheses and the #PCDATA declaration:

```
<!ENTITY % parts "(#PCDATA | prologue | detail | moral |
punchline | joke)*">
<!ELEMENT STORY %parts;>
<!ELEMENT TALE %parts;>
<!ELEMENT FABLE %parts;>
```

Each approach has its advantages in different situations. In this case, because the STORY, TALE, and FABLE elements have the exact same content model, including the extra content works well. If you needed to add extra elements to some of the content models, the first approach — leaving out #PCDATA, the parentheses, and the asterisk — would give you more flexibility. Adding another element possibility would require only a vertical bar and the name of the element:

```
<!ELEMENT STORY (#PCDATA | %parts; | aside)*>
```

XML enables you to make either choice.

Attribute List Declarations

Attributes are most useful for storing information that is of more interest to computers than to humans. Attributes enable you to annotate element structures without having to modify those structures significantly. Attributes remain a key part of XML, offering flexibility beyond that of elements and solidifying underlying structures. Attribute declarations use some syntax similar to that of element declarations but tend to offer more precise definitions of the content they allow.

Attributes are defined using attribute list declarations. Each attribute list declaration defines zero or more attributes for a single element, using the following syntax:

```
<!ATTLIST ElementName
    AttributeName Type Default
    (AttributeName Type Default...)>
```

The first value in an attribute declaration is the name of the element to which the attributes apply. Although it makes a DTD more readable to include the attribute declaration right after the element declaration, this is not required. In fact, there can be multiple attribute declarations for the same element: All declarations for that element will be combined into one large set. If the same attribute is declared multiple times in that set, only the first appearance will be used. This makes it easy to extend existing DTDs without having to change them drastically.

After the element is named, an attribute definition or a list of attribute definitions may follow. Although they don't do anything as far as parsing, empty attribute list declarations can be useful placeholders:

```
<!ATTLIST MyElement>
```

A definition consists of the name of an attribute, its type, and its default value (or a specification for that value). Names of attributes must obey the same rules as names for entities and elements: They must contain only letters, digits, periods, dashes, underscores, and colons, and must start with a letter or underscore. Again, colons should be reserved for use with namespaces. Attribute types define the kinds of data permitted in an attribute the attribute is used in an element instance. (An element instance is just a use of the element in the document.) Table 6-2 lists all the acceptable values for attribute types.

Table 6-2 *Attribute Types*

Type	Explanation
CDATA	The attribute may contain only character data.
ID	The value of the attribute must be unique, identifying the element. If two attributes within a document of type ID have the same value, the parser should return an error. (Note that attributes of type ID may not have default values or fixed values.)
IDREF	The value of the attribute must refer to an ID value declared elsewhere in the document. If the value of the attribute doesn't match an ID value within the document, the parser should return an error.
ENTITY, ENTITIES	The value of an ENTITY attribute must correspond to the name of an external unparsed entity declared in a DTD. An ENTITIES attribute is similar but allows multiple entity names separated by whitespace.
NMTOKEN, NMTOKENS	The value of the attribute must be a name token like CDATA, but the characters used in the value must be letters, digits, periods, dashes, underscores, or colons. NMTOKENS is similar but allows multiple values separated by whitespace.
Enumerated, e.g. (thisone | thatone)	The value of the attribute must match one of the values listed. Values must appear in parentheses and be separated by OR (|) symbols.
NOTATION (enumerated)	The value of the attribute must match the name of one of the NOTATION names listed. For example, an attribute with type NOTATION (picture | slide) must have a value of picture or slide, and NOTATION declarations must exist for both picture and slide.

Most of the time, developers will need to use CDATA, ID, and enumerated types, although the other possibilities are available. The last necessary part of an attribute declaration is the default. The default may take one of the four values listed in Table 6-3.

Table 6-3 *Attribute Defaults*

Value	Explanation
`#REQUIRED`	Indicates to the parser that this attribute must have a value in all instances of the element. Failure to include the attribute results in parsing errors.
`#IMPLIED`	Allows the parser to ignore this attribute if no value is specified. The XML working draft states that "The XML processor must inform the application that no value was specified; no constraint is placed on the behavior of the application."
`#FIXED` `"value"`	Announces that element instances that specify that a value for this attribute must specify the listed value. If an element instance doesn't include this attribute, its value will be presumed to be the value specified.
`"defaultvalue"`	Provides a default value for the attribute. If the attribute is not declared explicitly in an element instance, the attribute will be assumed to have a value of *defaultvalue*.

Now that you understand all these parts, it's time to see what they do. Attributes of type ID are becoming more and more common as scripting tools, and other processors have scrambled to find a way to address elements individually in documents. Making these systems work effectively, however, usually requires that all elements (or at least the elements to be manipulated) have an ID value, usually listed in the id attribute. Declaring a required ID value for an element takes little effort:

```
<!ELEMENT DATABRICK (#PCDATA)>
<!ATTLIST DATABRICK
     id   ID   #REQUIRED>
```

All DATABRICK elements created in documents resulting from this DTD will be required to have unique values for their id attribute. Other attributes might enable a processing application to treat DATABRICK elements differently, based on their type. Defining a list of possible types will make it much easier for a processing application to run smoothly.

```
<!ELEMENT DATABRICK (#PCDATA)>
<!ATTLIST DATABRICK
    id   ID   #REQUIRED
    status   (proceeding | accepted | rejected
|deferred) "proceeding">
```

DATABRICK elements now have a status attribute that informs the processing application of their status. If an element is created that doesn't specify a value for this attribute, the DATABRICK is assumed to be "proceeding" along a path of eventual acceptance, rejection, or deferral to a later date. A document-management system or a database could use this attribute to limit its activities to DATABRICK elements whose status is appropriate to their work.

In cases in which an attribute's presence isn't critical to proper processing, implied default values are acceptable. An application that translates documents from one DTD to another might use a comments field of some kind to keep track of the activities it has performed on the document. Only documents that have been through this process will need such a comment; documents created directly in the target DTD might have no such need. To create this comment attribute, you can use the following declaration:

```
<!ELEMENT MASTERPIECE (#PCDATA)>
<!ATTLIST MASTERPIECE
    TranslationNote   CDATA   #IMPLIED>
```

This might be adequate for many situations. It might be better, however, to supply a default value instead of leaving the parser to report no value.

```
<!ELEMENT MASTERPIECE (#PCDATA)>
<!ATTLIST MASTERPIECE
    TranslationNote   CDATA   "None">
```

"None" is a slightly stronger affirmation that no translation was done than is a notice that the attribute contained no value. "None" is easier to check for in a program and relieves the programmer of wondering whether the parser had a problem or whether there really was no value.

Fixed attribute types are somewhat unusual. They might be useful in situations in which documents are fed into processors that use attributes for formatting to ensure that the results of processing all the documents created with this DTD will look similar. By specifying a fixed attribute value, a particular DTD can be sure of preserving its identity in collections of documents that use similar DTDs.

```
<!ELEMENT ARTICLE (#PCDATA)>
<!ATTLIST ARTICLE
    FormatModel    CDATA    #FIXED "Contemporary">
```

Another DTD file uses a similar declaration but with a different fixed value:

```
<!ELEMENT ARTICLE (#PCDATA)>
<!ATTLIST ARTICLE
    FormatModel    CDATA    #FIXED "Country">
```

A processing application can take note of the FormatModel attribute and choose a set of styles appropriate to that model. It can also use the information to sort the documents in a library, enabling browsers to choose only articles that fit the user's design mood of the moment.

Attribute values that refer to external data sources can also be useful for processing. Although the parser itself will do nothing with the information (except pass it along), a processing application can combine that information with the markup material to create, for example, a document with pictures:

```
<!NOTATION ourFormat1SYSTEM
"http://www.simonstl.com/ourViewer.exe">
```

Continued

```
<!NOTATION ourFormat2 SYSTEM
"http://www.simonstl.com/pictures/ourPlayer.exe">
<!ELEMENT DOCUMENT (#PCDATA | PICTURE)*>
<!ELEMENT PICTURE empty>
<!ATTLIST PICTURE
     TYPE      NOTATION (ourFormat1 | ourFormat2)
"ourFormat1"
     IMAGE CDATA #IMPLIED>
```

In this case, the editor of a set of documents has decreed that all pictures must be in one of two formats. The XML document that uses this DTD might look like the following:

```
<DOCUMENT>I hate my boss. He makes me use this picture
all the time:
<PICTURE TYPE="ourFormat2" IMAGE="FROGS.fm2"/>
Sometimes he lets me use this image:
<PICTURE TYPE="ourFormat1" IMAGE="BIRDS.fm1"/>
But I hate it more, so I usually stick with the frogs.
</DOCUMENT>
```

Although DTDs don't understand namespace processing, the attributes used to declare namespaces must themselves be declared in the DTD. To a validating XML processor, a namespace declaration is an attribute like any other—the fact that it begins with xmlns doesn't provide it any special status. In some cases, a namespace value can be declared as #FIXED, though this isn't required:

```
<!ATTLIST myDoc
     xmlns  CDATA  #FIXED
"http://www.example.com/myDoc">
```

Microsoft Internet Explorer version 5.*x* expects all declarations for namespace attributes to provide fixed values, and reports an error if the same attribute is declared as shown in the following:

```
<!ATTLIST myDoc
     xmlns  CDATA  "http://www.example.com/myDoc">
```

This error reporting is unnecessary and reports false problems in a large number of the W3C's own specifications, but it may be wise to use #FIXED if your target application is Internet Explorer 5.*x*. (The latest version of the MSXML parser, 3.0, fixes this problem.)

> **Caution**
>
> Although you can use DTDs to declare namespaces through the use of defaulted attributes, some non-validating parsers may never encounter the declaration if it appears in the external DTD subset. To improve interoperability and make your documents easier for humans to figure out, it's a good idea to include the namespace attributes explicitly in your documents even when a default value is provided in the DTD.

Similarly, the xml:lang and xml:space attributes will require declarations in the DTD when they are used in valid documents.

Comments

Comments perform a similar function in DTDs to the one they perform in documents, but in DTDs their role may be even more critical. Comments in documents typically indicate revision information or occasional warnings to other authors, but documents rarely need explicit documentation. In DTDs, comments are the only easily accessible way to report why you chose to use the structures you did and how the pieces all fit together.

Comments use the same syntax inside DTDs that they use inside documents. They can appear between declarations but cannot appear inside declarations. There isn't a fixed convention regarding which comments apply to which declarations, but comments frequently appear before declarations:

```
<!--The given_name element contains the given name
        (sometimes called first name) of a person.-->
<!ELEMENT given_name(#PCDATA)>
```

XML Authority, a DTD editor from Extensibility, uses a set of conventions that identify different kinds of comments providing additional information about DTDs. Although comments are an excellent addition to DTDs, you should probably consider even well structured comments only as a first line of documentation, not as the sole documentation. Remember that a DTD without an explanation is just a list of names and structures.

Notation Declarations

Notation declarations provide extra information about information. DTDs already provide information about information, but notations provide an extra layer of abstraction that can be used to provide identifiers for information or to bluntly specify applications that can be used to process information. Notation processing beyond basic syntax is entirely up to the application, not the XML parser, making notations a tool that works well in specific applications but doesn't do much in generic processing.

Notation declarations must be used with external unparsed entities to identify the type of information represented by the entity, can be used as an attribute value, and are sometimes used to provide additional information about processing instructions. The notation declaration tells the processor what kind of information there is; the processing instruction announces what process should be used to handle it. Notation names can also be used as attribute values.

The syntax for notation declarations is similar to the document type declaration:

```
<!NOTATION Name ExternalID>
```

The name of the notation must be composed of letters, digits, periods, dashes, underscores, or colons, and begin with a letter or an underscore. (The use of colons is discouraged because of namespaces, described in Chapter 3.) A typical notation declaration might read as follows:

```
<!NOTATION image_gif
SYSTEM 'http://www.isi.edu/in-
notes/iana/assignments/media-types/image/gif'>
```

Tip

John Cowan maintains a list of NOTATION identifiers for MIME types at http://home.ccil.org/~cowan/XML/media-types.dtd. These identifiers use the registration directories set up by the IANA (Internet Assigned Numbers Authority) for URLs representing different content types.

The parser itself does nothing to check the information at the external ID; it just passes the information on to the processing application. If the processing application can handle the information, that's wonderful. If it can't, it doesn't matter to the parser. The SYSTEM keyword may be followed by a reference to an application that can present the data, but the processing application is definitely not required to use that application. (If a Macintosh or UNIX user is reading this file, a Windows executable won't help him or her much anyway). More typically on the Web, notation declarations will specify MIME content types. PUBLIC identifiers may also be used to identify notations, even without a URL. Notations that the processing application cannot understand may be errors, but they aren't XML errors. The parser continues its work without announcing an error. The application, of course, may announce its own errors.

Entities

XML offers two kinds of entities: general entities and parameter entities. HTML developers will be familiar with using predefined general entities for encoding unusual characters and characters used for markup (the infamous <, >, and &). Although defined in DTDs, general entities are used to add information to documents, substituting their value for the entity reference, which takes the form &name;. Parameter entities are defined and used only in external DTDs. They can save developers typing, as do general entities, but they can also give developers tremendous power to include other DTDs and other information in their DTD. Parameter entities enable developers to reuse and subset older DTDs, avoiding the perpetual reinvention of the wheel and making the expansion of previously existing DTDs easier.

General entities

Developers can define entities, which contain content, just as they can define elements. General entities are simple and make many complex and annoying tasks very simple, especially when it comes to filling in boilerplate text. The syntax for defining a general entity is fairly simple:

```
<!ENTITY name "EntityContent">
```

The name of the entity must be composed of letters, digits, periods, dashes, underscores, or colons, and begin with a letter or an underscore. (The use of colons is discouraged because of namespace, described in Chapter 3.) The entity definition may contain any valid markup and must be enclosed in quotation marks. The syntax for using an entity in the markup is also simple:

```
&name;
```

The ampersand must appear at the start and the semicolon at the end. No additional whitespace is permitted around or inside the entity.

Creating entities this way is useful for reusing repetitive information that is prone to change during the lifetime of the document. For example, during the development of a manual for the first version of a product, the developers may not even know the name of the product. Rather than introduce possible errors by doing a search-and-replace when the product is finalized, the developers can use an entity reference to make sure that the product is referred to correctly. For example, the code name of a project might be Crystal. In the prerelease version of the documentation, developers can create the following entity reference:

```
<!ENTITY ProdName "Crystal">
```

Whenever the product is referred to they can use an entity reference rather than the actual name of the product. For example,

```
&ProdName; is a remarkable advance, guaranteeing users
happier days.
```

is interpreted as

```
Crystal is a remarkable advance, guaranteeing users
happier days.
```

When the final product name is finalized, transforming Crystal into RF-2000-QJ-46, the developers can just change the entity reference:

```
<!ENTITY ProdName="RF-2000-QJ-46">
```

The text would then be interpreted as

```
RF-2000-QJ-46 is a remarkable advance, guaranteeing users
happier days.
```

It sounds a bit stilted, but determined developers can even create entities that address different grammatical positions (the possessive, for example), if they needed to go that far. Entities are extremely useful for legal contracts and other such documents that are mostly boilerplate text. A simple contract in which the only parts that change are the name of one of the parties and the amount of money involved can be written as

```
<CONTRACT>&boilerplate1; <PAYMENT>$100,000.00
(US)</PAYMENT>&boilerplate2;<RECIPIENT>Lucky
Author</RECIPIENT></CONTRACT>
```

Most contracts are open to more change than this form would allow, but many contracts can be broken down into standard clauses, enabling the regular use of entities.

Nevertheless, the main use of general entities is still for presenting characters that aren't in the usual (normally ASCII) set. Character references enable developers to include characters that aren't easily inputted or that might not be understood consistently. For example,

```
<!ENTITY THORN "&#222;" >
```

when used on systems using Latin-1 or Unicode encoding, will produce an Icelandic thorn, a character not frequently seen on American keyboards. The built-in ampersand entity is declared as

```
<!ENTITY amp "&#38;">
```

Although developers could use these codes directly in XML without going to the trouble of creating an entity declaration, naming these characters tends to produce a much cleaner document. ISO 8879 (SGML) includes a full set of standard named entities used in SGML. The SGML markup uses codes, however, which most early XML parsers probably won't be able to process.

A large set of entity DTDs written for XML is available at `http://www.schema.net/entities/` and includes a wide variety of different characters and marks. You can either examine the code and add the parts you need to your own DTD or use parameter entities (described later in this chapter) to include the entire entity DTD in your own DTD.

Note

Entities have their own quirks. You can use markup inside an entity, but using entities inside entities takes some extra effort. The parser will examine the entity for markup when it is added to the document text, and errors in entity coding can produce mysterious parsing errors. Always test your entities before using them, and always make sure that the content of an entity is appropriate to its destination in the document.

XML parsers interpret entities according to a strict set of rules, which tends to result in entities being parsed more than once. This multiple parsing can make it difficult to include entities within entities in certain situations, because some entities — all the parameter entities and character references — are parsed when the computer parses the DTD. When the entity is placed in the document, all entities are parsed. This situation is highly unusual (happening mostly when developers use the character reference equivalents for ampersands and less-than signs), but developers whose entities mysteriously wreak havoc on their documents should parse their entities separately and inspect their results.

Unparsed entities

Not all entities refer to XML data. Unparsed entities must refer to information in files stored outside the XML document itself. In the SGML world, unparsed entities connect images and other files to SGML documents in a more formal way than HTML's <IMG SRC="*filename*"> approach.

Entities that refer to binary (non-textual) data must be external (that is, they must use SYSTEM or PUBLIC identifiers) and use the NDATA keyword after the entity definition to specify the entity's data type with a notation identifier. An external binary entity referring to a GIF file, for example, should conclude with NDATA gif. External unparsed entities may not appear directly in XML documents using the &*name*; syntax. Instead, the name of the entity should appear in an attribute that has been declared to be of type ENTITY or ENTITIES. The application can then decide what to do with the information in the external unparsed entity.

To declare an unparsed entity representing a GIF file, you might use the following syntax:

```
<!NOTATION image_gif
SYSTEM 'http://www.isi.edu/in-
notes/iana/assignments/media-types/image/gif'>
<!ENTITY myPic SYSTEM "mypic.gif" NDATA image_gif>
<!ELEMENT picture EMPTY>
<!ATTLIST picture
    pictRef  ENTITY  #IMPLIED>
```

Then you could reference the myPic entity in the document:

```
<picture pictRef="myPic" />
```

The W3C hasn't made much use of this feature, preferring the XLink approach described in Chapter 16.

> **Note**
>
> The XML Working Group left external unparsed entities in the specification to accommodate legacy SGML documents. The "SGML way" of including binary data requires many more steps than the "HTML way," which relies on the server (and file extensions) to identify content types. Many XML users will never need to declare these entities or support this kind of processing – it depends on the style demanded by the applications they use.

Parameter entities

The parameter entity is for use only within DTDs. Parameter entities carry information for use in the markup declaration, often a set of common attributes shared by several elements or a link to an outside DTD. Parameter entities whose references are purely within the DTD are known as internal entities, whereas references that draw information from outside files are external entities. Even though parameter entities may considerably simplify the creation of a DTD, you should use them with caution. Entities by their nature require a lookup to determine their contents. This isn't too difficult for computers, but it can become extremely complex for unfortunate humans who have to sort out obfuscated XML.

Parameter entries use a percent sign (%) both in their references and in their declaration. The percent sign differentiates a general entity from a parameter entity. The syntax for a parameter entity declaration is as follows:

```
<!ENTITY % Name EntityDefinition>
```

The space between the percent sign and the name of the entity is mandatory. As with general entities, the name of the entity must be composed of letters, digits, periods, dashes, underscores, or colons, and begin with a letter or an underscore. The entity definition may contain any valid markup and must be enclosed in quotation marks.

The value of the entity definition must resolve to something that makes sense in the context in which the entity will be used; otherwise, the parser will fail to understand the DTD and will return errors.

Internal parameter entities behave much like general entities but operate in the DTD rather than the document content. For example, a DTD for a document set that contains a variety of quoted materials might use a common set of attributes for all the different kinds of materials — letters, diaries, novels, poems, and quotations. To make the documents more readily searchable, all these elements must have attributes that identify the language in which they are written and a copyright date to determine whether they remain in copyright. An entity declaration that provides these attributes might look like the following:

```
<!ENTITY % sourceinfo
"LANGUAGE CDATA #REQUIRED
COPYRIGHTDATE CDATA #REQUIRED">
```

To use that entity in a declaration all you need to do is call it with the %name; syntax:

```
<!ELEMENT LETTER (#PCDATA)>
<!ATTLIST LETTER %sourceinfo;>
<!ELEMENT QUOTATION (#PCDATA)>
<!ATTLIST QUOTATION %sourceinfo;>
```

(There is no space between the percent sign and the entity name when the entity is used; the space is used only when the entity name is declared.) The language and copyright date information will flow right into the QUOTATION and LETTER attribute declarations. When the parser encounters the %sourceinfo; notation it will expand the entity to include the full value announced elsewhere in the DTD. QUOTATION and LETTER and any other elements that use the contents of the sourceinfo entity will require attributes indicating language and copyright date. This feature becomes more useful as the number of repetitive elements and the length of the attributes list grow.

Caution

The XML 1.0 Recommendation places a somewhat tricky restriction on the use of parameter entities in the internal subset (that is, the DTD information declared directly in a document). Parameter entities that are used in the internal subset may contain only complete declarations, not the partial declarations used previously. This places severe restrictions on the flexibility of parameter entities in the internal subset and is yet another good reason to keep your DTDs in external files.

External entities enable developers to link to materials entirely outside their documents or DTD and use the same syntax as the document type declaration described previously for linking to outside files. Entity values must use SYSTEM identifiers and may also use PUBLIC identifiers when appropriate. Most XML developers will probably find themselves linking to external documents using SYSTEM identifiers unless document-management systems become common enough that most document users have access.

The contents of the files linked to by external entities are required only to make sense in the context in which they are used. Generally they will consist of declarations or parts of declarations, although under certain circumstances they may also contain binary data, like GIF files. Parameter entities are frequently used to combine several DTD subsets or to include large lists of general entities. The files referred to by external entities may also include other external entities. Parsers will return an error if these references are circular — if document A refers to document B, which refers to document C, which refers to document A again, the parser will stop. External entities may resemble trees with many branches, but those branches are not allowed to grow back into the trunk. Too many branches, of course, will produce unwieldy DTDs that are difficult to understand.

My example for external entities will simply combine two lists of general entities for use in a single DTD. (The use of parameter entities to nest more complex DTDs is covered in later chapters.) It is

always a good idea to include comments with external entity declarations: the URLs in SYSTEM identifiers and even the more complete
information in PUBLIC identifiers are often cryptic. The first entity
file, companies.dtd, includes the following:

```
<!ENTITY GLW "Corning Incorporated">
<!ENTITY IBM "International Business Machines">
<!ENTITY T "American Telephone and Telegraph">
```

The second file, states.dtd, includes the following:

```
<!ENTITY NC "North Carolina">
<!ENTITY ND "North Dakota">
<!ENTITY NJ "New Jersey">
<!ENTITY NM "New Mexico">
<!ENTITY NY "New York">
```

The DTD, although simple, is also stored in an external file:

```
<!-The following entity connects to a list of companies
using stock-ticker symbols as entity references. ->
<!ENTITY % companies SYSTEM "companies.dtd">
<!-The following entity connects to a list of states
using postal abbreviations as entity references. ->
<!ENTITY % states SYSTEM "states.dtd">
<!ELEMENT DOCUMENT (#PCDATA)>
%companies;
%states;
```

The sample XML file that uses these references looks like this:

```
<?xml version="1.0" encoding="UTF-8"?>
<!DOCTYPE DOCUMENT SYSTEM "penex.dtd">
<DOCUMENT>The company &GLW; is headquartered in &NY;, as
is &IBM;. &T; is headquartered in &NJ;.</DOCUMENT>
```

Parsing this file should yield the results shown in Figure 6-9.

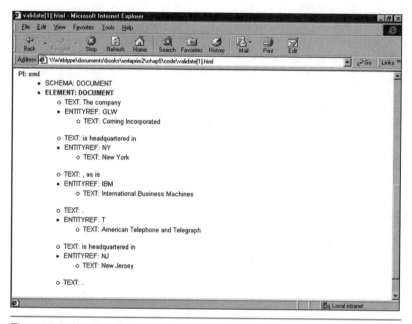

Figure 6-9 *Internet Explorer 5.0 resolves general entities referenced by parameter entities.*

As you see in later chapters, parameter entities can be a very useful tool for simplifying complex markup and managing multiple DTDs.

Marked Sections in DTDs: IGNORE and INCLUDE

Developers who need to test different structures while keeping track of alternatives may want to use the IGNORE and INCLUDE marked sections in DTDs. IGNORE and INCLUDE enable developers to turn portions of a DTD on and off. IGNORE and INCLUDE are particularly useful for developers who are combining several DTDs and need to limit the side effects of multiple files colliding, or for developers who need to create a single core DTD with optional subsets.

IGNORE and INCLUDE sections may be nested inside other IGNORE and INCLUDE sections, but, like elements, their beginnings and ends may not overlap.

> **Note**
>
> Although IGNORE and INCLUDE may seem somewhat obscure, they are critical tools in the W3C's XHTML modularization effort. If you're creating your own relatively simple DTDs these tools may not seem critical, but developers creating XHTML modules will need to understand this feature.

The syntax for IGNORE and INCLUDE resembles that of CDATA:

```
<![IGNORE[ declarations ]]>
<![INCLUDE[ declarations ]]>
```

Neither IGNORE nor INCLUDE may appear in the middle of a declaration; both must address a single declaration or set of declarations. For example,

```
<![IGNORE[<!ELEMENT YUCK (#PCDATA)>]]>
<![INCLUDE[<!ELEMENT HOORAY (#PCDATA)>]]>
```

would keep the YUCK element from being parsed and would allow the HOORAY element to be parsed normally. Applied in this way, IGNORE seems like a handy way to edit out useless parts of a DTD, and INCLUDE seems to be just plain useless. Parameter entities give INCLUDE and IGNORE the power they need to be meaningful additions to the XML vocabulary. Rather than use INCLUDE and IGNORE directly to change code throughout a DTD, developers can use parameter entities to make all those changes in one place. This makes INCLUDE and IGNORE far more convenient and occasionally even necessary. The following example provides a simple demonstration:

```
<!ENTITY % invoice "IGNORE">
<!ENTITY % receipt "INCLUDE">
<![%invoice; [
```

Continued

```
<!ENTITY notice "Please remit the following payment
within thirty days.">]]>
<![%receipt; [
<!ENTITY notice "Thank you for your prompt payment. The
sums below have been collected and recorded.">]]>
<!ENTITY address "555 Twelvetwelve Lane">
```

Depending on the values assigned to invoice and receipt, the general entity notice will provide either the voice of a bill collector or that of a grateful vendor. To change the output, just switch the values of the two entities. The value of the address entity (probably that of the company), on the other hand, will be the same in either case. Similar markup could continue throughout the DTD, with parts inappropriate for receipts being deleted. Switching the DTD over to receipts would require editing only two lines of the file instead of demanding a search-and-replace of the entire document. In the next chapters I explore more uses of this limited but powerful tool.

Note

In SGML, IGNORE and INCLUDE also work in documents, but XML has banished them to the DTD.

Chapter 7

Schemas: The Next Generation?

DTDs provide a solid foundation for some kinds of XML document processing, but are only a starting point for other kinds of processing. They were designed as a general framework for document structures, not as a precision instrument for distinguishing different types of numbers or for representing object-oriented structures and all their properties. As a result, many developers have been clamoring for a new approach to describing document structures, leaving DTDs behind and starting anew. At the same time, however, there is little consensus on what exactly needs to be done to make that new start, and the schemas landscape is somewhat fragmented and uncertain.

Note

All of the material discussed in this chapter and the next three chapters should be considered "under construction" and downright contentious. There seems to be less and less consensus around schemas, though supporters of the leading contenders are definitely pushing forward with their plans.

Limitations of DTDs

Although DTDs provide document-oriented developers with control over structure labeling and organization, they don't provide data-oriented developers with much of the control they are used to having in typical relational database and software contexts. Perhaps because of these limitations, the W3C hasn't updated DTDs for reliable interoperability with later additions to XML, notably XML namespaces. On top of these issues, some developers building complex document structures find the mechanisms used by DTDs for extensibility (notably parameter entities and notations) both unfamiliar and inadequate.

Data typing

The limited range of data types in XML 1.0 is probably the largest complaint most developers have with DTDs. Although DTDs constrain the element and attribute structures that XML elements may contain, there is no built-in way to require that an element named quantity contain an integer value, for instance. Developers exchanging information between type-sensitive programs and databases need to write extra (and repetitive) code to handle simple issues such as making sure that a date contains a properly formatted numeric value rather than textual interpretations such as yesterday. Although XML makes a wonderful interchange format, developers often find themselves filling in a lot of understandings that aren't described by XML itself.

XML 1.0 does support some kinds of data types, notably in attribute values, but those types often refer to document-oriented information (ID, IDREF, IDREFS), provide generic but under-specified functionality (NOTATION), or provide only a limited mechanism for constraining content (NMTOKEN, NMTOKENS, and enumerated types). Although #REQUIRED, #IMPLIED, #FIXED, and default values provide some control over the presence of attributes, and content models provide some control over element content, these mechanisms don't go very far toward preventing common problems such as missing or incorrect values. An element may be required in a content model, for instance, but it can be empty even if it's supposed to be holding a number.

In response to these needs, the XML Schema Working Group has developed a set of rules for specifying and creating data types within schemas. This specification, which I describe in the next chapter, provides both primitive types — a needed foundation — and rules for extending these types into types that more precisely reflect the needs of applications. Using these data types, developers can require that string content meet particular formats, or that numbers fall inside a given range. The data-types specification uses these rules internally to create a number of predefined types, including types that support the XML 1.0 types.

Namespace handling

XML 1.0 was finished for more than a year before the *Namespaces in XML* Recommendation was published, and the authors of *Namespaces in XML* chose not to explain how to integrate namespace processing with XML 1.0 validation. DTDs are not namespace-aware; no mechanisms have been defined that would make DTDs namespace-aware. Although you can create documents that use namespaces and can be validated against DTDs, doing so generally requires compromise.

The simplest compromise is the use of a consistent prefix (or consistently no prefix), thereby ignoring the promise of *Namespaces in XML* that prefixes wouldn't matter and that only the mappings to namespace URIs would identify the true name of an element or attribute. By sticking to fixed namespace prefixes and including them in the DTD, developers can create documents that use namespaces but that also validate against the DTD. If any of those prefixes needs to change, however, the document will no longer validate.

A more complex possibility uses parameter entities and INCLUDE and IGNORE sections to enable document authors to control the use of prefixes in the DTD. This approach pushes the use of these tools to the limit, and hardly enhances the readability of the resulting DTDs. For an example of this approach, see the W3C's *Modularization in XHTML* at http://www.w3.org/TR/xhtml-modularization/dtd_module_rules.html#s_module_namespace.

The newer schema specifications, which have the advantage of having been developed after *Namespaces in XML* was published, include built-in support for namespaces, including an understanding of namespace prefixes. Although "native" namespace processing requires parsers to have a different understanding of document markup than DTDs are permitted to see in the confines of XML 1.0 validation, namespaces themselves aren't difficult to handle.

Extensibility

XML itself is extensible, but describing extensible vocabularies with DTDs is difficult. For the most part, DTD best practice involves defining a vocabulary as precisely as possible, and the options for defining "loose" DTDs are pretty limited. The ANY content model provides a combination of too much flexibility and too little flexibility, and using parameter entities to provide flexibility requires a lot of planning ahead and understanding on the part of users to make it work.

The ANY content model doesn't provide any control over what contents may appear within it, except that elements appearing in an ANY section must still be declared somewhere in the DTD. There is no way to limit child elements to those within a particular namespace, or to elements in DTDs other than the one that includes the ANY element, or to elements defined elsewhere in a particular DTD.

Developers who want to add flexibility to their DTDs may want to use parameter entities for things such as element content models, making it easier for other developers to override those entities and add their own content to the DTD. This makes it easier for people to modify a DTD without copying it and modifying the copy, but also can make DTDs far more difficult to read, especially when multiple layers of parameter entities are involved. Parameter entity usage is somewhat controversial: Some developers consider it a powerful tool for DTD management and creation, whereas others regard its text substitution approach to be a weak tool better replaced by more thorough-going models of inheritance, extension, and restriction.

Schemas have an opportunity to create their own models for extensibility, taking advantage of namespaces for simplifying the mixing of vocabularies while developing their toolsets for describing relationships between vocabularies. Two of the goals stated in the W3C's *XML Schema Requirements* were "integration with name-spaces" and "definition of incomplete constraints on the content of an element type," which together seem to promise a more comprehensive approach to mixing vocabularies.

Management

One feature common to all the schema proposals that have appeared since XML 1.0 itself came out is that they use XML syntax to describe XML documents. XML 1.0, like SGML, uses a different syntax for the declarations inside DTDs from the one it uses for document content. This allows DTDs to be far more compact than they are when expressed in XML document syntax, and to be (to some extent) more readable. It's easy to distinguish between parameter entities (used in DTDs) and general entities (used inside documents), and lets parsers avoid naming collisions.

On the other hand, processing DTDs requires different tools from processing XML documents. Most XML parsers read DTDs and use the information in validation, but then throw away the contents. Reading the contents of a DTD requires special-purpose tools, which have received far less development (and use) than XML parsers. Although there are certainly tools (document editors,

DTD and schema editors, and some kinds of document-object mappers) that use DTDs at some phase in their processing, DTDs remain something of an underused relic because they use a different syntax.

Tip

If you need to parse a DTD, try Mark Wutka's DTDParser, available at `http://www.wutka.com/dtdparser.html`. It's a Java-based standalone DTD parser that gives you a report of all the declarations inside a given DTD.

Using XML as the syntax for describing XML documents does-n't magically enable applications to understand those descriptions with just an XML parser. On the other hand, it makes it much easier to layer on top of an XML parser components that do understand the descriptions, and that can then either apply those descriptions to documents (for validation) or pass that information to the application (to help in querying or other kinds of document processing). It also means that XML-based schemas can be stored, queried, and managed with the exact same set of tools used to manage XML documents. Instead of being something different (such as DTDs), schemas blend into XML fairly comfortably.

XML syntax also offers another significant advantage over DTDs — much greater flexibility in documenting the description. The only documentation mechanism built into DTDs is comments, and that in a limited way. Developers *can* create and use conventions using comments to document DTDs, perhaps sticking to a "comments before the declaration" rule and even sometimes using HTML markup inside the comments, but these conventions are really only conventions, with no guaranteed meaning across projects. Developers often go their own way in documenting (or not documenting) DTDs, and different sets of conventions can lead to confusion over which documentation belongs to which convention. Because XML syntax permits the use of containment for identification and XML vocabularies for subtlety, XML-based schemas can provide a much more precise set of tools for documenting descriptions of documents.

Schema Schisms

Although it seems clear that there are plenty of developers who'd like more control over document descriptions, there are lots of different ways to satisfy to that need. Even before the W3C started its XML Schemas Activity four different specifications were available:

- XML-Data, XML Data Reduced (XDR) — Developed by Microsoft, ArborText, and DataChannel, XDR is the schema built into versions 5.0 and 5.5 of Microsoft Internet Explorer and the MSXML parser (`http://www.w3.org/TR/1998/NOTE-XML-data-0105`).

- Schema for Object-Oriented XML (SOX) — Developed by CommerceOne, SOX uses an object-oriented framework to describe XML documents. It has been deployed in a number of e-commerce frameworks and XML tools (`http://www.w3.org/TR/NOTE-SOX/`).

- Document Content Description (DCD) — A joint project of Microsoft and IBM, this schema language used concepts from XML-Data and syntax from the W3C's Resource Description Framework (RDF) (`http://www.w3.org/TR/NOTE-dcd`).

- Document Description Markup Language (DDML, formerly XSchema) — Developed on the XML-Dev mailing list, this schema language expressed DTD concepts in XML syntax with a focus on simplicity. The author of this book was one of the editors (`http://www.w3.org/TR/NOTE-ddml`).

Although these four schema vocabularies have been deployed in various products, the W3C focused on creating a single standard vocabulary, commonly referred to as XML Schema, W3C XML Schemas, or XML Schema Description Language (XSDL). It no longer looks very much like any of its four predecessors, though concepts from the predecessor languages have influenced its design. XSDL has the benefit of announced backing from Microsoft, Oracle, and the Apache Group, though at present it isn't yet complete.

During the development of XSDL, three new contenders emerged, each taking a different approach to validation and document description:

- Document Structure Description (DSD)—This proposal from AT&T Labs builds on assertion grammars, a concept used in Cascading Style Sheets (CSS), to describe document structures of varying depths (http://www.brics.dk/DSD/).

- Regular Language Description for XML (RELAX)—Developed by the Japanese Standards Association, RELAX is based on a mathematical model known as hedge grammars and provides a relatively simple way to describe complex document structures (http://www.xml.gr.jp/relax/).

- Schematron—Initially developed by Rick Jelliffe, a member of the W3C XML Schemas Working Group, the Schematron uses XPaths and XSLT processing to describe tree patterns, and is especially notable for its use in creating human-friendly validators (http://www.ascc.net/xml/resource/schematron/schematron.html).

RELAX is moving forward through ISO processes and is still in development, whereas Schematron has an active core of developers building tools and documentation. RELAX and XML Schema Description Language are often seen as competitors, offering very different sets of tools to perform similar tasks; Schematron is typically described as a supplemental tool, capable of fitting in any kind of XML environment, whether it uses DTDs, XML Schemas, RELAX, or none of the above. In the next few chapters, I describe XML Schemas and RELAX; in Chapter 15, I look at Schematron and XSLT.

Note

If you like DTDs but really need to add data types, you might also want to explore the Data Types for DTDs (DT4DTDs) note at http://www.w3.org/TR/dt4dtd.

This may sound like an overload of schema possibilities, and for some people it is, but keep in mind that XML itself is a very new technology, and that schemas are even newer. XML opens up an incredibly large set of possibilities, and it isn't yet clear that a single approach will fit all of those possibilities cleanly. Some developers have already picked a single schema foundation — some DTD stalwarts are sticking with DTDs, some database and object-oriented folks are happy to use the W3C's XML Schemas, and some document-oriented people are excited about RELAX. Add Schematron — and the ever-present option of just sticking to well-formed XML with no DTD or schema — and there are lots of different communities making lots of different choices.

The costs of those choices may seem significant, especially if you pour resources into learning and implementing one schema option only to find that the rest of the world has taken a different route. Fortunately, those risks are lessened somewhat by tools for converting among different schema languages. Commercial developers such as TIBCO Extensibility see an opportunity in creating tools that can operate with all of these schema vocabularies while each community is busy developing free tools for converting other schema languages into its particular schema language. There will be costs, and you may want to focus on a particular choice, but for starters you may want to explore the options.

Note

As this book was going to press, another schema contender, TREX, appeared. Originally created by James Clark, author of the expat parser and editor of XSLT, TREX takes an approach more like RELAX but with a slightly different foundation and syntax. For more information, see `http://www.thaiopensource.com/trex/`.

Schema-Building Tools

Whatever schema strategy you choose, you may not want to create your complex descriptions of document structures in a text editor.

Trying to keep track of the potentially enormous number of connections among different parts of a document structure is a difficult task that grows rapidly more difficult as structures grow. Although this book focuses on handcrafting XML documents and schemas — in the belief that developers at this phase of XML's emergence should have a solid grounding in the underpinnings of XML — hand-coding doesn't necessarily scale well to large projects.

Note

New tools for writing and processing schemas appear regularly. The descriptions provided here represent some of the tools available in January 2001. For a much more complete list of possible tools, see `http://www.xmlsoftware.com/dtd/`.

Hand-crafting schemas

Developers with especially sharp memories and a fondness for detail may want to use a text editor or a generic XML editor to edit schemas. It definitely works — schemas, like all XML, are just text files — and it definitely provides finely tuned control. Developers who want to use advanced features of or extensions to schemas that may not yet be supported by schema editors may find direct editing the easiest way to get results immediately. Developers working in emergency situations — late at night, attempting to figure out why documents are being rejected — may also find a hand-editing strategy worth having.

Hand-tuning may be another option worth considering on a large scale. Though they may use graphical schema editors to create schemas initially, developers can then massage the results by hand. Using the generated schema as a foundation developers can add extra constraints, fine-tune document types, or optimize the schema for particular processors. This approach offers developers both the support of the tools and the precision of hand-crafting, but they risk running into difficulties if schemas have to go back and forth between tool- and hand-modification. Tool developers seem to be aware of this possibility, however, and generally attempt to design tools that preserve additional material even if they don't provide an interface for editing it directly.

XML Authority

TIBCO Extensibility's XML Authority uses a graphic interface for editing schemas in a wide variety of flavors. It can process DTDs as well as XDR, DCD, SOX, and W3C XML schemas natively, and imports and exports in those formats plus a variety of options from RELAX to COBOL copybooks to Java data structures to delimited text files to ODBC databases. A graphic interface supplemented by text tables enables you to work with either pictures or formal descriptions of your structures, data types, and content models. XML Authority is available for Windows, Macintosh, and Unix systems. For more information about XML Authority, visit `http://www.extensibility.com/`.

TIBCO Extensibility offers trial downloads of all of its software, letting you give it a test run. They also provide a Web site (free, but registration required), `http://apps.xmlschema.com/`, where you can use some of their conversion and validation tools.

XML Spy

Altova's XML Spy combines an XML document editor with an XML Schema editor. Although XML Spy includes some support for editing DTDs, XML Data Reduced, and Document Content Description, the product's schema-editing tools are primarily focused on W3C XML schemas. Developers can use a graphical editing environment to modify their schemas, and the document editor will immediately reflect the changes. The document editor uses document schemas to provide choices for users, presenting available options based on the contents of the schema. XML Spy is available for Windows systems. For more information about XML Spy, including trial downloads, visit `http://www.xmlspy.com`.

Chapter 8

W3C XML Schemas: Datatypes

The loudest complaint about XML 1.0 DTDs is their near-total lack of support for data typing. Programmers exchanging information between programs may find textual, enumerated, and document-oriented types useful occasionally, but generally they want to be able to specify different kinds of types — such as integers, floats, Booleans, dates, and times — and sometimes they want to be able to constrain the content within those types as well.

The W3C XML Schemas Working Group broke its development work into two pieces: Structures and Datatypes. The Structures document describes how to create schemas describing complex document structures, for which containment, sequence, and other interactions between XML element and attribute structures are the primary concern. The Datatypes document concentrates on the smaller pieces of information contained inside of those element and attribute structures, and information that doesn't use structural markup.

The Datatypes specification has proven far less controversial than the Structures specification, which is covered in the next chapter. XML Schema datatypes used by RELAX, for instance, can be integrated to some extent with DTDs, and may be a part of future incarnations of Schematron. Although some developers are only using subsets of XML Schema Datatypes (just primitive types, or just the types defined in the spec itself), even those subsets provide a solid basis for interoperability.

> **Note**
>
> This discussion of *XML Schemas Datatypes* is based on the 24 October 2000 Candidate Recommendation (`http://www.w3.org/TR/2000/CR-xmlschema-2-20001024/`). Although this document seems fairly stable, it may be subject to change. For the latest draft, see `http://www.w3.org/TR/xmlschema-2/`.

Primitive Datatypes

Primitive datatypes provide the foundation on which all of the rest of XML Schemas Datatypes are built. Each of these types has aspects that cannot be expressed generically with the rest of the constraints available in the specification, so the primitives are defined individually as base types. Table 8-1 lists these types.

Table 8-1 *Primitive Datatypes Defined by XML Schemas*

Type	Contents	Facets
string	Textual information – hello, 1234e43d, the weather is cloudy!	length, minLength, maxLength, pattern, enumeration, whiteSpace
boolean	True/false values –	pattern, whiteSpace true, false
float	32-bit decimal numbers with optional mantissa exponent – 1.23345, 2.3E22, 9.12E-31, -34.2 – along with INF (infinity) and NaN (not a number)	maxInclusive, minInclusive, maxExclusive, minExclusive, pattern, enumeration, whiteSpace

Type	Contents	Facets
double	64-bit decimal numbers with optional mantissa exponent – 1.23345, 2.3E42, 9. 12E-51, -34.2 – along with INF (infinity) and NaN (not a number)	maxInclusive, minInclusive, maxExclusive, minExclusive, pattern, enumeration, whiteSpace
decimal	Arbitrarily precise decimal numbers. Processors must support at least 18 digits. No exponent is permitted – 1.223345, 74.37593, -21.01	precision, scale, maxInclusive, minInclusive, maxExclusive, minExclusive, pattern, enumeration, whiteSpace
timeDuration	A positive or negative time duration expressed with ISO8601 notations in Year, Month, Day, Hour, Minutes, Seconds – P2Y1M10D5H11M45. 13s, P2Y1M, -P27H	maxInclusive, minInclusive, maxExclusive, minExclusive, pattern, enumeration, whiteSpace
recurring Duration	A recurring time. This type is only used as a base type to derive other types, and may not be used directly.	duration, period, maxInclusive, minInclusive, maxExclusive, minExclusive, pattern, enumeration, whiteSpace
binary	A binary number. This type is only used as a base type to derive other types, and may not be used directly.	encoding, length, minLength, maxLength, pattern, enumeration, whiteSpace
URIReference	A URI reference, such as http://www.w3.org/	length, minLength, maxLength, pattern, enumeration, whiteSpace

Continued

Table 8-1 *Continued*

Type	Contents	Facets
ID	A unique identifier, exactly like the ID in DTD attribute declarations.	length, minLength, maxLength, pattern, enumeration, whiteSpace, maxInclusive, minInclusive, maxExclusive, minExclusive
IDREF	A reference to a unique identifier, exactly like the IDREF in DTD attribute declarations.	length, minLength, maxLength, pattern, enumeration, whiteSpace, maxInclusive, minInclusive, maxExclusive, minExclusive
ENTITY	A reference to an unparsed entity, exactly like ENTITY in DTD attribute declarations. (You will have to declare the entity in a separate DTD, since XML schemas don't support entity declarations.)	length, minLength, maxLength, pattern, enumeration, whiteSpace, maxInclusive, minInclusive, maxExclusive, minExclusive
Qname	A namespace-qualified XML name, including a namespace name (the URI) and a local part.	length, minLength, maxLength, pattern, enumeration, whiteSpace, maxInclusive, minInclusive, maxExclusive, minExclusive

These primitive types are a foundation for other types, but can also be used (except where the table indicates otherwise) directly. By themselves, these types represent a substantial advance over the types supplied by XML 1.0, but they don't answer all needs or even all basic needs. The additional types in the *XML Schemas Datatypes* specification offer more solutions.

> **Note**
>
> In some sense it would be possible to derive all of these types from the string type. The *XML Schemas Datatypes* specification doesn't include a rich enough vocabulary to perform that kind of derivation, however, and it's probably fortunate that the Schema Working Group didn't attempt it.

Other Built-in Datatypes

The primitive datatypes include a wide variety of useful types, but many developers need more — types representing dates rather than time intervals, different types of numbers, and the rest of the XML 1.0 DTD datatypes. XML Schemas provides a set of built-in types that address these needs and that can themselves be further refined. Table 8-2 lists these types.

Table 8-2 *Derived Datatypes Defined by XML Schemas*

Type	Contents	Derived from
CDATA	Same as DTD CDATA type. Whitespace has been normalized to remove line feeds, tabs, and carriage returns.	string
token	Like CDATA, except that two spaces may not appear consecutively.	CDATA
language	RFC 1766 language identifiers, used by the xml:lang attribute.	token
IDREFS	Same as DTD IDREFS type.	IDREF
ENTITIES	Same as DTD ENTITIES type.	ENTITY
NMTOKEN	Same as DTD NMTOKEN type.	token
NMTOKENS	Same as DTD NMTOKENS type.	NMTOKEN

Continued

Table 8-2 *Continued*

Type	Contents	Derived from
Name	Strings that follow the rules for element and attribute names.	token
NCName	A name, but with colons prohibited. Used to describe the prefix and local part of names using namespaces.	Name
NOTATION	Same as DTD NOTATION type. In order to use this, however, you *must* derive a type that includes an enumeration.	Qname
integer	A number with no digits after the decimal point.	decimal
nonPositive Integer	An integer that is either negative or zero.	integer
negative Integer	An integer with a value of less than zero.	nonPositiveInteger
long	Integers between 92233720368 54775807 and -9223372036 854775808.	integer
int	Integers between 2147483647 and -2147483648.	long
short	Integers between 32767 and -32768.	int
byte	Integers between 127 and -128.	short
nonNegative Integer	Integers that are either positive or zero.	integer
unsignedLong	An integer with a value between zero and 18446744073709551615.	nonNegativeInteger
unsignedInt	An integer with a value between zero and 4294967295.	unsignedLong
unsignedShort	An integer with a value between zero and 65535.	unsignedInt
unsignedByte	An integer with a value between zero and 255.	unsignedShort

Type	Contents	Derived from
positive Integer	An integer with a value greater than zero.	nonNegativeInteger
timeInstant	A specific time, expressed relative to UTC: 2009-07-34T15: 10:00-06:00, for example.	recurringDuration
time	A time of day with no date expressed, in UTC: 2:00:10-05:00, for example.	recurringDuration
timePeriod	A period of time. This type cannot be used directly; schemas must derive types specifying a duration.	recurringDuration
date	A time period representing one full day, expressed as YYYY-MM-DD where all digits must appear. 2006-04-02 represents April 2, 2006.	timePeriod
month	A time period representing a month, expressed as YYYY-MM. 2010-06 represents June 2010.	timePeriod
year	A time period representing a year, expressed as YYYY. 1998 represents the year 1998.	timePeriod
century	A century, expressed as the first two digits of a YYYY year representation. The value 18 represents the century 1800-1899.	timePeriod
recurringDate	A date specified without a year to indicate the same day of multiple years. --04-02 represents April 2nd.	recurringDuration
recurringDay	A recurring day of the month, used to indicate meanings such as "the 15th of every month," represented as ---15.	recurringDuration

Developers who need even more control over their datatypes can derive types from these built-in types just as they can from the primitive types. (A number of the derived types in the specification are already derived from derived types.) The facets provided by the root primitive type remain available to developers, making it possible to focus these types even more tightly.

Caution

Right now, most approaches for integrating XML Schema Datatypes with document structure descriptions other than XML Schemas itself work best (or only) when you stick with the types built into the specification. Deriving your own types may not work in other environments, though support for datatype derivation is on a number of to-do lists.

Datatype Extension

Deriving new datatypes from existing ones means adding constraints through the facets provided on the primitive types. Each facet has its own set of rules for using it. The pattern facet, for instance, uses a regular expression language to express restrictions, whereas the maxInclusive and minInclusive facets take numbers. Some types are easy to create, whereas others may require substantial work in developing appropriate patterns and choosing types. The syntax XML Schemas uses is fairly simple, but the nuances of creating types (and processing such definitions) remain as complex as types have always been in computer programming.

The integerPercent type that follows demonstrates the basic approach used to derive a simple numeric datatype:

```
<simpleType name='integerPercent'>
  <restriction base='nonNegativeInteger'>
    <maxInclusive value='100'/>
  </restriction>
</simpleType>
```

The new `integerPercent` type is a simple type, with only data and no element structures. It is based on `nonNegativeInteger`, which means it has a foundation of integers from zero to infinity, which is then restricted to an upper limit of 100.

Extended types offer developers a number of options, from creating templates that users can then fill in to offloading concerns over data formats from applications to parsers and schema checkers. Although this level of control isn't needed by every application, it meets critical needs for some classes of developers.

Note

The business of deriving datatypes moves beyond the scope of an XML primer and is a field subject to change. The *XML Schemas Datatypes* specification includes examples and uses derivation to create a number of built-in types as well. You may also want to explore the XML Schemas Best Practices documents that Roger Costello is creating at http://www.xfront.com.

Chapter 9

Getting Started with W3C XML Schema: Structures

W3C *XML Schema: Structures* represents two years of development time at the W3C, where vendors have gathered to create a more powerful and more flexible approach to document structure description than DTDs allow. Unlike the Datatypes portion of the Schemas specification, which focuses on atomic data, the Structures portion gives developers tools to describe more complex structures which may then contain the atomic types defined in Datatypes. The focus of the Structures specification is on documents and document structures, creating a means of describing documents and reusing those descriptions.

Caution

This discussion of *W3C XML Schema: Structures* is based on the 24 October 2000 XML Schemas Candidate Recommendation, available at `http://www.w3.org/TR/2000/CR-xmlschema-1-20001024/`. For the latest version of W3C *XML Schema: Structures*, see `http://www.w3.org/TR/xmlschema-1/`.

Describing XML Using an Object Approach

DTDs use a combination of a simple (some would say stark) notation for describing content models and a text-substitution approach (parameter entities) for reusing and managing those descriptions. In place of these tools, W3C XML Schemas defines a type structure whose foundations operate using approaches taken from object-oriented development: containment, inheritance, restriction, and extension. XML Schemas is not an object-oriented development environment—they only define data structures without methods, and there is (for example) no concept of encapsulation.

The XML Schemas approach is designed to appeal to programmers familiar with object-oriented design and (to some extent) database structures. Although strictly applying concepts from object-oriented development and database schema design will probably lead to substantial confusion, XML Schemas builds its structures for describing document structures on those foundations. Much like building a program using objects, defining document structures using XML Schemas requires evaluating the information being processed to break it down into similar and dissimilar types, and choosing appropriate containers for those types.

Note

XML Schemas is about only document structures, not document content, though attribute defaulting is still a feature. Most important, the XML Schemas specifications explicitly leave out the entity definitions provided by DTDs. If you need to use parsed entities in your documents you'll still need to define them in a DTD and associate that DTD with the document using the DOCTYPE declaration.

Understanding Structures

Unlike the datatypes explored in the previous chapter, XML Schemas structures are designed to let you create complex nested structures, containing many different kinds of components. XML Schemas structures enable developers to work at a number of levels, allowing them to start with relatively simple types and build to more complex structures when modularization, reuse, and differentiation are needed.

Namespaces and W3C XML Schemas

W3C XML Schemas is namespace aware and use namespaces to define both their own structures and the structures they describe.

The specification identifies two namespaces. The first is used for components of XML Schemas themselves:

```
http://www.w3.org/2000/10/XMLSchema
```

Although that namespace is often assigned the prefix xsd, it is often used as the default namespace as well. XML Schemas can support any of these three approaches:

```
<xsd:schema
    xmlns:xsd="http://www.w3.org/2000/10/XMLSchema"
    xmlns="http://www.example.com/schemas/atom">
  <xsd:element name="atom" type="xsd:string"/>
</xsd:schema>
```

or:

```
<xsd:schema
    xmlns:xsd="http://www.w3.org/2000/10/XMLSchema"
    xmlns:atom="http://www.example.com/schemas/atom">
  <xsd:element name="atom:atom" type="xsd:string"/>
</xsd:schema>
```

or:

```
<schema
    xmlns="http://www.w3.org/2000/08/XMLSchema"
    xmlns:atom="http://www.example.com/schemas/atom">
  <element name="atom:atom" type="string"/>
</schema>
```

The second namespace (which typically uses the prefix xsi) is used inside document instances described by schemas to add schema-specific functionality:

```
http://www.w3.org/2000/10/XMLSchema-instance
```

This namespace is used to indicate datatypes within XML instance documents, and also to build a replacement for the DOC-TYPE declaration, the xsi:SchemaLocation attribute. When used on an XML element, it tells a validator where to find the XML Schema that should be used to check the document structure.

Note

Schema location mechanisms are controversial at present, and this mechanism is only one of several, all of which are subject to change. For more details on the intricacies of schema location mechanisms, see http://www.w3.org/ TR/xmlschema-1/#schema-loc.

Caution

Both of these namespace URIs are likely to change, as the XML Schema WG appears to be changing them with each new draft.

Basic element structures

For the first XML schema, I start by describing a very simple document from Chapter 2:

```
<product_list>
  <product>
    <product_number>S127.29</product_number>
    <description>
      <species>Maple</species> -
      <height unit="inches">1"</height>x
      <width unit="inches">1"</width>x
      <length unit="feet">2'</length>
    </description>
```

```
  <price>$4.25</price>
</product>
<product>
  <product_number>S128.29</product_number>
  <description>
    <species>Oak</species> -
    <height unit="inches">1"</height>x
    <width unit="inches">1"</width>x
    <length unit="feet">2'</length>
  </description>
  <price>$5.75</price>
</product>
<product>
  <product_number>S130.29</product_number>
  <description>
    <species>Pine</species> -
    <height unit="inches">1"</height>x
    <width unit="inches">1"</width>x
    <length unit="feet">2'</length>
  </description>
  <price>$2.00</price>
</product>
</product_list>
```

I leave off the attributes at first and focus exclusively on the elements. The top-level element in this document is product_list, so I start there and work down through its components. The declaration, though short, introduces some key pieces:

```
<xsd:element name="product_list">
   <xsd:complexType>
      <xsd:sequence>
         <xsd:element ref="product" minOccurs="1"
            maxOccurs="unbounded"/>
      </xsd:sequence>
   </xsd:complexType>
</xsd:element>
```

The xsd:element identifies this as a declaration for an element structure, just as <!ELEMENT> did in the DTD. The name of the element being defined appears in the name attribute. Because product_list is a complex type, containing other structures, you need to enclose its content model in an xsd:complexType element. The contents of product_list are a sequence of elements named product — there must be at least one of these, but there is no upper limit on quantity, so minOccurs is set to 1, whereas maxOccurs is set to unbounded.

Whereas xsd:sequence contains sequences, xsd:choice contains choices. These can be nested inside each other to reflect structures as necessary. If a choice reflects mixed content (text and elements in any sequence), a mixed attribute with a value of true is added to the xsd:choice attribute. The following example shows what the declaration for the description element might look like if you were to use mixed content rather than a simple sequence:

```
<xsd:element name="description">
  <xsd:complexType mixed="true">
    <xsd:choice minOccurs="0" maxOccurs="unbounded">
      <xsd:element ref="species"/>
      <xsd:element ref="height"/>
      <xsd:element ref="width"/>
      <xsd:element ref="length"/>
    </xsd:choice>
  </xsd:complexType>
</xsd:element>
```

Next, you need to define the product elements that appear inside the product_list. This definition uses structures similar to the previous example, but has more options for content:

```
<xsd:element name="product">
  <xsd:complexType>
    <xsd:sequence>
      <xsd:element ref="product_number"/>
```

```
          <xsd:element ref="description"/>
          <xsd:element ref="price"/>
      </xsd:sequence>
    </xsd:complexType>
  </xsd:element>
```

This time the sequence contains three elements. Because no minOccurs or maxOccurs attributes appear on the child xsd:element declarations, each of these items must occur once and only once.

Each of the elements identified by the ref attributes must have its own declaration. Initially you can treat all atomic content as strings, which enables you to declare product_number and price:

```
<xsd:element name="product_number" type="xsd:string"/>
<xsd:element name="price" type="xsd:string"/>
```

The description element is more complex, though it uses features you're already familiar with:

```
<xsd:element name="description">
  <xsd:complexType>
    <xsd:sequence>
       <xsd:element ref="species"/>
       <xsd:element ref="height"/>
       <xsd:element ref="width"/>
       <xsd:element ref="length"/>
    </xsd:sequence>
  </xsd:complexType>
</xsd:element>
```

The rest of the elements are all simple strings:

```
<xsd:element name="species" type="xsd:string"/>
<xsd:element name="height" type="xsd:string"/>
<xsd:element name="width" type="xsd:string"/>
<xsd:element name="length" type="xsd:string"/>
```

Assemble all this inside an xsd:schema element and you get the following:

```
<?xml version="1.0" encoding="UTF-8"?>
<xsd:schema
     xmlns:xsd="http://www.w3.org/2000/10/XMLSchema">
   <xsd:element name="product_list">
      <xsd:complexType>
         <xsd:sequence>
            <xsd:element ref="product" minOccurs="0"
               maxOccurs="unbounded"/>
         </xsd:sequence>
      </xsd:complexType>
   </xsd:element>
   <xsd:element name="product">
      <xsd:complexType>
         <xsd:sequence>
            <xsd:element ref="product_number"/>
            <xsd:element ref="description"/>
            <xsd:element ref="price"/>
         </xsd:sequence>
      </xsd:complexType>
   </xsd:element>
   <xsd:element name="product_number" type="xsd:string"/>
   <xsd:element name="description">
      <xsd:complexType>
         <xsd:sequence>
            <xsd:element ref="species"/>
            <xsd:element ref="height"/>
            <xsd:element ref="width"/>
            <xsd:element ref="length"/>
         </xsd:sequence>
      </xsd:complexType>
   </xsd:element>
   <xsd:element name="price" type="xsd:string"/>
   <xsd:element name="species" type="xsd:string"/>
```

```
<xsd:element name="height" type="xsd:string"/>
<xsd:element name="width" type="xsd:string"/>
<xsd:element name="length" type="xsd:string"/>
</xsd:schema>
```

Now that you have the elements under control, it's time to look at that unit attribute. Without the unit attribute the declaration for the height element is pretty simple:

```
<xsd:element name="height" type="xsd:string"/>
```

Adding an attribute means changing the type from a simple string to a complex type combining the string and an attribute value whose type is itself (for now) a string. The type attribute disappears, replaced by a child xsd:complexType structure.

```
<xsd:element name="height">
   <xsd:complexType>
      <xsd:simpleContent>
         <xsd:extension base="xsd:string">
            <xsd:attribute name="unit"
              type="xsd:string"/>
         </xsd:extension>
      </xsd:simpleContent>
   </xsd:complexType>
</xsd:element>
```

Although this approach is much more verbose than the original, it will help with reuse and to some extent with schema management. To demonstrate how this works, I add some enumerated values to the attribute to specify appropriate units in this DTD.

```
<xsd:element name="height">
   <xsd:complexType>
      <xsd:simpleContent>
         <xsd:extension base="xsd:string">
            <xsd:attribute name="unit">
               <xsd:simpleType>
```

Continued

```
                    <xsd:restriction base="xsd:string">
                        <xsd:enumeration value="feet"/>
                        <xsd:enumeration value="inches"/>
                        <xsd:enumeration value="yards"/>
                    </xsd:restriction>
                </xsd:simpleType>
            </xsd:attribute>
        </xsd:extension>
    </xsd:simpleContent>
  </xsd:complexType>
</xsd:element>
```

That looks a bit extensive for a simple string plus an attribute value, especially since three elements are present that all use the same combination of possibilities. Fortunately, this is where the typing system in XML Schemas rides to the rescue. You can pull that complex type out from this element declaration, assign it a name, and use it as a type within your schema. That way you declare it once and use it repeatedly, thus eliminating a lot of redundancy. The complex type looks like this:

```
<xsd:complexType name="measurement">
    <xsd:simpleContent>
        <xsd:extension base="xsd:string">
            <xsd:attribute name="unit">
                <xsd:simpleType>
                    <xsd:restriction base="xsd:string">
                        <xsd:enumeration value="feet"/>
                        <xsd:enumeration value="inches"/>
                        <xsd:enumeration value="yards"/>
                    </xsd:restriction>
                </xsd:simpleType>
            </xsd:attribute>
        </xsd:extension>
    </xsd:simpleContent>
</xsd:complexType>
```

The `type` declaration now contains all the complexity of the original, but your element declarations return to their former simplicity:

```
<xsd:element name="height" type="measurement" />
<xsd:element name="width" type="measurement" />
<xsd:element name="length"  type="measurement" />
```

Exploring Advanced Features

The declarations in the previous section are only the tip of the iceberg — *XML Schema: Structures'* 228 pages contain an incredible number of options for defining types, reusing types, testing types, establishing scope, and building structures that must be unique within a given scope. In the next few sections I describe a few of the options available to you in the current specification, though they are all definitely subject to extension or removal themselves.

Structures: Extension, restriction, and re-use

The example in the previous section used extension and restriction in some very limited ways — to define a type and add an attribute to it or to restrict the appropriate values of a string to the approved list of measurements. XML Schemas enables developers to use these same techniques on all kinds of structures, even complex ones. The mechanism for extensions has shown more staying power than the mechanism for restrictions, because it's usually easier to add things than it is to remove them. XML Schemas also enables developers to create types that prohibit modification — barring extension and/or restriction with the `xsd:final` attribute.

These capabilities make it possible to build libraries of schema components — both structures and datatypes — and customize them as needed for particular usage. The measurement type in the previous section might need extra possibilities for units, particularly if support for metric units matters at all. Products might have more sophisticated descriptions than the extremely simple set provided in this catalog schema, and a generic description model might provide a foundation for more complex solutions while allowing simple descriptions to remain simple.

Open content models

XML Schemas supports more controllable and more open ANY content models than did XML 1.0 DTDs. DTDs require that any element used inside an ANY content model must still be declared somewhere in a DTD, and provides no mechanisms whatsoever for limiting which elements may appear in those content models. XML Schemas allows for the possibility of any well-formed XML inside a content model, and also provides an option for developers who want to limit such content to *any* elements in a particular namespace. The following declaration demonstrates a content model in which zero or more elements from the XHTML namespace may appear, but nothing else may.

```
<xsd:complexType>
    <xsd:sequence>
        <xsd:any namespace="http://www.w3.org/1999/xhtml"
            minOccurs="0" maxOccurs="unbounded"
            processContents="skip"/>
    </xsd:sequence>
</xsd:complexType>
```

The namespace attribute sets the allowable namespace, and minOccurs and maxOccurs indicate how many elements may appear there. The processContents attribute enables developers to specify what level of content checking is permitted. The skip value tells the processor not to validate the contents at all. The strict value requires that there be declarations for the contents, and that they be valid — effectively, this produces the same results as the XML 1.0 DTD ANY content model. The lax value allows validation processing of the contents if and only if declarations are available. You can also mix multiple namespaces using multiple `xsd:any` elements.

Substitution groups

Sometimes, you may need to treat two different types as potential substitutes for each other. This doesn't mean that they are equivalent—in fact, the XML Schemas WG changed the name of the tool from *equivalence classes* to *substitution groups* because the original name seemed inaccurate. You should use substitution groups carefully because they can be a prime source of confusion when users read a document expecting one thing and find another.

Substitution groups are defined in element declarations. For example, if you want to create a French version of your height, width, and length elements, and make them substitutable, you can use the following:

```
<xsd:element name="height" type="measurement" />
<xsd:element name="width" type="measurement" />
<xsd:element name="length"  type="measurement" />
<xsd:element name="taille" type="measurement"
substitutionGroup="height" />
<xsd:element name="largeur" type="measurement"
substitutionGroup="width" />
<xsd:element name="longueur"  type="measurement"
substitutionGroup="length" />
```

This won't solve all of your translation problems, but it may work in a lot of cases.

Annotations for documentation and extension

XML Schemas enables you to include an `xsd:annotation` element in any declaration. These elements may contain human-readable documentation stored inside `xsd:documentation` elements and machine-readable metadata stored inside `xsd:appInfo` elements. Both of these elements may take source attributes that identify referenced content with a URI, and the `xsd:documentation` element may also take an `xml:lang` attribute to support multilingual documentation.

```
<xsd:annotation>
    <xsd:documentation xml:lang="en"
     source="http://www.example.com/schemadocs/desc.htm">
        human-readable description
    </xsd:documentation>
    <xsd:appInfo source="myAppInfo.xml"><!--machine-
readable annotation-->
    </xsd:appInfo>
</xsd:annotation>
```

The content models for both `xsd:documentation` and `xsd:appInfo` are wide open, making them prime territory for developers seeking to extend XML Schemas.

Path-based tests

Although typing and extensions give developers all kinds of control over content models, they don't provide a means for a type to control the content of its content. Content models are one layer deep — parent elements can define which child elements they have, but not what content those child elements have. In many cases this is perfectly acceptable, and developers used to working with DTDs won't find it surprising. On the other hand, it can raise some substantial problems if different parent elements must share the same child element, and the appropriate content of the child element depends on context.

Content models aren't very useful for checking for such situations, but three other structures can manage these tasks — CSS Selectors, XPaths, and XPointers. The XML Schemas approach uses XPaths, enabling developers to test structures for uniqueness and to set scopes within which identifiers (keys) must have unique values. This XPaths approach goes well beyond the ID/IDREF combinations allowed by DTDs, because those always had document-wide scope. These features haven't been widely implemented in tools supporting XML Schemas yet, but they may come to play an important role in the future. Schematron, which I discuss in Chapter 14, is entirely based on this XPaths approach, and may be a useful supplement to W3C XML Schemas.

Note

Although there will undoubtedly be books explaining W3C XML Schemas when they come closer to completion, several online references that can help you get started. The W3C's own *XML Schemas: Primer* http://www.w3.org/TR/xmlschema-0/) provides a walkthrough of several different approaches to schema development while providing an overview of the syntax. Roger Costello has also created a set of XML Schemas Best Practices documents, available from http://www.xfront.com.

Chapter 10

Getting Started with RELAX

RELAX's origins are very different from those of W3C XML Schemas. Instead of starting from a features list expressed as requirements, RELAX started from a small core of mathematical theory for describing ordered and unordered sets of information. Although the foundation, hedge automata, is fairly difficult reading for nonmathematicians (this author included), it provides a workable base of concepts on which to build lightweight but powerful tools, as well as some potentially significant features that W3C XML Schemas don't offer.

Note

RELAX is currently being considered for publication as an ISO Technical Report. You won't find information on RELAX at the W3C, and may have to pay for information from ISO, but you should be able to find all you need to work with RELAX at the main RELAX Web site, http://www.xml.gr.jp/relax/.

Hedging Your Schema Bets

Although W3C XML Schemas are popular with some developer communities, others find XML Schemas too large, too complex, and too unwieldy for their projects. As a result, some technologies from outside the W3C are receiving serious attention. It isn't clear whether XML Schemas will replace DTDs and take over their work, or if RELAX will stage an upset, or if the XML world will find itself contentedly divided among DTDs, XML Schemas, and RELAX, with Schematron perhaps as a key supplementary technology.

Certain classes of developers seem more excited about using RELAX than others. Document-oriented developers seem to find hedges more approachable than type hierarchies inspired by object-oriented design. Certain features made possible by RELAX's model, notably context-sensitive content models and content models that can be varied based on attribute values, are excellent fits for many kinds of document design. Exclusions, for example, are used several times in XHTML, but can't be expressed with DTDs or XML Schemas.

RELAX's mathematical foundations also make it possible for programmers to explore RELAX document descriptions as sets — developers who need to find the unions and intersections of schemas can do this in RELAX quite simply, because underneath RELAX schemas are hedge grammars, easily manipulated with simple algorithms. Developers who need to manipulate their schemas, perhaps even at runtime, may find RELAX more appropriate for some kinds of projects.

Tip

Mathematically-inclined readers who want more information may want to explore "Hedge Automata: A Formal Model for XML Schemata" at `http://www.xml.gr.jp/relax/ hedge_nice.html`. You don't need to know anything about hedges to use RELAX, however.

Caution

Using RELAX is something of a risk, if only because of the widespread credence XML developers give tools developed at the W3C, the home of XML 1.0, XSLT, XLink, etc. You'll need to evaluate your project needs to determine whether RELAX's formal but approachable style is for you.

Using the RELAX Vocabulary

Like XML Schemas, RELAX is built with XML syntax, and relies on the data types defined in *XML Schemas Part 2: Datatypes*. The rest of RELAX, though it performs similar tasks to XML Schemas, — defining element and attribute structures — uses a very different vocabulary, so knowing one schema language doesn't help much if you're trying to learn the other. (A basic understanding of DTDs can help, however.)

Like XML Schemas, RELAX does both more and less than XML 1.0 DTDs. Murata Makoto, editor of RELAX, describes RELAX as:

> (DTD – entities – notations + datatypes + namespaces) in XML.

RELAX is designed to describe document structures, not to modify their content, so it doesn't support entities and notations. As with XML Schemas, you can still support these features by supplementing your schemas with DTDs. Data typing is an added feature, as is support for namespaces (though the specification for mixing namespace modules is still being written.) RELAX documents are built as modules, each of which defines a set of elements and attributes that share a common namespace.

Creating modules

The root element of a RELAX module is always the `module` element. The `module` element has a number of attributes that identify features of the module as a whole as well as which version of RELAX it conforms to. For example, the `module` element in the following code specifies that this is version 2.0 of a given module, that it is using version 1.0 of the RELAX Core, and that the target namespace of the content it describes is `"http://www.example.com/paragraph"`. It also identifies the default namespace for the RELAX content.

```
<module moduleVersion="2.0" relaxCoreVersion="1.0"
targetNamespace="http://www.example.com/paragraph"
xmlns="http://www.xml.gr.jp/xmlns/relaxCore">...</module>
```

Inside that module you can define document structures that can be validated against the module. The module's attributes provide some metadata about the module as a whole, but there is another piece of module-wide information that should appear next: the acceptable root elements of documents conforming to this module. The `interface` element may contain `export` elements whose `label` attribute identifies possible root elements:

```
<interface>
<export label="paragraph"/>
<export label="quote"/>
</interface>
```

After these preliminaries, the actual definitions may follow.

Defining elements within modules

RELAX describes elements more flexibly than does XML 1.0 DTDs. The `elementRule` element, which defines the content model of an element type, may provide both a label and a `role` attribute for the element, giving developers two different ways to classify the element. This separation makes it much easier to reuse content types and to define context-sensitive document structures. If you don't need that separation, you can simply leave off the label `attribute`, and the value given for the `role` will be used for the label:

```
<elementRule role="paragraph">
....
</elementRule>
```

Elements that contain only data (no child elements) use the `type` attribute to describe their content with one of the built-in datatypes from XML Schema Datatypes:

```
<elementRule role="word" type="string"/>
```

Note

RELAX adds two possibilities to the list of data types: none and `emptyString`. Neither of these is exactly a data type, but they can be useful in certain situations in which nulls of a particular type are needed. There is presently no way to use user-derived types, however.

Elements with more complex content models can define them using syntax that in turn uses principles similar to those of DTDs: empty elements, sequences, and choices. The simplest, as usual, is the empty content model:

```
<elementRule role="nothing">
  <empty/>
</elementRule>
```

Sequences are defined using a sequence element containing the sequence as a list:

```
<elementRule role="bookInfo">
  <sequence>
    <ref label="title"/>
    <ref label="author"/>
    <ref label="pubDate"/>
  </sequence>
</elementRule>
```

In this case, ref elements contain label attributes that point to the permissible child elements. Just as in DTDs, these element types must be defined elsewhere in the schema. The sequence element can be treated as parentheses around a list of comma-separated values, and (like the ref element, choice element, and anything else that might represent repeatable element content) it takes an occurs attribute that can contain XML 1.0 DTD occurrence indicators: *, +, and ?. (No occurs attribute means that the element must appear only once.) These occurrence indicators have the same meaning as in DTDs. For example, if a book might have a required title and multiple authors, and if the publication date is optional, the declaration for bookInfo might look like this:

```
<elementRule role="bookInfo">
   <sequence>
     <ref label="title"/>
     <ref label="author" occurs="+"/>
     <ref label="pubDate" occurs="?"/>
   </sequence>
</elementRule>
```

Choices work similarly, using containment by a choice element to express a set of possibilities. If the content of a document came in paragraphs, figures, and perhaps multimedia presentations, the model below might be appropriate:

```
<elementRule role="content">
   <choice occurs="*">
     <ref label="paragraph" />
     <ref label="figure" />
     <ref label="multimedia" />
   </choice>
</elementRule>
```

To define mixed content, where text and attributes appear together, use a mixed element that contains a list of options.

```
<elementRule role="sentence">
    <mixed>
        <choice occurs="*">
           <ref label="subject"/>
           <ref label="verb"/>
           <ref label="object"/>
        </choice>
    </mixed>
  </elementRule>
```

RELAX places the same limitations on mixed content as XML 1.0 DTDs, limiting the kinds of constraints you can impose on their sequence. The choice element must specify an occurs attribute value of *.

All elementRule elements must also have tag elements to identify their attributes, even if the element being defined has no attributes. If the content element contains no attributes you can use an empty tag element whose name attribute contains the element name:

```
<tag name="content" />
```

Defining attributes within modules

If elements need attributes, adding them is a simple process. The tag element accepts attribute child elements, each of which takes a name and a type attribute to identify the name and type of the attribute:

```
<tag name="content">
   <attribute name="id" type="ID" />
   <attribute name="creator" type="string"/>
</tag>
```

The attribute element can also contain data type facets such as enumeration values, making it possible for the programmer to add constraints to an attribute value:

```
<tag name="location">
   <attribute name="state" type="string">
      <enumeration value="NY" />
      <enumeration value="PA" />
      <enumeration value="MA" />
      <enumeration value="CT" />
      <enumeration value="VT" />
   </attribute>
</tag>
```

RELAX supports all of the facets specified by *XML Schemas Datatypes*, though no user-defined data types per se can be created — just attributes with a particular set of facets.

Note

Element types can also be refined through facets.

RELAX also enables you to create attribute pools, collections of attributes that may be used by more than one element. If that `state` attribute needs to be used on multiple attributes (and especially if it lists all 50 states, not just New York and its neighbors), you might define it as part of an attribute pool:

```
<attPool role="CityStateZipUS">
   <attribute name="city" type="string" />
   <attribute name="state" type="string">
      <enumeration value="NY" />
      <enumeration value="PA" />
      <enumeration value="MA" />
      <enumeration value="CT" />
      <enumeration value="VT" />
   </attribute>
   <attribute name="zip" type="string" />
</attPool>
```

Any element that needs a `city`, `state`, and `zip` attribute can then use this attribute pool:

```
<tag name="location">
   <ref role="cityStateZipUS" />
</tag>
```

Documentation through annotation

RELAX provides an `annotation` element that works much like the `xsd:annotation` element of W3C XML Schemas, and has the

same contents: documentation and appInfo. If annotation elements are used, they must generally appear only once as the first
child element:

```
<attPool role="CityStateZipUS">
   <annotation>
     <documentation>
         This collection of attributes is used for
addresses in the USA to identify the city, state, and
postal ZIP code.
     </documentation>
   </annotation>
   <attribute name="city" type="string" />
   <attribute name="state" type="string">
      <enumeration value="NY" />
      <enumeration value="PA" />
      <enumeration value="MA" />
      <enumeration value="CT" />
      <enumeration value="VT" />
   </attribute>
   <attribute name="zip" type="string" />
</attPool>
```

As in W3C XML Schemas, the contents of these elements are
loosely defined. The documentation element is for human-readable
content, whereas the appInfo element is for application processing.
The RELAX modules for RELAX make considerable use of the
documentation mechanisms — see http://www.xml.gr.jp/relax/
relaxCore.rlx.

Hedge rules for complex content models

RELAX enables developers to create sets of rules for content models that can be reused and modified. These rules, called hedge rules,
use the same vocabulary for defining content models that element
rules use, and can be included into elements by reference. Although

the hedge rules themselves cannot contain mixed content, they can be included in mixed content declarations.

Defining a hedge rule looks much like defining an element rule:

```
<hedgeRule label="document_metadata">
  <sequence>
    <ref label="title"/>
    <ref label="author" occurs="+"/>
    <ref label="pubDate" occurs="?"/>
  </sequence>
</hedgeRule>
```

After you define the rule you can use it in other declarations:

```
<elementRule role="description" label="book-content">
  <sequence>
    <hedgeRef label="document_metadata" />
    <ref label="binding" />
  </sequence>
</elementRule>
<elementRule role="description" label="article=content">
  <sequence>
    <ref label="magazine" />
    <hedgeRef label="document_metadata" />
  </sequence>
</elementRule>
```

Hedge rules give RELAX much of its power, both for designing modules and for processing them.

Roles, labels, and context-sensitivity

Because RELAX makes a key distinction between roles and labels, it's possible to define different content models for the same element and then identify which content model should be used where. The role attribute always defines the name of the element, but the `label` attribute provides a separate identifier, which enables developers to specify which `elementRule` they really mean, even while using the same element name. This means that developers can define element content models to precisely fit particular contexts with concern that the "extra parts" used for one context will be reused/abused in another context.

The rules in the previous section for magazine article and book content both define an element named `description`. You may want to use the two variations in different contexts. A `magazineArticle` element might contain the `article-content` version, whereas a book might contain the `book-content` version. Implementing this is easy:

```
<elementRule role="magazineArticle">
    <sequence>
        <ref label="article-description" />
        <ref label="article-content" />
    </sequence>
</elementRule>
<elementRule role="book">
    <sequence>
        <ref label="book-description" />
        <ref label="book-content" />
    </sequence>
</elementRule>
```

The `magazineArticle` element and the `book` element must each have a description element as its first child element, but the content types are different, building on the types described in the previous section.

Rebuilding the wood catalog

We can easily rebuild the example from the previous chapters using RELAX. The following version doesn't do anything fancy structurally, since the documents are pretty simple. The `attPool` at the end provides support for the enumerated value on the units attribute.

```
<module moduleVersion="1.2"
    relaxCore="1.0"
    targetNamespace=""
    xmlns="http://www.xml.gr.jp/xmlns/relaxCore">
    <interface>
        <export label="product_list"/>
    </interface>
    <annotation>
        <documentation>Wood Catalog
fragment</documentation>
    </annotation>
    <elementRule role="product_list">
            <sequence>
                <ref label="product" occurs="+"/>
            </sequence>
    </elementRule>
    <tag name="product_list"/>
    <elementRule role="product">
        <sequence>
            <ref label="product_number"/>
            <ref label="description"/>
            <ref label="price"/>
        </sequence>
    </elementRule>
    <tag name="product"/>
    <elementRule role="product_number" type="string"/>
    <tag name="product_number"/>
    <elementRule role="description">
        <sequence>
            <ref label="species"/>
            <ref label="height"/>
            <ref label="width"/>
```

```
            <ref label="length"/>
        </sequence>
    </elementRule>
    <tag name="description"/>
    <elementRule role="price" type="string"/>
    <tag name="price"/>
    <elementRule role="species" type="string"/>
    <tag name="species"/>
    <elementRule role="height" type="string"/>
    <tag name="height">
        <ref role="unitConstrained" />
    </tag>
    <elementRule role="width" type="string"/>
    <tag name="width">
        <ref role="unitConstrained" />
    </tag>
    <elementRule role="length" type="string"/>
    <tag name="length">
        <ref role="unitConstrained" />
    </tag>
    <attPool role="unitConstrained">
        <attribute name="unit" type="string"/>
            <enumeration value="inches" />
            <enumeration value="feet" />
            <enumeration value="yard" />
        </attribute>
    </attPool>
</module>
```

Building on the RELAX Core

RELAX Core defines the creation of modules that describe elements in a single namespace. It doesn't intrinsically support documents containing multiple namespaces. The next phase of RELAX development, RELAX Namespace, defines rules for interactions between modules, establishing the relationships permitted between different vocabularies, and establishing a framework in which different structures can be combined and processed. That work is still in the early stages, though formal drafts should be appearing in 2001. Further work may extend RELAX in new directions, though most current work is focused on building applications that will take advantage of the simple foundation RELAX provides.

Note

For more information on RELAX, including the latest developments, standards status, and links to software and tutorials, see the main RELAX site at `http://www.xml.gr.jp/relax/`.

Part III

Supporting Specifications

Chapter 11

Processing Approaches: Browsers, DOM, SAX, and More

The architecture of distributed applications is changing once again. We've moved from text-based systems to complex client-server systems built on complex communications systems to the text-based Web and now may be on the verge of custom applications that use Web technologies as a foundation for transporting XML-based information. As always, each generation builds on foundations created for a previous one, and XML takes considerable advantage of technologies and architectures used by HTML. Although at this point XML isn't exactly the "SGML for the Web" that many thought it would be, processing models for XML have inherited much from—and are now contributing to—the Web browser experience.

Note

Even if you only plan to develop documents and not applications, you may want to explore this chapter. Applications that use different styles of parsing occasionally need slightly different document structures, and different styles of parsing can make it easier to process long, complex documents. You'll be better able to communicate with developers, and may develop a different perspective on how to structure information within documents.

HTML and XML Parsing In Browsers

The explosive growth of the Web was made possible by several different factors: the simplicity of HTML, the relative ease of setting up an HTTP (Web) server, and the rapid proliferation of browsers, of which Netscape and Microsoft Internet Explorer are the most prominent. Even the earliest browsers, created at CERN in 1991, were meant to give users quick access to documents, letting them move from document to document without any complex transactions getting in the way. This was one of HTML's most significant breaks from SGML; it was as significant a break as using markup tags for formatting as well as structure.

Web browsers combine a parsing engine with a presentation engine, though they typically use a very loose set of rules for parsing. HTML browsers don't validate HTML even against their internal definitions. Instead, they parse the file and do what they can with the tags they can understand. If they can't understand a tag, they ignore it. If there's a missing closing tag, they take their best guess at where it would most likely have been. Attributes may have an effect or may be ignored, depending on whether the browser understands them. This uncontrolled model has made it much easier for amateurs to publish Web pages, and has increased the number of Web authors dramatically. The downside is a lot of poorly written HTML. The ugliness may not show up in the screen presentation but lie instead in the code used to create it, which is information that is difficult to reuse.

Grossly simplified, browsers consist of four key parts: a communications engine that can send requests and receive information using HTTP and other network protocols, a parser that interprets that information, a presentation engine that displays the elements found by the parser, and an interface that controls user interaction with the information provided. Figure 11-1 shows a simple model of how a browser processes HTML documents.

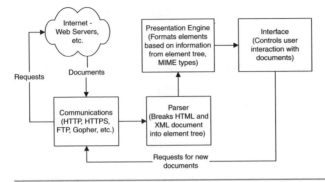

Figure 11-1 *The structure of a simple browser*

The communications engine gets HTML files from Web servers and passes them to the parser, which breaks them down into a tree of discrete elements. The presentation engine examines the contents of those elements and formats them properly for the screen, downloading additional materials as necessary. The interface provides the browser window in which the document is displayed, with its menus, navigation aids, scroll bars, and other features. It handles user actions and, when necessary, opens new pages, which go through the same communications — parsing and processing.

Browsers today are far more complicated than this simple model. They include scripting engines, style-sheet interpreters, Java Virtual Machines, plug-in interfaces, and all kinds of graphics engines, along with an ever-growing number of attachments to provide mail, news, groupware, HTML editing, and other integrated features. The channel features I describe in Chapter 20 have added some extra overhead. Because it has to handle all these parts, the browser has grown dramatically since its origin as a very small, simple program. Browsers today dwarf their predecessors, and most continue to grow larger and larger.

Competition between the browser vendors has also changed the rules for parser, presentation, and interface: documents are becoming dynamic. They are no longer static entities incapable of changing after they've reached the browser. Scripts can add and remove elements, change their appearance, modify their contents, and move them around the screen. The parsing engine still reads in code as it arrives, but the resulting tree it produces is now open to manipulation and modification. Effectively, scripts have been given read and write access to the document tree, making possible a whole new category of browser-based interfaces.

The W3C is currently in the process of standardizing the competing approaches to this technique. The Document Object Model Working Group is creating an Applications Processing Interface (API) for accessing and manipulating the contents of HTML and XML documents. Level 1, which provides a foundation, is now a W3C Recommendation, and largely implemented in Internet Explorer 5, Mozilla, and Netscape Communicator 6. DOM Level 2 has just reached W3C Recommendation status, though it hasn't yet been widely implemented, and work on Level 3 is beginning. The abstract for DOM Level 1 presents neatly the impact the Document Object Model will have on the simplified model presented in Figure 11-1:

> The Document Object Model (DOM) Level 1 provides a mechanism for software developers and Web script authors to access and manipulate parsed HTML and XML content. All markup as well as any document type declarations are made available. Level 1 also enables the creation "from scratch" of entire Web documents in memory; saving those documents persistently is left to the programmer. DOM Level 1 is intentionally limited in scope to content representation and manipulation; rendering, validation, externalization, etc. are deferred to higher levels of the DOM.

The parser creates an initial state for the browser. After that, the element tree it creates may be modified, reorganized, or even rebuilt. Our XML documents, and perhaps even their DTDs or schemas, may change shape (which may cause problems, at least until Level 3 of the DOM appears to clarify validation processing).

These developments are the latest stimuli for the continuing expansion of the browser. Netscape's long-held dream of creating a browser that provides a complete interface is on the verge of being realized, although battles between Netscape and Microsoft continue. The implications of this extreme new flexibility are enormous. The browser environment is reaching the point at which it is rich enough to handle a variety of data presentation and processing jobs, most of which used to be the domain of applications built with specialized client-server tools. Although it remains to be seen whether the DOM will provide enough flexibility for developers to write a word processor in a browser, the DOM certainly promises enough flexibility to make it possible to create far more powerful client interfaces than we can now.

XML's demands for conformance to standards may come as a shock to HTML developers. XML parsers (which may rest underneath browsers that display the parsed information) are far pickier about syntax and structure than are HTML browsers. By demanding that authors get the syntax and structure right, rather than forcing the browser to figure out what's supposed to be in the document, XML makes it much easier for parsers, in terms of both performance and reliability. XML documents are intended to parse consistently, every time. There are a few variations in output depending on the type of parser, but even these are limited.

Because the parsers don't have to spend time rebuilding broken documents, they can perform their tasks far more efficiently than their HTML cousins. They have the luxury of focusing on the tree structure already included in a document rather than on creating a presentation structure based on a mixed-up stream of information. XML standards refer to processors (parsers), not browsers, because much XML development will be intended for machine-readable data applications rather than graphically exciting Web pages. Any kind of application may be built on top of a parser, and browsers are only a small, though important, part of the XML vision. Browsers remain extremely useful, presenting XML workers with a friendly and accessible tool for reading information, but they are only windows to a much larger project.

Beyond Browsers: Parsers in Applications

Although Netscape and Microsoft are both integrating XML into their browsers, browsers will only be one small part of the XML toolset. Viewing XML in a browser using style sheets can be very useful, but browsers have some serious limitations. They aren't very good at letting users manipulate and change information, and provide only limited tools for sending information retrieved by the browser on to other applications for processing. While many developers have focused on building Web applications inside the browser, XML seems to be inviting developers to connect other kinds of software directly to the Web.

Some of the tools for doing this have come directly from the Web. Microsoft's MSXML parser, for example, has been integrated with Internet Explorer since version 4.0, and provides XML parsing services to the browser. It's always had a second life, however, as a separately downloadable package that can be used without the rest of the browser. MSXML has its own Software Development Kit (SDK), which includes examples of how to use it within both Web browsers and other kinds of applications.

Going in the other direction, Mozilla and Netscape 6 have incorporated James Clark's expat parser into their browsers, using it to read XML documents into the browsers' internal structures. The Mozilla and Netscape 6 browsers actually use XML and XML tools to describe and manage their user interfaces, as part of a planned transition from being pure Web browsers to being customizable XML-based application-development platforms. Mozilla and Netscape 6 enable developers to process and manipulate XML through the browser, and these browsers use the same tools to actually create the browser.

Even parsers that have no direct connection with browsers, like the Apache Project's Xerces, use technologies that evolved in Web browsers, notably the Document Object Model. Other kinds of applications — from word processors to agents to electronic-commerce facilitators to games to content-management systems — are using this Web-originated technology for purposes far beyond the browser. Models that work in browsers aren't appropriate to every application, however. While browsers need to keep a complete picture of a document in memory, many applications need only to extract information from documents, or prefer to map documents to internal structures that may be more efficient than a model of an XML document. Event-based parsers take a different approach, though one that (like expat) can feed into the tree-based model used by browsers.

Building and manipulating trees: DOM

Applications that receive a Document Object Model (DOM, or sometimes DOM tree) from the parser have the luxury of having the entire document available to them at any time. This approach works extremely well when users expect to have the entire document at their disposal for viewing or other manipulation, or when a processor needs to retrieve information from the end of a document to correctly process information at the beginning of a document.

The Document Object Model presents applications with a model of a document, representing elements, attributes, text, and other components as individual nodes that are part of a tree. Where order matters (as with element content), order is preserved, but random access is available where order doesn't matter (as with lists of attributes). All XML document components are abstracted as nodes, but different kinds of nodes can have different properties as well as different rules about which kinds of nodes they can contain. Element nodes, for example, can contain nodes representing elements, text, comments, processing instructions, CDATA sections, and entity references, whereas attribute nodes are treated as properties of element nodes and may contain only text and entity-reference nodes. Applications can "walk the tree" — move from node to node in search of particular structures and content — or use search features provided as extensions in some parsers.

The in-memory representation of a document is typically many times larger than the original XML document itself. Some parsers can keep memory consumption within a factor of five times the original size, but early parsers have been known to expand a document to 40 to 100 times its original size. For many applications this is perfectly acceptable — the tradeoff between memory and manipulability pays off very well, especially when only a few documents are open at any given time. For browsers and editors, the DOM (or models like it) makes a lot of sense. On the other hand, if you're working with a system that processes tens of thousands of sizable documents simultaneously you may find that the costs of the DOM are too extreme, and need to move to a model like SAX or some combination of SAX and the DOM.

Note

Applications using the DOM have a significant advantage because they receive the document only after well-formedness checking and, optionally, after validation. DOM-based parsers typically handle all the parsing before returning any results to the application, helping you to avoid being unpleasantly surprised by a glitch at the very end of a document.

While the DOM Core describes how to represent and manipulate XML document structures, the DOM also includes modules for handling HTML documents, views, styles, events, and content models (like DTDs and schemas), and loading and saving document content. Some of this work is plainly browser-oriented, while other parts will be useful in non-browser contexts as well. The DOM is written in three flavors: JavaScript, Java, and CORBA IDL. Implementations are available in other environments as well, though creating a full-scale DOM implementation is a difficult task.

Tip

The Document Object Model isn't described in a single document. Instead of one spec, there are several levels, some of which are further broken down into modules. The easiest place to find information on all these different parts as well as their status is the DOM page at the W3C: `http://www.w3.org/DOM/`.

Listening to events: SAX

Although the DOM is very useful in many cases, there are also plenty of times when applications want to manage the document representation themselves. In some cases, especially in large or large-scale document processing, applications want to avoid building an entire object model in memory, but still need to do something with the document. In other cases, applications want to map document content and structures directly to their internal structures without creating an internal representation of the document modeled as a document. For these cases, a different approach to parsing, called event-based parsing, is usually more appropriate.

The Simple API for XML (SAX) is the dominant event-based interface for XML parsers. It originated on the XML-Dev mailing list, under David Megginson's editorial guidance. SAX has no institutional home, though it may find one in the near future. SAX version 1 provided a basic API for reporting the contents of a parsed document, and SAX version 2 revised and extended that model to support features like namespaces, event filters, and additional extensions to the API. Although SAX is defined as a Java API, SAX-based APIs have appeared in a number of other environments including Microsoft's MSXML parser, Perl modules, and Python modules. (James Clark's expat parser uses its own event-based API, developed before SAX appeared.)

To use the SAX API developers create handlers for events that happen during the parsing of a document. These events represent things like the start and end of the document, the start and end of elements, and textual content inside those elements. The application receives the document as a series of method calls rather than as a single large chunk of information representing the document. The application is in charge of interpreting the events as they flow by, keeping track of document structures as appropriate and, typically, mapping them to internal application structures. Some applications — filters — accept a stream of events and then pass on some version of that stream to another part of the application. Other applications can take SAX events and generate XML documents from them, making it possible to create SAX-based document transformation tools that start with one document and return another.

Note

Some parsers generate SAX events that optionally feed into a DOM creator. The two models are different, but not mutually exclusive.

SAX is used in a wide variety of processing situations, from tiny systems running in a few hundred kilobytes to massive systems processing huge volumes of documents. Because the API is much smaller than the DOM API, it is both easier to learn and less capable than the DOM, giving developers plenty of room to wrap their own systems around XML documents. Some developers have gone so far as to create applications that exchange SAX events internally, without creating XML document representations. Other applications include parsers that report SAX events while parsing non-XML data streams, like tab-delimited data and EDI.

Developers using SAX do have to watch out for a few issues, however. Unlike applications using the DOM, applications using SAX-based parsers may encounter errors in a document after the application has already accepted information from the parser. Rolling back information that has been processed earlier can be difficult. Perhaps most important, however, is the amount of work developers have to do to implement handlers for SAX. Developers need to manage context by themselves, because the parser returns documents as fragments whose structure is described by the order of arrival, not as a neat tree. Handling these fragments and making sure they end up where they belong can become a challenge as the number of possible document structures grows.

Tip

For more on SAX, visit `http://www.megginson.com /SAX/index.html`. SAX and its documentation are in the public domain, and you can use it free of charge. You'll probably want to make sure you use a SAX2 parser (see `http://www.megginson.com/Software/` for a list), though SAX1 is often sufficient if namespace processing isn't important.

New contenders

SAX and DOM aren't the only options available to developers integrating XML with their applications, and the event-based and tree-based models aren't mutually exclusive. As the XML community has grown new needs and new communities have emerged, and some groups have developed new tools. Given XML's enormous flexibility and the number of different ways in which it's been used, this isn't entirely surprising.

JDOM (`http://www.jdom.org/`) is a community-developed API that provides a tree-based model that has a more Java-centric API than does the W3C's Document Object Model. While it provides much of the same functionality as the DOM Core modules, it has also taken greater advantage of Java API conventions and features like collections. The JDOM package uses SAX events to build its tree. It focuses on integration with applications other than browsers, which frees it from much of the design baggage the DOM has had to carry.

JAXP, the Java API for XML Parsing, was developed through Sun Microsystems' Java Community Process and provides a generic wrapper around SAX and the DOM. It incorporates those specifications by reference, and fills in a few holes regarding loading and saving documents. It is also growing to include additional functionality. For more on JAXP, visit http://java.sun.com/xml/.

The Perl community has developed a wide array of tools for parsing and processing XML. XML::Parser is built on James Clark's expat, and is probably the dominant parser in Perl, but a number of other parsers and approaches are also popular. XML::Twig supplements XML::Parser by letting developers identify which parts of a document they find interesting and discard the rest of the document tree. Other modules give developers support for XPath querying, XSLT processing, and simplified text-oriented XML processing.

The Python community has also been very active on the API front, as SAX-based parsing is built into the core distribution and a growing community of developers is building DOM, RDF, XPath, and XSLT tools in Python. EasySAX, an approach that combined a SAX-event approach with tree results, offered a promising alternative to pure event- and tree-based parsing.

Tip

For more on Perl modules and architectures, see xmlhack.com's Perl archive at http://xmlhack.com/list. php?cat=10. For more on Python modules, see http://www. python.org/topics/xml/, or xmlhack.com's Python archive at http://xmlhack.com/list.php?cat=18.

Chapter 12

Structure-Based Formatting: Cascading Style Sheets (CSS)

Although some developers use XML only to transfer information among applications, others are using it to distribute information to humans, often using existing Web browsers. Even developers who need to look at their data only occasionally may find this infrastructure convenient, because it makes it easy to render a raw XML document as a friendlier table or human-readable document, basing presentation on the markup instead of making people read documents that include all the pointy brackets. A set of styling tools developed for HTML can make formatting XML much easier, requiring only the creation of style sheets that identify how particular document structures content should be presented. Cascading Style Sheets (CSS) is relatively simple but can address a wide variety of XML formatting needs.

Note

CSS is easy to approach, but all its possibilities could fill a book of their own. *Cascading Style Sheets: Designing for the Web*, by Hakon Lie, Bert Bos, and Robert Cailliau (Addison-Wesley, 1999), is a good tutorial written by some of the editors of the Cascading Style Sheets specifications.

Connecting Style Sheets to Documents

Unlike HTML, XML documents don't (necessarily) include formatting information. Styling information is generally stored outside the XML document itself, which makes it much easier to share formatting across a group of documents. Applications sometimes apply style sheets to XML documents if they know the XML vocabulary being used, but the W3C also provides a mechanism that documents can use to point to style sheets the document authors consider appropriate, using a processing instruction.

The `xml-stylesheet` processing instruction, described in *Associating XML Documents with Stylesheets* (`http://www.w3.org/TR/xml-stylesheet`), enables developers to connect XML documents with CSS and XSL stylesheets, and may eventually be used with additional style sheet formats. It must appear before the root element in the prolog of an XML document, and it tells applications that understand it (typically browsers) where to find style sheets and what types of style sheets they will find.

Tip

If you already understand the HTML `LINK`-element syntax for including style sheets, you'll find that the `xml-stylesheet` processing instruction has very similar attributes and behavior.

An `xml-stylesheet` processing instruction including all the pseudo-attributes might look like this:

```
<?xml-stylesheet href="http://www.example.com/
mystyle.css" type="text/css" title="My Stylesheet"
media="screen" charset="utf-8" alternate="no" ?>
```

The only required pseudo-attributes are `href` and `type`, which identify the location and MIME content type of the style sheet. The `href` value must be a URI, which can point to a separate document or even to a fragment identifier in the current document, permitting style sheets embedded in the original document. (The fragment identifier usage is possible, but not widely supported.) The type is typically "text/css" for CSS or "text/xml" for XSL.

The other attributes are optional. The title provides a human-readable description of the style sheet, which might be used in an application that enables users to choose which style sheet to apply to a document. The media value specifies which type of output the style sheet describes — "screen" and "print" are the most commonly used values, but a list of media descriptors is available at http://www.w3.org/TR/REC-html40/types.html#type-media-descriptors. The charset value identifies the character set used for the style sheet, just as the charset value in the XML declaration identifies the character set used for an XML document. The alternate pseudo-attribute tells the application if this is a default style sheet for the document ("no"), or an optional style sheet that may be applied by the application or the user ().

Tip

For more details on these values, see the HTML 4.01 recommendation at http://www.w3.org/TR/REC-html40/struct/links.html#h-12.3.2.

Applications that encounter XML documents containing an xml-stylesheet processing instruction will, if they understand the processing instruction and the style-sheet language used, present the document according to the rules in that style sheet.

Applying Styles Using Structured Formatting

Cascading Style Sheets makes it possible to specify formatting information separately from document content, though HTML developers often include the information inside the document. *Cascading* refers to CSS's ability to combine multiple style sheets and inline styling, simplifying the task of creating master templates and then making modifications as needed. Cascading Style Sheets uses the document structure as a framework that is then annotated with formatting information and displayed (or printed, or read, or presented somehow) by an application, typically (for now) a Web browser.

Evolving specifications

As part of a general effort by the W3C to recall HTML's more structured past while still addressing the needs of Web designers for whom lack of control of overall appearance is the largest obstacle to effective Web use, the W3C released the Cascading Style Sheets Level 1 specification in late 1996. Cascading Style Sheets Level 2, which became a recommendation in May 1998, continued the development of this technology, and Cascading Style Sheets Level 3 is currently in development. Though CSS was originally developed for HTML, it works quite well—some would even say better—with XML.

Microsoft jumped on the CSS bandwagon immediately, implementing some CSS features in Internet Explorer 3.0 and adding more robust though still incomplete functionality in 4.0, 5.0, and 5.5. Netscape, which originally proposed its own JavaScript Style Sheets standard, has also lined up behind CSS, implementing some of CSS in Netscape Communicator 4.0, and all of CSS Level 1 along with parts of Level 2 in Netscape Communicator 6.0. Opera has also substantially implemented CSS in its version 4 and 5 browsers.

CSS uses selectors—which in their simplest form correspond to element names—to identify targets for formatting. The information in curly braces following the selector is a set of properties and their values, which will be applied to all elements that meet the criteria established by the selector. The general syntax is as follows:

```
selector {property-name: value; property-name: value;}
```

Whitespace is unimportant—designers can format style sheets in whatever way is most convenient for readers. Many designers use one line per property value, making it easy to see the information as a list and to pick out particular properties. For the most part, reading style sheets is simple. The style sheet might include the following line:

```
H1 {font-family: Arial, Helvetica; font-weight: bold;
font-size: 24pt}
```

In this case, the selector refers to all H1 elements. H1 elements will be displayed in the font family Arial if available, and Helvetica if not. (If neither of them is available, the browser will revert to its default. Using `sans-serif` as the value simplifies this process.) H1 elements in the document to which this style sheet is applied will be bolded, and displayed as 24-point type.

The rules for applying style sheets offer developers considerable flexibility, and, to a limited degree, the ability to create their own formatting-tag vocabularies. Style sheets are said to be *cascading* because you can apply multiple style sheets to the same document. The style sheets are applied in a sort of reverse precedence, where the most recent definition is applied instead of the first. Although the word *cascading* may conjure up images of waterfalls and rapids, it really just means that an XML element will accept formatting from the style that is closest to it. The most immediate style is embedded directly in the element, as a `STYLE/style` attribute, though that attribute works reliably only in a limited number of W3C-created vocabularies. If present, the `STYLE` attribute overrides all other style information. Styles (and style sheets) can be applied in several ways, though the `xml-stylesheet` processing instruction described previously is the standard for XML vocabularies other than HTML. Although they don't yet, browsers may soon enable users to choose among multiple styles connected to a document. In that way, users will be able to choose large print if they need it, or a style that hides all the graphics in a document for an unvarnished look at the text. (Recent browsers also support user-specified style sheets, which can override the styles specified by a document.)

Note

You can also combine multiple style-sheet files from within a style sheet, using the @IMPORT URL (*stylesheetURL*) syntax.

In practice, an organization can create style sheets for use by its entire group, but individual documents can override the look of the site. For example, a large company can create a standard style sheet for all its documents but enable departments to create their own style sheets that override the corporate standard. Individual page designers (at the risk of getting fired, of course) could then apply both the corporate and the department style sheets to their documents, while making changes through the cascade.

Integrating CSS with XML

Although you can use style sheets to go wild and format your documents every which way, I don't recommend it. CSS can do a lot more than replace the HTML FONT element, but more complex actions require cooperation and coordination. Integrating CSS with XML vocabularies means creating standards that work across documents, making it easy for a designer (or a group of designers) to create specifications that you don't need to rebuild from the ground up every time someone needs a new page. The ID attribute can help fine-tune such models, helping designers implement one-on-a-page models that can highlight the latest news or create a new design twist. Even though CSS is all about formatting, it emphasizes structure in order to place formatting into a repeatable, controlled environment. This structure may not matter very much for small sets of documents, but it can make managing large document sets infinitely easier.

HTML and several other XML vocabularies developed at the W3C include ID, CLASS, and STYLE (or id, class, and style) attributes on all of their presentable element types to enable developers to create style-sheet rules that apply to particular elements or types of elements within a document, but these are somewhat less necessary and certainly less accepted in the XML world.

XML elements may have ID attributes, identified as type ID in the schema or DTD, but the use of the CLASS attribute is less necessary in most XML work because developers have control over their own vocabularies. Support in CSS2 for selectors based on other attribute names and values also makes CLASS less critical.

Use of the STYLE attribute in HTML to attach CSS properties directly to elements is a controversial technique that raises some complex issues involving vocabulary design and namespaces. The W3C has published a Working Draft, *Syntax of CSS rules in HTML's "style" attribute* (http://www.w3.org/TR/css-style-attr), which explains how the style attribute works, but it isn't clear that style will be supported in other XML vocabularies.

The "classic" HTML way of formatting involved putting formatting information directly into documents. This approach demands an incredible amount of fine-tuning every time a designer wants to change a typeface or a color in the overall design. Style sheets are the answer to this site-level problem. They enable you to manage your styles on the grand scale. Rather than putting the style information directly in the document, style sheets use selectors and pseudo-elements to identify formatting for particular elements in particular locations on the document tree. For the most part, XML documents created with non-W3C vocabularies rely entirely on this approach when they want to use CSS.

Note

Cascading Style Sheets is becoming an integral part of XML-based W3C projects like Synchronized Multimedia Integration Language (SMIL) and Structured Vector Graphics (SVG). See http://www.w3.org/Style/CSS for the latest information. The www-style@w3.org W3C mailing list (subscribe by e-mailing www-style-request@w3.org) and comp.infosystems.www.authoring.stylesheets newsgroup are forums for discussing CSS issues and implementations.

Because style information is stored outside the actual document, designers need some fairly precise tools to tell applications which formatting to apply to which part of the document. Although CSS selectors were originally developed for HTML, they work very well with XML. A complete list of CSS selectors and pseudo-classes, which behave much like selectors, is shown in Table 12-1.

Table 12-1 *Cascading Style Sheets Selectors*

Selector	Meaning	Level
elementName	Selects every element whose name is elementName.	1, 2
elementName1 elementName2	Selects all elements named elementName2 that are descended from (not necessarily children of) elements named elementName1.	1, 2
elementName1, elementName2 [, elementName3...]	Selects any elements that match the selector in the list.	1, 2
elementName1> elementName2	Selects all elementName2 elements that are directly children of elementName1 elements, not all descendants.	2
elementName1+ elementName2	Selects elementName2 elements are direct siblings to elementName1 elements.	2
[attName]	Selects elements that specify a value (it doesn't matter what value) for the attribute attName.	2
[attName= "attValue"]	Selects elements that have the particular value attValue for the attribute attName.	2
[attName~= "attValue"]	Selects elements when the value attValue is contained anywhere in a list (separated by whitespace) of tokens in the attribute attName.	2

Selector	Meaning	Level
`[attName|="attValue"]`	Selects `elementName` elements with attributes named `attName` when their value begins with `attValue` followed by a hyphen. (Used to select particular language types.)	2
`.className`	Selects `elementName` elements that contain an attribute named `class` or `CLASS` whose value is `className`.	1, 2 (HTML and XHTML only)
`#Idvalue`	Selects `elementName` elements that contain an attribute of type `ID` (in HTML, named `ID`) whose value is `IDvalue`.	1, 2
`*`(asterisk)	Selects all elements, whatever their name or content. The asterisk can be used instead of an element name anywhere within a selector.	2
`:first-child`	Selects elements that are the first child elements to appear inside their parent elements.	2
`:link`	Selects elements that represent hypertext links that have not yet been visited by the user.	1, 2
`:visited`	Selects elements that represent hypertext links that have already been visited by the user.	1, 2
`:active`	Selects hypertext links when the user is activating them.	1, 2
`:hover` `:focus`	Selects elements when the user is interacting with them (usually in a browser) in particular situations.	2
`:lang(language)`	Selects element content of the language specified. The CSS 2 specification suggests that this selector will work in conjunction with the `xml:lang` attribute identifying element language content.	2

Building style sheets requires choosing formatting properties that are applied to content identified by selectors. Style sheets enable developers to specify formatting precisely, giving them exact control over fonts, colors, positioning, and whitespace issues. Table 12-2 lists a subset of properties that will be especially useful as browser vendors finish implementing CSS for XML.

Table 12-2 *Cascading Style Sheets Properties*

Property	Notes	Acceptable Values	Level
`background`	Specifies all the possibilities for a background in one value.	A collection of the values for the other background properties	1, 2
`background-attachment`	Specifies whether the background scrolls with the content or remains fixed in one place.	`scroll`, `fixed`, `inherit`	1, 2
`background-color`	Specifies the background color of the element.	A color name (like `white`) or hex representation (like `#FFFFFF` for white)	1, 2
`background-image`	Specifies the background image of the element.	A URL identifying the image	1, 2
`background-repeat`	Specifies whether the background should repeat.	`repeat`, `repeat-x`, `repeat-y`, `no-repeat`, `inherit`	1, 2
`border`	Specifies all border properties in one property.	A collection of the values for the other border properties	1, 2
`border-bottom-color`	Sets the color value for the bottom border.	A color name or hex value	2
`border-bottom-`	Sets the style for the border on the bottom of the block.	`none` (default), `dotted`, `dashed`, `solid`, `double`, `style` `groove`, `ridge`, `inset`, `outset`	2
`border-bottom-width`	Sets the width for the border on the bottom of the block.	`thin`, `medium`, `thick`, or an explicit measurement	1, 2

Property	Notes	Acceptable Values	Level
border-color	Sets the color value for the entire border.	A color name or hex value	2
border-left-color	Sets the color value for the left border.	A color name or hex value	2
border-left-style	Sets the style of the border on the left of the block.	*none* (default), *dotted*, *dashed*, *solid*, *double*, *groove*, *ridge*, *inset*, *outset*	2
border-left-width	Sets the width of the border on the left of the block.	*thin*, *medium*, *thick*, or an explicit measurement	1, 2
border-right-color	Sets the color value of the right border.	A color name or hex value	2
border-right-style	Sets the style for the border on the right of the block.	*none* (default), *dotted*, *dashed*, *solid*, *double*, *groove*, *ridge*, *inset*, *outset*	2
border-right-width	Sets the width of the border on the right of the block.	*thin*, *medium*, *thick,* or an explicit measurement	1, 2
border-style	Sets the style of the entire border	*none* (default), *dotted*, *dashed*, *solid*, *double*, *groove*, *ridge*, *inset*, *outset*	1, 2
border-top-color	Sets the color of the top border.	A color name or hex value	2
border-top-style	Sets the style of the border on the top of the block.	*none* (default), *dotted*, *dashed*, *solid*, *double*, *groove*, *ridge*, *inset*, *outset*	2
border-top-width	Sets the width of the border on the top of the block.	*thin*, *medium*, thick, or an explicit measurement	1, 2
clear	Specifies whether floating blocks are allowed along the sides of the object.	*none*, *left*, *right*, *both*, or *inherit*	1, 2

Continued

Table 12-2 *(Continued)*

Property	Notes	Acceptable Values	Level
`color`	Specifies the color value for the element foreground.	A color name or hex value	1, 2
`direction`	Identifies the direction of text flow (important for internationalization).	`ltr` (left-to-right), `rtl` (right-to-left), or `inherit`	2
`display`	Provides a basic description of how an element should be formatted.	`block`, `inline`, `listItem`, `none`, `run-in`, `compact`, `marker`, `inherit`, `table`, `inline-table`, `table-row-group`, `table-header-group`, `table-footer-group`, `table-row`, `table-column-group`, `table-column`, `table-cell`, or `table-caption`	1, but much enhanced in 2.
`float`	Makes a block float.	`none`, `left`, `right`, or `inherit`	1, 2
`font-family`	Identifies the font or font family for an element.	`serif`, `sans-serif` and `monospace` are common; may also be a particular family name (`Arial`, `Times`), though not all fonts are available on all computers	1, 2
`font-size`	Sets the font size for an element.	May use `small`, `medium`, `large`, or point sizes	1, 2
`font-style`	Sets the style of the font, where `style` refers to the level and type of italicizing.	`normal`, `italic`, or `oblique`.	1, 2
`font-variant`	Creates small-caps formatting.	`normal` or `small-caps`	1, 2

Property	Notes	Acceptable Values	Level
font-weight	Specifies a weight for the font.	integer values from 100 to 900 (if supported), or *normal*, *bold*, *bolder*, or *lighter.*	1, 2
height	Specifies the height of the element; used for positioning elements in a space, typically a browser window.	Measurement	1, 2
left	Specifies the position of the left edge of the element from the left edge of the window; used for positioning elements in a space, typically a browser window.	Measurement	2
letter-spacing	Provides additional spacing between letters and text.	Measurement	1, 2
line-height	Specifies distance between baselines of text, enabling linespacing within blocks.	May be *normal*, number to multiply by point size, absolute measurement, or percentage.	1, 2
list-style-image	Enables display of an image (rather than a standard bullet character) as a bullet.	Takes a URL, *none*, or *inherit*	1, 2
list-style-position	Specifies how bullets should fit into a list of bulleted items	Takes *inside*, *outside*, or *inherit*	1, 2
list-style-type	Sets the default bullet appearance. (If an image is specified, it will override this property.)	*disk*, *circle*, *square*, *decimal*, or *inherit.*	1, 2
margin	Specifies all margin properties in a single property.	A collection of the values for the other margin properties	1, 2
margin-bottom	Specifies how much empty space to leave below the bottom of the element.	Measurement	1, 2
margin-left	Specifies how much empty space to leave to the left of the element.	Measurement	1, 2

Continued

Table 12-2 *(Continued)*

Property	Notes	Acceptable Values	Level
margin-right	Specifies how much empty space to leave to the right of the element.	Measurement	1, 2
margin-top	Specifies how much empty space to leave above the element.	Measurement	1, 2
overflow	Tells the presenting application what to do if an element's contents go beyond the *height* and *width* specified.	May be *visible* or *scroll*	2
page	Identifies pages for printing.	takes an identifier or *auto* (the default)	2
page-break-after	Specifies how page breaks (in printouts) should appear after the appearance of the element.	*auto, always, avoid, left, right,* or *inherit.*	2
page-break-before	Specifies how page breaks (in printouts) should appear before the appearance of the element.	*auto, always, avoid, left, right,* or *inherit.*	2
page-break-inside	Specifies how page breaks (in printouts) should be handled within the element.	*auto, always, avoid, left, right,* or *inherit.*	2
text-align	Specifies text alignment.	*left, right, center,* or *justify.*	1, 2
text-decoration	Specifies additional marking (typically lines) for the element text.	*none, underline, overline, line-through,* or *blink.*	1, 2
text-indent	Specifies how much to indent the first line of an element.	Measurement or percentage	1, 2
text-transform	Enables the transformation of text.	*none* (default), *capitalize, uppercase, lowercase,* or *inherit.*	1, 2

Property	Notes	Acceptable Values	Level
top	Specifies the position of the top edge of the element relative to the top edge of the window; used for positioning elements in a space, typically a browser window.	Usually a measurement; may also be *auto* or *inherit*	2
vertical-align	Specifies how to align element content with respect to the baseline; used in creating subscripts and superscripts.	*baseline* (default), *sub*, *super*, *top*, *text-top*, *middle*, *bottom*, *text-bottom*, or a percentage or measurement above the baseline	1, 2
visibility	Specifies whether or not to render an object transparently. Unlike *display:none*, doesn't prevent child elements from appearing.	*inherit*, *collapse*, *visible*, or *hidden*	2
white-space	*Pre* tells the browser to respect all whitespace in the element content, including line breaks, without requiring * * tags. *Nowrap* tells the browser not to break lines unless explicitly told to with a * *, *<P>*, or other line-break-forcing element.	*normal*, *inherit*, *pre*, or *nowrap*	1, 2
width	Specifies the width of an image.	Measurement	1, 2
word-spacing	Specifies additional spacing between words.	Measurement, *normal*, or *inherit*	1, 2
z-index	Identifies the z-layer of a positioned block; higher values are layered on top of lower values.	An integer	2

Note

Because CSS deserves a book (or several) of its own, this table is hardly complete. For complete lists of properties and values, with much lengthier descriptions of their meanings, visit the CSS Level 1 specification at `http://www.w3.org/TR/REC-CSS1` or the CSS Level 2 specification at `http://www.w3.org/TR/REC-CSS2`. The properties in Table 12-2 provide a basic set of tools for making XML pages attractive.

Creating style sheets

I start with a simple example from Chapter 2, the lumber catalog fragment:

```
<product_list>
  <product>
    <product_number>S127.29</product_number>
    <description>
      <species>Maple</species> -
      <height unit="inches">1"</height>x
      <width unit="inches">1"</width>x
      <length unit="feet">2'</length>
    </description>
    <price>$4.25</price>
  </product>
  <product>
    <product_number>S128.29</product_number>
    <description>
      <species>Oak</species> -
      <height unit="inches">1"</height>x
      <width unit="inches">1"</width>x
      <length unit="feet">2'</length>
    </description>
    <price>$5.75</price>
  </product>
```

```
<product>
  <product_number>S130.29</product_number>
  <description>
    <species>Pine</species> -
    <height unit="inches">1"</height>x
    <width unit="inches">1"</width>x
    <length unit="feet">2'</length>
  </description>
  <price>$2.00</price>
</product>
</product_list>
```

Despite the multiple levels of structure added, this document represents a table in its original form:

```
S127.29 Maple - 1"x1"x2'    $4.25
S128.29 Oak - 1"x1"x2'      $5.75
S130.29 Pine - 1"x1"x2'     $2.00
```

You can create a style sheet that recreates this presentation as closely as possible, using CSS selectors to assign different table-related display properties to the document structure. First, the product_list represents the table as a whole:

```
product_list {display:table}
```

The product elements are table rows:

```
product {display:table-row}
```

The product_number, description, and price elements are all table cells. The following code adds a bit of padding to make the distinctions clearer:

```
product_number {display:table-cell; padding:5px}
description {display:table-cell; padding:5px}
price {display:table-cell; padding:5px}
```

The height, width, and length are all parts of the description, and you don't want them rendered as separate cells or paragraphs, so assign their `display` property the value `inline`:

```
height, width, length {display:inline}
```

Finally, you can render the entire document in the monospace type in the original example, using the asterisk (*) selector to make it apply to all elements:

```
* {font-family:monospace}
```

Assembled, the style sheet looks like this:

```
product_list {display:table}
product {display:table-row}
product_number {display:table-cell; padding:5px}
description {display:table-cell; padding:5px}
price {display:table-cell; padding:5px}
height, width, length {display:inline}
* {font-family:monospace}
```

If you put it in a file called lumber.css, you can tell the browser to use that style sheet by adding the following processing instruction to the beginning of the main lumber.xml file:

```
<?xml-stylesheet href="lumber.css" type="text/css"?>
```

The results, rendered in the Mozilla browser, should be familiar, as you can see in Figure 12-1:

Caution

At present, table-rendering with CSS works in the Mozilla, Netscape 6, and Opera 4 browsers. It does not work in Internet Explorer 5.x or earlier.

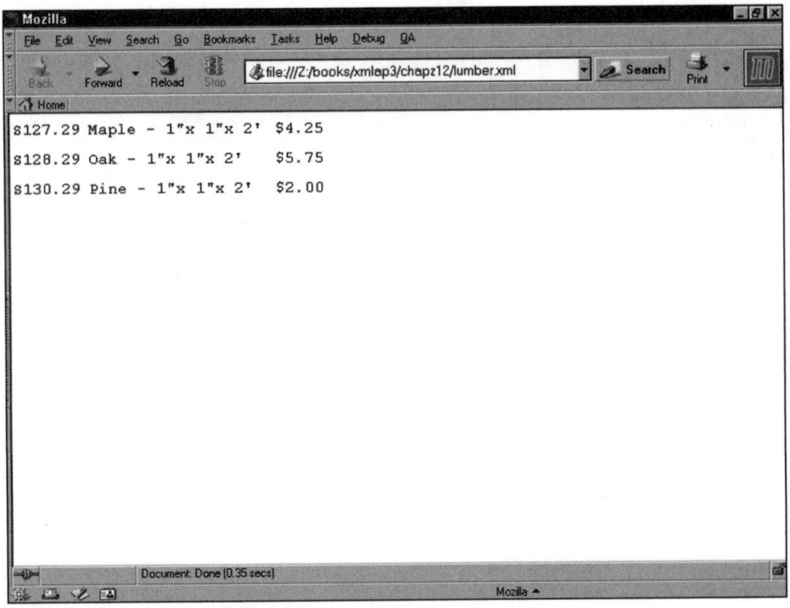

Figure 12-1 *Rendering a table from XML using CSS in Mozilla*

If you want to present your information as a list of items, you can use a different style sheet. The following style sheet uses a different set of display properties to render the contents of the XML document as a sequential list rather than as a table:

```
product_list {display:block}
product {display:block; padding:5px}
product_number {display:block;}
description {display:block;}
price {display:block;}
height, width, length {display:inline}
```

Though the information is the same, the results in Figure 12-2 are displayed quite differently.

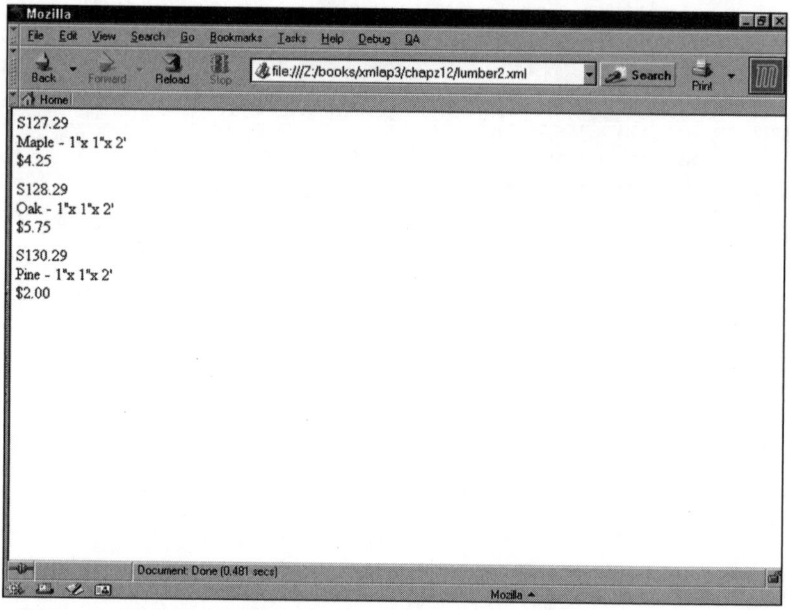

Figure 12-2 *Rendering a list from XML using CSS in Mozilla*

This time Internet Explorer 5.*x* also presents the same formatting, as shown in Figure 12-3.

Cascading Style Sheets has been far in advance of actual implementation, which is giving it something of a mixed reputation. Browsers are catching up to the specification, though slowly, and CSS offers developers as much control over formatting as HTML ever has — more, in fact. If you need to present XML documents over the Web, or even just explore documents visually, CSS offers a powerful but conveniently lightweight set of options. I use CSS in examples later in this book to provide a visual presentation of document structure.

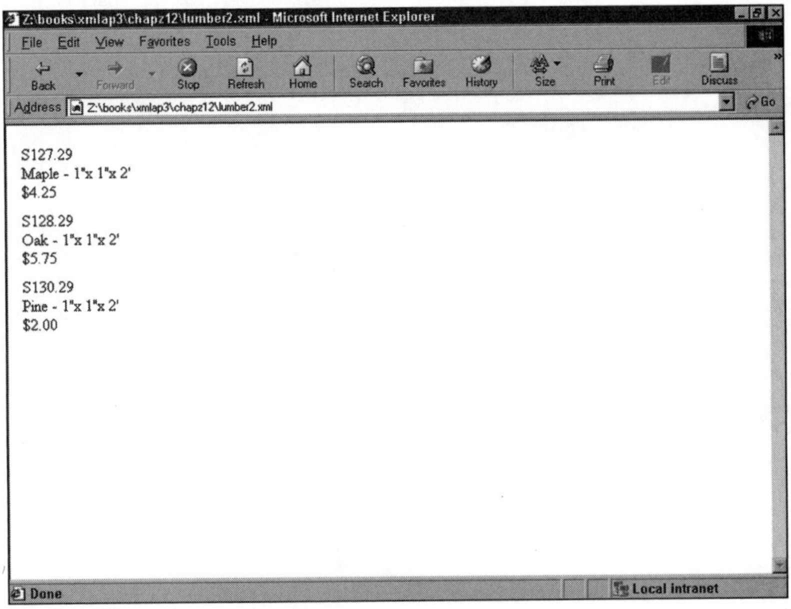

Figure 12-3 *Rendering a list from XML using CSS in Internet Explorer 5.5 for Windows*

Chapter 13

XPath: Identifying Document Parts

XML's cleanly labeled structures add a generous dose of predictability to document processing. Rather than walk through an entire document to find information, developers can ask for parts of a document that conform to a particular structure and then work on those parts. XPath defines a syntax for making those requests, giving developers a convenient and easily processed means of working with document parts. Although XPath was originally created for use with Extensible Stylesheet Language (the subject of the next chapter), it has also been used for a variety of projects that have very little to do with styling in general and XSLT in particular.

A standard syntax for identifying document parts is useful in a number of different situations, some of which involve processing those parts, some of which require retrieving those parts, and some of which only "mark" those parts as having special properties. XPath creates descriptions that may (or may not) lead to portions of documents, rather than requiring developers to write code that specifies how to explore a DOM tree or listen to a SAX event stream. This approach — often described as declarative, rather than procedural — makes it much easier to concisely describe the results you want while relying on a generic processor to do the actual work.

You can use XPath in a variety of different environments, with varying degrees of declarative and procedural contexts. XSLT uses

XPath to identify which parts of a document a given template should be applied to, while some DOM implementations provide extensions that let procedural scripts and programs retrieve document fragments using XPath identifiers. XPointer uses XPath as a foundation vocabulary for describing which parts of documents are connected by hypertext links.

Note

You may have noticed that XPath and CSS selectors perform similar functions. No one has worked much on reconciling the two approaches, which both emerged from different working groups within the W3C Style Sheet Activity. Both approaches work well with XML, though XPath has achieved more of an independent existence, largely because of XSLT's use outside of formatting applications.

Describing Locations

XPath expressions describe a route through a document to the desired structure. Every legal XPath expression contains at least one and potentially more location steps, separated from each other by slashes. An XPath expression containing only one location step might look like this:

```
locationStep
```

whereas an expression containing three location steps might look like this:

```
locationStep/locationStep/locationStep
```

The first location step applies to the entire document, and each subsequent step applies to results from the location step or steps to its left. Location steps don't necessarily identify a single piece of document content; they can also identify sets of content, even sets that weren't next to each other in the original document. If an XPath starts from the root of a document, it should begin with a slash (/).

Location steps themselves are composed of three parts, though these are sometimes abbreviated. The first part of the location step identifies the axis to which the step applies, the second identifies the node test (typically an element or attribute name), and the third part contains a predicate or predicates in square brackets. The third part of the location step is used only when additional information is needed to make claims such as "the 4th instance of a `paragraph` element that is a sibling to the current element." Predicates may also contain functions.

XPath provides 13 different axes, listed in Table 13-1.

Table 13-1 *Axes Available in XPath*

Axis	Meaning
child	Contains all the immediate child elements and other nodes of the current node (you can abbreviate it by leaving off `child::` entirely).
descendant	Contains all the elements and other nodes (except namespace nodes and attributes) contained by the current node.
parent	Contains the parent node of the current node, if one exists. (Can be abbreviated as `..` (dot dot), as is common in file-system usage.)
ancestor	Contains all nodes that contain the current node, if any exist.
following-sibling	Contains all nodes that share a common parent element with the current node, and that appear after the current node.
preceding-sibling	Contains all nodes that share a common parent element with the current node and that appear before the current node.
following	Contains all nodes that appear after the current node, but that are not descendants of the current node, if any.
preceding	Contains all nodes that appear before the current node, but that are not ancestors of the current node, if any.
attribute	Contains attribute nodes of the current node. (Can be abbreviated as `@`.)
namespace	Contains namespace nodes of the current node.
self	Contains the current node.
descendant-or-self	Contains the current node and its descendants.
ancestor-or-self	Contains the current node and its ancestors.

These axes are then combined with node tests and predicates to describe a step from the current node. Node tests typically involve checking against the name of a structure, but there are also options that offer more complex possibilities, as listed in Table 13-2.

Table 13-2 *Node Tests Available in XPath*

Node Test	Meaning
QName (qualified name)	A namespace-qualified name. (This just means that XPath uses XML namespaces when processing nodes.)
*	Any name. If the axis is `attribute`, it will be applied to attribute names; if the axis is `namespace`, it will be applied to namespace names. Otherwise, it applies to element names.
NCName:*	Allows testing for all nodes inside a given namespace whose prefix is *NCName*.
`text()`	Allows retrieval of text nodes.
`comment()`	Allows retrieval of comment nodes.
`processing-instruction()`	Allows retrieval of processing instructions. An optional argument limits the retrieval to processing instructions whose target is equal to that argument.

With just these two parts, specifying a lot of structural information in XPath is already possible. Unless an abbreviated form is used the axis must appear before the node test, separated from it by two colons (`::`). (A single colon may appear in the node test, separating a namespace prefix from the local name.)

```
child::date
ancestor::memo
self::text()
attribute::id
descendant::names:firstName
descendant::MyNS:*
```

Predicates enable developers to use these tools far more precisely, making the tools useful in a wider variety of situations. Predicates resolve to `true` or `false` for all the nodes specified by the axis and node test, and only the nodes for which the predicate resolves to `true` are included in the results of the location set. Predicates may be just numbers (in which case they restrict the results to a given node in the set), additional node set requirements, or expressions. Expressions allow a wider variety of conditions including mathematical operations and comparisons to be tested.

Predicates are always enclosed in square brackets (`[ ]`), and multiple predicates may appear after a given location set. Nodes must satisfy all the conditions set by the predicate to be members of the final location set. Predicates are the area where most of XPath's complexity sets in, so for the examples in this primer I settle for numeric predicates and tests of attribute values when necessary.

Note

For more comprehensive explanations of XPath predicates and especially their interactions with XSLT, you may want to explore Michael Kay's *XSLT Programmer's Reference* (Wrox Press, 2000) or Ken Holman's *Practical Transformation Using XSLT and XPath*, available from `http://www.cranesoftwrights.com/training/index.htm`.

Creating Paths from Location Tests

Although location tests provide a foundation for describing document parts, you often need multiple tests in order to arrive at a particular node. In some cases (as in much XSLT work), those paths are specified by multiple separate XPath expressions, and the current node from one operation is passed to another operation. In other cases, as in XPath's use within XPointer, a series of location tests walks a document tree all the way from its root node (or a node identified by an `ID` value) to its final destination. XSLT style sheets call upon XPath from a particular context within style-sheet processing, whereas XPointers have no expectation of a current processing context and need to describe a path from the fixed starting points, the origin of the document, or an element clearly identified with an attribute of type ID.

Here, I return to an earlier example document to explore different paths for locating information, modified slightly to demonstrate more XPath possibilities.

```
<!--sample product list managed by Jim-->
<product_list>
  <product id="S127.29">
    <product_number>S127.29</product_number>
    <description>Maple - 1"x1"x2'</description>
    <price currency="USD" sale="no">4.25</price>
  </product>
  <product id="S128.29">
    <product_number>S128.29</product_number>
    <description>Oak - 1"x1"x2'</description>
    <price currency="USD" sale="yes"
reg_price="7.75">5.75</price>
  </product>
  <product id="S130.29">
    <product_number>S130.29</product_number>
    <description>Pine - 1"x1"x2'</description>
    <price currency="USD" sale="no">2.00</price>
  </product>
</product_list>
```

You can start by creating some simple expressions containing node sets representing parts of the document that might be useful to manipulate. First I present some fairly self-explanatory expressions (though some things that look obvious are not) followed by a few more subtle ones.

Creating absolute XPaths

The simplest XPath (that returns any nodes) is /, which returns the root node. It might seem as though the root node is the product_list element, but it isn't. The root node contains both the product_list element and the comment that precedes it. To select the product_list element, you need to specify /product_list or at least /*. You can also write this XPath as /child::product_list or /child::*, but the abbreviated form is far more commonly used.

Tip

If you want to see an explicit demonstration of the nodes contained in XML documents, try the SHOWTREE XSLT Tree Display Stylesheet developed by Crane Softwrights. Documentation and the style sheet are available at http://www.cranesoftwrights.com/resources/ showtree/index.htm.

To create a list of all of the descriptions included in this document, you can retrieve the description elements (and only the description elements) using the XPath expression /product_list/product/description. The resulting node set will contain three element nodes: one a description for Maple; another a description for Oak; and the last a description for Pine. Similarly, to retrieve all the prices, you can use the expression /product_list/product/price. If you want to retrieve only products that are on sale, you can use the expression /product_list/product[price/@sale="yes"].

For product numbers, however, you have two options. (Although redundancy in document content isn't typically a great design choice, it's sometimes unavoidable and is very useful for examples like this one.) You can retrieve the product number from the id attribute, the product element, or the product_number element. The XPath pointing to the product_number elements is /product_list/product/product_number, whereas the XPath pointing to the id attribute is `/product_list/product/attribute::id` or (more commonly) `/product_list/product/@id`.

You can also use product numbers to limit the results returned by an XPath expression to a single node. (Within this document, product numbers are unique.) For starters, you can retrieve only product elements whose id attribute is S128.29:

```
/product_list/product[@id="S128.29"]
```

If you want to refine this search a little so as to get the description element for that product, you can use the following expression:

```
/product_list/product[@id="S128.29"]/description
```

Alternatively, you can retrieve description nodes first and then test the attribute value of the description element's parent to produce the same result:

```
/product_list/product/description[../@id="S128.29"]
```

For pretty much everything in XPath, there is more than one way to do it. To get just the text of the description, you can use the following expression:

```
/product_list/product[@id="S128.29"]/description/text()
```

or

```
/product_list/product/description[../@id="S128.29"]/text(
)
```

When you're certain where you are in the document or you need more flexibility, you can also leave off element names:

```
/*/*/description[../@id="S128.29"]/text()
```

This version looks for all description elements three layers down in the document tree whose parent elements have an id attribute value of S128.29 and returns their textual content. If you know that the description will always be the second child element there, or are concerned only with retrieving the second child attribute, you can abbreviate further to the following:

```
/*/*/[2][../@id="S128.29"]/text()
```

or

```
/*/[@id="S128.29"]/[2]/text()
```

 Caution

Although these many possibilities give XPath powerful capabilities, they also make it very easy for developers to create severely obfuscated style sheets. If you expect your applications of XPath to have any production lifetime, be certain to use readable XPath expressions when possible and document any creative usages. That way, someone else might be able to modify, fix, or reuse your XPath expressions without having to start over from scratch.

Creating relative XPaths

So far, all the XPath expressions you have created start from the top of the document tree, because they begin with a slash (/). Although these XPaths are perfectly acceptable and quite unambiguous, there are lots of times when XPaths must operate from a particular context. Most sophisticated XSLT style sheets include at least some context-based XPaths, and many other XPath applications support XPath testing against a given node's contents rather than against the entire document. XPath includes a variety of tools (mostly the axes) for moving through a document tree from someplace inside it.

For all the examples in this section, you start from the product element for Oak, identified by the absolute XPath:

```
/product_list/product[@id="S128.29"]
```

This product element has a parent element (product_list), three child elements (product_number, description, and price), and two siblings (a product element before and after.)

To get the parent element of this product element, you can specify the following:

```
parent::.
```

The single period (.) refers to the current node. You can also abbreviate that XPath this way:

```
..
```

If you want to reach the first child of the parent element (product_list), you can specify this:

```
../*[1]
```

or this:

```
../product[1]
```

You can reach that element directly using the preceding-sibling axis:

```
preceding-sibling::.[1]
```

To reach the sibling product element that describes Pine, you can use the following-sibling axis:

```
 following-sibling::.[1]
```

Working with the child elements of this element is much like identifying them within the document as a whole, except that /product_list/product[2] is already assumed. To reach the price element, you can just write this:

```
price
```

Because of the context, that would be equivalent to

```
/product_list/product[2]/price
```

To reach the `currency` attribute of the `price` element, you would write this:

```
price/@currency
```

XPath offers a lot of functionality, and you'll see in the next chapter that it makes XSLT very flexible.

Chapter 14

XSL

Cascading Style Sheets work by annotating existing document structures with presentation information. Extensible Style Language (XSL) takes a much more dramatic approach, transforming the original document into a new document tree that may be composed of formatting objects, which an application can then display. XSL uses XML syntax for its style sheets, and is focused entirely on XML, not HTML or other possible input formats.

XSL is derived in large part from the Document Style Semantics and Specification Language (DSSSL), which is commonly used to provide formatting information for SGML documents. DSSSL is an enormously powerful and complex standard capable of providing very precise formatting for all kinds of documents. Learning and implementing DSSSL, however, is an enormous task. As XML is SGML for the Web, so XSL is DSSSL for the Web. (There is also DSSSL-O, a lightweight online profile of DSSSL, that could contend with XSL.) DSSSL and its derivatives use SGML rather than XML, and their syntax is quite incompatible with XML. XSL's developers are trying to build a style language as powerful (or nearly so) as DSSSL, but one that uses XML syntax and is simple enough for common use on the Web. How compatible (or convertible) the two standards will be will remain a mystery until the final recommendation is issued. Unlike XML, whose designers specified compatibility with SGML as an explicit goal, XSL isn't bound by backward compatibility.

Cross-Reference

For an excellent tutorial on DSSSL, see Paul Prescod's "Introduction to DSSSL" at `http://www.prescod.net/dsssl/`. For information on DSSSL-O, see `http://sunsite.unc.edu/pub/sun-info/standards/dsssl/dssslo/dssslo.htm`. An open-source project enhancing a DSSSL engine has its headquarters at `http://www.netfolder.com/DSSSL/`. DSSSL does have its fans, and may prove useful if XSL isn't enough for you.

XSL is comprised of two key tools: a transformation engine that converts the original document tree into a document tree that can be presented, and a formatting vocabulary that describes the presentation of information for layout, typesetting, and so forth. The transformation engine moved through development much more rapidly and is useful for more than formatting, so the W3C split it into a separate document, XSL Transformations (XSLT). So far, most implementations have focused on XSLT, not formatting objects. As a result, most of the people currently working with XSL are developers making the transition from one XML vocabulary to another, not designers laying out document templates.

You can use XSLT to generate HTML (which is convenient if you need to present XML information to users who don't have XML support in their browsers) or to present XHTML, but "the HTML way" receives very little consideration from the XSL Working Group.

Caution

Some of the information in this chapter regarding XSL is subject to change. Although XSLT 1.0 is stable and has been for a while, XSLT 1.1 is currently in development – the latest draft is available at `http://www.w3.org/TR/xslt11/`. The parent XSL specification, which describes the interactions between XSLT and formatting objects as well as the details of formatting, is a Candidate Recommendation, and some changes may take place there as well – the latest version will always be at `http://www.w3.org/TR/xsl/`. Complete implementations of XSLT have been available for over a year, but similarly complete XSL implementations are still on the horizon.

Cross-Reference

For a list of tools that you can use to process XSL, visit `http://www.xmlsoftware.com/`.

Understanding Tree Construction (Transformations)

When an application invokes an XSL processor, the processor loads a style sheet. That style sheet contains rules in XSLT for transforming the original document structure into a new document structure. The rules are expressed as a set of templates that apply to various elements in the original document and produce a new document based on the original document. XSLT never annotates a document tree; instead, it builds a new document from an old one, according to the templates in the style sheet. This approach makes it very easy to do things such as reorder documents, hide and display information, convert tables into graphs (using a vector graphics markup language such as the W3C's Structured Vector Graphics, or SVG), or just convert XML documents into HTML for presentation in older browsers (which is what I do in my examples).

XSLT has a bright future as a transformation tool, regardless of how the rest of XSL does. XSLT already plays a key server-side role, simplifying the transition from HTML to XML by converting "alien" XML to "friendly" HTML (or even HTML+CSS) for browsers that don't understand XML. XSLT may also have a role to play in a number of the server-side processing tools, from Active Server Pages to Java servlets and CGI programming, giving programmers a generic tool for creating templates and modifying document structures that doesn't require explicit coding.

XSLT uses XPath to identify parts of the document tree that need processing and template rules to describe the processing that should take place. In some ways XSL is like a programming language, with structures that test equality and perform processing based on the results of that processing, but its overall approach is very different. Using XPath to find its way through source documents, XSLT can rearrange documents in all kinds of ways. XSLT includes a large set of rules that can be combined to convert attribute values to element text, recombine content in different sequences (including sorting), add numbering and other document-centered information, build macros for later reuse, respond to different conditions, and perhaps eventually provide capabilities for extending XSL itself, possibly with ECMAScript.

Caution

XSLT is quite new but already has some interoperability problems. The first set came from the version of XSL built into Internet Explorer, which isn't much like the final version of XSLT. The MSXML 3.0 parser conforms to the new specification, but won't appear in new downloads of Internet Explorer until version 6.*x*. The other issues tend to come from extension functions, typically those of extensions that rely on scripting engines or other environment-specific tools.

Take a look at a simple XSLT style sheet, converting an XML memo to HTML. First, the memo:

```
<?xml version="1.0"?>
<memo>
  <from>Jim</from>
  <to>Joe</to>
  <subject>Donuts</subject>
  <date formal="2001-04-13">April 13, 2001</date>
  <content>Thanks for those very fine donuts. Could you
    please bring two dozen to the management meeting?
    Everyone wants more. Thanks.</content>
</memo>
```

Although this is a fairly simple document, it presents some challenges that make the XML version not quite presentable in a Web browser or on paper. There aren't any labels on the from and to information, and most presentations aren't going to include the markup directly, so people will have to guess whether this is to or from Jim or Joe. The XSLT style sheet will add those labels and put this document into an HTML framework, making it easy to present in a browser.

```
<xsl:stylesheet
xmlns:xsl="http://www.w3.org/1999/XSL/Transform"
version="1.0">
  <xsl:output method="html"/>
  <xsl:template match="/">
    <html>
     <body>
       <xsl:apply-templates select="memo"/>
     </body>
    </html>
  </xsl:template>

  <xsl:template match="memo">
    <p>From:
      <xsl:value-of select="from"/>
    </p>
    <p>To:
      <xsl:value-of select="to"/>
    </p>
    <p>Re:
      <xsl:value-of select="subject"/>
    </p>
    <p>Date:
      <xsl:value-of select="date"/>
    </p>
    <hr />
    <p><xsl:value-of select="content"/></p>
  </xsl:template>
</xsl:stylesheet>
```

I'm working with these two documents inside Architag's XRay, a Windows-based tool that enables you to edit XML documents and XSLT stylesheets while watching the results of your work in separate windows. (XRay is free and available at http://architag.com/xray.) Loaded into XRay, with windows for the original XML, the XSLT transform, the results of the transform, and an HTML view, the documents produce the results shown in Figure 14-1.

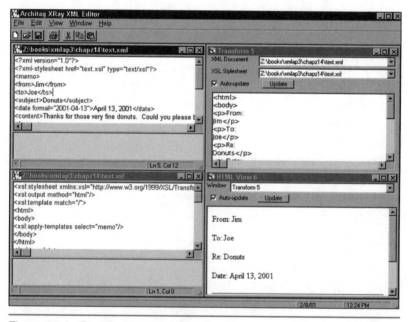

Figure 14-1 *Transforming the memo in XRay, with access to all the pieces and results*

To see the full results of the transformation, you may want to enlarge the result windows, as shown in Figure 14-2.

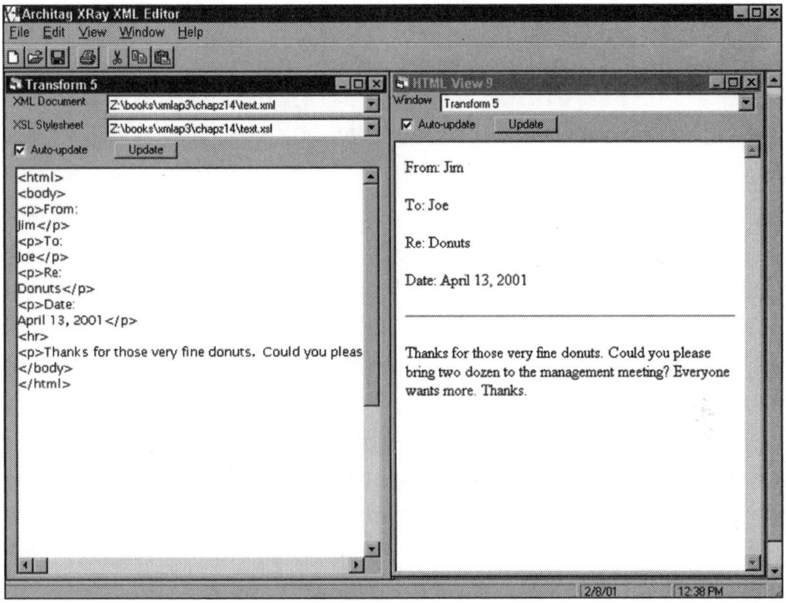

Figure 14-2 *Transformation results in XRay*

The results look good, but it's probably not exactly clear how you got there. The XSLT style sheet combines both the markup of the result and the rules for processing the original document, in a template form that isn't immediately comprehensible to those used to working with the start-to-finish text-generation approach more common in the Web-development world.

The XSLT style sheet starts off with an `xsl:stylesheet` element that sets the namespace for the XSLT components, and specifies which version of XSLT you're using. (Because 1.1 is in development, the version number is becoming more important.)

```
<xsl:stylesheet
xmlns:xsl="http://www.w3.org/1999/XSL/Transform"
version="1.0">
```

Caution

If you encounter style sheets that use the namespace `http://www.w3.org/TR/WD-xsl`, they were built using an older flavor of XSL that works only in Internet Explorer and environments built using the MSXML parser.

The next piece of the style sheet identifies the kind of content you want to produce—in this case, HTML. (XML and text are also options, and some XSLT processors provide additional options.)

```
<xsl:output method="html"/>
```

The next two child elements, the xsl:template elements, are where all the action in the style sheet takes place. They identify which part of the document they apply to in their match attributes, and their contents describe what should happen to that part of the document. The first rule sets the stage for the HTML-ization of the memo:

```
<xsl:template match="/">
  <html>
  <body>
    <xsl:apply-templates select="memo"/>
  </body>
  </html>
</xsl:template>
```

The match in this case is to /, the root of the document, which contains all the top-level content. The XSLT processor will generate the html and body elements but inside those elements is another XSLT instruction, xsl:apply-templates, which tells the processor that it should process memo elements, identified in the select attribute, according to the template rule that applies to them. That rule follows as the next xsl:template element (though it could have been anywhere in the style sheet). The rule for processing the memo element does most of the heavy lifting in the style sheet:

```
<xsl:template match="memo">
  <p>From:
    <xsl:value-of select="from"/>
  </p>
  <p>To:
    <xsl:value-of select="to"/>
  </p>
  <p>Re:
    <xsl:value-of select="subject"/>
  </p>
  <p>Date:
    <xsl:value-of select="date"/>
  </p>
  <hr />
  <p><xsl:value-of select="content"/></p>
  </xsl:template>
</xsl:stylesheet>
```

This template rule matches the memo element and wraps all its contents into labeled paragraphs, creating the HTML memo shown in Figure 14-2. The xsl:value-of element enables you to pick content out of various nodes for inclusion in the final document. The result of applying that template rule to the memo element is the following HTML pieces:

```
<p>From:
Jim</p>
<p>To:
Joe</p>
<p>Re:
Donuts</p>
<p>Date:
April 13, 2001</p>
<hr>
```

```
<p>Thanks for those very fine donuts. Could you please
bring two dozen to the management meeting?  Everyone
wants more. Thanks.</p>
```

The XSLT processor fills in the blanks created by the `xsl:value-of` elements with the content they identified. That select attribute can use any XPath that starts in the current (`memo`) context. For example, if you want the date to use the attribute value `formal` instead of the element content, you just need to change:

```
<p>Date:
  <xsl:value-of select="date"/>
</p>
```

to:

```
<p>Date:
  <xsl:value-of select="date/@formal"/>
</p>
```

This produces the result shown in Figure 14-3.

There's almost always more than one way to do it in XSLT, and that applies even to this extremely simple style sheet. Instead of including the rules for the subelements of `memo` inside the template for `memo`, you can fragment them into their own rules:

```
<xsl:template match="memo">
  <xsl:apply-templates />
</xsl:template>

<xsl:template match="from">
  <p>From:
  <xsl:value-of select="."/>
  </p>
</xsl:template>
```

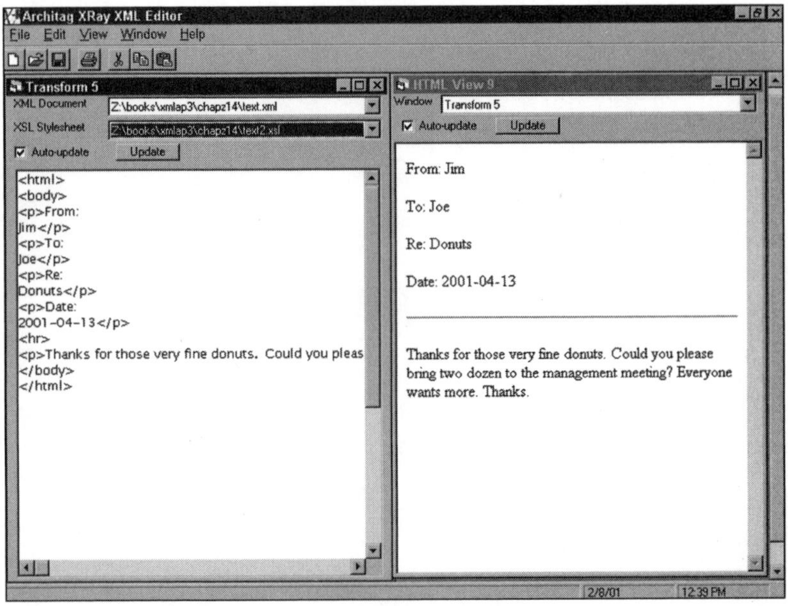

Figure 14-3 *Transformation results reflecting attribute content for the date*

```
<xsl:template match="to">
  <p>To:
    <xsl:value-of select="."/>
  </p>
</xsl:template>

<xsl:template match="subject">
  <p>Re:
    <xsl:value-of select="."/>
  </p>
</xsl:template>
```

```
<xsl:template match="date">
  <p>Date:
    <xsl:value-of select="@formal"/>
  </p>
</xsl:template>

<xsl:template match="content">
  <hr />
  <p><xsl:value-of select="."/></p>
</xsl:template>
```

The rule for memo is now just a shell, though you can use it to frame the memo if you want:

```
<xsl:template match="memo">
  <xsl:apply-templates />
</xsl:template>
```

Because no `select` attribute is provided, the XSLT processor will apply any rules whose `match` XPath fits the current context. As it encounters the from, to, subject, date, and content elements, it will apply those rules. Because the context has changed, the XPath in the `select` attributes of these rules has changed. The period (.) references the current element, and since you're already in the from, to, subject, and so on element, there's no need to specify the element name again. (XPath would go searching for a child element with that name if you specified it, and there's no from/from in this document.)

The new flavor of the style sheet works as well as the old, as shown in Figure 14-4.

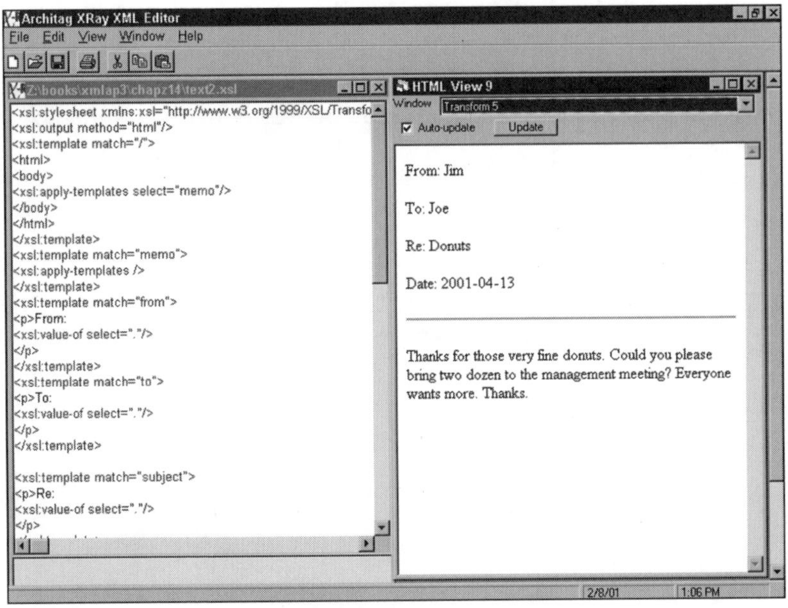

Figure 14-4: *Transformation results with the more fragmented style sheet*

If you have MSXML 3.0 installed on a computer running Internet Explorer 5.*x* you can add an xml-stylesheet processing instruction to the document prolog:

```
<?xml-stylesheet href="text2.xsl" type="text/xml"?>
```

and see the results, shown in Figure 14-5, in your browser.

XSLT offers far more than simple match-based processing, including function processing and a variety of control structures. Although it isn't meant to be an all-purpose transformation language, many developers are applying it in situations far removed from the formatting for which it was originally intended.

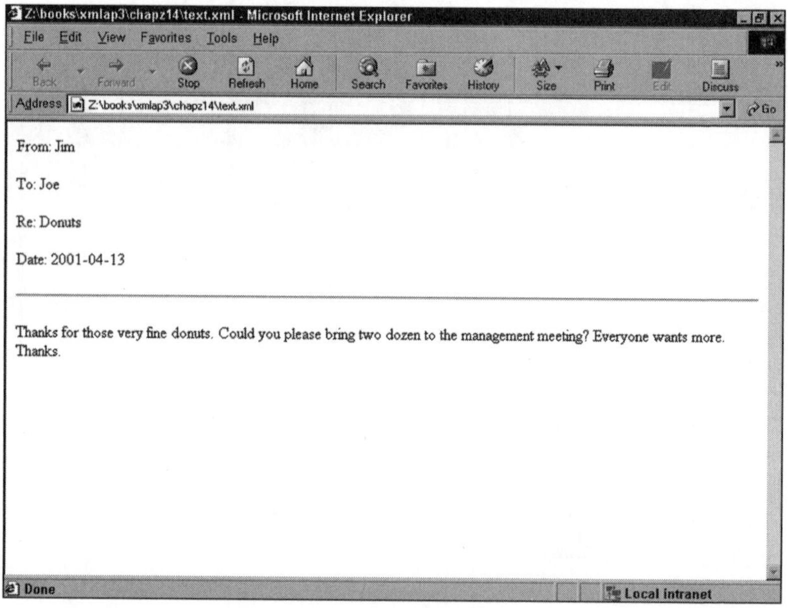

Figure 14-5 *Internet Explorer 5.5 displaying a document styled with XSLT*

Formatting Objects

The other side of XSL, formatting objects, has moved far more slowly than XSLT. XSL has seen some changes, notably the change of formatting objects from an abstract set of objects to a concrete XML vocabulary, as well as plenty of negotiation between the different formatting approaches of DSSSL and CSS. Although XSL aims to provide more capabilities than CSS, it also does many of the same things, and some kind of reconciliation would simplify the work of developers and make conversions easier. XSL is also taking on a remarkably difficult task, because formatting can become almost infinitely complex as the community of users with different needs grows larger and larger.

Note

For an interesting contrast to the XSL approach, see Håkon Wium Lie's "Formatting Objects Considered Harmful" at `http://www.operasoftware.com/people/howcome/1999/foch.html`.

An XSL style sheet transforms a document into a new vocabulary of formatting objects, an XML vocabulary that specifies only how information is to be presented, not how it is structured. All the meaning in an XSL-FO document (as it is often abbreviated) is about presentation. Effectively, XSL's formatting objects are a presentation-centered vocabulary for XML, no better than HTML for search-ability and reuse, but designed purely as a front-end for presentation. To give you some idea of how much control you have over formatting structures, the following list presents XSL formatting objects, all of which are represented in XSL documents as elements:

`fo:root`	`fo:external-graphic`
`fo:declarations`	`fo:instream-foreign-object`
`fo:color-profile`	`fo:inline`
`fo:page-sequence`	`fo:inline-container`
`fo:layout-master-set`	`fo:leader`
`fo:page-sequence-master`	`fo:page-number`
`fo:single-page-master-reference`	`fo:page-number-citation`
`fo:repeatable-page-master-reference`	`fo:table-and-caption`
`fo:repeatable-page-master-alternatives`	`fo:table`
`fo:conditional-page-master-reference`	`fo:table-column`
`fo:simple-page-master`	`fo:table-caption`
`fo:region-body`	`fo:table-header`

`fo:region-before`	`fo:table-footer`
`fo:region-after`	`fo:table-body`
`fo:region-start`	`fo:table-row`
`fo:region-end`	`fo:table-cell`
`fo:flow`	`fo:list-block`
`fo:static-content`	`fo:list-item`
`fo:title`	`fo:list-item-body`
`fo:block`	`fo:list-item-label`
`fo:block-container`	`fo:basic-link`
`fo:bidi-override`	`fo:multi-switch`
`fo:character`	`fo:multi-case`
`fo:initial-property-set`	

Each of these formatting objects may be further defined using formatting properties — attributes much like the properties of CSS. Formatting properties range from the simple, such as `color`, `font-family`, `font-size`, and `line-height`, to the more sophisticated, such as `line-spacing-precedence`, `escapement-space-end`, `hyphenation-char`, and `contents-rotation`.

XSL's usefulness on the Web will depend heavily on how much support the browser vendors provide. Although Microsoft has moved forward aggressively with its XSL transformation engine for Internet Explorer 5, its incompatibilities with the final draft of XSLT have made it of limited use with any but purely Microsoft environments, and Microsoft has shown no sign that it intends to implement formatting objects. Netscape has shown even less interest, having built its new engine on an XML+CSS combination, and Opera also appears content to stay with XML+CSS. Whether XSL can supplement or replace CSS in the Web environment is questionable, though the XSL development process may contribute to the CSS property list as well.

XSL does seem to be finding favor with some communities, however. Large-scale document-management systems that need to present multiple versions of the same document, often reorganized to meet different needs, are definitely exploring XSL. Typesetters and designers who need precise layout and features such as footnotes, floating paragraphs, and tight control over text presentation are also exploring XSL avidly. A variety of tools for generating Portable Document Format (PDF) files, used by Adobe Acrobat, are already available, and tools that render directly from XSL formatting objects to PostScript are also in development.

Tip

A mailing list for XSL discussion is also available — see http://www.mulberrytech.com/xsl/xsl-list/ for archives and information. This is a very active list, with participants at all levels of experience.

Using Schematron to Create Rules

As developers got used to using XPath to identify document structures and XSLT to create result documents based on those structures, a few of them had some slightly unconventional ideas about how to use these tools in a very different way. Instead of creating result documents representing a conversion of the document from one form to another, developers could treat those result documents as reports on the content and structure of the documents. XSLT style sheets could do this work, but they were a bit unwieldy, and Schematron emerged as a vocabulary for expressing assertions that could be compared to documents through an XSLT processor.

Schematron enables developers to create rules. The rules contain an *assertion*, which is an XPath expression, and a *report*, which provides information to humans if the assertion is true, as well as a *context*, which enables developers to specify where in a document these rules apply. Rules can be grouped into *patterns*, which are themselves grouped into *schemas*. A schema provides a set of assertions that can be tested against a document, providing human readers with a report on document contents as detailed (or not) as the schema developer would like.

Unlike other forms of schema validation, which are largely intended to return true/false results to programs before they continue processing, Schematron schemas are intended for human usage. This makes it much easier for developers to create various levels of warnings, or provide clearer information about how to fix a particular problem and what its causes might be. Schematron's XSLT foundation also makes it much easier than other forms of schema validation to implement in a wide variety of environments, since it requires only an XSLT processor, not a specialized schema processor.

Tip

For more information on Schematron, see `http://www.ascc.net/xml/resource/schematron/schematron.htm1`. An interview about Schematron with Rick Jelliffe, its creator and maintainer, is available from `http://xmlhack.com/read.php?item=121`. A tutorial is available at `http://zvon.vscht.cz/HTMLonly/SchematronTutorial/General/contents.html`.

Chapter 15

Identifying Document Fragments with XPointer

Because XML document structures are so neatly organized, developers can use them to reference portions of a document without having to add labels inside the document. Unlike linking into HTML documents, which requires the document author to add anchoring names inside the document, anyone can link to any portion of an XML document without having to modify the document at all. If the document has internal labels — typically attributes of type ID — that's an added convenience, but it isn't necessary. Although the approach isn't perfect, because document structures can change independently of the XPointers that pointed to them, it offers an enormous new level of flexibility, and integrates tightly with the URIs at the foundation of Web-document identification.

URLs and URIs

Uniform Resource Locators, or URLs, along with HTML and HTTP, were among the key parts of the early Web that made the Web browser such a tremendous success. Users can type in these odd strings and retrieve all kinds of information — resources — without needing to know anything about the underlying protocol handling the transaction. Developers could use URLs inside documents to point to other resources, making URLs the foundation of Web site construction.

Over time, URLs have grown beyond their original world of retrievable resources to a larger set of possibilities. Resources now include documents, but they also include graphics, other types of files, and much more abstract concepts as well. URLs have been subsumed into Uniform Resource Identifiers (URIs), and now have the much weightier task of identifying information (think namespaces) rather than merely locating them.

Absolute URIs begin with a scheme, which describes the protocol used to interpret the URI. Commonly used schemes include `http:`, `ftp:`, `gopher:`, `mailto:`, `nntp:`, `file:`, and `urn:`. The information applicable to the scheme follows the scheme. In many cases (where something is expected to be retrievable), this information will appear as a reference to a server or a file on a server, prefixed by two slashes. For example, an absolute URL using the HTTP protocol implements the following syntax:

`http://hostcomputer:port/path?query#fragmentidentifier`

`port`, `path`, and `query` are optional. The host computer must contain a valid DNS name or IP address, and `port` optionally specifies a port on the host computer (80 is the default for http). `path` specifies a path to a particular file on the host computer: Only numbers, letters, and the characters $, -, _, +, !, *, ', (,), and the period and comma can appear in the path. Any other character may be escaped by the % sign followed by its hexadecimal value. The optional `query` provides additional information to the server, enabling it to respond appropriately to form or other information. The content of `query` is limited to the same characters as `path`.

Relative URI references use the URI of the current page (or the value set by `xml:base`, which I describe in the next chapter) as a prefix, and URI-aware processors should treat relative URIs as their absolute URI equivalents. Relative URIs do not include schemes.

Tip

For more information on URI syntax, see the complete official syntax for URIs defined in RFC 2396 (`http://www.ietf.org/rfc/rfc2396.txt`).

An absolute or relative URIs may include a fragment identifier at the end in place of the query. Fragment identifiers in HTML include a pound sign (#) and a value that should connect to the NAME attribute of an A element in the target document. For example, in

```
<A HREF="#laterlink">Skipping around is fun!</A>
...

...
<A NAME="laterlink">Aren't you glad you skipped ahead?
```

you could click on "Skipping around is fun!" to scroll the document to the location of the A element with the NAME attribute laterlink. Of course, you can also use fragment identifiers in combination with URIs.

```
<A HREF="zip.html#nothingness">
```

would take a user who clicked it to the line in the zip.html file that contained

```
<A NAME="nothingness">
```

Even though XPointer supports a notation similar to this HTML approach, it implements a much more powerful fragment identifier syntax capable of far more interesting things. XPointer enables authors and developers to treat elements, rather than documents, as the primary unit involved in linking. XPointers make it possible for XLink to be considerably more robust than that of HTML, providing a number of tools that can address parts of documents by structure, ID, HTML anchor, or even text content. Thanks to these features, XLinks can specify links from outside the structure or even outside the document it is linking from.

XPath Extensions

XPointers originally used a syntax of their own, derived from the Text Encoding Initiative. As XSLT emerged, XPath started to seem like a more appropriate base, so the entire syntax shifted between working drafts. The basic approach is similar, as are the capabilities and the integration with XLink. XPointer defines itself as a set of extensions to XPath, with a set of rules for escaping characters used by XPath into the forms permitted by the rules for URI syntax.

Note

The Text Encoding Initiative (TEI) is an academic project building tools for marking up literary and historical documents. For more information on TEI, visit their Web site at `http://www-tei.uic.edu/orgs/tei/`.

Escaping characters

Because URIs and XML are both particular about the characters that can appear in their domains, and because XPointers themselves rely on parentheses, developers may be forced to modify the contents of their XPointers to preserve their meaning. The set of rules presented at `http://www.w3.org/TR/xptr#escaping` describes how to handle non-ASCII characters in URIs using % escaping and also how to use built-in XML entities to handle the <, >, ', ", and & characters.

URI encoding uses a percent sign and a Unicode hexadecimal reference to escape characters that are outside the ASCII (0-127) range. Spaces, for example, are encoded as %20, whereas an opening square bracket ([) is encoded as %5B. These rules are changing to some extent as the IETF and other organizations open up the URI space to more internationalized possibilities, but will likely remain in effect for some time to come.

Two non-XPath approaches

The simplest forms of XPointer fragment identifiers don't actually use XPath at all. The first, bare names, looks much like HTML fragment identifiers and uses ID attributes as stable hooks into documents; the second, child sequences, uses a very simple numeric notation to let developers move down a document tree. I apply these two approaches to a modified version of an example from Chapter 2:

```
<!DOCTYPE product_list SYSTEM "productlist.dtd">
<product_list>
  <product id="S127.29">
    <product_number>S127.29</product_number>
    <description>Maple - 1"x1"x2'</description>
    <price>$4.25</price>
  </product>
  <product id="S128.29">
    <product_number>S128.29</product_number>
    <description>Oak - 1"x1"x2'</description>
    <price>$5.75</price>
  </product>
  <product id="S130.29">
    <product_number>S130.29</product_number>
    <description>Pine - 1"x1"x2'</description>
    <price>$2.00</price>
  </product>
</product_list>
```

XPointer enables you to point directly to any of the elements with an attribute of type ID using a notation called bare names. To refer to the first product, you can use a fragment identifier such as:

```
#S127.29
```

To refer to the last product, you can use the fragment identifier:

```
#S130.29
```

Both of these reference the id attribute of the product element. There's one hitch: that attribute must be declared to be of type ID in a DTD or XML Schema. For example, you hope that the productlist.dtd has a declaration like:

```
<!ATTLIST product
    id    ID    #IMPLIED>
```

If there's no DTD (or if a nonvalidating parser doesn't read the external DTD), the reference to id won't work.

If you don't want to use ID values but don't want to have to use XPath either, you can use the child sequence notation. Child sequences always start with a slash and a number 1, and use decimal numbers separated by slashes to move through the tree structure of a document. The first slash represents the root element of a document, and the numbers represent child elements. Slashes separate numbers indicating children of children to whatever depth in the document you require. For example, you can link to the root element, product_list, with the following fragment identifier:

```
#/1
```

To link to the first child of the root element, product, you can use this fragment identifier:

```
#/1/1
```

This identifier will point to the first product element, which is the same thing that will happen if you use the following code:

```
#S127.29
```

To point to the last (third) child of the root element, the last product element, you can use the following fragment identifier:

```
#/1/3
```

which will, again, point to the same place that the following code will point to.

```
#S130.29
```

You can reach any element in a document with this approach, because there is no limit on depth except the limit built into a document. If you want to reach the description element for the oak, you can use the following identifier:

```
#/1/2/2
```

Child sequences give developers an easy way to point into documents without having to use attributes defined as type ID. Although they aren't as resistant to changes in documents, they work well enough in a wide range of situations. You can also combine them with the bare-name approach. For example, to reach the `description` element for the pine, you could use the following code:

```
#S130.29/2
```

Bare names are actually the equivalent of an XPath-based `xpointer()` syntax:

```
#xpointer(id("S130.29"))
```

If you want to use `ID` values but are concerned about the presence (or lack thereof) of DTDs, the specification suggests a workaround that combines the `ID` and a similar XPath version:

```
#xpointer(id("S130.29"))xpointer(//*[@id="S130.29"])
```

If XPointer can't find anything that matches the first option, it will try the second XPath version. The second version just looks for an element whose `id` attribute has the value you're looking for, whether or not it's actually of type `ID`.

XPath-based XPointers

All other types of XPointers use XPath as a foundation, with extensions where needed to make XPointer a more capable tool for indicating the origins and targets of hypertext links. Creating an XPointer can be as simple as wrapping an XPath inside `xpointer()`:

```
#xpointer(/product_list/product)
```

Caution

Remember that you'll need to perform URI encoding on any special characters inside your XPointer, whether or not they were legal in XPath itself.

Although XPath is very good at tracking down small pieces of a document, there are a few tasks for which it isn't very well suited, but which are critical for making hypertext work well. XPointer must be able to point to ranges of information (such as strings) that may cross element boundaries but aren't well-formed XML themselves, must be able to establish connections relative to the origin of the link, and must be able to differentiate unique results from sets of results. Instead of just dealing with nodes, XPointer works with nodes, points, and ranges. A point indicates a position within a document, whereas a range is the area between two (or more) points.

Caution

Although XPath enables you to select empty location sets, and this is a good thing in an XSLT context, XPointer reports these sets as errors because it can't do anything with an empty set. However, because the XPointer specification itself claims that "the specification does not constrain how applications deal with these errors," there's no telling what will appear in a given environment – perhaps nothing, perhaps a message to the user.

If you need to identify a range of content between two nodes, you can use the `range-to` function, as shown in the following example:

```
#xpointer(id("S127.29")/range-to(id("S130.29")))
```

You can reverse the IDs and still describe the same range, since it has the same endpoints:

```
#xpointer(id("S130.29")/range-to(id("S127.29")))
```

You can also identify string ranges by specifying an XPath in which the string might appear, followed by the string:

```
string-range(//product,"S130.29")
```

Sometimes you need to limit the range to the first appearance of that string with a number. To catch only the first appearance, adding [1] will do the trick:

```
string-range(//product,"S130.29")[1]
```

XPointer also provides functions for converting XPath location sets and their contents into ranges. The `range()` function returns ranges representing all the content in the location set it receives as an argument, whereas the `range-inside()` function returns ranges describing the contents inside the location set — the text nodes, not the element structures. The `start-point()` and `end-point()` functions return the starting and ending points, respectively, of ranges in the location set.

Two of XPointer's extensions enable developers to establish relative pointers from links. The `here()` function returns the node containing the XPointer, which can be useful when you're working from a link inside a document that points to another location inside the document. The `origin()` function, designed to work with XLink, returns the node from which the link was activated and makes it possible to build systems that take users to locations relative to the link's location.

The Promise of XPointers

In many ways, XPointers make XLink's features, which I describe in the next chapter, feasible. By providing a consistent way to reference document structures without having to add explicit labels, XPointers make it possible to create structures that define connections between those structures. Rather than use an approach that requires that links be embedded in documents (such as HTML), you can consider an approach that enables you to store links in separate documents, in much the same way that you can store scripts and style sheets.

XPointers may also lead the way to other approaches for presenting and processing XML. Because XPointers make it possible to reference fragments inside XML documents, they may lead to other kinds of processing that work with those fragments, not just with entire documents. Authors can subdivide a document into more manageable chunks with well-structured elements. You can display a long file in many smaller chunks rather than as an enormous file. This makes it easy to excerpt other documents using links — a feature known in other systems, notably Ted Nelson's Xanadu, as *transclusion*.

Cross-Reference

For more on transclusion and Xanadu, see Theodor Holm Nelson's article entitled "Embedded Markup Considered Harmful," in the Winter 1997 issue of *World Wide Web Journal*, available from O'Reilly and Associates.

For this to work efficiently, file structures will need to change so that the processing application loads the desired chunk rather than the entire document. The file system itself would have to be an XML processor (perhaps even an object database), storing XML documents as elements rather than as single files that must parse sequentially. I discuss these possibilities in greater detail in Chapter 23.

Note

XPointer makes it easy to identify document fragments of all kinds, but processing them is more difficult. The XML working group was addressing this issue, attempting to figure out exactly how to present and process document fragments of many different (and not necessarily well-formed) kinds. Although work seemed to have stopped for a while, XML Fragment Interchange just reappeared (without modification) as a W3C Candidate Recommendation: http://www.w3. org/TR/xml-fragment.

Chapter 16

Hypertext XML: XLink and XML Base

HTML's explosive growth probably had more to do with its capacity for linking than with any other single factor. Hundreds of people and organizations worked simultaneously on hypertext systems, some even using SGML, but no system had the simplicity of HTML's convenient linking system. <A HREF="*targetURL*"> has strung millions of pages together and built the World Wide Web. Still, there's definitely room for improvement. Hypertext specialists and other developers complained loudly about the limited abilities of these basic links, and at least some HTML developers looked at SGML's more complete (indeed, just about all-inclusive) HyTime specification and wished for some of its power, though not its complexity. XML presents a chance to strike a balance between HTML's simplicity and other hypertext systems' relative power, and the XML working group has focused on linking since early in the XML development process. XML linking builds on HTML's success and provides more powerful — yet more complex — tools.

Note

The discussion in this chapter is based on the 20 December 2000 Proposed Recommendation of the XLink specification, available at `http://www.w3.org/TR/2000/PR-xlink-20001220/`. The latest version of XLink is available from `http://www.w3.org/TR/xlink/`.

The XLink Namespace

XLink uses its own namespace to create an XML vocabulary for linking that you can use in concert with other XML vocabularies. Everything in XLink is done with attributes, so adding XLink to other XML-based specifications shouldn't require major redefinition of document structures. The XLink namespace, as of the 20 December 2000 Candidate Recommendation, is represented by the following URI:

```
http://www.w3.org/1999/xlink
```

Typically this URI is mapped to the xlink prefix, though that is not required:

```
<myDocument xmlns:xlink="http://www.w3.org/1999/xlink">
...
</myDocument>
```

Wherever the xlink prefix appears in this chapter, you can assume that it has been assigned to that namespace URI.

Simple Links

After six years of extensive use, HTML's linking systems are receiving mounting criticism for providing only the simplest of links. Conversely, many developers seem perfectly content with the current linking syntax, and a small army of development tools and Web-mapping tools have grown up around this key standard. HTML's HREF attribute has done well enough for most developers. Why change it? XLink doesn't require that developers unlearn the previous standard approach, rather it adds to that approach. It adds a lot, in fact, but the basic HTML link structure is still available in the XLink standard to make it easier for developers who only need that functionality. I start by examining the kinds of links available in HTML documents; then I look at how you can implement them in XML.

Links in HTML

The A element is the key to nearly all HTML linking, although the LINK element plays a limited role. Figure 16-1 displays a simple HTML link created with an A element.

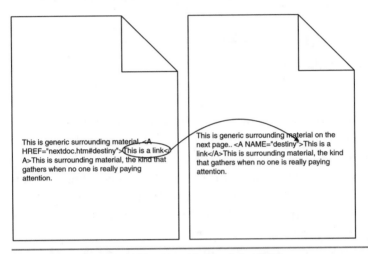

Figure 16-1 *Simple unidirectional in-line link, HTML*

The A element has several attributes, only one of which gets constant use from HTML developers: the all-powerful HREF (or href, in XHTML). HREF usually takes a URL (Uniform Resource Locator) for its value, which represents the target of the link. URLs may be absolute or relative.

The A element also allows for REV and REL attributes, whose purpose is to show the relationship between the anchor and the target URL. REL indicates the relationship of the URL to the anchor (moving forward along the link), whereas REV indicates the relationship of the anchor to the URL (moving backward along the link). Neither of these attributes is widely used in anchor tags.

HTML uses hypertext linking beyond the familiar A element as well. The LINK element, which appears in the HEAD element of HTML documents, also supports the HREF, REL, and REV attributes. In the case of LINK , REL indicates that the target URL represents a style sheet. LINK also provides a TYPE attribute to indicate the MIME type of the target URL. Unlike an A element, a LINK element doesn't take the user anywhere — it just connects outside resources to the document, in much the same way that the IMG, APPLET, SCRIPT, or OBJECT elements can with their SRC attributes.

Simple links in XML

In XLink, links like those used in HTML are called *simple links*. Simple links point from the linking element to a target resource, identified by the xlink:href attribute. Like the classic HTML href link, this link is unidirectional because it points only from the element that provides the link to the target location and is called an in-line link because the A element is involved as a resource. (The Back button doesn't count, in this example, as providing two-way linking.) *Traversing* describes the action that takes place when a link is actuated, even if the link doesn't "take" the actuator (which may be a user or a program) to a new document.

In XLink, you can define a simple link using any element whose xlink:type attribute is set to simple. In this example, for convenience, I define an element called simpleLink that represents a simple link and includes the basic attributes for a simple link, but you don't have to call simple link elements simpleLink — any element can be a link element.

```
<!ELEMENT simpleLink (#PCDATA)>
<!ATTLIST simple
    xlink:type      #FIXED 'simple'
    xlink:href      #IMPLIED
    xlink:title     #IMPLIED
    xlink:role      #IMPLIED
    xlink:show      (new | replace | embed |
                    other | none)      #IMPLIED
    xlink:actuate   (onLoad |onRequest |
                    other |none)       #IMPLIED
>
```

I use the `simpleLink` element declaration here only for illustration. In fact, any element can be a link—you do not need to create separate elements such as the HTML `A` that exist solely to implement simple links. You can use this element to create links easily, though:

```
<simpleLink xlink:type='simple'
xlink:href="http://www.example.com" xlink:title="link to
a non-existent example site" xlink:show="replace"
xlink:actuate="onRequest">Example.com</simpleLink>

<simpleLink xlink:type='simple'
xlink:href="http://www.example.com/icon.png"
xlink:title="Icon for Example.com" xlink:show="embed"
xlink:actuate="onLoad" />
```

In the first case you've created a user-activated link like the one shown in Figure 16-2.

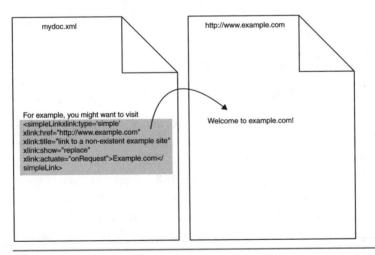

Figure 16-2 *A simple XLink*

This kind of link waits for the user to activate it (because `xlink:actuate` is set to `onRequest`), and takes the user to a new page (because `xlink:show` is set to `replace`) in the same window. A human-readable `xlink:title` describes the target of the link, and the URL for the link target is provided in the `xlink:href` attribute.

The second `simpleLink` behaves very differently — more like the HTML `IMG` element than like the HTML `A` element. Because `xlink:show` is set to `embed`, the content of the resource (an image) identified by `xlink:href` will be embedded at the `simpleLink` element's location when the link is activated — `onLoad`, according to the `xlink:actuate` attribute. You can mix and match these values as appropriate to create the kinds of behavior you need.

Caution

Most browsers don't yet support XLink. Mozilla and Netscape 6 will support simple XLinks where `xlink:actuate` is set to `onRequest` and `xlink:show` is set to `replace`, but nothing else. Microsoft Internet Explorer 5.x doesn't recognize XLink at all. Using Opera with XLink requires using a CSS workaround; for more information, go to `http://www.xml.com/pub/a/2000/04/19/opera/index.html`.

Conflicts between XHTML and XLink

Simple links can handle the tasks expected of documents by Web developers, but there are some substantial issues separating the HTML (and now XHTML) syntax from XLink, and some things that HTML does easily in attributes and XLink can't do without the more complex multi-element extended link structure. Most complaints fall into two categories: XLink's insistence on its own namespace, and its support for only a single URI in its simple link structure.

XLink's use of its own namespace for its attributes — called a *global attributes strategy* — works very well when developers need to integrate XLink with their own vocabularies and no prior linking mechanism exists. Developers can pull XLink "off the shelf" and apply it in XLink-aware applications immediately. On the other hand, developers who are already using vocabularies with their own link vocabularies specified in their own namespaces face a change. The href attribute of the a element in this bit of XHTML:

```
<html xmlns="http://www.w3.org/1999/xhtml">... <a
href="nextfile.htm">next</a>... </html>
```

is not the href attribute of the a element in this bit:

```
<html xmlns="http://www.w3.org/1999/xhtml">... <a
xlink:href="nextfile.htm" xlink:type="simple"
xmlns:xlink="http://www.w3.org/1999/xlink">next</a>...
</html>
```

This shift may force changes in future generations of XHTML and other XML vocabularies that had their own simple linking equivalents.

The other complication lies in HTML constructions such as the following:

```
<img src="http://www.example.com/icon.png" alt="icon"
longdesc="http://www.example.com/icon_explanation.html"
/>
```

Several elements in HTML contain multiple linking-related URI-containing attributes. Simple XLinks can't support this at all — extended XLinks are the answer to the problem, but using them requires adding new child elements to the previously EMPTY img element.

The W3C's XLink Working Group has proposed a Note, *XLink Markup Name Control* (http://www.w3.org/TR/xlink-naming/), which proposes a solution to some of these problems, relying on W3C XML Schemas to resolve these issues. It isn't yet clear whether that approach will be used in future versions of XHTML and other W3C-sponsored XML vocabularies.

More Complex Links

Extended links give the world of linking entirely new geometries, making possible new architectures and new interfaces. Even though the "I am here — click to go there" model provided by the HTML A element has done an excellent job of getting the Web started, it's time to move on to "I am one part of a set — treat me as such and explore." Extended links, multidirectional links, and links stored in separate documents will enable developers to build more intricate structures that make managing links easier in the long run.

Extended links enable developers to create groups of links, effectively providing the user (or a processing application) with a set of choices from a link, rather than a single target. Even though the requirements for how an extended link must be treated by a processing application remain somewhat vague in the specification, you can easily picture an extended link as a set of choices that will appear on a pop-up menu (or other interface) to enable the user to select a direction. One example of this is a thesaurus that provides a pop-up menu of synonyms when the user clicks a word. The user chooses from among them and can view more information about the selected synonym.

Implementing these links is somewhat complex. As I did with simple links, I start by examining some sample declarations, in this case for an element that can represent an extended link. Extended links involve multiple elements, and the outermost element serves as both a container of the other components and a carrier of information about the link as a whole:

```
<!ELEMENT extendedLink ANY>
<!ATTLIST extendedLink
    xlink:type     #FIXED 'extended'
    xlink:title    #IMPLIED
    xlink:role     #IMPLIED
>
```

As for the previous simple example, elements implementing extended links do not need to be named extendedLink. The container can't carry much information, however — just a type, a title, and a role (which I discuss in the roles and arcroles section later in the chapter.) Inside this container you can hold four kinds of XLink information: locators, resources, arcs, and titles.

Locators and resources are similar, but an xlink:locator element may have an xlink:href attribute, whereas an xlink:resource element describes the originating resource — the point where the link appears — rather than any external content. Apart from that critical difference, the two types behave very similarly. For this example, I declare elements named locator and resource:

```
<!ELEMENT locator EMPTY>
<!ATTLIST locator
    xlink:type      #FIXED 'locator'
    xlink:href      #IMPLIED
    xlink:title     #IMPLIED
    xlink:label     #IMPLIED
    xlink:role      #IMPLIED
>


<!ELEMENT resource EMPTY>
<!ATTLIST resource
    xlink:type      #FIXED 'resource'
    xlink:title     #IMPLIED
    xlink:label     #IMPLIED
    xlink:role      #IMPLIED
>
```

The xlink:title attribute provides a human-readable description of the target of the element, whereas the xlink:label provides a short label that arcs can use to describe possible paths between the locators and resource contained by an extended link. To build links that point from and to various portions of documents, you will probably use XPointer fragment identifiers, which I describe in the previous chapter, inside the `xlink:href` attribute values.

An extended link built using the DTD fragments presented so far might look something like this:

```
<extendedLink>History Texts
<resource xlink:title="here" xlink:label="index" />
<locator xlink:title="African" xlink:href="african.xml"
xlink:label="african" />
<locator xlink:title="Asian" xlink:href="asian.xml"
xlink:label="asian" />
<locator xlink:title="European" xlink:href="european.xml"
xlink:label="european" />
<locator xlink:title="North American"
href="namerican.xml" xlink:label="northamerican" />
<locator xlink:title="Pacific" href="pacific.xml"
xlink:label="pacific" />
<locator xlink:title="South American"
href="samerican.xml" xlink:label="southamerican" />
</extended>
```

This extended link describes a set of documents that are part of the link, but hasn't yet specified how those documents are related. Is this link supposed to point outward from a single "History Texts" bit of text in an XML document? Or are all these documents related to each other somehow? Arcs provide a means for developers to tell applications not only what resources are members of a set, but what the connections between those resources are and how the connections should be presented to users. You can start by defining an arc element, which has some familiar components:

```
<!ELEMENT arc EMPTY>
<!ATTLIST arc
    xlink:type      #FIXED 'arc'
    xlink:title     #IMPLIED
```

```
xlink:from       #IMPLIED
xlink:to         #IMPLIED
xlink:arcrole       #IMPLIED
xlink:show       (new | replace | embed |
                 other | none)      #IMPLIED
xlink:actuate    (onLoad |onRequest |
                 other |none)       #IMPLIED
>
```

Like everything in the XLink world, arcs have human-readable title content. They have the same xlink:show and xlink:actuate attributes as simple links, offering a brief description of behavior. Instead of identifying resources, however, the arc uses its xlink:from and xlink:to attributes to describe the relationships between the locators and resources defined elsewhere in the link. The contents of the xlink:from and xlink:to attributes, if they appear, must correspond to xlink:label attribute values from locator and resource elements. If they don't appear, their values are understood to mean "everything." For example, to establish an outbound link in the History Texts example above, you need only to add this arc element:

```
<arc xlink:from="index"/>
```

Since the xlink:to element is missing, XLink processors would understand that the arc pointed from the resource labeled index to all the rest of the contents of the link. To make the arcs point in reverse, you can write the following:

```
<arc xlink:to="index"/>
```

Then all the other documents will be treated as pointing to the index, not the other way around. To make everything point to everything, you can write this:

```
<arc />
```

To make the index point to the African texts, and only the African texts, you can write this:

```
<arc xlink:from="index" xlink:to="african"/>
```

The title element exists solely to permit more complex title information than a single attribute can support. Arcs, locators, and extended links may use title child elements rather than title attributes in cases where multiple titles are needed or where the title itself contains subelements. Declaring a title element is pretty simple:

```
<!ELEMENT title ANY>
<!ATTLIST title
    xlink:type    #FIXED 'title'
>
```

The content model may be ANY, or it may be anything you find appropriate in your document structures.

Tip

If you're using hypertext to describe sets of documents, rather than just establishing connections between documents, you may want to explore Topic Maps. Topic Maps provide a set of tools for describing relations between topics and resources, at a higher-level perspective than with XLink. More information on Topic Maps is available at http://www.topicmaps.org.

Roles and Arcroles

Although the basic explanation of extended links I provide in the previous section is enough to get you started with XLinks, the XLink working group has added roles and arcroles to the model to give applications a hook for additional behavior beyond simple link processing. Like namespace declarations, these attributes take URI values that are used as identifiers for particular kinds of behavior —

to narrow down the kinds of handling a link might receive, or to identify special types of links or arcs. Again like namespaces, no rules are provided regarding the meaning of those URI values, leaving developers to create and process roles and arcroles according to their own rules.

The `xlink:role` attribute may appear on extended, simple, locator, and resource-type elements, whereas `xlink:arcrole` may appear on simple and arc-type elements. The `xlink:role` attribute identifies a role for the link as a whole; `xlink:arcrole` identifies a role for a particular traversal path.

Only one URI role is defined in the XLink spec: an `xlink:arcrole` of `http://www.w3.org/1999/xlink/properties/linkbase` whose purpose is to identify XLink linkbases.

Linkbases

As exciting as these new tools seem, they may make it even more difficult to manage links. An XML document cannot always "know" of other documents with which it shares links, especially if those links are stored in content owned by other people. Managing the mazes of links created by the ability to include more than one location in a link presents a logistical challenge that may call for centralization of linking information. XLink offers the prospect of *linkbases* to address this need, enabling developers to include pointers to collections of links rather than including all the links in documents along the way. The initial advantage of linkbases is that they make it easy for a processing application to obtain reasonably complete information about the documents to which an initial document is linked, instead of "discovering" links only when a user opens the new documents. You can arrange sets of documents in groups, making discovering related links easy.

Referencing linkbases just requires including an extended link pointing from a document to a linkbase, with the arcrole set appropriately.

```
<extendedLink>
  <locator xlink:label="thisdoc" xlink:href="thisdoc.xml"
    />
  <locator xlink:label="linkbase"
    xlink:href="linkbase.xml"
    />
  <arc xlink:from="thisdoc" xlink:to="linkbase"
    actuate="onLoad"
    xlink:arcrole=
    "http://www.w3.org/1999/xlink/properties/linkbase"
    />
</extendedLink>
```

When an application encounters a linkbase, it loads the referenced document and retains all the linking information in that document for application to the resource identified by the xlink:from
attribute. The application shouldn't do anything else with the information, such as present it to the user on load.

The implications of this approach are profound. Extended link
groups make it possible to centralize link information, replacing a
maze of links (shown in Figure 16-3) with a centralized hub-and-
spoke system (shown in Figure 16-4) that enables developers to
examine and manage links without having to read endless documents. It also reduces bandwidth overhead, enabling developers to
require an XML document to download only one extra document
(or perhaps a few) in order to create a complete list of links.

Extended link groups by themselves also make it possible to add
links from other documents to your own documents efficiently. As
long as the other document recognizes your document (that is, your
document referenced from a document element or connected
through a number of links no greater than the steps attribute
allows), links from your document to the target document will be
recognized by the target document and may appear as outgoing

links. Even if the target document does not recognize your document, links from your document may still be "remembered" by the processing application when traversed, enabling documents to reference each other easily. If the processing application remembers the links from document to document, the target document will become linked to your document, although only within the context of the processing application. This makes annotating documents much simpler than it has been in the past.

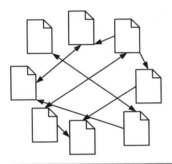

Figure 16-3 *Old-style linking, connecting a set of documents through decentralized links*

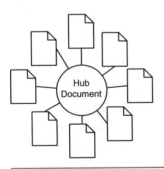

Figure 16-4 *Centralized linking, providing a hub for easy management of links*

From Specification to Practice

It may seem as though the XLink spec brings incredible power to the Web, but it still has a long way to go — and it's hardly clear that the Web represents the target application for those designing the XLink specification. Several communities have overlapped in the creation of XLink, all demanding different things and each with a different set of rules and preferences. Many people involved in the process like to cite "established practice" and "years of hypertext experience," but much of that collective experience conflicts at best, confuses at worst, and yet leaves an enormous number of possibilities open.

A number of key issues remain unresolved in XLink, many of them deliberately. The issue of "remembering" links across multiple documents is somewhat hazy, explained in detail in the linkbase sections but not at length elsewhere. Creating multidirectional links and specifying links from documents other than the ones being linked is going to demand a good deal of applications, and it isn't entirely clear how they should manage the information describing the links.

The relationship of style sheets to links isn't especially clear either. Both CSS and XSL formatting objects include tools for formatting the origins of links, but a method for specifying more complex behavior, perhaps by means of pop-up menus for links pointing to multiple target resources, isn't mentioned anywhere in those specifications. To complicate matters further, the relationship of links identified by XPointers and XSLT transformations of the original documents isn't clear. Effectively, transformation results don't have URIs, though those results might be derived from a document pointed into by an XPointer. If that content is moved, repeated, or deleted, it may not be clear how to present the document.

The last issue built into the specification, roles and arcroles, is probably the least of XLink's worries, but the continuing reverberations from the use of URIs as identifiers in namespaces suggests that using URIs for behavior identifiers is somewhat risky. Although it does an excellent job of letting applications do their own thing, it also makes it trickier to define a "conformant" set of behaviors that work across multiple applications. XLink's vocabulary isn't especially tightly fixed, and it's not entirely clear how this feature will interact with other kinds of XML processing.

Finally, it's worth remembering that XLinks don't have to be used with humans and browsers in mind. Many developers who see links as sets treat them as amorphous sets without traversal paths because traversal isn't important to their applications. You may find link sets extremely useful for many modeling applications that have nothing to do with Web browsers, describing resources and their behavior in a variety of different contexts. Specifying traversal behavior — in fields where traversal may not exist — can prove a distraction at best and a hindrance at worst to these developers, though it may be useful for certain kinds of modeling.

Tip

Have a question about the XLink spec? Want to make a contribution? The comments list for the XLink specification has become something of a discussion area for XLink issues. You'll find the archives at `http://lists.w3.org/Archives/Public/www-xml-linking-comments/` and sub-scription information at `http://www.w3.org/Mail/Request`.

XML linking may seem complicated, but further development of the specification and use will make them friendlier. As XML moves out into the world, the implications of these linking schemes may prove as dramatic as the implications of XML itself.

XInclude: Adding Content, Not Just Embedding

The availability of the embed value for the xlink:show attribute led to some early controversies over how that "embedded" content should be handled. Would it be part of the document? Ought it to be handled by the document's style sheet? Would it affect validation? Partly to keep these issues out of XLink and partly because XML Schemas doesn't provide a mechanism for defining external entities, the W3C began work on a project that includes XML content using URI references directly inside the content of a document. XML Inclusions (XInclude) has its own set of controversies, but the provision of an alternative mechanism for inclusion has simplified XLink work considerably.

Note

This discussion of XInclude is based on the 26 October 2000 Working Draft (`http://www.w3.org/TR/2000/WD-xinclude-20001026`). The basic concepts underlying XInclude haven't changed very much, but its syntax has changed repeatedly, and 21 "open issues" are listed in the draft. For the latest version of XInclude, see `http://www.w3.org/TR/xinclude`.

At its simplest, XInclude is a single element type with its own namespace and an `href` attribute that points to a URI containing content that is to replace that element.

```
<xinclude:include
xmlns:xinclude="http://www.w3.org/1999/XML/xinclude"
      href="source.xml">
```

When this element is encountered in an XML document, the parser should load the resource identified by the `href` attribute and replace the `xinclude:include` element with its contents. An optional `parse` attribute may take values of `xml` or `text`, identifying whether the content referenced by the `href` attribute should be parsed as XML and its structure then merged with the structure of the containing document, or simply loaded as text and added as a text node. Inclusions may use XPointers in their URIs when including XML-based content.

XML Inclusions are processed after validation against a DTD, and the relationships with XML Schemas are undefined. Whereas XML Inclusion is a relatively simple concept when used in uncomplicated situations, it's not entirely clear how it will mesh with XPointers and XLinks working on documents that use XInclude.

XML Base: Working with Relative URIs

XML Base gives XLink projects control over their base URI that's similar to the control HTML projects have had over their base URIs — a little more, in fact. XML Base enables XML document creators to define the base URI that will be added to relative URIs at any point in an XML document. By default, the base URI for the contents of an XML document is the URI that was used to access that document. If that behavior isn't appropriate — perhaps because a document has multiple access points, because it's in a temporary location, or simply because the document author doesn't feel like typing full URIs — adding the xml:base attribute to a document can change the base URI within the scope of the element using it.

If the element hosting the xml:base attribute is the root element, it applies to the entire document unless overridden by a child element with its own xml:base attribute. If the xml:base attribute appears in any other element, it applies to the contents of that element, unless, once again, overridden by another xml:base attribute. xml:base scoping works exactly like that used for namespace declarations, xml:lang, and xml:space. There's one other trick to this processing: If an xml:base attribute value is itself a relative URI, it is combined with the current base URI to form a new base URI, as shown in this example:

```
<doc xml:base="http://www.example.com">
<extendedLink xml:base="/history/">History Texts
<resource xlink:title="here" xlink:label="index" />
```

```
<locator xlink:title="African" xlink:href="african.xml"
xlink:label="african" />
<locator xlink:title="Asian" xlink:href="asian.xml"
xlink:label="asian" />
<locator xlink:title="European" xlink:href="european.xml"
xlink:label="european" />
<locator xlink:title="North American"
href="namerican.xml" xlink:label="northamerican" />
<locator xlink:title="Pacific" href="pacific.xml"
xlink:label="pacific" />
<locator xlink:title="South American"
href="samerican.xml" xlink:label="southamerican" />
<arc xlink:from="index"/>
</extended>

<extendedLink
xml:base="http://www.example.com/language/">Language
Texts
<resource xlink:title="here" xlink:label="index" />
<locator xlink:title="African" xlink:href="african.xml"
xlink:label="african" />
<locator xlink:title="Asian" xlink:href="asian.xml"
xlink:label="asian" />
<locator xlink:title="European" xlink:href="european.xml"
xlink:label="european" />
<locator xlink:title="North American"
href="namerican.xml" xlink:label="northamerican" />
<locator xlink:title="Pacific" href="pacific.xml"
xlink:label="pacific" />
<locator xlink:title="South American"
href="samerican.xml" xlink:label="southamerican" />
<arc xlink:from="index"/>
</extended>
</doc>
```

The root element of this document declares the base URI for all of its contents to be `http://www.example.com`. The link for history texts provides an `xml:base` attribute value of `/history/`. That will be added to the base URI from the root element to form `http://www.example.com/history/` as the base URI for all the components of that link. The link for language texts uses a slightly different approach, providing the absolute URI `http://www.example.com/language/` instead of relying on combining an attribute value with the root element's base URI. That absolute URI will be the base for all links coming from its child elements.

XML Base is not yet widely implemented, but it may reach larger audiences as use of XLink spreads. This discussion is based on the 20 December 2000 Proposed Recommendation, which is still subject to change. For the latest on XML Base, see `http://www.w3.org/TR/xmlbase/`.

Caution

XML Base does not apply to namespace URIs.

Chapter 17

Querying XML

XML enables developers to store information in a labeled structured format, but using structures that are different from the relational database structures many organizations are used to working with. Although most developers recognize that there is a mismatch between the tools they use to work with relational databases (notably Structured Query Language, or SQL) and the structures of XML documents, they would also like to perform the same kind of work on XML structures that they perform on relational databases Such work may include asking questions across multiple documents, retrieving particular kinds of information, and manipulating that information into summaries and other compiled forms.

A demand for XML query mechanisms definitely exists, but progress in this field has been fairly slow and is still only getting started. The W3C held a meeting — QL '98, the Query Languages Workshop — in December 1998, but the XML Query Working Group formally got started only in early 2000. So far, it has managed to publish working drafts of XML Query Requirements (`http://www.w3.org/TR/xmlquery-req`), a data model (`http://www.w3.org/TR/query-datamodel/`), and a query algebra (`http://www.w3.org/TR/query-algebra/`), but all of these are still in formative stages and subject to major change. In this chapter I take a look at what might be coming in XML query, and how it might affect XML development in general.

Note

Information about QL '98, including 66 position papers from various different participants, are available online at http://www.w3.org/TandS/QL/QL98/. The spectrum of different (though often overlapping) requirements is enormous. A mailing list, www-ql@w3.org, also came out of that meeting, and its archives are publicly available at http://lists.w3.org/Archives/Public/www-ql.

Managing All Kinds of Data

XML promises to help developers manage the kinds of information that doesn't fit in table structures. Relational databases have been an incredible boon for organizations that need to create, store, analyze, and process information that has a very regular form. On the other hand, relational databases aren't designed to store documents efficiently. Web developers have used a variety of strategies for integrating relational databases with document structures, typically using templates, but many XML developers want to be able to manage documents with tools more like the ones they presently use for databases. At the same time, relational database users want to be able to process query results with XML's flexibility.

To meet all these needs, the XML community needs some means of describing its document content structures, and relational database vendors and users need some way of mapping their content to the document structures of XML. The first problem is technically difficult, whereas the second problem is largely a political problem involving too many different ways to represent information. Most of the focus so far is on making XML query language work for XML, because it isn't that difficult to use SQL and some form of record set formatting tools to at least get started with representing relational database structures as XML.

SQL was able to build on a very mathematical foundation built on table structures and descriptions of table structures, but XML has no such mathematical base. W3C XML Schemas, often described as a key component of XML query techniques, are built on an ad hoc set of requirements, not a clean mathematical framework. As a result, developers building tools on top of Schemas may encounter problems when modeling document structures algorithmically. Despite these issues, the W3C has moved ahead with a query algebra that formally describes structures and processes for finding information inside XML documents.

Note

If you have experience with database and query internals, you may want to explore the W3C's XML Query Algebra, at `http://www.w3.org/TR/query-algebra/`. You'll find it easier reading if you have a background in computer science and mathematics. If you don't, remember that the query language syntax itself should be simpler than the algebra, leaving the algorithms to the underlying implementation.

Reconciling the XML "way of syntax" with the relational "way of structure" is going to take some work. Relational databases and the tools for working with them are well established, well understood, and well appreciated. Developers who expect querying XML to be just like querying relational databases are likely to be disappointed, at least in the short term. On the other hand, developers who need to work with document structures are likely to find XML querying to be a substantial improvement over the capabilities they had before.

Note

Although a number of proposals for a "grand unification of query" have been put forth, XML Query doesn't seem likely to replace SQL any time soon, even on "XML-enabled" databases. SQL does an excellent job in its field, and XML Query will likely be treated as a supplement, something useful for tasks that SQL doesn't handle by design.

Paths, Pointers, and Querying

Some XML developers are perfectly content with XPath and XPointer as tools for retrieving information fragments from documents. Developers can combine them with a bit of extra processing logic using the DOM, XSLT, or other approaches to extract information from documents and present it in a final result form that meets their needs. Infrastructures for building such systems are readily available, and "home-grown" querying systems are in widespread use.

This approach has some substantial drawbacks, however—drawbacks similar to the ones that drove development communities to standardize the declarative SQL approach instead of the procedural approach used by many databases. Procedural code isn't very portable, especially when it may be dealing with local definitions of XML document sets and using features from a variety of tools that may not exist on other platforms. Procedural code can also be difficult to maintain, especially when ownership of the code is transferred from one person to another. Declarative queries often are easier to read and figure out than inputs and outputs.

Developers have been using a mixture of strategies, but companies that want to build larger-scale systems—and especially larger-scale interoperable systems—have been waiting for a more comprehensive solution. The solution needs to comprise something that enables them to move beyond simple one-document structural queries built for style-sheet creation and hypertext linking to an approach that enables them to connect disparate systems containing large numbers of documents.

The requirements established by the working group seem to address most of these issues. The new XML query language will have to work in environments dealing with the following:

- Human-readable documents
- Data-oriented documents

- Documents that mix human-readable and data-oriented content
- Administrative data (such as log files)
- Streams (feeds of multiple consecutive XML documents)
- DOM trees
- XML repositories and Web servers
- Catalog systems
- Multiple development languages and environments

That's already a fairly tall order, and it doesn't even suggest how the queries will have to operate. The current list of rules for the query language is quite substantial:

- It must have at least one human-readable/writable syntax expressed in XML
- It must be declarative, and cannot enforce a particular processing approach
- It must not be bound to a particular protocol
- It must report errors
- It must be updateable
- It must be defined for finite instances of the data model, and may also be defined for infinite instances

The requirements document details the features of XML processing that must be supported, including the core XML Infoset, datatypes, collections of documents, references inside and between XML documents, namespaces, and XML Schemas (though query processing must also be possible when there is no schema). The functionality that the Working Group proposes to build on these foundations is pretty ambitious:

- Data-type-aware operations
- Recognition of text and element boundaries
- Universal and existential quantifiers for collections

- Operations based on hierarchies and sequences
- Combinations of parts from single or multiple documents
- Summary information on sets of information
- Sorted query results
- Operation composition using result sets as operands
- Null values
- Preservation of hierarchy and sequence in results
- Transformation of XML structures
- Reference traversal
- Identity preservation
- Operations on literal data
- Operations on XML names (elements, attributes, processing instructions)
- Operations on schemas
- Room for developers to add extra functionality beyond the built-in set

It's a tall order, but the XML Query WG is marching forward.

Note

For the latest news from the XML Query Working group, visit their site at `http://www.w3.org/XML/Query`. They have a quick reference list of their specifications and information on query-related presentation and information.

Under Construction

The XML Query working group has divided its work into two pieces: a data model, which describes the underlying structure of the information as seen by XML Query, and an algebra, which defines the semantics that will underlie the eventual query language. The algebra is not itself the query language — rather, it provides a formal description of the operations that users of the query language will be able to perform. The algebra isn't tightly bound to XML, but it should be reasonably familiar to developers who have worked with relational algebras (not just relational queries).

While this process moves forward, a number of interim solutions are available that you may find worth exploring. Vendors of XML repositories and relational databases extending themselves into XML have had to develop tools to perform similar work to that which will be done by XML Query. These solutions may meet your needs if your projects operate across a limited number of environments, and some of these solutions will probably be supported after XML Query has been completed.

Looking Forward: Quilt

One query language in particular that might be worth exploring as a precursor to XML Query is Quilt — among other things, it's being created by members of the XML Query Working Group, though that doesn't mean the rest of the group will accept it. Quilt has received a fairly warm welcome at XML conferences, though it should probably be considered a work in progress. You may find that Quilt is the easiest query language to implement today, however, and unusual for being vendor-independent.

Tip

Quilt's creators have been showing Quilt at various conferences and writing papers that describe Quilt in some substantial depth. Much more information on Quilt, including presentations, papers, and implementations, is available from `http://www.almaden.ibm.com/cs/people/chamberlin/quilt.html`.

Quilt is "an XML query language for heterogeneous data sources." Translated, that means that Quilt uses XML syntax to describe queries that may be applied to a variety of different kinds of information, which may be stored in a variety of different kinds of repositories. XML documents might be stored in file systems, hierarchical document repositories, or object stores, whereas tabular information might be stored in relational databases. Quilt uses other query languages as foundations, assembling these parts into a whole sheet much as a patchwork quilt combines different kinds of fabrics into a single pattern.

Quilt's heritage is extremely diverse. On the XML side, XPath and XQL (`http://www.w3.org/TandS/QL/QL98/pp/xql.html`) provide tools for working with the hierarchical element structures of XML documents. XML-QL, a proposed query language from AT&T Labs (`http://www.research.att. com/~mff/ files/ final.html`) that was focused on XML for business communications, provides a structure for binding variables to result structures. SQL itself contributes a grammatical structure composed of clauses for structuring results, and OQL (object query language) provides a functional framework. In combination with pieces from other sources, these parts give Quilt a rich heritage.

Quilt processors accept XML documents containing Quilt queries and return XML documents (or fragments or sets of documents) containing the results of those queries. There isn't any concept of a record set, for instance, as something separate from an XML document. Quilt talks about "forests of nodes," building on the metaphor of XML documents as tree structures, so applications using Quilt will have to be prepared to accept responses that include more than one top-level node, much as applications using XPath have to be prepared to accept node sets rather than single nodes.

Quilt queries can include a number of components. Path expressions, based on XPath, let developers specify locations in documents based on the document's node structure and content. Element constructors let developers wrap results in elements created as part of the query. FOR-LET-WHERE-RETURN (FLWR, pronounced "flower") expressions work much like their SQL equivalents. Mathematical operators and the SQL operators (UNION, INTERSECT, EXCEPT) are also available, as are conditional expressions and a small set of functions from XPath and SQL.

Quilt's patchwork nature hasn't interfered with implementations, though some developers have implemented subsets. Quilt's being composed of disparate parts makes that much easier, a fairly sharp contrast to the difficulty of subsetting monolithic specs like XML Schemas. Although Quilt lacks a solid mathematical foundation, its style of ad hoc reuse of existing technologies makes it immediately useful and relatively easy to implement quickly.

Note

As this book goes to press, Quilt looks likely to be the foundation for XQuery, the W3C's query language. The first draft of XQuery shares authors and even some text with the Quilt drafts. For the latest on XQuery, see `http://www.w3.org/TR/xquery`.

Part IV

Building Your Own Markup

Chapter 18

Plan in the Present, Save in the Future

Now that you've seen what XML looks like and the enormous power it gives the designer, it's time to look at the implications of what I've covered so far. XML enables designers to create their own tags. Cascading Style Sheets (CSS) and Extensible Style Language (XSL) can combine very nicely with XML to enable you to define your own formatting for your XML vocabularies. You can do almost anything you want without having to pay attention to what someone you've never met said on a committee years ago in a distant land about your particular subject area. The grammar of XML is fixed, but the vocabulary is open. XML is an extremely powerful tool, capable of amazing things. Unfortunately, XML is something like a chainsaw — incredibly powerful, capable of getting the job done without too much effort, and remarkably dangerous. Chainsaws require regular maintenance and skilled users or they inflict tremendous damage. XML (probably) won't cause you bodily harm, but it can inflict damage as a result of poorly thought-out projects. Users who think they can just start it up and go to work without learning about it and how best to apply it are in for some dark days.

XML has the potential to become the worst disaster yet to hit the Web. Sites composed of poorly written XML may look okay on the surface (if the style sheets are any good), but they will rapidly deteriorate into maintenance nightmares that require small armies of developers who must sort out the incompatibilities between documents that claim to be similar but really aren't. Millions of people may choose to spend their time reinventing the wheel, wasting time that could have been spent coding productively. Companies may continue to waste millions of dollars converting information from one poorly thought-out system to another. HTML isn't always beautiful, but badly written XML can be much uglier.

XML is about much more than creating documents that look good on someone's screen. You can use it for data transfers of any kind, including data transfers embedded in what used to be treated as "ordinary" documents. Unfortunately, that means that many more people must be involved in the process. When the Web first began creeping into businesses, it usually started with whatever group or person handled computers and networking and migrated slowly toward marketing and design. Even though different divisions of a company might all contribute to a Web site, their content didn't all have to look identical, and data could arrive in different formats. Web applications so far have been mostly driven by relational databases, each of which has its own format and structures. XML promises to unify all these different pieces, making the transfer of information between divisions and departments much smoother and the transfer to the Web much easier. As these transfers increase, however, more coordination will be necessary.

Caution

If you just want to use XML to extend your existing Web development toolset and have no interest in coordinated document management, you will see how to do so as you read the rest of this book. The ability to create your own vocabularies is exciting, but it's only the beginning of what's possible. Additionally, you're setting yourself up for bigger problems in the long run if you've written and used your own DTD and schemas for documents and your company develops a new, incompatible set and requires that you use it. Fortunately, XML is relatively easy to process and transform, but it's probably wise to look around as you build your projects.

Making this process work requires cooperation from many parts of an organization or even an industry. SGML has been mired down in committees from its very beginning, and XML will probably inspire many committee meetings of its own. This organizational quagmire doesn't have to mean endless meetings and continual reorganization or perpetually slipping release dates for your new company Web site. XML can greatly enhance collaboration, but it also takes a certain amount of collaboration to get things moving at the beginning. Developing an XML vocabulary doesn't have to be a company-wide (or industry-wide) initiative, but involving more people than the Web development staff (or database administration staff) is an important first step.

Who Should be Involved in XML?

Because XML has the potential to become a standard format for virtually all documents in an organization as well as for interchange of all kinds of data, many people who never thought about data formats before (and probably don't want to think about them now) are likely to be affected by XML development. Companies that have standardized on commercial document-management (mostly word-processing) tools now have the opportunity to switch to a far more flexible and indeed customizable solution. Planning for a change of this magnitude will probably take years of consideration and slow conversion from the old ways to the new.

The good old days when the Web development team was a strange group of techies and designers isolated in a former storage room, separate from the rest of the company, are mostly over, and other developers are also facing substantial Web-related change. When the Web moves inside the company, rather than just projecting data outward, the development team can no longer live at the borders of the organization. The increasing number of intranets heralds the integration of the company and the Web. Employees who might not even have computer backgrounds have become grassroots Webmasters, using personal Web servers and other small-scale tools to distribute data. Some corporations have established central Web servers for departments or divisions, giving the smaller organizations responsibility for their own content. Web-based intranets are an excellent means of deploying applications at minimal cost.

XML has the potential to penetrate enterprises far more deeply than even the latest wave of intranet applications, becoming a standard format on nearly every desktop. XML is more than just a format for Web and printed documents; it can provide a database format, a container for control instructions, a generic interchange format, and a variety of other applications that will undoubtedly come along. XML's extreme flexibility gives it incredible power to reach into nearly every data-processing application, not just word-processing and Web-development applications. Even XML documents that were created for the limited worlds of word processing and Web development may end up mined for useful information, a much easier task when documents are created using well-crafted XML.

This potential for expansion means that in order to develop standards that meet an organization's needs, developers must talk to many more people inside an organization than they have had to in the past. Organizing Web development has traditionally been mostly a matter of interface design and content automation — taking content from various sources, converting it to HTML, and presenting it attractively. Organizing XML development requires close examination of both content design and workflow automation. Web development, database development, and even network administration are blurring together like never before. Presentation may still be important, but XML enables developers to ask that documents use XML and a standard vocabulary as their native format, thereby making conversion unnecessary and opening up powerful new possibilities for document management and data interchange. This obviously won't happen immediately; the process may take years, but it probably won't happen at all if developers lurch forward with poorly designed document structures that cause more mayhem than they fix.

Avoiding that mayhem requires considerable consultation with users. Even if your Web-application development efforts have been moved from the computing department to marketing, it's time to go back to computing and talk about what can be done to ensure compatibility in the long run. Designers who have spent the past few years forcing HTML to present pages precisely the way they want them must talk with database managers whose data are organized in enormous tables, and agree on some common solutions. Companies that may have standardized on a particular desktop applications suite to avoid the headaches of constant file conflicts may find that their large investment was merely an interim solution and that the real tools for document interchange are only starting to appear. Convincing users of the need to change will be a difficult process, even if software vendors extend support (as several have promised) for the new tools XML makes available.

Focus on Structure

The most difficult demand that XML makes of developers is that they standardize their document structures. This doesn't mean that every single document must look the same; it means that developers must examine the components that go into their pages and create standards. HTML provided some tools for creating structures such as paragraphs, lists, and headings, but never demanded that developers apply structures rather than formatting. HTML tags had to work in concert at times, but a headline tag never required that a paragraph follow it, for example. XML can make such demands and (with a validating parser) enforce them. Taking full advantage of XML requires developers to examine their document and data structures closely and to restate them more explicitly.

Document structure

This chapter is somewhat structured. It opens with a title followed by some paragraphs. A heading follows, with some more paragraphs, and then another heading appears, followed by an introductory paragraph and a subhead. The text you are reading now is the paragraph below that subhead, so you are several layers down in the document hierarchy, as shown in Figure 18-1.

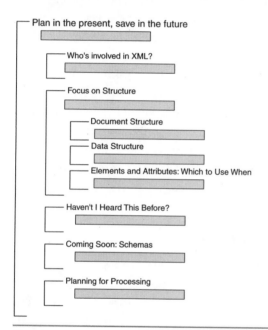

Figure 18-1   *A map of this chapter*

Not every document has a structure as complex as this chapter's, but most documents have some kind of structure. Memos, for example, begin with the names of the recipient(s) and the sender(s), as well as the date and other company information. The text that follows is generally less structured. Letters frequently provide more information, especially in a business environment, such as the sender's and recipient's addresses as well as a salutation (Dear John), a closing (Sincerely), a signature, and a printed version of the name of the sender. Attachments may be noted, as may typists and others involved in the preparation of the document. Documents may be more complex than these basic examples, but they are very rarely any simpler.

Don't take this discussion to mean that your Web development team should be enforcing standards for company memos and other documents, even though that might eventually be a reasonable goal. (It's a project we tackle in Chapter 21, as well.) Many companies' attempts to standardize formats of commonly used documents have been met with resistance. For a wide variety of reasons, people often do not like to format their memos uniformly. When developing standards for company documents, try to allow for some flexibility — at least on stylistic matters such as font and size, if not on header information. Pushing standardization too hard is likely to keep the standard from ever being applied, especially in these early stages when friendly tools for applying standards have yet to appear.

HTML took a relatively simple approach to documents: identifying distinct components and creating tools for reproducing them. However, it did not link the parts in any particular way (with the significant exceptions of lists, forms, and tables). Most elements in the BODY section of an HTML document can appear anywhere, in any order. There are no rules declaring that H2 elements must appear only after H1 elements; H2 elements can appear anywhere in the document, with or without other headlines. The only limitations in HTML are those that create block elements. For example, H2 elements don't work well inside H1 elements.

```
<H1>This is the top<H2>This is the middle</H2>This is the
end</H1>
```

This line of code fails to produce a single line with two sizes of header. Figure 18-2 shows the results.

Apart from this kind of misbehavior, HTML puts very few constraints on the way its document parts are used. List elements are expected to appear in a list, but the browser will cope if they aren't; the same is true of form elements. Table elements (rows and columns) are ignored outside the context of a table because they don't make sense. HTML's lack of structural constraints makes it much easier for beginners to create pages that resemble their creators' expectations. Even if HTML had such structures they wouldn't be enforced, because HTML has no requirement for document validation.

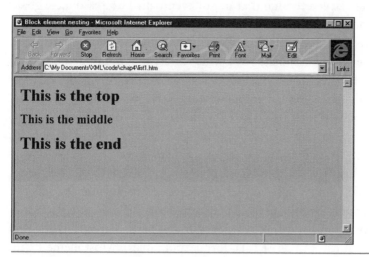

Figure 18-2 *Block-element nesting misbehavior*

XML enables developers to create document structures many times more complex than those available in HTML. Document structures are useful because they guarantee that documents have all their required elements, and that document authors haven't run completely amok, creating their own wild formats and putting information in the "wrong" places. These XML structures enable document-management systems to check on completeness and to assist formatting engines in producing visually appealing representations of XML documents. Combined with style sheets, document structure elements make it possible to use XML to create readable, highly formatted Web pages, complete with headlines, subheads, paragraphs, citations, indented blocks, and all the structures previously available in HTML.

You can identify a document structure fairly easily by looking at a document. The structure's primary mission is to provide a roadmap to the information, enabling readers to find the information they need at a glance. Not surprisingly, most SGML implementations have been designed for documentation projects, which tend to produce enormous amounts of information that need structure to help readers find their way through. Documentation usually follows strict conventions, often resorting to paragraph numbering for easy references (such as "see paragraph 1.3.2 for detailed information about widgets"). Projects that already have strong structures are easy targets for markup languages; the real challenges are less structured documents that contain many different types of information.

When developing DTDs based on document structures, developers should check to see what has already been done. Large companies and other organizations may already have their own SGML standards. Organizations of every size may need to adhere to standards to enable them to circulate information easily. Document structures are much less likely than data structures to demand their own unique DTDs (a memo is pretty much a memo, whatever organization or individual produced it).

Developers in need of some inspiration may want to examine the work of the Text Encoding Initiative (TEI) at `http://www.uic.edu/orgs/tei`. This academic organization has produced an enormous set of standards for scholarly document encoding. Written to provide standards for the conversion of printed books to electronic formats that scholars can use more readily, the TEI DTDs provide extensive frameworks for all kinds of materials from prose to poetry to plays to commentaries. TEI standards regularly cross the boundaries between document structure encoding and data encoding. In fact, they demonstrate how blurred the distinctions can be. Nevertheless, their adaptations of markup structures to a variety of document types are generally well thought-out and informed by implementation as well as prior planning.

In general, good document structure systems are more obvious than good data structure systems. Many organizations have already given some thought to document-management issues, and many have even considered their impact on document presentation, storage, and management. Desktop publishers have had to develop a sense of the structures pertaining to their materials, Web developers have had to build homes for a variety of different types of information, and technical writers and other documentation writers have generally had to work with preset document structure expectations. XML offers developers the chance to codify these structures and possibly make them more interoperable than they have traditionally been. XML's freedom from formatting information gives it the flexibility to deal with all these situations, making it possible for newsletter information to reappear on a CD-ROM, the Web, or even in a printed company history without too much mangling and rebuilding along the way. Building abstract document structures makes producing and managing documents much easier in the long run.

Data structure

If the document structures provide a table of contents for documents, the data structures provide the index. Document structures organize your document to help readers understand the structure of an argument or follow an extended discussion without getting lost. Data structures reflect the content directly, with little concern for where the structures appear in an overall document structure. A DTD or schema may require that they appear in a particular document structure, but they often have more freedom to "float" within a document.

The ability to create structures based on data content gives XML most of its practical advantage over HTML. Even though document structures are useful, they have little direct effect on the ways that computers can reuse the information in documents. They may enable management systems to identify the locations of information more precisely, but they do very little to help them actually retrieve the information. Document structures help humans read documents, but they do very little to help computers find the critical pieces of data they need without human assistance. A program may be able to identify a table easily, but without additional information it cannot extract data from that table for reuse in later analysis. Table headers may be useful to a certain extent, but as soon as multiple tables with similar headers appear in a document, which is common, the computer is stuck once again when it tries to determine what information is relevant.

XML promises to help both computers and humans assess the data in a document and extract them for reuse or modification. Best of all, XML enables users to collect data scattered throughout a document as well as data carefully collected in a table or other formatting structure. When working on a suitably marked-up document parsers can return information in a variety of formats, transforming textual data into more structured database and spreadsheet formats. Even though XML lacks tools for manipulating data (calculated fields, for example) within a document, it provides the raw materials necessary for building applications around an independent data format.

Elements based on content provide document-structuring abilities as well. Apart from the fact that they can (in concert with style sheets) provide formatting based on content, these elements can be linked together with DTDs to provide datasets, not just individual atoms of data. A catalog document, for example, might contain lots of structured information:

```
<ITEM><PRODNAME>Jimbo's Super Clock</PRODNAME>:
<PART>SC45-A</PART>   <PRICE>$199.95</PRICE>
(<AIRF>$19.95</AIRF> freight/air,
<GROUNDF>$7.95</GROUNDF> ground) <WARRANTY>Twenty-five
year</WARRANTY> Warranty. Made in
<ORIGIN>Canada</ORIGIN></ITEM>
```

Continued

```
<ITEM><PRODNAME>Lamp Controller</PRODNAME>: <PART>LC45-
X</PART> <PRICE>$25.95</PRICE> (<AIRF>$9.95</AIRF>
freight/air, <GROUNDF>$4.95</GROUNDF> ground)
<WARRANTY>Ten-year</WARRANTY> Warranty. Made in
<ORIGIN>Canada</ORIGIN></ITEM>
<ITEM><PRODNAME>Electroshock Clips</PRODNAME>:
<PART>ES45-L</PART> <PRICE>$59.95</PRICE>
(<AIRF>$9.95</AIRF> freight/air, <GROUNDF>$4.95</GROUNDF>
ground) <WARRANTY>One-year</WARRANTY> Warranty. Made in
<ORIGIN>USA</ORIGIN></ITEM>
```

Each ITEM element includes a set of other elements, any of which can be made to be required with a DTD. These sets of elements could be treated as rows in a database, as shown in Table 18-1.

Table 18-1 *Sets of Elements Treated as Rows in a Database*

Prodname	Part	Price	AirF	GroundF	Warranty	Origin
Jimbo's Super Clock	SC45-A	$199.95	$19.95	$7.95	25 years	Canada
Lamp Controller	LC45-X	$25.95	$9.95	$4.95	10 years	Canada
Electroshock Clips	ES45-L	$59.95	$9.95	$4.95	1 year	USA

These datasets can be stored in any order within the database. The sequence in which information is presented in XML is not bound by the sequence within the database, nor is the database bound by the sequence in the XML. Use whatever sequence seems most appropriate for each medium. Making datasets like these work effectively requires more coding than the well-formed piece we originally used, but the XML version certainly provides a much stronger starting point than you can get with HTML. The relational model of tables of data will not always be appropriate to XML, which offers considerably more flexibility than HTML, but the groundwork for easy transfers between the two information models is easy to build.

Previously, tools for data interchange using basic text (usually ASCII) formats relied on one of two scenarios: fixed-length fields or delimiters. Fixed-length fields were designed for older technologies, such as mainframes that stored all their information in tightly coded tables. For situations where information fits a tightly restricted container and can be counted on never to exceed a preset maximum length, fixed fields can be handy. The receiving machine needs to know the boundary positions between the fields; then it can chop the long string of characters it receives into usable fields. If one character slips, however, the data become useless. Delimiters use a different technique for indicating boundaries, inserting a previously agreed-on character (such as a comma) between each field and a different character (often a carriage return) between each record. The first line of the file containing the data is usually a list of field names, themselves delimited. Delimiters remain very popular, though converting between delimited text data and XML isn't very difficult.

Neither of these solutions is very useful for data that must be mixed with less structured information or data that aren't strictly text and numbers. Both solutions have served well as interim techniques for managing information transfers, but XML promises a much more flexible and indeed much more reliable mechanism for information transfers.

Note

Given a large enough binary file, the code for the delimiter is likely to creep in at some point, disrupting the program trying to read the delimited file. This could happen with XML as well, even though XML provides an entity mechanism that should prevent it from happening with either valid or well-formed XML.)

Consider the following data table:

FirstName	LastName	ClassName
John	Nickelson	Introductory French
John	Nickelson	Introductory Geometry
Sarah	Angleton	Advanced Calculus
Carrie	Milton	Introductory French
Carrie	Milton	Advanced Calculus
Timothy	Shore	Introductory Geometry

If exported to a text file, delimited by commas, the information would look like this:

```
FirstName,LastName,ClassName
John,Nickelson,Introductory French
John, Nickelson,Introductory Geometry
Sarah,Angleton,Advanced Calculus
Carrie,Milton,Introductory French
Carrie,Milton,Advanced Calculus
Timothy,Shore,Introductory Geometry
```

In an XML file, this information could appear mixed with other information carrying additional meaning to both humans and computers:

```
<?xml version="1.0" standalone="yes"?>
<HEADER><HEADLINE>Alert!</HEADLINE>
To:<TO>All teachers</TO>
From: <FROM>Registrar's Office</FROM>
Re: <SUBJECT>Students left off rosters</SUBJECT>
Date: <DATE>9/13/1997</DATE></HEADER>
<MESSAGE>The following students were inadvertently left
off the course lists previously distributed. Please add
them to your lists. If you have any questions, please
contact the Registrar's Office.</MESSAGE>
```

```
<COURSELIST>
<COURSEITEM>
<STUDENT IDNUM ="A0653B"><FIRSTNAME>John</FIRSTNAME>
<LASTNAME>Nickelson</LASTNAME></STUDENT>
<CLASSNAME>Introductory French</CLASSNAME>
</COURSEITEM>
<COURSEITEM>
<STUDENT IDNUM ="A0653B"><FIRSTNAME>John</FIRSTNAME>
<LASTNAME>Nickelson</LASTNAME></STUDENT>
<CLASSNAME>Introductory Geometry</CLASSNAME>
</COURSEITEM>
<COURSEITEM>
<STUDENT IDNUM ="A0653C"><FIRSTNAME>Sarah</FIRSTNAME>
<LASTNAME>Angleton</LASTNAME></STUDENT>
<CLASSNAME>Advanced Calculus</CLASSNAME>
</COURSEITEM>
<COURSEITEM>
<STUDENT IDNUM ="A0653D"><FIRSTNAME>Carrie</FIRSTNAME>
<LASTNAME>Milton</LASTNAME></STUDENT>
<CLASSNAME>Introductory French</CLASSNAME>
</COURSEITEM>
<COURSEITEM>
<STUDENT IDNUM ="A0653D"><FIRSTNAME>Carrie</FIRSTNAME>
<LASTNAME>Milton</LASTNAME></STUDENT> <CLASSNAME>Advanced
Calculus</CLASSNAME>
</COURSEITEM>
<COURSEITEM>
<STUDENT IDNUM ="A0653E"><FIRSTNAME>Timothy</FIRSTNAME>
<LASTNAME>Shore</LASTNAME></STUDENT>
<CLASSNAME>Introductory Geometry</CLASSNAME>
</COURSEITEM>
</COURSELIST>
```

The XML version, even the section that carries the same information as the delimited text version, is considerably more verbose; however, it is capable of serving multiple purposes. With the help of a style sheet, this document can be posted to a Web site, printed, or sent as e-mail to MIME-enabled mail readers. Even though transmissions directly to humans are important, the automation potential of this document has advantages that go beyond humans reading it. This XML provides both document and data structures, which overlap and reinforce one another. The traditional style of the memo is preserved, and the HEADER element contains information that normally appears at the top of a memo. However, the information is marked up to indicate smaller chunks of data, enabling a document-management system to store this memo and provide access to it in a number of ways. Readers can find it in lists sorted by recipient, sender, date, subject, or even headline. Searches can find information here on students whose first name is "Carrie" or who are taking "Introductory Geometry."

An enterprising teacher maintaining a database of students can connect to the XML information provided in the COURSELIST elements and import the list directly, without retyping student names. A good parser can even grab a student's ID number from the IDNUM attribute of the STUDENT element and store it along with the name and class information, enabling the teacher to link to other information in a central database regarding that student. Perhaps most exciting of all, the school's central database can generate these files automatically, creating an easy way for administrators to "push" information out to teachers' own databases without maintaining constant connections to them or linking everyone to a gigantic central system. If you can imagine a cut-and-paste mechanism that reliably transfers information between dramatically different systems and applications, you can see a small bit of the promise of XML.

These systems don't exist yet; even the few places that use SGML extensively probably haven't connected their data from the central documents to distributed databases via memos. Office automation on this level promises to build many new data-driven workflow applications, as well as finally reducing the amount of repetitive data entry that remains a demanding task even in today's ubiquitous computing environments. According to the September 1997 issue of *Byte*, 90% of business data currently lives outside databases — as memos, spreadsheets, letters, proposals, documentation, and assorted other forms of information. The prospect of connecting those documents with a document-management system (as opposed to a database) is much of what makes XML so promising. Making the document-management system meaningful will require considerable effort in building infrastructure, a significant part of which will be devoted to creating DTDs that provide information about the information in the document.

Developing DTDs that reflect data structures is frequently more difficult than developing document structures. Like relational data-bases, data structures are very clear in highly structured environ-ments, but they can be extremely murky in ordinary documents. Deciding what counts as data and finding ways to mark them meaningfully are both difficult tasks. Different sectors of an organi-zation may apply data very differently. For example, the individual parts listed on an order are critical information to a shipping depart-ment. Nevertheless, they are of only marginal interest to accounts receivable and are interesting only in the aggregate to corporate management. Different priorities can lead to different proposals for data structures and data management, much as they have in other applications of information technology.

One element missing in XML is data typing. An enormous number of developers, especially database developers and program-mers, have found the lack of this feature to be a difficult stumbling block. This issue of this "missing feature" appears regularly on XML development mailing lists and is probably the heaviest burden XML bears as a result of coming from document processing rather than data processing. Because the SGML world was tightly focused on documents, document management, and making document presen-tation easier, data typing was never really an issue there. XML 1.0's position as a subset of SGML made it difficult to add features like this, and they are only now arriving in the schema proposals I dis-cuss at the end of this chapter. The early rush to XML by program-mers (rather than Web developers and other document creators) has created new demands that XML was not originally well equipped to handle; the retrofit is in progress.

Note

XML does provide some support for describing data types through notations, which I describe in the next chapter. Notations are fairly controversial and widely held to be both underspecified and better at describing the type of large chunks of information (such as file formats), than the type of small chunks (such as integers). Regardless, notations may be a useful stopgap until schemas actually arrive.

Despite the potential for chaos, some basic rules for data design remain useful in deciding which pieces of data rate their own elements and how they should be broken down. Data should always be broken down into the smallest parts that will ever be needed, as is done in creating a normalized relational database. The preceding class-roster example could have provided the first name and last name as one element, NAME, instead of as two elements, FIRSTNAME and LASTNAME. This would certainly be easier for the document creators, who must mark up each element separately, but would cause problems for anyone else who needed to sort the class lists by last name. You can build more complex structures by nesting these smaller pieces in container elements (the STUDENT element, in this case). If the information were actually coming from a database, this structure would be easy to automate, both for exporting the data to XML and for importing it from XML. Hand-coders and document authors forced to deal with the complexity of nested tags may disagree, requiring compromise in many cases. To accommodate the varied needs of different users you may also have to compromise on the nesting of subelements within larger container elements.

Making these data structures work requires more than just creating a DTD or schema; it requires continuous negotiation between developers and their user communities. Developers lucky enough to build standards only for themselves will be a distinct minority in the XML community. Bringing XML's promise of content-based documents to pass will require considerable political as well as technical skill in addition to teams that can handle both sides of the equation.

Processing Plans

XML is "bigger" than HTML and SGML in a number of ways, capable of reaching into more areas of computing, from Web browsers to word processors to resource files to databases to control systems. As a result, developers need to be aware of the possibility that structures designed for one purpose will end up being processed for another purpose entirely. XML removes the moorings that had attached data permanently to particular applications. Its simple unambiguous document structures enable applications to reach into any XML document and explore and process it. XML makes it possible to create powerful generic frameworks capable of storing information of wildly different types. Although this may not be the goal of everyone creating XML document structures — after all, short-term goals remain vividly important — it's something to keep in mind in the XML document structure and application development processes.

Web developers, document authors and managers, and application programming developers have so far been hampered by a lack of tools. XML creation is still a pioneering effort: developers have little to work with because programs that support XML have just begun to appear. Nonetheless, one of the most magical features of XML is that today's documents can work with tomorrow's applications: the basic element and attribute structures are strongly fixed, but flexible enough to keep up with a wide variety of needs. XML developers also have a rich heritage of examples to draw on from the SGML world and the promise of ever-increasing XML support from major vendors.

Cross-Reference

Developers who need a heavy-duty introduction to the process of building large-scale document standards in XML may want to explore *Developing SGML DTDs: From Text to Model to Markup*, by Eve Maler and Jeanne El Andaloussi (Prentice-Hall, 1996). Although the book is about SGML (it came out before XML existed), it provides a useful and readable guide to information modeling and to the processes — both political and technical — that are part of building standards and applications with SGML.

Chapter 19

Recreating Web and Paper Documents with XML

Now that I've covered all the parts involved, it's time to create some valid XML documents with reasonably complex structures and use DTDs to describe them. Despite the many parts involved, creating a DTD doesn't have to be painful. Developers converting documents from HTML or a word-processor style sheet often find that their document structures are actually simplified. This chapter examines the production and implementation of two sample DTDs for document production, including DTD development, document coding, and style-sheet creation for browser viewing of the documents, as well as a wrapper DTD for working with legacy-text content.

Note

This chapter uses only DTDs to describe document structures. Schemas of whatever flavor don't offer much additional functionality that applies to these kinds of projects. Schemas are used in the next few chapters, however.

To XML from HTML

Many organizations already store huge quantities of information in HTML. After spending hours converting it to HTML from some other format, many of these information keepers probably aren't thrilled to hear about this great new development that promises to sweep away HTML (not to mention the rest of their document formats). However, most of the HTML information already created will probably never be formally converted to XML, and if it is, that conversion is likely to be automated. Because HTML files have often been developed to look a certain way, the appearance of finished HTML on the screen has taken precedence over the structure underlying the code. Developers on a deadline must have something to show the client; if broken code doesn't bother the browsers in which it's viewed, it isn't likely to bother the client. Add to that the fact that much HTML is coded by hand, created by tools that litter the page with extra markup, or generated by programs that may not consistently create cleanly structured documents, and the odds of HTML pages being close to well-formed XML drop precipitously.

HTML provides a set of structures that represent generic structures for documents, plus a set of tools for formatting these structures. HTML doesn't provide vocabulary for features specific to particular kinds of documents or data. For a time it seemed that HTML was losing its status as a vocabulary for describing structures and becoming a vocabulary for describing formatting. With the rise of style sheets and the W3C's return to prominence as the keeper of HTML specifications, HTML has returned to its roots describing structures, leaving (much) formatting to style sheets. Recent HTML standards have used SGML as their formal vocabulary, creating a description of "valid" HTML in SGML. The next revision of HTML, called XHTML, which I discuss in greater depth in Chapter 13, is converting HTML to a set of XML modules. If all that you need is technically valid XML documents, you might consider simply converting from current forms to this XML-ized version of valid HTML. But remember that valid XML is not necessarily easily managed. Targeted vocabulary that reflects specific content rather than generic structure (or worse, presentation) is the main advantage of using XML as a file format, and using the HTML DTDs will not provide that.

Note

If you want to use some of the HTML elements in your documents, you may want to explore XHTML Modularization, which provides pre-fabricated DTD fragments of the HTML vocabulary (http://www.w3.org/TR/xhtml-modularization/). If that's too complex, John Cowan's Itsy-Bitsy Teeny-Weeny Simple Hypertext (IBTWSH) DTD may be useful. It describes a smaller subset of HTML and is compatible with XHTML. It's available at http://www.ccil.org/~cowan/XML/ibtwsh.dtd.

For many Web documents, the conversion process will probably take place by hand, as it would with paper documents. Tools can "learn" the format of a set of pages and extract the needed content, but sets of HTML pages that aren't generated by machines rarely follow a format consistently. The text on one page may include five paragraphs, whereas another page may have no text at all. For example,

```
<HTML>
<HEAD><TITLE>Joe's Catalog - Money
Counters</TITLE></HEAD>
<BODY BGCOLOR="#FFFFFF">
<H1>Money Counting Equipment</H1>
<H2>Basic Money Counter</H2>
<H4>Count your cash without spending all of it!</H4>
Joe's is pleased to announce this NEW addition to our
line. People with piles of change can sort their money
easily, and wrap it for the bank. Makes the change box
a lot more useful!<BR>
```

Continued

```
Price:<B>$14.95</B>, <FONT SIZE=1>plus $4.95 shipping and
handling. </FONT><P>
Also available: Paper Coin Wrappers, bag of 100:
<B>$2.95</B><P>
<H2>Standard Money Counter</H2>
<H3>Count and collect your cash automatically!</H3>
This money counter wraps your change automatically --
just feed it the plastic change rolls. You'll feel just
like the bank when you read its LED display announcing
how much change you've gathered.<P>
Special guarantee: 100% accuracy on wrapping or your
money back!<BR>
Price:<B>$64.95</B>, <FONT SIZE=1>plus $7.95 shipping and
handling. </FONT><P>
Also available: Plastic Coin Wrappers, box of 400:
<B>$10.95</B><P>
<H2>Super-Duper Money Counter</H2>
Tired of change? This machine counts bills as well. Feed
it the take from a cash register and watch it count away.
Spits out old bills in a separate tray for easy counting.
Saves hours of effort spent counting pennies -- and
twenties!<BR>
Price:<B>$649.95</B>, <FONT SIZE=1>plus $29.95 shipping
and handling.</FONT><P>
Uses plastic coin wrappers above, and Paper Bill
Wrappers, box of 1000: <B>$10.95</B><P>
</BODY></HTML>
```

This document, viewed in a browser, presents a simple catalog page of money counters, as shown in Figure 19-1.

Even though this document has some clear parts that could easily be converted to a DTD, the style of coding isn't exactly conducive to automatic conversion to XML. The text is littered with "extra guarantees" and "also availables" that neither appear consistently nor use the same format. This looks like an old hand-coded HTML document, which uses the <P> tag at the end of a paragraph rather than enclosing paragraphs in <P>...</P>. Although it might be possible to write a program to convert this document, Joe will probably be better off either developing a DTD and having someone convert it by hand or making it well-formed by adding closing tags.

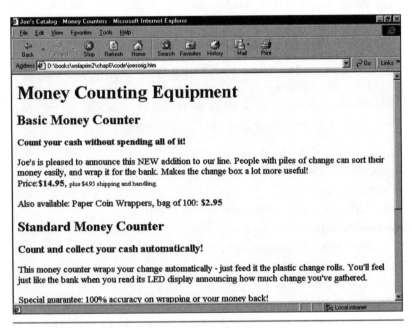

Figure 19-1 *The HTML version of Joe's Catalog*

A DTD for Joe's catalog that is based on its content rather than its presentation could read like the following:

```
<!ELEMENT CATALOGPAGE (HEADER,CATALOGITEM+)>
<!ELEMENT HEADER (#PCDATA)>
<!ELEMENT CATALOGITEM (ITEMNAME, ITEMSUBHEAD?,
ITEMDESCRIPTION*,ITEMPRICING,SUBITEM*)>
<!ELEMENT ITEMNAME (#PCDATA)>
<!ELEMENT ITEMSUBHEAD (#PCDATA)>
<!ELEMENT ITEMDESCRIPTION (#PCDATA)>
```

Continued

```
<!ELEMENT ITEMPRICING (#PCDATA|ITEMNOTE|PRICE|SHIPPING)*>
<!ELEMENT PRICE (#PCDATA)>
<!ELEMENT SHIPPING (#PCDATA)>
<!ELEMENT ITEMNOTE (#PCDATA)>
<!ELEMENT SUBNAME (#PCDATA)>
<!ELEMENT SUBITEM (#PCDATA|SUBNAME|PRICE|SHIPPING)*>
```

Joe's catalog page would need to undergo some extensive modification. For example, the DTD adds a SHIPPING element that wasn't formally represented before. Additional layers of elements must be added where there wasn't any markup before. For those reasons, Joe's catalog probably needs to be recreated by a human rather than a machine. The new page looks like the following:

```
<?xml version="1.0" encoding="UTF-8"?>
<!DOCTYPE CATALOGPAGE SYSTEM "joes.dtd">
<CATALOGPAGE>
<HEADER>Money Counting Equipment</HEADER>
<CATALOGITEM>
<ITEMNAME>Basic Money Counter</ITEMNAME>
<ITEMSUBHEAD>Count your cash without spending all of
it!</ITEMSUBHEAD>
<ITEMDESCRIPTION>Joe's is pleased to announce this NEW
addition to our line. People with piles of change can
sort their money easily, and wrap it for the bank. Makes
the change box a lot more useful!</ITEMDESCRIPTION>
<ITEMPRICING>Price:<PRICE>$14.95</PRICE>, plus
<SHIPPING>$4.95</SHIPPING> shipping and
handling.</ITEMPRICING>
<SUBITEM>Also available: <SUBNAME>Paper Coin Wrappers,
bag of 100</SUBNAME>: <PRICE>$2.95</PRICE></SUBITEM>
</CATALOGITEM>
<CATALOGITEM>
<ITEMNAME>Standard Money Counter</ITEMNAME>
<ITEMSUBHEAD>Count and collect your cash
automatically!</ITEMSUBHEAD>
```

```
<ITEMDESCRIPTION>This money counter wraps your change
automatically -- just feed it the plastic change rolls.
You'll feel just like the bank when you read its LED
display announcing how much change you've
gathered.</ITEMDESCRIPTION>
<ITEMPRICING><ITEMNOTE>Special guarantee: 100% accuracy
on wrapping or your money back!</ITEMNOTE>
Price:<PRICE>$64.95</PRICE>, plus
<SHIPPING>$7.95</SHIPPING> shipping and
handling.</ITEMPRICING>
<SUBITEM>Also available: <SUBNAME>Plastic Coin Wrappers,
box of 400</SUBNAME>: <PRICE>$10.95</PRICE></SUBITEM>
</CATALOGITEM>
<CATALOGITEM>
<ITEMNAME>Super-Duper Money Counter</ITEMNAME>
<ITEMDESCRIPTION>Tired of change? This machine counts
bills as well. Feed it the take from a cash register and
watch it count away. Spits out old bills in a separate
tray for easy counting. Saves hours of effort spent
counting pennies -- and twenties!</ITEMDESCRIPTION>
<ITEMPRICING>Price:<PRICE>$649.95</PRICE>, plus
<SHIPPING>$29.95</SHIPPING> shipping and
handling.</ITEMPRICING>
<SUBITEM>Uses plastic coin wrappers above, and
<SUBNAME>Paper Bill Wrappers, box of 1000</SUBNAME>:
<PRICE>$10.95</PRICE></SUBITEM>
</CATALOGITEM>
</CATALOGPAGE>
```

This is still not a complete solution, although it may be all the solution Joe's Catalog wants. A more thorough DTD design might change the kinds of information presented and the order in which they appear, making the code look more like the Jimbo's Super Clock catalog example in Chapter 3 with its part numbers and freight information. The catalog as it stands now is reasonably useful for people to read, but it is still not very effective for use in an inventory system or catalog-management tool.

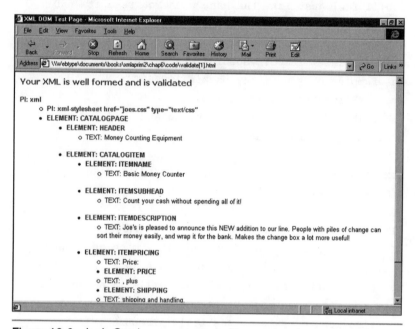

Figure 19-2 *Joe's Catalog represented with a content-focused notation*

Tip

Pages that are already generated by a computer will be fairly easy to convert, at least if the code or markup is written intelligibly. Search-and-replace mechanisms may be able to convert static machine-generated pages if all the material uses precisely the same markup. Better yet, if the data are still available in the original structure (database form, most likely) and are used to create pages on the fly, the scripts that create HTML can be easily modified to produce XML. Instead of placing certain formatting tags around a price, the script can place the price within a PRICE element.

A few HTML documents are probably ready for XML now, and HTML developers can plan ahead by designing pages that will convert easily. In Chapter 2, I discussed how Cascading Style Sheets provide a CLASS attribute that HTML developers can use to create their own tags effectively. Developers who have been using CSS classes to reflect categories of content and not just formatting will be in good shape. The main difference between the structure created by CSS CLASS attributes and the structure created by XML is in enforcement: CSS can't require classes to nest in a particular order. Still, because CSS provides formatting inheritance between elements (child elements will by default receive many of the style properties of their parents), many pages created with CSS reflect good XML structure and are in a good position to be converted. They work well in the newer (since version 5) versions of the Netscape and Internet Explorer browsers. The following example uses a small segment of a catalog to show how CSS CLASS attributes could work for Joe:

```
<HTML>
<HEAD><TITLE>Joe's Catalog - Money Counters</TITLE>
<STYLE TYPE="text/css">
DIV.HEADER {font-size:24pt;font-weight:bold}
DIV.ITEMNAME {font-size:18pt;font-weight:bold}
DIV.ITEMSUBHEAD {font-size:14pt;font-weight:bold}
DIV.ITEMDESCRIPTION {font-size:12pt}
DIV.ITEMPRICING {font-size:10pt}
SPAN.PRICE {font-weight:bold}
SPAN.SHIPPING {font-weight:normal}
DIV.SUBITEM {font-size:11pt}
SPAN.SUBNAME {font-weight:bold}
</STYLE></HEAD>
<BODY BGCOLOR="#FFFFFF">
<DIV CLASS="HEADER">Money Counting Equipment</DIV>
<DIV CLASS="ITEMNAME">Basic Money Counter</DIV>
```

Continued

```
<DIV CLASS="SUBHEAD">Count your cash without spending all
of it!</DIV>
<DIV CLASS="ITEMDESCRIPTION">Joe's is pleased to announce
this NEW addition to our line. People with piles of
change can sort their money easily, and wrap it for the
bank. Makes the change box a lot more useful!</DIV>
<DIV CLASS="ITEMPRICING">Price:<SPAN
CLASS="PRICE">$14.95</SPAN>, plus <SPAN
CLASS="SHIPPING">$4.95</SPAN> shipping and
handling.</DIV>
<DIV CLASS="SUBITEM">Also available: <SPAN
CLASS="SUBNAME">Paper Coin Wrappers, bag of 100</SPAN>:
<SPAN CLASS="PRICE">$2.95</SPAN></DIV>
<!--listing truncated-->
</BODY></HTML>
```

If the catalog is organized like this, converting to XML might require custom code that could take the DIV and SPAN elements, replace them with the appropriate elements (in this case, their CLASS attributes), and group them under appropriate parent elements. Most developers, however, won't be this lucky, unless they've just begun building their HTML documents. The page (abbreviated here for the example) looks much like the original version, as shown in Figure 19-3.

 Cross-Reference

A much more complete analysis of the needs of a catalog document appears in the next chapter. Joe's Catalog has crossed over from HTML, but still faces a much more dramatic restructuring.

Building a style sheet for Joe's catalog using CSS won't be too difficult. The parts are easily identified, and the formatting already exists in the HTML version. Linking a style sheet to an XML document requires some extra markup. Every document that uses style sheets needs to include the following line before the appearance of the root element:

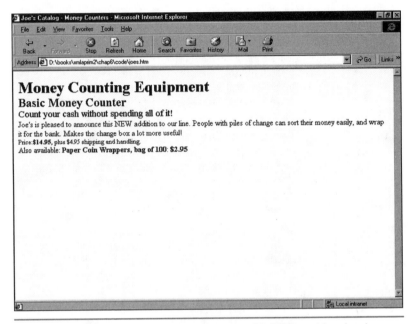

Figure 19-3 *Using* DIV *and* SPAN *elements with CSS enables developers to identify both formatting and content within HTML.*

```
<?xml-stylesheet href="joes.css" type="text/css"?>
```

The big question now is whether Joe wants to change the look of his catalog. If not, it's pretty easy to create an appropriate style. CSS display properties, shown in Table 19-1, make it possible for browsers to figure out a basic structure for rendering the XML elements in the document.

Table 19-1 *Display Property Values for Building Document Presentation Structures*

Display Value	Meaning	Notes
block	Identifies the element as a separate block, which will start its text on a new line and end with a break at the end of the element. The root element is usually formatted with block, as are many paragraph-like subelements.	Appeared in Level 1, but was not supported until recently. Similar to the HTML DIV element in behavior.
inline	The default value; formats the element as part of the current block, without a break before or after. Typically used with elements that apply formatting to parts of sentences or paragraphs.	Appeared in Level 1, but was not supported until recently. Similar to the HTML SPAN element in behavior.
listItem	Makes the element behave like an HTML list-item (LI) element, indenting it and possibly bulleting it, depending on other CSS properties.	Appeared in Level 1, but was not supported until recently. Similar to the HTML LI element in behavior.
none	The element isn't displayed. No child elements will be displayed, either. (To hide elements but allow their children to appear, use the visible property.)	Appeared in Level 1. Commonly used in Dynamic HTML.
run-in	If the element is followed by a block element, this element joins that element as if it were declared inline. If it isn't, this element is formatted as if it were declared as block.	New to Level 2.
compact	Makes lists fit in a tight space.	New to Level 2.
marker	Identifies an element with CSS content generation.	New to Level 2.

Display Value	Meaning	Notes
inherit	Makes the element use the display properties of its parent element (which may also be inherited).	Appeared in Level 1.
table, inline-table, table-row -group, table-header-group, table-footer-group, table-row, table-column-group, table-column, table-cell, table-caption	Used to make elements into components of tables.	New to Level 2.

By combining these display properties with other formatting properties, you can build a simple style sheet for Joe's Catalog.

```
HEADER {
     display:block;
     font-size:24;
     font-family:serif;
     font-weight:bold
}
CATALOGITEM {
     display:block;
     font-family:serif
}
ITEMNAME {
     display:block;
     font-size: 18;
     font-weight:bold
}
ITEMSUBHEAD {
     display:block;
```

Continued

```
        font-size:14
}
ITEMDESCRIPTION {
        display:block;
        font-size:12
}
ITEMPRICING {
        display:block
}
PRICE {
        display:inline;
        font-family:bold
}
SHIPPING {
        display:inline
}
SUBITEM {
        display:block
}
```

The main tool used here is the style `display` attribute, which enables you to declare whether each element should be its own paragraph or flow with the text. If the element rates its own paragraph or line, it's styled as `block`. If it doesn't, it is styled as `inline`. The `list-item` option provides yet another choice: separate lines, with less spacing than a block. Using the `none` option suppresses display of an element and all of its content. Other options (discussed in greater detail in Chapter 2) provide table structures and other features. Although it might take a little tweaking, the styles shown in the preceding code produce a reasonable first draft of the catalog, as shown in Figures 19-4 and 19-5.

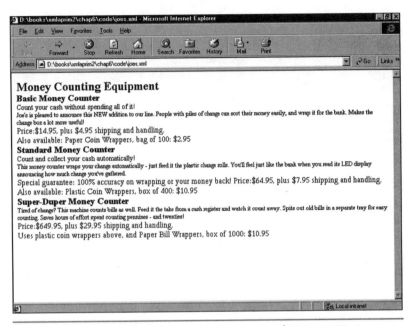

Figure 19-4 *A styled version of the XML document (in Microsoft's Internet Explorer 5) presents a prettier version of the same information without losing the underlying structure.*

After you have built a style sheet, making changes is easy—just make changes at the style sheet and they will flow through to the documents that call the style sheet. Extending the style sheet isn't as easy. Suppose that the PRICE element is to be displayed in red, but only for markdowns. CSS2 provides support for selectors that can respond to attribute values. (With XML, however, the CLASS attribute has no special privileges, as it did in HTML.)

```
PRICE.[status="markdown"] {
    display: inline;
    font-weight:bold;
    color:red
}
```

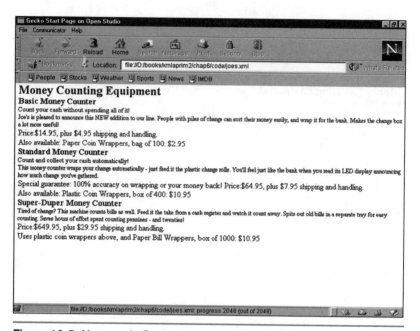

Figure 19-5 *Netscape's Gecko browser preview presents a similar view of the document.*

Remember that to use the attribute, you have to declare it in the DTD if you're using validation. With this style declared, the browser or other formatting application will turn the following price red, indicating a great bargain:

```
<PRICE status="markdown">$1.25</PRICE>
```

This will work for a while — until someone decides that the price color should also change if it's eligible for a bulk discount. Prices need to be either fixed or byquantity. Even though the following style might work for a little while, it can hardly be called elegant:

```
PRICE{
    display:inline;
    font-weight:bold;
}
PRICE.[status="set"]{
    color:blue;
}
PRICE.[status="byquantity"] {
    color:green;
}
PRICE.[status="markdownset"] {
    color:red;
}
PRICE.[status="markdownbyquantity"] {
    color:brown;
}
```

Building This Book

In writing the first edition of this book, I used two kinds of style notation. Most of the styling was done using Microsoft Word's built-in style tools and a style sheet provided by MIS:Press. Some of the information — such as notes, output, warnings, and sidebars — used markup notation very similar to XML. Notes, for instance, started with <NOTE> and ended with </NOTE>. Although these solutions work reasonably well, there are many ways in which they could improve. XML addresses most of those possibilities, simplifying the style-sheet structure and opening up new media to this document at the same time.

The styles defined in Word are a combination of structural information and formatting information, as shown in Table 19-2.

Table 19-2 *A Sample Style Sheet for a Book Chapter*

Style	Usage
TOC0 CT	Chapter number and title. This text will be used in the table of contents when it is generated.
TOC1 A	A-head – the top level of headings in a chapter. This text will be used in the table of contents when it is generated.
TOC2 B	B-head – the level of headings under A heads. This text also appears in table of contents.
C	C-head – the level below B. Not in the table of contents.
D	D-head – the level below C. Not in the table of contents.
E	E-head – the level below D. Not in the table of contents.
BT	Body text – the first paragraph of text after a header, icon, list, figure caption, or other free-standing graphic. Not indented.
BT INDENT	Body text following a **BT** element. Indented.
BL/NL1 TOP	Bulleted or numbered list – top line. (Formatted with extra space above.)
BL/NL2 MID	Bulleted or numbered list – middle lines. (Formatted with no extra space above or below.)
BL/NL3 BOT	Bulleted or numbered list – bottom line. (Formatted with extra space below.)
GL	Glossary text – word defined should be in bold, the definition in normal text.
CC1 TOP	First line of multiline code listing. Formatted with extra space above.
CC2 MID	Middle lines of multiline code listing. No extra space above or below.
CC3 BOT	Last line of multiline code listing. Formatted with extra space below.
CC4 SINGLE	Single line of multiline code listing. Formatted with extra space above and below.
ICON	Icon text – used in combination with markup (**<NOTE>**, **<WARNING>**, and so on) to identify text to be called out from body text.
FG	Figure caption – Figure *chapterNum.FigureNum* should be in bold, rest of text plain.
LC	Listing caption – goes above code listing.
TBC	Table caption – goes above table.
TBH	Table heads – goes above each column.
TB	Table body.
UL	Unnumbered list.
SN	Source notes – footnotes or notes at bottom of table.

The structures defined with markup are mostly icons and bullets. Bullets are indicated as <b> on PCs to avoid collisions between operating systems. Note icons are indicated as <NOTE>. A few structures are indicated with simple formatting. Keystrokes and menu items are supposed to be in bold, and titles are in italic.

Even though the current model worked well for MIS:Press, you may be able to indicate document structures more easily and more clearly in XML. XML offers opportunities that weren't available in traditional word processors. Structural styles can avert some of the redundancy required to make formatting styles work and make converting documents from format to format easier.

Pass 1: A DTD That Looks Like the Old Styles

You can start by setting up a chapter structure. (Chapters will eventually become part of the larger book structure.) The chapter will include a title, a brief introduction, and a series of sections marked by A-heads. In the interest of ensuring a smooth transition, the original style names are used where possible, although spaces must be stripped out:

```
<!ELEMENT CHAPTER (TOCOCT, INTRODUCTORY, ALEAF*)>
```

The TOCOCT element performs the same duty as the TOCO CT style: It identifies the chapter title. It contains only text:

```
<!ELEMENT TOCOCT (#PCDATA)>
```

The INTRODUCTORY element is new, introducing a chapter feature that wasn't included in the previous definition. All chapters start with text after the chapter headline. The INTRODUCTORY element is required and must consist of at least one body text (BT) paragraph. (No code listings or other subelements should appear in the introduction for now.)

```
<!ELEMENT INTRODUCTORY (BT+)>
```

The BT element is a bit more complicated because the text in it can include italic items (such as citations) and bold items (such as keystrokes and menu clicks — user actions). To address these needs, create a few elements and a parameter entity that includes them, making it easier to include them in other elements.

```
<!ELEMENT CITATION (#PCDATA)>
<!ELEMENT USERACTION (#PCDATA)>
<!ENTITY % textual-elements
"(#PCDATA|CITATION|USERACTION)*">
<!ELEMENT BT %textual-elements;>
```

Note

Because the `textual-elements` entity describes a mixed-content model, it cannot be used in combination with other content models or appear in parentheses.

The next target is the ALEAF element. To avoid confusion with the HTML tags A and B, I've added the word LEAF to the letters for all of these sections. Because the leaves may contain a variety of content types, it's time to plan ahead and create a parameter entity. The `content-elements` entity will contain a list of all types of content available to a LEAF element, which includes only the PARAGRAPH element at present.

```
<!ENTITY % content-elements "BT">
```

All the LEAF elements will contain a header and paragraphs or sublevels.

```
<!ELEMENT ALEAF (TOC1A,BT,(%content-elements;|BLEAF)*)>
<!ELEMENT BLEAF (TOC2B,BT,(%content-elements;|CLEAF)*)>
<!ELEMENT CLEAF (C,BT,(%content-elements;|DLEAF)*)>
<!ELEMENT DLEAF (D,BT,(%content-elements;|ELEAF)*)>
<!ELEMENT ELEAF (E,BT,(%content-elements;)*)>
<!ELEMENT TOC1A (#PCDATA)>
<!ELEMENT TOC2B (#PCDATA)>
```

```
<!ELEMENT C (#PCDATA)>
<!ELEMENT D (#PCDATA)>
<!ELEMENT E (#PCDATA)>
```

Note that you don't include the LEAF elements as part of the content-elements entity. Doing so would have allowed authors to put ELEAF elements directly below ALEAF elements, violating the desired hierarchy. Instead, these elements remain separate, making it easier for the designer to see the structure. Using the (%content-elements | XLEAF)* structure allows zero or more layers of content: ALEAFs aren't required to have BLEAF elements, but you can't have a CLEAF element unless it's included in a BLEAF element. (Later in this chapter you change this, simplifying the structure considerably.)

You have just provided the basic structure for a chapter, building a basic outline form that can be up to five levels deep. (If a chapter moves beyond five levels, it will be time to either reconsider the chapter's organization or add another level to the DTD.) Now it's time to go back and add content beyond basic text paragraphs. The easiest type of information to manage in this context is code. The current style sheet uses one of four different styles for code, depending on the position of the line of code. In XML, what matters most is not the position of the code, but that the information is code. Style sheets clean up the presentation and apply the extra space before and after the code element. Your code element, to match the style sheet, will be named CC. By default, your CC element's TYPE attribute will be CODE because very few books still have textual output. For those books that do, you provide an OUTPUT value option for the TYPE, enabling the designer to format these two similar types slightly differently. A CC element may contain a listing caption (LC) and must include at least one CLINE (code line) element, with multiple lines to store code as necessary.

```
<!ELEMENT CC (LC?,CLINE+)>
<!ATTLIST CC TYPE (CODE|OUTPUT) "CODE">
<!ELEMENT LC (#PCDATA)>
<!ELEMENT CLINE (#PCDATA)>
```

The next set of styles that needs an interpretation is the list styles. Currently, this style sheet includes a combined set of entries for bulleted and numbered lists, along with a separate style for unnumbered lists. This presents you with several options. You can maintain the style sheet as it exists now, creating one element to handle numbered and bulleted lists and another for unnumbered lists. You can break up the numbered and bulleted lists, keeping all the list styles separate. Finally, you can combine all the elements under one large umbrella.

Even though the large-umbrella idea produces cleaner code (and you use it in the next pass), for now compatibility is important. Given the latest developments in style sheets (especially XSL), however, it seems likely that you'll want to separate bulleted and numbered lists for separate style processing. That way the style mechanism can apply numbers and bullets as appropriate, making it easier for writers to move items around without renumbering them. Unnumbered lists will remain their own category.

```
<!ELEMENT BL (BLINE+)>
<!ELEMENT NL (NLINE+)>
<!ELEMENT UL (ULINE+)>
<!ELEMENT BLINE (#PCDATA)>
<!ELEMENT NLINE (#PCDATA)>
<!ELEMENT ULINE (#PCDATA)>
```

The next style you implement is GL, which is for glossary text. GL by itself doesn't do very much, and the author has to make the glossary entry bold. Because glossaries are one of the best types of documents for manipulation, it seems reasonable to improve on this approach. The new GL element will contain a GLITEM and a GLDEF-INITION, which explains the word contained in GLITEM.

```
<!ELEMENT GL (GLITEM,GLDEFINITION)>
<!ELEMENT GLITEM (#PCDATA)>
<!ELEMENT GLDEFINITION %textual-elements;>
```

ICON text is a somewhat difficult case. The ICON text by definition has a graphic floating to the left of it, but the graphic is not
specified in the style sheet. Although it might be possible to create
separate NOTE, SHORTCUT, WARNING, and TIP elements for each type
of text instead of an ICON element, this doesn't correspond well to
current practice. For now, create an ICON element that contains an
attribute identifying its type, allowing the application to add the
graphic later, identify it, and use BT information for the content.

```
<!ELEMENT ICON (BT+)>
<!ATTLIST ICON
    TYPE  (NOTE|SHORTCUT|WARNING|TIP) "NOTE">
```

Tables are the next challenge—a challenge XML is not exactly
prepared to face. Tables are often as much about formatting as about
content, and they are necessary for the presentation of many types
of content. The style sheet offers TBC for the table caption (which
should go above the table), TH to hold the column headings, TBH for
the column headings, TB for the table body text, and SN for source
notes at the bottom. In an ideal world authors would be able to create their own mini-DTD for every table, identifying cell contents
with their own element. Unfortunately, a publishing style sheet
doesn't offer much room for that kind of extension. For now you can
improvise, using the HTML-style TR and the style sheet's TB
(which is treated much like TD in HTML). Unlike in HTML, you
require that TB elements always fit inside TR elements.

```
<!ELEMENT TABLE (TBC*,TH?,TR+,SN*)>
<!ELEMENT TBC (#PCDATA)>
<!ELEMENT TH (TBH+)>
<!ELEMENT TBH (#PCDATA)>
<!ELEMENT TR (TB+)>
<!ELEMENT TB %textual-elements;>
<!ELEMENT SN %textual-elements;>
```

Note

Creating table elements in XML is a tricky business. Declaring these elements is not nearly the end of this process. Making tables work requires connecting these elements to styles that reflect their nature.

The last major element you need to deal with is figures. Figure images are not embedded directly in the file. Only a limited number of formats are acceptable. Figures include three parts: the picture, the figure number, and the caption describing the figure. The picture will be an empty element with attributes that explain to the processing application where to find the figure file and what kind of figure file it is. You define the kind of file using an attribute that matches a previously defined NOTATION declaration. The figure number will be part of the caption.

```
<!NOTATION tiff SYSTEM "image/tiff">
<!NOTATION bmp SYSTEM "image/bmp">
<!NOTATION eps SYSTEM "image/eps">
<!ELEMENT FIGURE (FIGREF, FG)>
<!ELEMENT FIGREF EMPTY>
<!ATTLIST FIGREF
    SRC    CDATA      #REQUIRED
    TYPE   NOTATION (tiff | bmp | eps) "tiff">
<!ELEMENT FG (FIGNUM, FDESC)>
<!ELEMENT FDESC %textual-elements;>
<!ELEMENT FIGNUM (#PCDATA)>
```

Now that you've created all these content elements, it's time to update the content-elements parameter entity to include them.

```
<!ENTITY % content-elements "(BT | CC | BL | NL | UL | GL
| ICON | TABLE | FIGURE)*">
```

Combining all this into one gigantic DTD file gives you something you can work with.

```
<!--Chapter DTD, version 1 -->
```

```
<!--Mandatory starting elements -->
<!ELEMENT CHAPTER (TOC0CT, INTRODUCTORY, ALEAF*)>
<!-- Chapter Title -->
<!ELEMENT TOC0CT (#PCDATA)>
<!--Chapter Introduction -->
<!ELEMENT INTRODUCTORY (BT+)>
<!--Common text elements. -->
<!ELEMENT CITATION (#PCDATA)>
<!ELEMENT USERACTION (#PCDATA)>
<!--Textual elements allows mixing w/ regular data -->
<!ENTITY % textual-elements
"( #PCDATA| CITATION| USERACTION )*">
<!--BT - Body text. Used for each paragraph -->
<!ELEMENT BT %textual-elements;>
<!--Content element allows multiple content types in
section contents-->
<!ENTITY % content-elements "(BT | CC | BL | NL | UL | GL
| ICON | TABLE | FIGURE)*">
<!--XLEAF elements behave like X-heads in previous-->
<!--Note the structure for XLEAF elements - BLEAF
elements can only appear in ALEAF elements, CLEAF
elements can only appear in BLEAF elements, etc. -->
<!ELEMENT ALEAF (TOC1A,BT,(%content-elements;|BLEAF)*)>
<!ELEMENT BLEAF (TOC2B,BT,(%content-elements;|CLEAF)*)>
<!ELEMENT CLEAF (C,BT,(%content-elements;|DLEAF)*)>
<!ELEMENT DLEAF (D,BT,(%content-elements;|ELEAF)*)>
<!ELEMENT ELEAF (E,BT,(%content-elements;)*)>
<!--Headers for leaf sections -->
<!--A Head - appears in Table of Contents -->
<!ELEMENT TOC1A (#PCDATA)>
<!--B Head - appears in Table of Contents -->
<!ELEMENT TOC2B (#PCDATA)>
<!--C, D, E heads do not appear in Table of Contents-->
<!ELEMENT C (#PCDATA)>
```

Continued

```
<!ELEMENT D (#PCDATA)>
<!ELEMENT E (#PCDATA)>
<!--Declarations for marking code listings -->
<!ELEMENT CC (LC?,CLINE+)>
<!--TYPE attribute differentiates code listings from text
output-->
<!ATTLIST CC TYPE (CODE|OUTPUT) "CODE">
<!--LC is list caption -->
<!ELEMENT LC (#PCDATA)>
<!--CLINE represents a single line of code-->
<!ELEMENT CLINE (#PCDATA)>
<!--Declarations for lists (bulleted, numbered, unordered
lists) -->
<!ELEMENT BL (BLINE+)>
<!ELEMENT NL (NLINE+)>
<!ELEMENT UL (ULINE+)>
<!--List contents (bulleted, numbered, unordered lists)--
>
<!ELEMENT BLINE %textual-elements;>
<!ELEMENT NLINE %textual-elements;>
<!ELEMENT ULINE %textual-elements;>
<!--Glossary Declarations -->
<!ELEMENT GL (GLITEM,GLDEFINITION)>
<!--Word being defined-->
<!ELEMENT GLITEM (#PCDATA)>
<!-Definition-->
<!ELEMENT GLDEFINITION %textual-elements;>
<!--Icon/Note Declarations -->
<!ELEMENT ICON (BT+)>
<!ATTLIST ICON
     TYPE     (NOTE|SHORTCUT|WARNING|TIP) "NOTE">
<!--Table Declarations -->
<!ELEMENT TABLE (TBC*,TH?,TR+,SN*)>
<!--Table Caption -->
<!ELEMENT TBC (#PCDATA)>
```

```
<!--Table Headers -->
<!ELEMENT TH (TBH+)>
<!ELEMENT TBH (#PCDATA)>
<!--Table Rows -->
<!ELEMENT TR (TB+)>
<!--Table Body (sim to HTML TD) -->
<!ELEMENT TB %textual-elements;>
<!--Table Source Note -->
<!ELEMENT SN %textual-elements;>
<!--Graphic Type Declarations -->
<!NOTATION tiff SYSTEM "viewer.exe">
<!NOTATION bmp SYSTEM "viewer.exe">
<!NOTATION eps SYSTEM "viewer.exe">
<!--Figure Declarations -->
<!ELEMENT FIGURE (FIGREF, FG)>
<!ELEMENT FIGREF EMPTY>
<!ATTLIST FIGREF
    SRC   CDATA      #REQUIRED
    TYPE  NOTATION (tiff | bmp | eps) "tiff">
<!--FG is figure description -->
<!ELEMENT FG (FIGNUM, FDESC)>
<!ELEMENT FDESC %textual-elements;>
<!ELEMENT FIGNUM (#PCDATA)>
```

Unfortunately, a gargantuan DTD requires a gargantuan document to test it. The following code is clearly only test code, not a real chapter (although I could increase the thickness of this book dramatically by including another one). Nevertheless, this code should test most of these elements in their natural habitats.

```
<?xml version="1.0" encoding="UTF-8"?>
<!DOCTYPE CHAPTER SYSTEM "chapter.dtd">
<CHAPTER>
<TOCOCT>How to code XML</TOCOCT>
<INTRODUCTORY>
```

Continued

```
<BT>This is a chapter on how to code XML.</BT>
<BT>This is another bit of intro info.</BT>
</INTRODUCTORY>
<ALEAF>
<TOC1A>Subhead A1</TOC1A>
<BT>This is A1, from <CITATION>my
document</CITATION>.</BT>
<CC><LC>This is a listing</LC>
<CLINE>I don't know what to do in this program!</CLINE>
<CLINE>I don't know what to do in this program!</CLINE>
</CC>
<BT>You could have typed <USERACTION>exit</USERACTION>
instead of running the parser.</BT>
</ALEAF>
<ALEAF>
<TOC1A>Subhead A2</TOC1A>
<BT>This is A2. We'll start with a table, and move on to
a B leaf.</BT>
<TABLE><TBC>This is a sample table</TBC>
<TH><TBH>Column 1: Time</TBH><TBH>Column 2:
Money</TBH></TH>
<TR><TB>Never enough</TB><TB>Can always use
more</TB></TR>
<TR><TB>More than enough</TB><TB>Had enough to begin
with</TB></TR>
<SN>From <CITATION>The book of nonsense</CITATION></SN>
</TABLE>
<BLEAF>
<TOC2B>Subhead B1</TOC2B>
<BT>A C leaf will follow, after the bulleted list.</BT>
<BL>
<BLINE>This is the first item of a bulleted list</BLINE>
<BLINE>This is the second item of a bulleted list</BLINE>
</BL>
<CLEAF>
```

```
<C>Subhead C1</C>
<BT>This is a C leaf that contains a numbered list and
a figure.</BT>
<NL>
<NLINE>1. This is the first item.</NLINE>
<NLINE>2. This is the second item.</NLINE>
</NL>
<FIGURE><FIGREF SRC="image.tif" TYPE="tiff"/>
<FG><FIGNUM>101.12</FIGNUM><FDESC> - The wild boar at
rest.</FDESC></FG></FIGURE>
</CLEAF>
<CLEAF>
<C>Subhead C2</C>
<BT>This C leaf contains an unnumbered list and a
glossary item.</BT>
<UL>
<ULINE>This isn't in any order.</ULINE>
<ULINE>Who needs order?</ULINE>
<ULINE>Order just gets in the way.</ULINE>
</UL>
<GL><GLITEM>Order</GLITEM><GLDEFINITION> Something that
gets in the way frequently.</GLDEFINITION></GL>
</CLEAF>
</BLEAF>
<ICON TYPE="NOTE"><BT>Hope you enjoyed the
chapter!</BT></ICON>
</ALEAF>
</CHAPTER>
```

Figure 19-6 shows the top portion of the validated XML in the
Internet Explorer 5.0 browser.

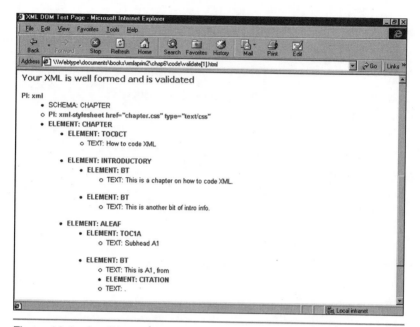

Figure 19-6 *A validated (though not necessarily meaningful) chapter*

A CSS Style Sheet for the Chapter DTD

A style sheet for the Chapter DTD won't be too hard to develop in XML, even though the publishers may grumble about losing the fine control they had with previous desktop publishing tools such as QuarkXPress. Even though XML's supporting style technologies will enable some fairly intricate formatting, it's still not quite what print designers are used to.

Note

For more general information about Cascading Style Sheets, including lists of selectors and properties, see Chapter 12.

The format of this particular style sheet has very little to do with the way the document is presented in the final printing — it is just a generic representation that helps the author and the editors see the book. After the editing is over, the production staff can in theory just replace the style sheet with a style sheet customized for the look of a particular book and have the same elements fall into their proper place for printing.

 Note

Documents created with the Chapter DTD will probably be combined with other chapters as part of a larger structure, which may have its own formatting rules. For the purposes of this style sheet, assume that chapters start and end on their own pages and that the larger document's structure will not interfere with any of the styling.

The style for the CHAPTER element marks itself as a block element, making itself a unit of text separate from any surrounding material. It also sets the default font information for the entire document:

```
CHAPTER {
        display:block;
        font-family:serif;
        font-size:12pt;
        font-weight: normal;
        font-style:normal;

}
```

I've avoided using actual font names throughout this style sheet, preferring to use generic family names such as serif and monotype. You can substitute real font names if you prefer, but keep in mind that not all computers will have your chosen set of fonts.

The TOCOCT opening headline is displayed in bold 24-point type. Note the padding-bottom attribute, which specifies the amount of space that should follow the headline.

```
TOCOCT {
    display:block;
    font-size:24pt;
    font-weight:bold;
    padding-bottom:9pt;
}
```

The CITATION and USERACTION elements will italicize words within the text, but they don't create separate blocks. Setting the display to inline (which is the default) makes it clear that these elements will not break up paragraphs.

```
CITATION {
    display:inline;
    font-style:italic;
}
USERACTION {
    display:inline;
    font-weight:bold;
}
```

BT is the primary element for displaying text. Each BT unit is the rough equivalent of a paragraph, so the BT element is clearly a block.

```
BT {
    display:block;
    line-height:24pt;
}
```

The XLEAF elements all share similar formatting. Each begins a block element, separated from the previous element by a preset amount of space, which is set in the padding-top value of CSS.

```
ALEAF {
    display:block;
    padding-top:12pt;
}
BLEAF {
```

```
    display:block;
    padding-top:9pt;
}
CLEAF {
    display:block;
    padding-top:9pt;
}

DLEAF {
    display:block;
    padding-top:9pt;
}

ELEAF {
    display:block;
    padding-top:9pt;
}
```

The headlines for the leaf elements are themselves block elements, each with its own set of formatting.

```
TOC1A {
    display:block;
    padding-bottom:6pt;
    font-size:18pt;
    font-weight:bold;
}

TOC2B {
    display:block;
    padding-bottom:6pt;
    font-size:14pt;
    font-weight:bold;
}
C {
```

Continued

```
    display:block;
    font-size:14pt;
    font-weight:bold;
    font-style:italic;
}

D {

    display:block;
    font-size:12pt;
    font-weight:bold;
    font-style:italic;
}

E {

    display:block;
    font-size:14pt;
    font-style:italic;
}
```

The code elements, the elements most dramatically simplified compared to the original chapter style sheet, take the most advantage of the power of CSS and XML. The extra spacing, which in Word required four different styles, is easily included in the definition of the CC element. Because the CC element encloses the caption and the code completely, it can supply the necessary padding at the top and bottom of the code listing without requiring that the author apply extra styling to the actual code.

```
CC {

    display:block;
    padding-top:9pt;
    padding-bottom:9pt;
    text-indent:.5in;
    font-family:monospace;
    line-height:18pt;
}
```

```
LC {
    display:block;
    padding-bottom:6pt;
    font-weight:bold;
}
```

```
CLINE {display:block}
```

The list elements can set the styles necessary for the list items they enclose using Cascading Style Sheets' fairly comprehensive set of list styles.

```
BL {
    display:block;
    text-indent:1in;
    line-height:18pt;
    list-style-type:disc;
    list-style-position:outside;
}
```

```
NL {
    display:block;
    text-indent:1in;
    line-height:18pt;
    list-style-type:decimal;
    list-style-position:outside;
}
```

```
UL {
    display:block;
    line-height:18pt;
    list-style-type:square;
    list-style-position:outside;
}
```

The content of those lists needs only to identify itself as a list item.

```
BLINE {display:list-item}
NLINE {display:list-item}
ULINE {display:list-item}
```

The GL element is a little more complex. Because glossary entries have a one-line item description followed by a multiline indented definition, the GL element sets its text indent to −1 inch, which produces the required hanging indent.

```
GL {
    display:block;
    text-indent:-1in;
    padding-bottom:9pt;
    line-height:24pt;
}


GLITEM {
    display:inline;
    font-weight:bold;
}


GLDEFINITION {display:inline}
```

The ICON element simply indents its text one inch and applies appropriate padding and spacing. The NOTE, SHORTCUT, WARNING, and TIP elements don't need styles at this point because they have no content at all. In final production, they must be replaced with graphics.

```
ICON {
    display:block;
    text:indent:1in;
    padding-top:9pt;
    padding-bottom:9pt;
    line-height:18pt;
}
```

Although Cascading Style Sheets Level 1 provided formatting only for text objects in the main flow of a document, relying on HTML's TABLE element and its children to build tables, CSS Level 2 provides a complete set of display properties for assembling tables from arbitrary elements. The `table`, `inline-table`, `table-row-group`, `table-header-group`, `table-footer-group`, `table-row`, `table-column-group`, `table-column`, `table-cell`, and `table-caption` values for the display property provide a construction kit much more flexible than the HTML model.

```
TABLE {display:table;
    padding-top:9pt;
    padding-bottom:6pt;
    }


TBC {
    display:caption;
    font-weight:bold;
    font-style:italic;
    padding-bottom:9pt;
}


TH{
    display:table-header-group;
    padding-bottom:9pt;
}


TBH {
    display:table-cell;
    font-weight:bold;
}


TR {
    display:table-row;
```

Continued

```
        line-height:18pt;
}


TB {display:table-cell}

SN {display:table-footer-group;
        font-size:10pt;
        padding-top:6pt;
        padding-bottom:6pt;
}
```

FIGURE elements are always centered on the page. The FIGREF
element that actually places the figure picture doesn't need a style,
unless extra padding is necessary. The FIGREF will inherit the centering from the FIGURE element. The figure caption (the FG element) will also inherit the centering, and the FIGNUM will appear
in bold.

```
FIGURE {
        display:block;
        text-align:center;
}


FG  {
display:block;
font-style:italic;
}
FIGNUM {
display:inline;
font-weight:bold;
}


FDESC {
display:inline;
}
```

Eventually, you will be able to use styles like these to present complex XML documents in a browser with little difficulty. Changing styles with Cascading Style Sheets is extremely simple, making it easy to present documents in different formats aimed at different media. Although CSS doesn't provide all the answers, it provides enough structure to build a reasonably well-formatted XML document. More complex documents (such as those requiring transformations) may need XSL's more powerful tools, but for this level of formatting CSS is just fine.

Pass 2: Toward a Cleaner DTD

The real test of the previous DTD will come as authors and the production department put it to use, stretching it and finding its weaknesses. Several significant weaknesses arose during the preceding discussion, but we overlooked them for the sake of compatibility with the original Word-based version. A second round, unhindered by the political need for compatibility, may improve the DTD to make it more extensible. Three areas could definitely use some structural improvements — the leaf structure (ALEAF, BLEAF, and so on), lists, and icons — and many elements could use friendlier names.

Note

These improvements are mostly technical improvements that demonstrate some of the more interesting features of XML. They are not guaranteed to improve user productivity, however. Some users may find the older structures easier to understand. DTD developers will frequently need to compromise between a more "elegant" technical solution and a solution that is more user-friendly. Automated tools for entering information will help bridge that gap, but it may be a while before they're accepted.

Even though the ALEAF/BLEAF/CLEAF structure makes sense to a reader who can scan through it, it requires a considerably larger number of elements than a more generic leaf version might. A more generic structure would use elements that behave similarly but aren't labeled A or B or C. Creating a generic leaf structure involves recursion — allowing an element to include another element of the same type within itself. Recursion has several meanings in different contexts, and in some of those contexts can lead to endless loops. XML permits elements to include themselves in the list of accepted child elements, but it does not, for example, permit entities to refer to files that then refer to the original file. For most purposes, the following example of recursion is the practical limit of recursion in XML.

In the following DTD, a LEAF element must contain a TITLE element and may contain additional LEAF elements and PCDATA.

```
<!ELEMENT TEST (LEAF+)>
<!ELEMENT LEAF (HEADER,(LEAF|CONTENT)*)>
<!ELEMENT CONTENT (#PCDATA)>
<!ELEMENT HEADER (#PCDATA)>
```

The following document takes advantage of the new LEAF element structure to create several layers of LEAF elements:

```
<?xml version="1.0" encoding="UTF-8"?>
<!DOCTYPE TEST SYSTEM "recurs.dtd">
<TEST>
<LEAF>
<HEADER>Top-layer Leaf 1</HEADER>
<CONTENT>This is a leaf.</CONTENT>
<LEAF>
<HEADER>Second-layer Leaf 1</HEADER>
<CONTENT>This is a leaf.</CONTENT>
</LEAF>
<LEAF>
<HEADER>Second-layer Leaf 2</HEADER>
<CONTENT>This is a leaf. </CONTENT>
<LEAF>
<HEADER>Third-layer Leaf 1</HEADER>
<CONTENT>This is a leaf.</CONTENT>
```

```
</LEAF>
</LEAF>
</LEAF>
<LEAF>
<HEADER>Top-layer Leaf 2</HEADER>
<CONTENT>This is a leaf.</CONTENT>
</LEAF>
</TEST>
```

Parsing this document reveals its layers of structure, as shown in Figure 19-7.

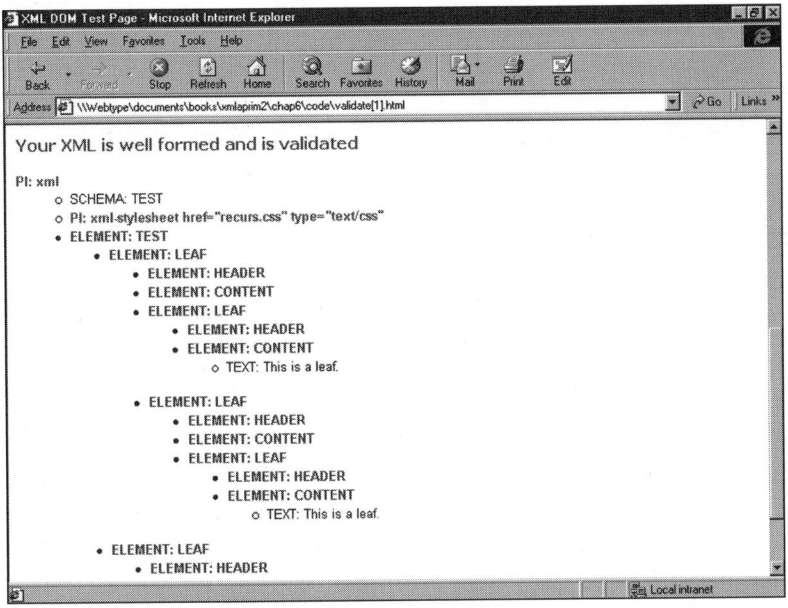

Figure 19-7 *Using a leaf structure provides a cleaner and more abstract means of nesting content.*

Using this structure enables you to simplify the following code from this:

```
<!ELEMENT ALEAF (TOC1A,BT,(%content-elements;|BLEAF)*)>
<!ELEMENT BLEAF (TOC2B,BT,(%content-elements;|CLEAF)*)>
<!ELEMENT CLEAF (C,BT,(%content-elements;|DLEAF)*)>
<!ELEMENT DLEAF (D,BT,(%content-elements;|ELEAF)*)>
<!ELEMENT ELEAF (E,BT,(%content-elements;)*)>
<!ELEMENT TOC1A (#PCDATA)>
<!ELEMENT TOC2B (#PCDATA)>
<!ELEMENT C (#PCDATA)>
<!ELEMENT D (#PCDATA)>
<!ELEMENT E (#PCDATA)>
```

to this:

```
<!ELEMENT LEAF (HEADER,BT,( %content-elements;| LEAF)*)>
<!ELEMENT HEADER (#PCDATA)>
```

The LEAF element replaces all its predecessor leaf structures, and the HEADER element replaces TOC1A, TOC2B, and C, D, and E. Whenever an author creates a new leaf, it acts as a subsection of the document. The level at which it appears (such as A, B, C, D, or E) is determined purely by context. This may be disorienting at first, at least until the tools catch up to the possibilities.

This approach also requires some minor changes in the styles I presented previously. The CSS specification allows for contextual selectors, which enable you to define styles based on the element type and also on the elements in which the element you're styling is nested. In this example, because all the subleaves (below the AHEAD) use the same padding value, the new style for the LEAF element is reasonably simple.

```
LEAF {
    display:block;
    padding-top:12pt;
}

LEAF LEAF {
```

```
    display:block;
    padding-top:9pt;
}
```

This style definition states that all LEAF elements will start out with a default padding of 12 points on top. However, all LEAF elements that are enclosed by other LEAF elements (which includes all layers below the top) will have 9 points of padding on top. The headers are more difficult, but they use the same rule.

```
LEAF HEADER {
    display:block;
    padding-bottom:6pt;
    font-size:18pt;
    font-weight:bold;
}


LEAF LEAF HEADER {
    display:block;
    padding-bottom:6pt;
    font-size:14pt;
    font-weight:bold;
 }


LEAF LEAF LEAF HEADER {
    display:block;
    font-size:14pt;
    font-weight:bold;
    font-style:italic;
}


LEAF LEAF LEAF LEAF HEADER {
    display:block;
    font-size:12pt;
    font-weight:bold;
```

Continued

```
        font-style:italic;
}


LEAF LEAF LEAF LEAF LEAF HEADER {
        display:block;
        font-size:14pt;
        font-style:italic;
}
```

The top line of these style settings is the old TOC1A header—a header inside one layer of LEAF elements. The second line is TOC2B, and so forth. Instead of being tied to a specific named element, the style of the headline is dependent upon its position in the hierarchy of LEAF elements, as shown in Figure 19-8.

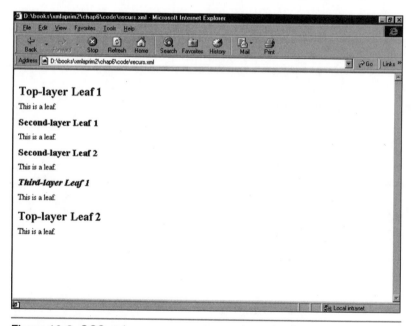

Figure 19-8 *CSS styles can use context to determine formatting.*

The lists could also stand significant improvement. For compatibility, I created three elements: BL, NL, and UL. You can combine these into a single LIST element with an attribute identifying the type of list.

```
<!ELEMENT LIST (LINE+)>
<!ATTLIST LINE
    TYPE CDATA (BULLETED|NUMBERED|UNORDERED)>
```

Even though this approach is tempting, for now it is limited by the ability of the processing application to keep up with the attribute. Cascading Style Sheets, for example, can respond to element context, but can react to the CLASS attribute only. (Renaming TYPE as CLASS would, of course, solve this problem, but a CLASS attribute might need to reflect more than the type of list.) When XSL and other more context-sensitive style systems come into more general use, it may or may not be time for this change, depending to a large extent on the preferences of those using the tools.

At present, the list items all have their own elements: NLINE, BLINE, and ULINE. You can combine these into one LINE element as long as the processing software can keep up. The resulting declarations are as follows:

```
<!ELEMENT BL (LINE+)>
<!ELEMENT NL (LINE+)>
<!ELEMENT UL (LINE+)>
<!ELEMENT LINE %textual-elements;>
```

The BL, NL, and UL elements keep their previous style definitions, and the line element uses a style declaration very similar to that of its predecessors.

```
LINE {display:list-item}
```

The last improvement I suggest is using longer names for most of the styles. XML doesn't offer a SHORTREF declaration, as SGML does, to provide for abbreviated versions of full names, so longer names will result in more markup and longer files. Still, if anyone must read the actual files, he or she will have a much easier time figuring out what's going where.

Creating Wrapper Documents

Although creating new XML formats for information seems like the right solution in many cases, moving from legacy formats to XML is a lot of work and not something that will always produce a return good enough to justify the effort. (I'm a very loud supporter of XML and believe quite firmly that breaking documents down into the smallest possible components is a good idea; even so, not every document is that valuable, and not every project can afford to throw away its legacy information.) In many cases, using an XML wrapper around the legacy information can be a good first step. It isn't appropriate for all information; information that isn't easily represented as a series of letters and numbers should usually be left alone. That still leaves an enormous amount of information passed in various non-XML text formats that are available for processing.

The simplest kind of information to wrap is a plain-text document. Although WYSIWYG editing may have driven out many common uses of plain-text formatting, many documents (including Internet Engineering Task Force RFCs) are still distributed as plain text, formatted with whitespace — tabs, line breaks, and ordinary spaces. The old typewriter-based ways live on as the simplest format on the Web. Converting these documents to heavily marked-up XML is difficult, but the first level of conversion isn't:

```
<?xml version="1.0" encoding="UTF-8"?>
<?xml-stylesheet href="wrap.css" type="text/css"?>
<wrapper xml:space="preserve">

Text with line breaks goes here.

</wrapper>
```

The style-sheet document is similarly simple:

```
wrapper {
    display:block;
    white-space:pre;
}
```

If the whitespace in the document isn't significant, the style-sheet processing instruction and the `xml:space` attribute can be dropped as well, making for a very simple wrapper. (Because the whitespace property won't permit automatic line breaking when whitespace is significant, as with the HTML PRE element, displaying documents like this that don't include line breaks can be problematic.) Table 19-3 lists the possible values of the whitespace property in CSS and their meanings. No `wrap` value is available — in all cases where whitespace is treated as significant, line breaks must be stated explicitly.

Table 19-3 *Values for the CSS2 Whitespace Property*

Whitespace Value	Meaning
normal	Whitespace characters will generally be treated as insignificant; multiple consecutive whitespace characters will be condensed to a single space. (This is the default, whether or not the `xml:space` attribute was set to `preserve`.) This behavior is the same as typical HTML browser behavior.
pre	All whitespace is treated as significant; lines break only at newline characters (or generated newline characters, as with **BR** in HTML) within the text. No condensing of multiple whitespace characters will take place.
nowrap	Whitespace is treated as significant, but newline characters are ignored. Lines are broken only at generated newline characters (as with **BR** in HTML).
inherit	This element will use the whitespace behavior of its parent element.

Wrapping entire documents in a single root element isn't a good long-term approach for document management — it does away with nearly all of XML's advantages. Still, it can be a good starting place for further markup. Strategies that permit processing of different levels of markup, from almost none to heavy-duty content-based markup, make it possible for organizations and people with varying levels of commitment and resources to get started using a standard. (It can also make it difficult to get them to move beyond the lowest common denominator, so be careful.)

Leaving legacy data intact within a genuinely marked-up XML document may still be a good idea. The Weather Observation Markup Format (OMF at `http://zowie.metnet.navy.mil/~spawar/JMV-TNG/XML/OMF.html`), for example, still keeps the text of the original legacy reports inside its more thoroughly processed versions of that data, making it easier for the new systems and the old to communicate. In some cases, XML is great as a format for representing additional information about a document—metadata like author, date created, copyright, and so on—but isn't necessary for the rest of the document, which already has its own encoding. Although in the long run it may be more sensible to migrate to a single standard, such hybrid solutions are likely to be around for a number of years.

In the next chapter you move on from simple documents based on print and Web models to more complex documents intended to enhance commercial document interchange. You use many of the same tools but expand on XML's ability to create machine-readable documents.

Chapter 20

XML for Commerce

Perhaps the biggest advantage of XML is that it enables people and companies to exchange information more clearly and completely than did previous formats. XML promises to capitalize on two key trends in the electronic world: the increasing use of Web sites for information distribution and the increasing use of electronic ordering and invoicing. XML can make Web sites more usable by providing more precisely described, easily searchable information while simultaneously making the process of business-to-business communication easier by providing an intelligible (and relatively cheap) foundation for data-interchange formats.

 Caution

With the first two examples in this chapter you explore the process of using XML to create commerce-focused DTDs and schemas. Although the prospect of creating your own DTDs for these functions may seem exciting, you should always check to see if an industry-standard DTD is already available. Creating your own DTD can give you a well-tailored solution to your system's particular needs, but it may also cut you off from the rest of your industry or require a budget for transformations between vocabularies. Commerce applications have the most at stake in standardization because search engines and other applications must be able to count on the same elements having the same meaning no matter what the source. Compatibility will be more important than a perfect solution in most cases involving multiple organizations. The final part of this chapter, where I discuss industry initiatives already in progress, should help you find what's been done already.

Who (and What) Will Be Reading My XML?

The documents in the previous chapter were meant, in the end, to be read by humans. XML makes the documents easier for machines to manipulate, providing a good way to apply formatting and possibly store the data, but in the long run all those documents will be read by people. The applications in this chapter take advantage of several additional advantages of XML. First, XML enables developers to create documents that both humans and machines can read. Markup tags may look like labels in English (or another language) to the developer, but to the computer they're simply labels that help direct it to the data it needs for processing, which is stored neatly in nested structures. Second, XML offers considerably more flexibility than the other options currently available for data interchange between systems. You can use XML to represent the contents of a relational database, or to represent the contents of an old hierarchical database or even the latest object-oriented database. At the same time, XML can easily represent document information, grouping information, or simple lists. Finally, XML provides a structure that programmers can easily manipulate using recursive structures that are widely available in most programming tools. The wide availability of XML parsers typically makes it easier to integrate an XML parser with a program than it would be to develop a custom format and write a parser for it.

These strengths give XML a range of capabilities far broader than those of other interchange formats. Although thousands of systems are already available for trading data between computers, none of them offers this much flexibility in a structure that is so easy to program. XML obviously won't solve all the problems involved in data interchange, but it still represents a major step forward. XML is definitely a generalist's tool. Given enough time and money, there will always be a more efficient or more beautiful way to perform the tasks I describe later in the chapter, but exquisite hand-crafting doesn't always pay off.

XML's combination of flexibility and structure suit it well to a group of applications that seek out information. Search engines and agents can consider the additional information available in the DTDs and schemas of these documents when they try to categorize or index them, and the labels inside documents themselves provide a rich source of information. Making full use of these capabilities will require some standardization of vocabularies — programs will have a hard time making sense of elements such as TODAYSVERYSPECIALPRICE and SALETODAYONLY. (PRICE probably makes considerably more sense).

Search engines have an especially difficult task gathering and sorting information in its current amorphous state. The addition of meaningful, even standardized vocabularies and structures should make search engines better at finding relevant information. Agents usually operate on a smaller scale, seeking out choice bits of information for particular users, but they stand to gain in the same way, possibly achieving the status computer scientists have claimed for them for so long.

Automated search tools bring up an additional issue — the dangers of letting programs surf the Web. Automated tools are happy to sort through megabytes of information they discard on their way to the piece of information they care about, and can generate a lot of traffic very quickly. If you expect your information to be handled by programs rather than by humans, you shouldn't use traffic expectations based on human-oriented Web sites, though you may still be using the same toolset.

Tip

The Web already has a partial solution to the problem of automated visitors, in the form of the robots.txt file. When an agent or search engine visits a site, it should examine this file to find out where on the site it is welcome and then avoid all proscribed areas. Details are available at `http://info.webcrawler.com/mak/projects/robots/norobots.html` or `http://www.searchtools.com/robots/robots-txt.html`. Although robots.txt is not an "official" standard, it is widely accepted by search-engine developers and should help prevent programs from crawling all over your site, slowing it down, or possibly crashing it.

Developing documents for computers to read really isn't much more difficult than developing documents for people to read. Computers are fairly predictable, and the strong structures of XML should make it easier to create information that can be used by many different—even extremely different—processing applications.

Presenting Goods or Services

Even though the HTML catalog in the previous chapter may have been acceptable as a way to present information on a page, and its XML transformation may have added some searchability, it can still stand some significant improvement. Jane's Catalog, the main competitor to Joe's Catalog, which I explored in the previous chapter, is embarking on this more difficult course. Building a new catalog format from the ground up may cost Jane some effort and adjustment, but it should create a more automatable catalog that is easier to manage.

As long as orders came in exclusively over the telephone, Jane was comfortable having a Web catalog that simply recreated her paper catalog. As the costs of her 800 number rose, she began to wonder whether she shouldn't revise her system and enable Web users to order over her cheaper Internet connection. At the same time, she's moving her catalog from the ragtag group of desktop publishing files they've used in the past into a new database system capable of holding her items and all their associated data — even pictures! Because Jane doesn't spend much on advertising, she would like automated tools that easily understand her catalog, making it easy for buyers to find the items they want. XML sounds as though it might give her a boost in that direction, and it should be a good fit for the database systems she's installing as well. The challenge is to create a catalog application that can present her data attractively to customers while lessening the demands on her order-entry department.

Instead of working from the catalog as it is currently presented on the Web, you can start by examining Jane's methods of assembling the catalog and processing orders. When Jane's computer receives an order (from a telephone operator at the moment), it processes payment, typically by credit card, and prints a packing slip in the warehouse. Workers in the warehouse find the items and ship them out immediately. The order-entry department would like to see the Web application feed their computer a simple set of information: payment information, shipping information, and the list of products to be ordered (by item number) and quantities. This is a fairly easy set of data to deliver with existing Web tools. Eventually, on the customer side, Jane would like the application to display a full invoice to the customer, complete with shipping costs. Part of the long-term motivation for moving to XML has to do with an interest in making the user's Web browser do as much work as possible, sparing her servers the trouble of processing information that client machines can handle just as easily. This saves Jane expensive bandwidth and processing effort. Even though XML may not be able to achieve this today, XML's flexibility will make it possible for humans (with the aid of a style sheet) to view the same information that computers are scouring.

At this point, XML has several drawbacks as a tool for Web application development. Browsers (and only the most recent browsers) provide different levels of support for XML styling and scripting, and issues such as user interaction with generic XML documents effectively prohibit XML documents from serving as comprehensive interfaces at present. Special-purpose XML vocabularies, such as Netscape's XUL, or the W3C's XHTML and SVG, may offer possibilities, but using them will require a transformation between the catalog vocabulary and the target vocabulary. For now, the catalog format will be a foundation for other efforts, not the interface itself, though enough interface information will be in the catalog for human readers to explore it. The fact that Jane's computers will be generating static XML from a database will also reduce difficulties by allowing some repetitive information to appear in the XML markup.

Jane's Catalog is loosely organized into pages that group together related products. The groups are determined informally by the team that builds the paper catalog. The electronic catalog should preserve these groupings, making it easy for customers to flip back and forth between the two versions. All the grouping information is stored in the database as well, making it much easier for a script to churn out pages based on a set of queries. Jane just needs a set of elements that can present the catalog data elegantly, with minimal processing overhead, and that can easily adapt to the upcoming improvements in scripting and document object models while still accommodating the needs of the present.

Describing the document structure with a DTD

You can start by building a DTD and then convert it to an XML Schema with some refinements. The top level of this DTD is the group—all members of a group will be presented in the same document.

```
<!ELEMENT GROUP (GROUPNAME, ITEM+,LEGALNOTICE)>
<!ATTLIST GROUP
      GROUPLINK CDATA #IMPLIED>
```

The GROUPLINK attribute holds a key value that will make it easy for a parser at Jane's to link to the original database record for troubleshooting or other information gathering. The GROUP element begins with a GROUPNAME element, which is effectively a headline for the page, and ends with a LEGALNOTICE element, which will contain the usual warnings about typos and pricing. It is probably unlikely that a search engine or agent would look for LEGALNOTICE as an element, but it does make formatting the fine print easier.

```
<!ELEMENT GROUPNAME (#PCDATA)>
<!ELEMENT LEGALNOTICE (#PCDATA)>
```

Under this headline are catalog ITEM elements. ITEM elements contain a variety of other elements, including ITEM subelements that represent products affiliated with their parent ITEM. Like the GROUP element, the ITEM element may have an attribute that connects it to its database entry.

```
<!ELEMENT ITEM (PRODUCTNAME, DESCRIPTION?,PRICING,
ITEM*)>
<!ATTLIST ITEM
      ITEMLINK CDATA #IMPLIED>
```

The PRODUCTNAME element, like the GROUPNAME element, is really just a headline. Because the elements receive different formatting and may need to be addressed differently through scripts, the two elements are created separately.

```
<!ELEMENT PRODUCTNAME (#PCDATA)>
```

The DESCRIPTION element must be able to handle a variety of content. (Remember that the DESCRIPTION element is optional — it won't be used for subitems.) Catalog entries don't often include italic or bold text, but periodically they do, mostly for book titles. Most product descriptions are single paragraphs, but occasionally an entry can go on for several paragraphs. Many descriptions even include pictures. As a result, the DESCRIPTION element must contain PARAGRAPH elements, which themselves contain a motley assortment of other elements, and IMG elements, which are modeled after their HTML equivalent.

```
<!ELEMENT DESCRIPTION (PARAGRAPH | IMG)*>
<!ELEMENT IMG EMPTY>
<!ATTLIST IMG
     SRC CDATA #REQUIRED
     HEIGHT CDATA #REQUIRED
     WIDTH CDATA #REQUIRED>
<!ELEMENT PARAGRAPH (#PCDATA | CITATION | EMPHASIS |
HIGHLIGHT)*>
<!ELEMENT CITATION (#PCDATA)>
<!ELEMENT EMPHASIS (#PCDATA)>
<!ELEMENT HIGHLIGHT (#PCDATA)>
```

This simple set of markup tags should enable Jane and staff to recreate the descriptions for all the items in the catalog. Although this is exciting for the design staff, it doesn't have nearly the effect on the order processing as the contents of the PRICING element. The PRICING element contains all the price, shipping-weight, delivery, availability, and warranty information, as well as the button that executes the script that adds the item to the shopping cart.

```
<!ELEMENT PRICING (PRODNUM,MARKER?,PRICE, MARKER?,
SHIPPING, MARKER?, DELIVERY, MARKER?, AVAIL, MARKER?,
WARRANTY)>
<!ELEMENT PRODNUM (#PCDATA)>
<!ATTLIST PRODNUM
      ID     id      #REQUIRED>
<!ELEMENT MARKER(#PCDATA)>
<!ELEMENT PRICE(#PCDATA)>
<!ATTLIST PRICE
      ID     id      #REQUIRED>
<!ELEMENT SHIPPING (#PCDATA)>
<!ATTLIST SHIPPING
      ID     id      #REQUIRED>
```

```
<!ELEMENT DELIVERY (#PCDATA)>
<!ATTLIST DELIVERY
        ID      id      #REQUIRED>
<!ELEMENT AVAIL (#PCDATA)>
<!ATTLIST AVAIL
        ID      id      #REQUIRED>
<!ELEMENT WARRANTY (#PCDATA)>
```

Jane is reasonably confident that her warehouse will have the items listed in stock and uses the AVAIL element mostly to generate advance orders by indicating when items are coming but haven't yet arrived in the warehouse. A company that runs out of stock more frequently would probably need to generate its pages dynamically and reflect its current stock situation with more precise tags, such as ONHAND for the number available or ONORDER to indicate when the item should arrive. Keep in mind, however, that you don't want to reveal your entire inventory to your competition.

The PRICING element is a list of the parts required for order processing, including all the non-customer information needed to build a packing list. Optional MARKER elements are interspersed throughout to enable descriptions such as Price: to appear without cluttering the PRICE element. This approach, though a bit verbose, averts the loose structure of a mixed content model and enables the content creators to retain control over the number and sequence of PRODNUM, PRICE, SHIPPING, DELIVERY, AVAIL, and WARRANTY elements. The MARKER information is really just formatting and must be kept separate from the content of the other elements.

Combining all this information produces a DTD that encapsulates the data required for Jane's Catalog to present its information to the customer and return that information to the order department:

```
<!ELEMENT GROUP (GROUPNAME, ITEM+,LEGALNOTICE)>
<!ATTLIST GROUP
        GROUPLINK CDATA #IMPLIED>
<!ELEMENT GROUPNAME (#PCDATA)>
```

Continued

```
<!ELEMENT LEGALNOTICE (#PCDATA)>
<!ELEMENT ITEM (PRODUCTNAME, DESCRIPTION?,PRICING,
ITEM*)>
<!ATTLIST ITEM
      ITEMLINK CDATA #IMPLIED>
<!ELEMENT PRODUCTNAME (#PCDATA)>
<!ELEMENT DESCRIPTION (PARAGRAPH | IMG)*>
<!ELEMENT IMG EMPTY>
<!ATTLIST IMG
     SRC CDATA #REQUIRED
     HEIGHT CDATA #REQUIRED
     WIDTH CDATA #REQUIRED>
<!ELEMENT PARAGRAPH (#PCDATA | CITATION | EMPHASIS |
HIGHLIGHT)*>
<!ELEMENT CITATION (#PCDATA)>
<!ELEMENT EMPHASIS (#PCDATA)>
<!ELEMENT HIGHLIGHT (#PCDATA)>
<!ELEMENT PRICING (PRODNUM,MARKER?,PRICE, MARKER?,
SHIPPING, MARKER?, DELIVERY, MARKER?, AVAIL, MARKER?,
WARRANTY)>
<!ELEMENT PRODNUM (#PCDATA)>
<!ATTLIST PRODNUM
      ID     ID      #REQUIRED>
<!ELEMENT MARKER(#PCDATA)>
<!ELEMENT PRICE(#PCDATA)>
<!ATTLIST PRICE
      ID     ID      #REQUIRED>
<!ELEMENT SHIPPING (#PCDATA)>
<!ATTLIST SHIPPING
      ID     ID      #REQUIRED>
<!ELEMENT DELIVERY (#PCDATA)>
<!ATTLIST DELIVERY
      ID     ID      #REQUIRED>
<!ELEMENT AVAIL (#PCDATA)>
<!ATTLIST AVAIL
```

```
     ID     ID     #REQUIRED>
<!ELEMENT WARRANTY (#PCDATA)>
```

The end result of this process is a structure that Jane's Catalog can use both for transmitting information to users and for processing this information to send orders back to the ordering system. (Those orders could be sent in an XML format, but that's another project. The preceding DTD includes just the information that a client-side processor would need to build a full packing list and invoice of ordered goods.)

A sample page from Jane's Catalog, generated by her database system, might look like the following:

```
<?xml version="1.0" standalone="no" encoding="UTF-8"?>
<!DOCTYPE GROUP SYSTEM "janes.dtd">
<GROUP GROUPLINK="23AA34FAB1">
<GROUPNAME>Pocket Calculating Devices</GROUPNAME>
<ITEM>
<PRODUCTNAME>Mortgage Calculator</PRODUCTNAME>
<DESCRIPTION><PARAGRAPH>Ever want to know precisely how
much of your house you own? What your monthly payments
would be if you refinanced? Mortgage-lovers will
appreciate this handy gadget. This calculator allows
comparisons between owning and renting, explores the
impact of inflation on your bank's profit margin, and
makes it easy to plan ahead.</PARAGRAPH></DESCRIPTION>
<PRICING><PRODNUM ID="I1024">1024</PRODNUM>
<MARKER>Price: $</MARKER>
<PRICE ID="I1024P">20.00</PRICE>
<MARKER>Shipping: $</MARKER>
<SHIPPING ID="I1024S">3.00</SHIPPING>
<MARKER>Delivery: </MARKER>
<DELIVERY ID="I1024D">Overnight</DELIVERY>
<MARKER>In Stock?: </MARKER>
<AVAIL ID="I1024A">Yes</AVAIL>
<MARKER>Warranty: </MARKER>
```

Continued

```
<WARRANTY>30 years</WARRANTY>
</PRICING>
<ITEM>
<PRODUCTNAME>Carrying Case</PRODUCTNAME>
<PRICING><PRODNUM ID="I1028">1028</PRODNUM>
<MARKER>Price: $</MARKER>
<PRICE ID="I1028P">2.00</PRICE>
<MARKER>Shipping: $</MARKER>
<SHIPPING ID="I1028S">1.00</SHIPPING>
<MARKER>Delivery: </MARKER>
<DELIVERY ID="I1028D">Overnight</DELIVERY>
<MARKER>In Stock?: </MARKER>
<AVAIL ID="I1028A">Yes</AVAIL>
<MARKER>Warranty: </MARKER>
<WARRANTY>2 years</WARRANTY>
</PRICING>
</ITEM>
</ITEM>
<LEGALNOTICE>Jane's Catalog is not responsible for
typographical errors. Prices and availability may change
at any time.</LEGALNOTICE>
</GROUP>
```

As you can see, nesting ITEM elements is simple. There is no need for the SUBITEM element that you use in the previous chapter, which makes for a more consistent structure. The ID elements duplicate information available elsewhere (the product number), but this evil is sometimes necessary as a transition.

Note

The next two sections explore modeling Jane's Catalog in XML Schemas and RELAX. If DTD's are enough for you, you can skip them both.

Describing the document structure with a W3C XML Schema

The catalog structure is fairly simple and offers very little room for optimization through creative reuse of typed structures. The following schema represents a straightforward conversion of the DTD into XML Schema notation, with the addition of a few data types. Prices and shipping costs must now be expressed as decimals, and the height and width of images must be expressed as integers.

```
<?xml version="1.0" encoding="UTF-8"?>
<xsd:schema
xmlns:xsd="http://www.w3.org/2000/10/XMLSchema">
  <xsd:element name="GROUP">
    <xsd:complexType>
      <xsd:sequence>
        <xsd:element ref="GROUPNAME"/>
        <xsd:element ref="ITEM" maxOccurs="unbounded"/>
        <xsd:element ref="LEGALNOTICE"/>
      </xsd:sequence>
      <xsd:attribute name="GROUPLINK" type="xsd:string"/>
    </xsd:complexType>
  </xsd:element>
  <xsd:element name="GROUPNAME" type="xsd:string"/>
  <xsd:element name="LEGALNOTICE" type="xsd:string"/>
  <xsd:element name="ITEM">
    <xsd:complexType>
      <xsd:sequence>
        <xsd:element ref="PRODUCTNAME"/>
        <xsd:element ref="DESCRIPTION" minOccurs="0"/>
        <xsd:element ref="PRICING"/>
        <xsd:element ref="ITEM" minOccurs="0"
maxOccurs="unbounded"/>
      </xsd:sequence>
      <xsd:attribute name="ITEMLINK" type="xsd:string"/>
    </xsd:complexType>
```

Continued

```
  </xsd:element>
  <xsd:element name="PRODUCTNAME" type="xsd:string"/>
  <xsd:element name="DESCRIPTION">
    <xsd:complexType>
      <xsd:choice minOccurs="0" maxOccurs="unbounded">
        <xsd:element ref="PARAGRAPH"/>
        <xsd:element ref="IMG"/>
      </xsd:choice>
    </xsd:complexType>
  </xsd:element>
  <xsd:element name="IMG">
    <xsd:complexType>
      <xsd:sequence/>
      <xsd:attribute name="SRC" use="required"
type="xsd:uriReference"/>
      <xsd:attribute name="HEIGHT" use="required"
type="xsd:integer"/>
      <xsd:attribute name="WIDTH" use="required"
type="xsd:integer"/>
    </xsd:complexType>
  </xsd:element>
  <xsd:element name="PARAGRAPH">
    <xsd:complexType mixed="true">
      <xsd:choice minOccurs="0" maxOccurs="unbounded">
        <xsd:element ref="CITATION"/>
        <xsd:element ref="EMPHASIS"/>
        <xsd:element ref="HIGHLIGHT"/>
      </xsd:choice>
    </xsd:complexType>
  </xsd:element>
  <xsd:element name="CITATION" type="xsd:string"/>
  <xsd:element name="EMPHASIS" type="xsd:string"/>
  <xsd:element name="HIGHLIGHT" type="xsd:string"/>
  <xsd:element name="PRICING">
    <xsd:complexType>
```

```xml
    <xsd:sequence>
      <xsd:element ref="PRODNUM"/>
      <xsd:element ref="MARKER" minOccurs="0"/>
      <xsd:element ref="PRICE"/>
      <xsd:element ref="MARKER" minOccurs="0"/>
      <xsd:element ref="SHIPPING"/>
      <xsd:element ref="MARKER" minOccurs="0"/>
      <xsd:element ref="DELIVERY"/>
      <xsd:element ref="MARKER" minOccurs="0"/>
      <xsd:element ref="AVAIL"/>
      <xsd:element ref="MARKER" minOccurs="0"/>
      <xsd:element ref="WARRANTY"/>
    </xsd:sequence>
  </xsd:complexType>
</xsd:element>
<xsd:element name="PRODNUM">
  <xsd:complexType>
    <xsd:simpleContent>
      <xsd:extension base="xsd:string">
        <xsd:attribute name="ID" use="required"
type="xsd:ID"/>
      </xsd:extension>
    </xsd:simpleContent>
  </xsd:complexType>
</xsd:element>
<xsd:element name="MARKER" type="xsd:string"/>
<xsd:element name="PRICE">
  <xsd:complexType>
    <xsd:simpleContent>
      <xsd:extension base="xsd:decimal">
        <xsd:attribute name="ID" use="required"
type="xsd:ID"/>
      </xsd:extension>
    </xsd:simpleContent>
  </xsd:complexType>
```

Continued

```
    </xsd:element>
    <xsd:element name="SHIPPING">
      <xsd:complexType>
        <xsd:simpleContent>
          <xsd:extension base="xsd:decimal">
            <xsd:attribute name="ID" use="required"
type="xsd:ID"/>
          </xsd:extension>
        </xsd:simpleContent>
      </xsd:complexType>
    </xsd:element>
    <xsd:element name="DELIVERY">
      <xsd:complexType>
        <xsd:simpleContent>
          <xsd:extension base="xsd:string">
            <xsd:attribute name="ID" use="required"
type="xsd:ID"/>
          </xsd:extension>
        </xsd:simpleContent>
      </xsd:complexType>
    </xsd:element>
    <xsd:element name="AVAIL">
      <xsd:complexType>
        <xsd:simpleContent>
          <xsd:extension base="xsd:string">
            <xsd:attribute name="ID" use="required"
type="xsd:ID"/>
          </xsd:extension>
        </xsd:simpleContent>
      </xsd:complexType>
    </xsd:element>
    <xsd:element name="WARRANTY" type="xsd:string"/>
</xsd:schema>
```

There are a few places in which more data typing is a possibility, but there are some complications. Availability is currently expressed as a yes/no Boolean structure, but XML Schemas requires `true` or `false` as values. On top of that, it might be preferable to express it as a date, but that's a business-level decision that Jane's catalog will have to make. The DELIVERY element requires some similar choices, involving how much information the catalog wants to put there and whether to provide multiple options.

There is one aspect of the schema that you might restructure slightly — you have a fair number of elements that currently involve a string value and an ID attribute. If developers really want to, they can do something like this:

```
<xsd:complexType name="stringWithID">
   <xsd:simpleContent>
      <xsd:extension base="xsd:string">
         <xsd:attribute name="ID" use="required"
type="xsd:ID"/>
      </xsd:extension>
   </xsd:simpleContent>
</xsd:complexType>
<xsd:element name="PRODNUM" type="stringWithID"/>
```

This may prove useful, or it may not. In the DTD, PRODNUM, PRICE, SHIPPING, DELIVERY, and AVAIL all looked quite similar. As you refine the schema with data types, however, those similarities seem to be disappearing. Establishing types too soon may cause its own problems.

Describing the document structure with a RELAX module

RELAX has similar capabilities for adding data types to the document structure, and programmers face pretty much exactly the same issues in choosing those types as with W3C XML Schemas. Because the structure of the catalog is simple, the RELAX schema can be expressed as a set of `elementRule` elements with attributes, without the need for anything fancy:

```
<module moduleVersion="1.0"
   relaxCore="1.0"
   targetNamespace=""
   xmlns="http://www.xml.gr.jp/xmlns/relaxCore">
  <interface>
    <export label="GROUP"/>
  </interface>
  <elementRule role="GROUP">
    <sequence>
      <ref label="GROUPNAME"/>
      <ref label="ITEM" occurs="+"/>
      <ref label="LEGALNOTICE"/>
    </sequence>
  </elementRule>
  <tag name="GROUP">
    <attribute name="GROUPLINK" type="string"/>
  </tag>
  <elementRule role="GROUPNAME" type="string"/>
  <tag name="GROUPNAME"/>
  <elementRule role="LEGALNOTICE" type="string"/>
  <tag name="LEGALNOTICE"/>
  <elementRule role="ITEM">
    <sequence>
      <ref label="PRODUCTNAME"/>
      <ref label="DESCRIPTION" occurs="?"/>
      <ref label="PRICING"/>
      <ref label="ITEM" occurs="*"/>
    </sequence>
  </elementRule>
  <tag name="ITEM">
    <attribute name="ITEMLINK" type="string"/>
  </tag>
```

```
<elementRule role="PRODUCTNAME" type="string"/>
<tag name="PRODUCTNAME"/>
<elementRule role="DESCRIPTION">
  <choice occurs="*">
    <ref label="PARAGRAPH"/>
    <ref label="IMG"/>
  </choice>
</elementRule>
<tag name="DESCRIPTION"/>
<elementRule role="IMG">
  <sequence/>
</elementRule>
<tag name="IMG">
  <attribute name="SRC" required="true"
type="uriReference"/>
  <attribute name="HEIGHT" required="true"
type="integer"/>
  <attribute name="WIDTH" required="true"
type="integer"/>
</tag>
<elementRule role="PARAGRAPH">
  <mixed>
    <choice occurs="*">
      <ref label="CITATION"/>
      <ref label="EMPHASIS"/>
      <ref label="HIGHLIGHT"/>
    </choice>
  </mixed>
</elementRule>
<tag name="PARAGRAPH"/>
<elementRule role="CITATION" type="string"/>
<tag name="CITATION"/>
<elementRule role="EMPHASIS" type="string"/>
<tag name="EMPHASIS"/>
<elementRule role="HIGHLIGHT" type="string"/>
```

Continued

```
<tag name="HIGHLIGHT"/>
<elementRule role="PRICING">
  <sequence>
    <ref label="PRODNUM"/>
    <ref label="MARKER" occurs="?"/>
    <ref label="PRICE"/>
    <ref label="MARKER" occurs="?"/>
    <ref label="SHIPPING"/>
    <ref label="MARKER" occurs="?"/>
    <ref label="DELIVERY"/>
    <ref label="MARKER" occurs="?"/>
    <ref label="AVAIL"/>
    <ref label="MARKER" occurs="?"/>
    <ref label="WARRANTY"/>
  </sequence>
</elementRule>
<tag name="PRICING"/>
<elementRule role="PRODNUM" type="string"/>
<tag name="PRODNUM">
  <attribute name="ID" required="true" type="ID"/>
</tag>
<elementRule role="MARKER" type="string"/>
<tag name="MARKER"/>
<elementRule role="PRICE" type="decimal"/>
<tag name="PRICE">
  <attribute name="ID" required="true" type="ID"/>
</tag>
<elementRule role="SHIPPING" type="decimal"/>
<tag name="SHIPPING">
  <attribute name="ID" required="true" type="ID"/>
</tag>
<elementRule role="DELIVERY" type="string"/>
<tag name="DELIVERY">
  <attribute name="ID" required="true" type="ID"/>
</tag>
```

```
<elementRule role="AVAIL" type="boolean"/>
<tag name="AVAIL">
  <attribute name="ID" required="true" type="ID"/>
</tag>
<elementRule role="WARRANTY" type="string"/>
<tag name="WARRANTY"/>
</module>
```

Because RELAX defines attributes separately from the element content type, there isn't much benefit to creating a new type for the String+ID elements. You can replace the single ID attribute with an attPool containing the ID attribute, but that doesn't have a substantial effect on processing or verbosity.

Taking Orders – Transacting Business

Electronic commerce over the Internet is just getting started, but it is the target of security threats and consumer skepticism. Instead of developing enormous systems for processing credit cards and handling customer inquiries, many Internet entrepreneurs have turned to the safer world of business-to-business transactions. Frequently, all parties involved in a deal already know and perhaps even trust each other, thus avoiding the anonymity issues associated with Internet commerce. Accounting systems already provide sales on credit to known customers, and shipping terms are already established. Not all transactions are financial, either; many systems out there use similar connections to exchange information securely.

Electronic data interchange (EDI) systems so far have tended to use structures from the database world: fixed-length or delimited fields ordered neatly into tables for processing. Transmission of this information has improved dramatically—whereas companies used to mail tapes to each other regularly, now they frequently connect over data networks—but the form of the information hasn't yet changed greatly. XML offers businesses more flexibility than their current systems can offer, along with an opportunity to create simple standards that can be extended to cover additional data structures as necessary.

> **Caution**
>
> The example presented in this section provides only a *very* basic outline of what you need to create a full-fledged commercial interchange system. The standards I propose here will probably be superceded in time by recommendations from standards bodies and industry organizations.

The use of EDI for commercial transactions has been expanding wildly over the last 20 years, and the structures it has created still have much to offer you in terms of your XML examples. XML is not the answer to every problem that arises in electronic order placement. Businesses may trust each other enough to ship each other goods, but must still place their orders over a secure channel. Doing this can be as simple as encrypting the XML documents with public-key encryption tools and sending them via e-mail, or as complex as sending them over a specially built private network. They can also send XML documents on magnetic tape by private courier to companies uninterested in making network connections to their financial systems.

After that channel has been established, the businesses can begin considering the format for their orders. All orders still need shipping and billing information, as well as contact information that can be used to reach a human if the computer fails. Dates are also critical, to give the recipient some idea of when the order was created and when it will arrive. A priority level for the order might be useful in some situations, although there might be separate priorities for the order as a whole and for parts of the order. A listing of the items to be ordered will follow, concluding with a total number of items and total bill. The conclusion is critical for making certain that items haven't been lost during processing. XML developers should probably look over their shoulders at the older forms of data interchange, if only to make certain that they haven't left out any key pieces that the older structures provided.

Designing a DTD for orders

Our initial DTD for XML transactions, which provides a shell for the order, is deliberately abstract. At this level, it doesn't matter what kinds of items are being ordered — apples, tractors, and concrete beams are all just items to be transferred between companies. The second DTD, which defines the items, will be much more focused on the goods in question.

You start by defining the ORDER element, which encompasses the entire document and defines its namespace, as follows:

```
<!ELEMENT ORDER (BILLTO, SHIPTO, CONTACT, PRIORITY,
ITEMS,TOTALS)>
<!ATTLIST ORDER
    xmlns CDATA #FIXED "http://example.com/orders">
```

The namespace defined on the ORDER element will help distinguish the shell from the items inside. The BILLTO and SHIPTO elements have similar contents:

```
<!ELEMENT BILLTO (REFERENCE | FULLADDRESS)>
<!ELEMENT SHIPTO ((REFERENCE |FULLADDRESS), SHIPVIA)>
<!ELEMENT SHIPVIA (REFERENCE | FULLADDRESS)>
<!ELEMENT REFERENCE (#PCDATA)>
<!ELEMENT FULLADDRESS (COMPANY, ADDRESSLINE+, CITY,
STATE, POSTALCODE, COUNTRY, CONTACT, PHONE, FAX?)>
<!ELEMENT COMPANY (#PCDATA)>
<!ELEMENT ADDRESSLINE (#PCDATA)>
<!ELEMENT CITY (#PCDATA)>
<!ELEMENT STATE (#PCDATA)>
<!ELEMENT POSTALCODE (#PCDATA)>
<!ELEMENT COUNTRY (#PCDATA)>
<!ELEMENT CONTACT (#PCDATA | REFERENCE)*>
<!ELEMENT PHONE (#PCDATA)>
<!ELEMENT FAX (#PCDATA)>
<!ELEMENT PRIORITY (#PCDATA)>
```

Most of this information is basic text, although the key REFER-ENCE element will probably be used for most transactions. By using a REFERENCE, an ordering company is announcing that it already has a record in the recipient's system. The processing application that receives these data will pass orders that use REFERENCE to the order system immediately—a relationship already exists. (If it's a bad relationship, because the company ordering doesn't pay the bills, or doesn't exist in the system, the order system can still reject the order.) Orders that arrive with full addresses will need further veri-fication. Contacts will be called, credit checks run if necessary, and the new buyer will be entered into the order system and given his or her own REFERENCE information for future use.

The ITEMS element contains a list of ITEM elements:

```
<!ELEMENT ITEMS (ITEM+)>
```

The TOTALS element contains a summary that can be used to check the order.

```
<!ELEMENT TOTALS (TOTALITEMS, TOTALQUANTITY, TOTALCOST)>
<!-NOTE TOTALS ARE FOR CHECKING DATA ONLY AND DO NOT
REFLECT FINAL COSTS OR QUANTITIES ->
<!ELEMENT TOTALITEMS (#PCDATA)>
<!ELEMENT TOTALQUANTITY (#PCDATA)>
<!ELEMENT TOTALCOST (#PCDATA)>
```

This basic shell could be useful to a variety of businesses, even though they will probably want to customize it to some extent to reflect their needs. The most important feature of this shell, how-ever, is what is left out. Because the ITEM element is never defined, this DTD is incomplete and needs a companion DTD to actually handle orders.

For this example, I use the publishing industry, the only industry in which I've personally encountered electronic ordering and all its associated benefits and costs. (Searching for hundreds of missing line items on thousands of orders for thousands of books each is not an experience I care to repeat, either.) The ITEM definition for this relatively simple industry will include only three pieces: BOOK, which carries the title information; QUANTITY, which specifies how many copies they want; PRIORITY, which enables the customer to request higher-priority treatment of certain titles; and EXTENDEDCOST, which provides the total cost the purchaser expects to pay if the other information is correct. EXTENDEDCOST in this case acts like a checksum, making sure that the purchaser's information makes sense. (If the purchaser has the wrong price, he or she will be billed for the correct amount, of course.)

```
<!ELEMENT ITEM (BOOK, QUANTITY, PRIORITY?, DISCOUNT,
EXTENDEDCOST)>
<!ELEMENT DISCOUNT (#PCDATA)>
<!ELEMENT EXTENDEDCOST (#PCDATA)>
```

The book industry standardized early on a notation for its products: the International Standard Book Number (ISBN). The ISBN for *XML: A Primer (Third Edition)*, for instance, is 0-7645-4777-1. The first digit indicates that the book is in English, and the next four digits indicate that the book was published by Hungry Minds, Inc. The next four digits (4777) uniquely identify the title for IDG Books, and the final digit (which could be a digit from 0–9 or an X) is a checksum. XML parsers won't process the ISBN to make sure the checksum is correct; that is the responsibility of the processing application. ISBNs uniquely identify books or book-related products, such as boxed sets of books and other packages that range from books that come with everything from stuffed animals to paper-making kits. Each ISBN is technically allowed to refer to only one item packaged as a unit for sale, although the contents of that package may include other items with their own ISBNs. (It's really a bar-code standard that makes it easy for stores to order and sell books.) In theory at least, this example's DTD shouldn't even need to include title or pricing information because that should all connect to the ISBN. In reality, titles and prices change regularly, and customers aren't always notified. Adding titles and prices to the information also provides some extra insurance that the order will be processed correctly and can be used to generate warnings to customers that the information they have is outdated without stopping the order completely or requiring human intervention. Redundancy may be annoying, but it often serves a purpose.

The BOOK element will include ISBN, title, and price. For most previous examples, I've avoided using any element names that conflict with HTML, but because this example uses namespaces you can let a TITLE be a child element of a BOOK when labeled with the namespace http://example.com/orders.

```
<!ELEMENT BOOK (ISBN, TITLE, PRICE)>
<!ELEMENT ISBN (#PCDATA)>
<!ELEMENT TITLE (#PCDATA)>
<!ELEMENT PRICE (#PCDATA)>
```

The other critical part of a line item is the quantity. It's more than likely that the company placing the order wants more than one copy of the book. Some large wholesalers and distributors want to receive books only in whole, unopened cartons. Because books come in all kinds of shapes and sizes, the number of books to a box varies from book to book. The same title can even come in different carton quantities when a printer who uses a different box size reprints it! In any case, you must provide options for customers to specify whether they want whole cartons, the size of the carton they are expecting, and rough instructions for how to adjust to any differences in carton quantities. Most small customers won't care about cartons because they'll be receiving repackaged boxes of mixed books from the warehouse.

```
<!ELEMENT QUANTITY (NUMBER, CARTON?)>
<!ATTLIST QUANTITY
        SHIPCQ     (NO | ROUNDUP | ROUNDDOWN |
ROUNDCLOSEST) "NO">
<!ELEMENT NUMBER (#PCDATA)>
<!ELEMENT CARTON (#PCDATA)>
```

Now that you have two complete DTDs, you can begin to create some orders. The first complete DTD provides the shell that you use:

```
<!ELEMENT ORDER (BILLTO, SHIPTO, CONTACT, PRIORITY,
ITEMS,TOTALS)>
<!ATTLIST ORDER
    xmlns CDATA #FIXED "http://example.com/orders">
<!ELEMENT BILLTO (REFERENCE | FULLADDRESS)>
<!ELEMENT SHIPTO ((REFERENCE |FULLADDRESS), SHIPVIA)>
<!ELEMENT SHIPVIA (REFERENCE | FULLADDRESS)>
<!ELEMENT REFERENCE (#PCDATA)>
<!ELEMENT FULLADDRESS (COMPANY, ADDRESSLINE+, CITY,
STATE, POSTALCODE, COUNTRY, CONTACT, PHONE, FAX?)>
<!ELEMENT COMPANY (#PCDATA)>
<!ELEMENT ADDRESSLINE (#PCDATA)>
<!ELEMENT CITY (#PCDATA)>
<!ELEMENT STATE (#PCDATA)>
<!ELEMENT POSTALCODE (#PCDATA)>
<!ELEMENT COUNTRY (#PCDATA)>
<!ELEMENT CONTACT (#PCDATA | REFERENCE)>
<!ELEMENT PHONE (#PCDATA)>
<!ELEMENT FAX (#PCDATA)>
<!ELEMENT PRIORITY (#PCDATA)>
<!ELEMENT TOTALS (TOTALITEMS, TOTALQUANTITY, TOTALCOST)>
<!--NOTE TOTALS ARE FOR CHECKING DATA ONLY AND DO NOT
REFLECT FINAL COSTS OR QUANTITIES -->
<!ELEMENT ITEMS (ITEM+)>
<!ELEMENT TOTALITEMS (#PCDATA)>
<!ELEMENT TOTALQUANTITY (#PCDATA)>
<!ELEMENT TOTALCOST (#PCDATA)>
```

The second DTD includes the first DTD through a parameter entity and provides the information for the actual line items.

```
<!ENTITY % ORDER SYSTEM "order.dtd">
%ORDER;
<!ELEMENT ITEM (BOOK, QUANTITY, PRIORITY?, DISCOUNT,
EXTENDEDCOST)>
<!ELEMENT DISCOUNT (#PCDATA)>
<!ELEMENT EXTENDEDCOST (#PCDATA)>
<!ELEMENT BOOK (ISBN, TITLE, PRICE)>
<!ELEMENT ISBN (#PCDATA)>
<!ELEMENT TITLE (#PCDATA)>
<!ELEMENT PRICE (#PCDATA)>
<!ELEMENT QUANTITY (NUMBER, CARTON?)>
<!ATTLIST QUANTITY
     SHIPCQ      (NO | ROUNDUP | ROUNDDOWN |
ROUNDCLOSEST) "NO">
<!ELEMENT NUMBER (#PCDATA)>
<!ELEMENT CARTON (#PCDATA)>
```

Now that you have a framework, it's time to learn how to use it. The order document calls only the book DTD directly. The order DTD is treated as a part of the book DTD and doesn't need to be called directly.

```
<?xml version="1.0" encoding="UTF-8"?>
<!DOCTYPE ORDER SYSTEM "book.dtd">
<ORDER xmlns="http://example.com/orders">
<BILLTO>
<REFERENCE>8345A</REFERENCE>
</BILLTO>
<SHIPTO>
<REFERENCE>8345A</REFERENCE>
<SHIPVIA><REFERENCE>2A</REFERENCE></SHIPVIA>
</SHIPTO>
<CONTACT>Burnie Orange</CONTACT>
<PRIORITY>Normal</PRIORITY>
<ITEMS>
<ITEM>
```

```
<BOOK><ISBN>155828592X</ISBN><TITLE>XML:A
Primer</TITLE><PRICE>$24.95</PRICE></BOOK>
<QUANTITY
SHIPCQ="ROUNDDOWN"><NUMBER>100</NUMBER><CARTON>20</CARTON
></QUANTITY>
<DISCOUNT>.42</DISCOUNT>
<EXTENDEDCOST>$1447.10</EXTENDEDCOST>
</ITEM>
<ITEM>
<BOOK><ISBN>1558285288</ISBN><TITLE>MIME, UUENCODE,
&amp; ZIP</TITLE><PRICE>$24.95</PRICE></BOOK>
<QUANTITY
SHIPCQ="ROUNDDOWN"><NUMBER>100</NUMBER><CARTON>20</CARTON
></QUANTITY>
<DISCOUNT>.42</DISCOUNT>
<EXTENDEDCOST>$1447.10</EXTENDEDCOST>
</ITEM>
<ITEM>
<BOOK><ISBN>1558514716</ISBN><TITLE>Graphical
Applications with Tcl &amp;
Tk</TITLE><PRICE>$39.95</PRICE></BOOK>
<QUANTITY><NUMBER>16</NUMBER><CARTON>16</CARTON></QUANTIT
Y>
<DISCOUNT>.42</DISCOUNT>
<EXTENDEDCOST>$370.74</EXTENDEDCOST>
</ITEM>
<ITEM>
<BOOK><ISBN>155828480X</ISBN><TITLE>World Wide Web
Bible</TITLE><PRICE>$29.95</PRICE></BOOK>
<QUANTITY><NUMBER>10</NUMBER><CARTON>10</CARTON></QUANTIT
Y>
<DISCOUNT>.42</DISCOUNT>
<EXTENDEDCOST>173.71</EXTENDEDCOST>
</ITEM>
```

Continued

```
<ITEM>
<BOOK><ISBN>1558284783</ISBN><TITLE>Introduction to
CGI/Perl</TITLE><PRICE>$19.95</PRICE></BOOK>
<QUANTITY
SHIPCQ="ROUNDDOWN"><NUMBER>24</NUMBER><CARTON>24</CARTON>
</QUANTITY>
<DISCOUNT>.42</DISCOUNT>
<EXTENDEDCOST>277.70</EXTENDEDCOST>
</ITEM>
</ITEMS>
<TOTALS><TOTALITEMS>5</TOTALITEMS><TOTALQUANTITY>320</TOT
ALQUANTITY>
<TOTALCOST>$3716.35</TOTALCOST>
</TOTALS>
</ORDER>
```

Although this format may not be as compact as the previous fixed-length or the more flexible delimited files, it's certainly easier for humans to read. Its extra flexibility also gives it a significant advantage because it doesn't require that all information be present all the time. The spread of networks has lowered the costs of transmission, making this kind of verbosity acceptable. Building a processing application around this DTD and connecting it to the order system will take some effort, but you can hope that the extra work will pay off in added flexibility, enabling customers to use any variety of XML processor they choose.

Tip

This format is really only the tip of the iceberg. Developers can add all kinds of additional information to meet particular needs – dates for canceling orders that haven't shipped yet, acceptable substitutes, and all kinds of other possibilities.

Moving to a schema for orders

To convert this DTD to a schema you use a new feature of XML Schemas, xsd:include, as well as the usual data-typing additions.

 Note

Again, if you're not interested in W3C XML Schemas, you can skip to the next section, "Direct Connections: Information Interchange."

The order is a straightforward conversion, with some added data types and an xsd:annotation/xsd:documentation element to represent the comment, as follows:

```
<xsd:schema
xmlns:xsd="http://www.w3.org/2000/10/XMLSchema">
  <xsd:element name="ORDER">
    <xsd:complexType>
      <xsd:sequence>
        <xsd:element ref="BILLTO"/>
        <xsd:element ref="SHIPTO"/>
        <xsd:element ref="CONTACT"/>
        <xsd:element ref="PRIORITY"/>
        <xsd:element ref="ITEMS"/>
        <xsd:element ref="TOTALS"/>
      </xsd:sequence>
      <xsd:attribute name="xmlns" use="fixed"
value="http://example.com/orders" type="xsd:string"/>
    </xsd:complexType>
  </xsd:element>
  <xsd:element name="BILLTO">
    <xsd:complexType>
      <xsd:choice>
        <xsd:element ref="REFERENCE"/>
        <xsd:element ref="FULLADDRESS"/>
      </xsd:choice>
    </xsd:complexType>
```

Continued

```
</xsd:element>
  <xsd:element name="SHIPTO">
    <xsd:complexType>
      <xsd:sequence>
        <xsd:choice>
          <xsd:element ref="REFERENCE"/>
          <xsd:element ref="FULLADDRESS"/>
        </xsd:choice>
        <xsd:element ref="SHIPVIA"/>
      </xsd:sequence>
    </xsd:complexType>
  </xsd:element>
  <xsd:element name="SHIPVIA">
    <xsd:complexType>
      <xsd:choice>
        <xsd:element ref="REFERENCE"/>
        <xsd:element ref="FULLADDRESS"/>
      </xsd:choice>
    </xsd:complexType>
  </xsd:element>
  <xsd:element name="REFERENCE" type="xsd:string"/>
  <xsd:element name="FULLADDRESS">
    <xsd:complexType>
      <xsd:sequence>
        <xsd:element ref="COMPANY"/>
        <xsd:element ref="ADDRESSLINE"
maxOccurs="unbounded"/>
        <xsd:element ref="CITY"/>
        <xsd:element ref="STATE"/>
        <xsd:element ref="POSTALCODE"/>
        <xsd:element ref="COUNTRY"/>
        <xsd:element ref="CONTACT"/>
        <xsd:element ref="PHONE"/>
        <xsd:element ref="FAX" minOccurs="0"/>
      </xsd:sequence>
```

```
      </xsd:complexType>
    </xsd:element>
    <xsd:element name="COMPANY" type="xsd:string"/>
    <xsd:element name="ADDRESSLINE" type="xsd:string"/>
    <xsd:element name="CITY" type="xsd:string"/>
    <xsd:element name="STATE" type="xsd:string"/>
    <xsd:element name="POSTALCODE" type="xsd:string"/>
    <xsd:element name="COUNTRY" type="xsd:string"/>
    <xsd:element name="CONTACT">
      <xsd:complexType mixed="true">
        <xsd:choice minOccurs="0" maxOccurs="unbounded">
          <xsd:element ref="REFERENCE"/>
        </xsd:choice>
      </xsd:complexType>
    </xsd:element>
    <xsd:element name="PHONE" type="xsd:string"/>
    <xsd:element name="FAX" type="xsd:string"/>
    <xsd:element name="PRIORITY" type="xsd:string"/>
    <xsd:element name="TOTALS">
      <xsd:complexType>
        <xsd:sequence>
          <xsd:element ref="TOTALITEMS"/>
          <xsd:element ref="TOTALQUANTITY"/>
          <xsd:element ref="TOTALCOST"/>
        </xsd:sequence>
      </xsd:complexType>
    </xsd:element>
    <xsd:element name="TOTALITEMS" type="xsd:string">
      <xsd:annotation>
        <xsd:documentation>NOTE TOTALS ARE FOR CHECKING
DATA ONLY AND DO NOT REFLECT FINAL COSTS OR QUANTITIES
</xsd:documentation>
      </xsd:annotation>
    </xsd:element>
```

Continued

```
<xsd:element name="TOTALQUANTITY" type="xsd:integer"/>
<xsd:element name="TOTALCOST" type="xsd:string"/>
<xsd:element name="ITEMS">
  <xsd:complexType>
    <xsd:sequence>
      <xsd:element ref="ITEM" maxOccurs="unbounded"/>
    </xsd:sequence>
  </xsd:complexType>
</xsd:element>
</xsd:schema>
```

The book-specific portion of the DTD undergoes a similar transformation, but the external parameter entity that you use to reference the order is changed to an xsd:include element.

```
<xsd:schema
xmlns:xsd="http://www.w3.org/2000/10/XMLSchema">
  <!--note change in following line-->
  <xsd:include schemaLocation="order.xsd"/>
  <xsd:element name="ITEM">
    <xsd:complexType>
      <xsd:sequence>
        <xsd:element ref="BOOK"/>
        <xsd:element ref="QUANTITY"/>
        <xsd:element ref="PRIORITY" minOccurs="0"/>
        <xsd:element ref="DISCOUNT"/>
        <xsd:element ref="EXTENDEDCOST"/>
      </xsd:sequence>
    </xsd:complexType>
  </xsd:element>
  <xsd:element name="DISCOUNT" type="xsd:decimal"/>
  <xsd:element name="EXTENDEDCOST" type="xsd:string"/>
  <xsd:element name="BOOK">
    <xsd:complexType>
      <xsd:sequence>
        <xsd:element ref="ISBN"/>
```

```
      <xsd:element ref="TITLE"/>
      <xsd:element ref="PRICE"/>
    </xsd:sequence>
  </xsd:complexType>
</xsd:element>
<xsd:element name="ISBN" type="xsd:string"/>
<xsd:element name="TITLE" type="xsd:string"/>
<xsd:element name="PRICE" type="xsd:string"/>
<xsd:element name="QUANTITY">
  <xsd:complexType>
    <xsd:sequence>
      <xsd:element ref="NUMBER"/>
      <xsd:element ref="CARTON" minOccurs="0"/>
    </xsd:sequence>
    <xsd:attribute name="SHIPCQ" use="default"
value="NO">
        <xsd:simpleType>
          <xsd:restriction base="xsd:NMTOKEN">
            <xsd:enumeration value="NO"/>
            <xsd:enumeration value="ROUNDUP"/>
            <xsd:enumeration value="ROUNDDOWN"/>
            <xsd:enumeration value="ROUNDCLOSEST"/>
          </xsd:restriction>
        </xsd:simpleType>
      </xsd:attribute>
    </xsd:complexType>
  </xsd:element>
  <xsd:element name="NUMBER" type="xsd:integer"/>
  <xsd:element name="CARTON" type="xsd:integer"/>
</xsd:schema>
```

Using schemas rather than DTDs may open up new possibilities for this document structure, especially if types for defining books and ordering structures already exist. Rather than your having to reinvent the wheel, using xsd:include may enable you to integrate such structures with your own work. It's usually best to decide on such things before building a library of documents, but transformation tools (such as XSLT) may be able to help you out if you change your mind too late.

Direct Connections: Information Interchange

Situations where multiple firms must organize multiple parts provide fertile ground for information interchange systems. Establishing this interchange may be difficult because some companies may feel that they have much to lose by revealing their proprietary information, but often there is more to be gained than lost by sharing. Even though much of the work involved in creating these interchange systems is similar to the work you put into the documents described in the previous chapter, sharing documents between multiple companies creates additional challenges. This section of the chapter won't build any more DTDs or schemas, which are likely to be even more industry-bound than the ordering processes I describe earlier in the chapter. Instead, you can explore some of the commerce-focused XML standards already in development.

Cross-Reference

To see a more comprehensive list of XML projects, visit http://www.oasis-open.org/cover/xml.html. For a directory of XML schemas, see http://www.schema.net.

The ebXML initiative (http://www.ebxml.org) is an XML-based project whose purpose is to build "a Single Global Electronic Market [that] enables all parties irrespective of size to engage in Internet-based electronic business and provides for plug and play shrink-wrapped solutions." The group has established and approved a Requirements document, and is currently building a Technical Architecture Specification and a Messaging Services specification.

ebXML is a joint project between OASIS-Open (`http://www.oasis-open.org`), a standards organization focused on vertical industry XML and SGML development, and the United Nations CEFACT (United Nations Centre for Trade Facilitation and Electronic Business, though the acronym is French.) (`http://www.unece.org/cefact`). UN/CEFACT previously developed EDIFACT, a standard for large-scale EDI transfers. Participation in ebXML is open—developers can join the project at `http://www.ebxml.org/participate.htm`. Both organizations and individuals are welcome. The scale of the project is enormous, so most developers are focusing on particular areas of specialty.

BizTalk (`http://www.biztalk.org`), under development by Microsoft, SAP, CommerceOne, Ariba, and others, provides a different framework, claiming that "the BizTalk Framework itself is not a standard. XML is the standard. The goal of the BizTalk Framework is to accelerate the rapid adoption of XML." BizTalk combines a set of rules for XML exchange with a repository of XML schemas representing the content of those exchanges. Microsoft itself plans to "natively support the BizTalk Framework in its product line and will publish XML schemas to the BizTalk Framework Web site for public use."

A number of vendors and marketplaces are developing their own standards and frameworks, and it isn't yet clear how different industries will support the wide variety of vertical and horizontal vocabularies and protocols under development. This area is often referred to as the Wild West of XML, as contending forces seek to make their mark on the landscape and collect their reward.

Chapter 21

XML for Document Management

XML promises a revolution in the way documents are managed. Document-management systems store documents, keep track of document contents, control access to those contents, and enable users to locate key information quickly. Many current document-management systems are just enormous electronic filing cabinets, storing documents with only a few keywords and a date provided for quick searching. XML documents carry within them the information and the structures needed to build more robust document systems, organizing collections of information that had previously been left to wither away in filing cabinets or trash cans.

Traditional file structures and even the Web have provided a minimum level of storage and accessibility, but more comprehensive systems are starting to become standard equipment in offices. By giving document-management systems a clearer picture of the contents of documents, markup languages make it possible to control larger sets of documents more efficiently. You can limit searches to individual elements, reducing both the amount of processing required to get to a document and the number of false matches. If XML can combine the extensive document systems already built using SGML and the ubiquity and ease of use of the Web, XML document management may eventually replace the file system as it currently exists.

Achieving this promise will require significant changes in the way organizations look at their documents and the development of new (and friendlier) tools for managing information. One of the reasons the paperless office has proven so elusive is the legacy that working with paper documents has left behind. Treating files as the basic unit of document management is much like treating single documents as the basic unit of a paper filing system. Documents, neatly stapled (or not), are stored in file folders in groups of related documents. Sometimes the same file must be stored in several places; sometimes you must search the entire file folder to track down a single document. Treating a document as a container of information rather than as a fundamental unit in itself is a huge first step in moving past the antiquated tools most people currently use to manage their documents, even their computerized documents. By changing focus from the document to the information within the document, management tools can finally provide the cross-referencing and searching tools needed to make computerized information systems genuinely useful.

Note

In this chapter I describe document structures using DTDs because these documents don't require the facilities provides by schemas. (The examples conform to the date data type to represent dates, however.)

XML's Inheritance: SGML and Document Management

XML inherits an enormous body of document-management development from SGML. Indeed, many SGML vendors are recasting their products as XML tools. SGML found its most comfortable niche in large-scale document-management systems, often for publishers and government (especially defense) organizations, and notably for IBM, which originally developed markup. This core of users has grown slowly over the last 20 years, and now includes users in smaller organizations, academia, engineering, and distributed projects. Linux documentation, for instance, is shifting to an SGML format based on the DocBook DTD.

Note

For an excellent overview of SGML document-management scenarios, including case studies from Grolier Incorporated, Sybase, United Technologies, and Mobil, see Chet Ensign's *$GML: The Billion Dollar Secret* (Prentice-Hall, 1997). For more on DocBook, see `http://www.docbook.org/`.

SGML document-management systems tend to be fairly large, often employing conversion from SGML to another format for presentation, and combining tools from multiple vendors to create a complete solution. "SGML-in-a-box" isn't available; instead, a variety of authoring and development tools, consulting services, document repositories, search engines, and custom-built applications need to be integrated to provide a complete solution for shared document systems. Because SGML has remained a tool for custom-built solutions, the prices of those solutions and their components have remained extremely high, which is a significant barrier to widespread SGML adoption. Not every SGML product is expensive, however; James Clark's SP parser is freely available from `http://www.jclark.com/`, for instance, and many versions of Corel's WordPerfect contain SGML tools, including a Visual DTD Builder.

Many SGML vendors are repositioning their products for use with XML. Although XML is technically a subset of SGML, some vendors are having an easier time than others. When buying these products for XML-focused solutions, always make certain that the output will be XML, without any of the many features of SGML that were removed in the XML creation process. The expertise gained from years of document design and information modeling, however, can be transferred directly from SGML to XML. After you've learned the basics of XML, and feel adventurous, exploring the resources available on SGML and data modeling can connect you to years of wisdom gained through hard work, helping you to avoid problems others have already solved.

Tip

A fantastic place to locate all kinds of SGML and XML resources is Robin Cover's extensive (indeed, overwhelming) SGML/XML Web page at `http://www.oasis-open.org/cover/sgml-xml.html`. The site lists books, papers, articles, software, and other resources in incredible detail.

The Future of XML Document Management

XML enables document-management systems to store documents as parts rather than as large clumps of (often indecipherable) information. Removing formatting information from the core of a document makes it far easier for search engines and similar tools to parse text without having to ponder formatting codes. Assigning element and attribute names that are meaningful in the context of information interchange is key to this process, as is the efficient storage and retrieval of the documents. A document-management tool written for XML from the ground up might even store documents as sets of elements within hierarchically organized databases. XML may force a move to repositories that are more sophisticated than files systems and that store XML documents in a way that reflects the structure of the document — a set of small pieces that can be manipulated, rather than a chunk of text that requires a full parsing every time it is accessed.

Cross-Reference

Repositories and XML document editors receive more attention in Chapter 23, in the fuller context of XML's place in client-server applications.

XML is only getting started as a document format. An essential piece of making the XML document-management dream real lies in the tools used to create the documents. If the XML tools are as clunky as the hand-coding you do throughout this book, no one will want to use them. Even though XML tools may require significant interface changes, many WYSIWYG tools are already providing support to handle the transition. Microsoft has announced support for XML as a common file format for Microsoft Office, though in a limited capacity, and it isn't clear how much freedom users will have to create documents using their own XML vocabularies in Office. Although the examples that follow are hand-coded, most of the people using them will not be entering tags directly. (Imagine an application . . . .)

Building document-management applications is well beyond the scope of this book. For the remainder of this chapter I will explore ways to create DTDs for real business needs, DTDs that create centrally stored documents that can be easily searched and that meet the needs of more than one part of a company. The first example standardizes the memo, perhaps the most commonly used business-document type. The second creates a custom solution to a problem common in larger companies: keeping track of completed projects. Both examples are small components of what will, with luck, grow into large interlocking systems that store information so that it can be readily accessed and easily processed. Afterwards, you can take a look at some approaches to using XML to distribute documents over Web infrastructures.

Small Steps toward the Paperless Office

The first document-management DTD will address one of the largest paper-wasters in business environments: the memos that perpetually fill in-boxes. Many companies produce small weekly newsletters in a memo format: this DTD disseminates chatty pieces of information as well as the boss's announcement that the company is cutting off the supply of free donuts. Although many people might question the wisdom of saving and managing memos, memos and other small-scale communications have grown dramatically in importance with the rise of litigation and the need to document processes. The Freedom of Information Act (FOIA), for example, requires that the federal government must maintain records of its activities and release them (in some form) to the public. At present, processing an FOIA request can take weeks or months as agencies contact their warehouses to gather old files. An XML-based system based on DTDs like the one we using for the memo can greatly reduce the time it takes to locate documents. You can reuse this DTD easily for a number of other tasks (for example, e-mail is typically formatted using a similar model).

Virtually no one will want to hand-code memos in XML. In the case of the memo, with its very simple structure, a program might be able to read the memo DTD and use it as a template, building a form around the needed information. XML parsers can use the information in a wide variety of ways, not just as document presentation information. An advanced XML processor might create the memo through an interview process rather than requiring users to click in fields in a document.

The first step in creating the memo DTD is interviewing people and collecting memos — lots of them — to examine how they are assembled. Most companies use a fairly standard format, with a letterhead of some kind at the top followed by a distribution list, the source of the memo, a brief headline, and then the contents. In some cases, the typist is indicated at the bottom of the memo if the typist was someone other than the original author. For this example, I use an imaginary company — Jimmy's Delectable Car Parts Design (JDCPD). JDCPD is a successful firm that sells after-market high-performance parts for all kinds of cars and trucks. A typical memo might look like the one shown in Figure 21-1.

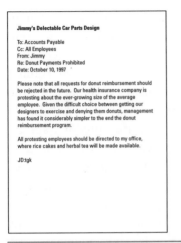

Figure 21-1 *A typical memo*

Some memos are more complex, like the one shown in Figure 21-2. Jimmy's Delectable Car Parts Design has a public relations office, which also puts out an internal weekly newsletter. In a friendly, informal style, the newsletter presents short items of interest to JDCPD employees.

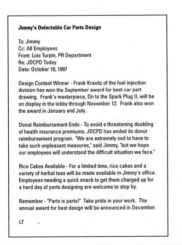

Figure 21-2 *A more complex memo*

The employees in the public relations department would like to be able to use the memo format for other presentations as well, although they haven't planned anything specific yet. They know that in future editions of the newsletter, especially the upcoming Intranet newsletter, they would like to include thumbnails of the award-winning drawings and dress up the page a bit with more logos and assorted clip art. Press releases are distributed in a similar format, although they probably won't be included in this project.

The human resources department has a few requests to make of the memo DTD project. Because all of these memos will eventually be going into a document-management system, the human resources director would like to be able to search the memo files for information created by particular employees and about particular employees and projects. This feature could come in handy in case of a lawsuit, saving a tremendous amount of time and money that would otherwise be spent searching through piles of memos for anything incriminating. Human-resources staff members obviously don't have time to read every memo in the firm, but this could help them to build an early warning system.

The mailroom is another critical customer for memos because they must distribute the memo. The mailroom's primary concern is that everyone on the distribution list receive a standard format, preferably one that can be switched over to e-mail painlessly so that they can get back to shipping packages instead of handing out memos. The rest of the company, including upper management, firmly believes that "memos are memos," although some of the designers would like to be able to add their drawings within the memos to provide reference material.

The humble memo apparently handles a variety of tasks, even though it does not need to carry much information. These tasks aren't all compatible, nor are they all likely to be accomplished on the first pass. Building a workable DTD will take some experimentation and approval from many people who do not wholly support electronic memos.

The best place to start on a document type definition is usually that area of a document that already has the most structure. In this case, that's the header area. The header always contains a distribution list, a source (the From: field), a topic, and a date. The distribution list at present can be anything the mailroom understands, but the prospect of using e-mail for all memos looms in the not-so-distant future. Initially, you can create a memo DTD that includes very little detail:

```
<!ELEMENT MEMO (HEADER, MAIN)>
<!--- MEMO DTD Version 0.1 - Experimental Use Only -->
<!ELEMENT HEADER (DISTRIBUTION, SUBJECT, DATE)>
<!ELEMENT DISTRIBUTION (TO+, CC?, FROM+)>
<!ELEMENT TO (#PCDATA)>
<!ELEMENT CC (#PCDATA)>
<!ELEMENT FROM (#PCDATA)>
<!ELEMENT SUBJECT (#PCDATA)>
<!ELEMENT DATE (#PCDATA)>
<!ELEMENT AUTHOR (#PCDATA)>
<!ELEMENT TYPIST (#PCDATA)>
<!ELEMENT MAIN (#PCDATA | AUTHOR | TYPIST)*)>
```

This is enough of a DTD for a simple demonstration of what is possible. To show what it can do, create a sample document:

```
<?xml version="1.0" standalone="no" encoding="UTF-8"?>
<!DOCTYPE MEMO SYSTEM "memo.dtd">
<MEMO>
<HEADER>
<DISTRIBUTION>
<TO>To: Jimmy</TO>
<FROM>From: Simon</FROM>
</DISTRIBUTION>
<SUBJECT>Re: Sample Document Created with Memo
DTD</SUBJECT>
<DATE>Date: 10/11/1999</DATE>
```

Continued

```
</HEADER>
<MAIN>
I just thought you might like to see what a memo in XML
looks like. Thanks for the vote of confidence at the last
meeting. With any luck, this will make our transition to
electronic documents reasonably painless.
<AUTHOR>SSL</AUTHOR>
</MAIN>
</MEMO>
```

Even though this parses well, it isn't flawless:

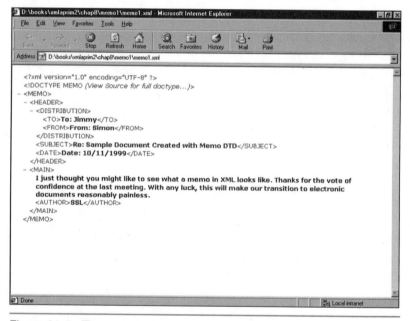

Figure 21-3 *The parsed memo*

The distribution fields are the main problem. Because they must include the To:, CC:, and From: headers, they don't quite make sense. This may be acceptable for paper documents, where humans can make sense out of the list just by reading it, but it will keep e-mail programs from working properly and make it difficult for the soon-to-arrive document-management system to keep track of senders and recipients. These fields must all be broken down some more. Fortunately, they all use the same kind of information, referring to individuals or organizations within the company. The solution clearly requires an extra element to identify senders and recipients. Because the two groups are composed of the same set of addresses of people and groups, they can share an element:

```
<!ELEMENT IDENTITY (#PCDATA)>
```

For now, it's not entirely certain what the address will be. The #PCDATA type lets us accept this uncertainty for the present, although JDCPD will probably want to move to a more specific model after it works out a directory structure. If it just needs to combine name and e-mail address, it could use the following:

```
<!ELEMENT IDENTITY (NAME, EMAIL?)>
<!NAME (#PCDATA)>
<!ELEMENT EMAIL (#PCDATA)>
```

Better yet, if it starts using some real directory-management tools, it might be able to use this:

```
<!ELEMENT IDENTITY (#PCDATA)>
<!ATTLIST IDENTITY NAMEID CDATA #REQUIRED>
```

The information contained in the IDENTITY element could be a description humans can understand, whereas the NAMEID attribute of the IDENTITY element would provide a unique identifier for an individual that corresponds to a listing in a central directory system. People distributing memos on paper could read the IDENTITY element text easily, whereas e-mail and document-management systems could pick up the NAMEID attribute. This combination of human-readable data and machine-readable data would ideally suit the needs of the human resources department I discuss earlier in the chapter, because IDENTITY elements could be used anywhere in a document to identify individuals and company divisions.

Including the IDENTITY element also requires a reworking of the elements in the DTD for the header. Even though they could be mixed declarations and just include addresses with other data, this approach wouldn't require addresses in the format that the document-management system would like. (The content of the address element will still be PCDATA, but a list of acceptable attributes could force the NAMEID, if one existed, to be meaningful.) Enforcing these requirements requires creating another layer of elements. The To:, CC:, and From: headers and the information can remain in PCDATA. These items can also be made into entities, although they're short enough that doing so is probably overkill. It might also be smart to convert the author/typist material at the bottom to IDENTITY elements.

Note

XSL and CSS Level 2 will be capable of handling the issue of text headers for a list of elements without needing extra text. E-mail systems won't be interested because they tend to provide that information automatically, and the document-management system won't need the extra text. For now, if the documents must be viewed in browsers that only support CSS Level 1, they will probably need to include the text. Later systems or dedicated applications can ignore it, but current systems may look better if it is included.

The last part of your document that may require significant improvement is the date. Dates have given programmers immense difficulty (for example, the Year 2000 problem) over the years. To make sure that your system handles dates reliably, you need to separate year, month, day, and possibly hour, minute, and second to create date fields that can be easily sorted and interpreted. The program in which the memos are written and read must recombine the dates in a way that people find acceptable, but that task is generally trivial compared to building code that handles multiple date formats interspersed throughout a collection of data.

Depending on the processing application, it may be smarter to use a date field of some type rather than atomizing the year, month, and day information. The W3C's XML Schema Working Group has focused on the rules in ISO 8601, *Representations of dates and times*. The rules for the date data type provide for a YYYY-MM-DD format, where YYYY is the year, MM is the month, and DD is the day, with all values expressed numerically. August 15, 2000 would be written as 2000-08-15, whereas April 1, 2006 would be written as 2006-04-01.

After you take all these considerations into account, your DTD looks like this:

```
<!ELEMENT MEMO (HEADER, MAIN)>
<!---MEMO DTD Version 0.2 - Experimental Use Only-->
<!ELEMENT HEADER (DISTRIBUTION, SUBJECT, DATE)>
<!ELEMENT DISTRIBUTION (TO, CC?, FROM)>
<!ELEMENT TO (#PCDATA |IDENTITY)*>
<!ELEMENT CC (#PCDATA |IDENTITY)*>
<!ELEMENT FROM (#PCDATA |IDENTITY)*>
<!ELEMENT IDENTITY (#PCDATA)>
<!--May add NAMEID attribute for easier connection to
directory structures later -->
<!ELEMENT SUBJECT (#PCDATA | DESCRIP)*>
<!ELEMENT DESCRIP (#PCDATA)>
<!ELEMENT DATE (#PCDATA)>
<!ELEMENT AUTHOR (IDENTITY+)>
<!ELEMENT TYPIST (IDENTITY+)>
<!ELEMENT MAIN (#PCDATA | AUTHOR | TYPIST)*>
```

The new document looks a bit different:

```
<?xml version="1.0" standalone="no" encoding="UTF-8"?>
<!DOCTYPE MEMO SYSTEM "memo.dtd">
<MEMO>
<HEADER>
<DISTRIBUTION>
<TO>To: <IDENTITY>Jimmy</IDENTITY></TO>
<FROM>From: <IDENTITY>Simon</IDENTITY></FROM>
```

Continued

```
</DISTRIBUTION>
<SUBJECT>Re: <DESCRIP>Sample Document Created with Memo
DTD</DESCRIP></SUBJECT>
<DATE>1999-10-11-</DATE>
</HEADER>
<MAIN>
I just thought you might like to see what a memo in XML
looks like. Thanks for the vote of confidence at the last
meeting. With any luck, this will make our transition to
electronic documents reasonably painless.
<AUTHOR><IDENTITY>SSL</IDENTITY></AUTHOR>
</MAIN>
</MEMO>
```

This parses well, although Figure 21-4 shows that it has a few more layers:

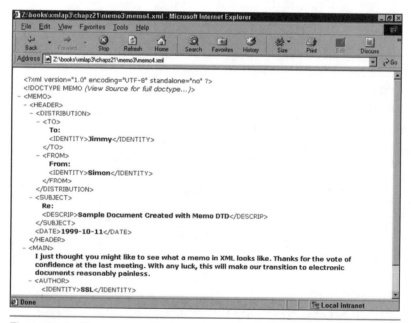

Figure 21-4 *The more sophisticated version of the memo, parsed*

This model should work for most simple documents. The header will keep the memos filed properly, making it easy for a document-management system to track them based on author, recipient, or title. The body content model remains a blank, however. The only kind of content that users can apply in the MAIN element right now is plain text. The body of the document needs some simple formatting elements to format the text and provide a few options for breaking up the tedium of the ordinary memo. JDCPD needs only three options to produce the memos it has now: PARAGRAPH, HIGHLIGHT (to give extra emphasis to important material), and HEADLINE.

```
<!ELEMENT PARAGRAPH (#PCDATA|HIGHLIGHT|IDENTITY)*>
<!ELEMENT HIGHLIGHT (#PCDATA)>
<!ELEMENT HEADLINE (#PCDATA)>
```

Note that the paragraph element enables writers to include IDENTITY information. Sorting out IDENTITY information from regular text is normally difficult, especially in informal documents. Encouraging the regular use of IDENTITY information will make it far simpler. All of these elements make it much easier for styles to connect to the users' documents.

The entire DTD now looks like this:

```
<!--MEMO DTD Version 0.3 - Experimental Use Only-->
<!ELEMENT MEMO (HEAD?,HEADER, MAIN)>
<!--HEADER information for addressing -->
<!ELEMENT HEADER (DISTRIBUTION, SUBJECT, DATE)>
<!ELEMENT DISTRIBUTION (TO, CC?, FROM)>
<!ELEMENT TO (#PCDATA | IDENTITY)*>
<!ELEMENT CC (#PCDATA | IDENTITY)*>
<!ELEMENT FROM (#PCDATA| IDENTITY)*>
<!ELEMENT IDENTITY (#PCDATA)>
<!--May add NAMEID attribute for easier connection to
directory structures later -->
<!ELEMENT SUBJECT (#PCDATA | DESCRIP)*>
<!ELEMENT DESCRIP (#PCDATA)>
```

Continued

```
<!ELEMENT DATE (#PCDATA)>
<!ELEMENT AUTHOR (IDENTITY+)>
<!ELEMENT TYPIST (IDENTITY+)>
<!ELEMENT PARAGRAPH (#PCDATA|HIGHLIGHT|IDENTITY)*>
<!ELEMENT HIGHLIGHT (#PCDATA)>
<!ELEMENT HEADLINE (#PCDATA)>
<!ELEMENT MAIN ((PARAGRAPH | HIGHLIGHT | HEADLINE)*,
AUTHOR?, TYPIST?)>
```

This will work well for most memos, but it might be useful to allow content outside the confines of textual memo data to use the memo DTD. The employees of the public relations department, for example, would also like to use the memo DTD for their newsletters. Even though they could use PARAGRAPH, HIGHLIGHT, and HEADLINE, they would prefer to have something more specific for their newsletter, which would show up separately in the document-management system. More important, they would like to be able to modify their DTD later without creating repercussions throughout the company. The best solution for their situation appears to be a separate DTD that includes their elements and that they can combine with the main memo DTD when necessary. Their newsletter DTD will look like this:

```
<!ELEMENT NEWSLETTER (STORY+)>
<!ELEMENT STORY (LEAD, PARAGRAPH*)>
<!ELEMENT LEAD (#PCDATA)>
```

Combining this with the memo DTD may be a bit of a problem. The easiest way to enable the NEWSLETTER element to replace the MAIN element in the memo is to change the MEMO element:

```
<!ELEMENT MEMO (HEAD?, HEADER, (MAIN | NEWSLETTER))>
```

Alternatively, they could change the MAIN element to include NEWSLETTER elements:

```
<!ELEMENT MAIN (((PARAGRAPH | HIGHLIGHT | HEADLINE)*,
AUTHOR?, TYPIST?) | NEWSLETTER)>
```

If it turns out, however, that another part of the company also wants to use the memo DTD for a different purpose, these declarations will grow incredibly unwieldy. If XML allowed a document to declare an element more than once (as it does with attributes), the solution would be simple: Override MAIN in the newsletters by making a new MAIN declaration in another DTD. This isn't possible — declaring elements more than once is an error in XML that prevents the document from being valid. The easiest way to avoid the duplication work is similar to your first attempt:

```
<!ELEMENT MEMO (HEAD?, HEADER, (MAIN | ALTERNATE))>
```

By using ALTERNATE, you make it possible for multiple users to take advantage of your DTD and use the memo for other applications. (ALTERNATE isn't a keyword — any element name, as long as the element is left undefined in that DTD, will do.) The public relations department can now create a DTD that uses and expands the memo DTD:

```
<!ENTITY % memo SYSTEM "memo.dtd">
%memo;
<!ELEMENT NEWSLETTER (STORY+)>
<!ELEMENT STORY (LEAD, PARAGRAPH*)>
<!ELEMENT LEAD (#PCDATA)>
```

The newsletter from earlier in the chapter can be converted to XML in a fairly straightforward way:

```
<?xml version="1.0" standalone="no" encoding="UTF-8"?>
<!DOCTYPE MEMO SYSTEM "news.dtd">
<MEMO>
<HEADER>
<DISTRIBUTION>
<TO>To: <IDENTITY>Jimmy</IDENTITY></TO>
<CC>CC: <IDENTITY>All Employees</IDENTITY></CC>
<FROM>From: <IDENTITY>Lois Turpin, PR
Department</IDENTITY></FROM>
```

Continued

```
</DISTRIBUTION>
<SUBJECT>Re: <DESCRIP>JDCPD Today  - Sample Newsletter
Created with Memo DTD</DESCRIP></SUBJECT>
<DATE>1999-10-10</DATE>
</HEADER>
<ALTERNATE>
<!--BEGIN ALTERNATE CONTENT TO REPLACE MAIN -->
<NEWSLETTER>
<STORY><LEAD>Design Contest Winner -
</LEAD><PARAGRAPH>Frank Kravitz of the fuel-injection
division has won the September award for best car-part
drawing. Frank's masterpiece, <HIGHLIGHT>On to the Spark
Plug II</HIGHLIGHT>, will be on display in the lobby
through November 12. Frank also won the award in January
and July.</PARAGRAPH></STORY>
<STORY><LEAD>Donut Reimbursement Ends -
</LEAD><PARAGRAPH>To avoid a threatened doubling of
health insurance premiums, JDCPD has ended its donut
reimbursement program. "We are extremely sad to have to
take such unpleasant measures," said Jimmy, "but we hope
our employees will understand the difficult situation we
face."</PARAGRAPH></STORY>
<STORY><LEAD>Rice Cakes Available - </LEAD><PARAGRAPH>For
a limited time, rice cakes and a variety of herbal teas
will be available in Jimmy's office. Employees needing a
quick snack to charge up for a hard day of parts
designing are welcome to stop by.</PARAGRAPH></STORY>
<STORY><LEAD>Remember - </LEAD><PARAGRAPH>"Parts is
parts!"  Take pride in your work. The annual award for
best design will be announced in December.</PARAGRAPH>
</STORY>
</NEWSLETTER></ALTERNATE>
</MEMO>
```

This newsletter XML file parses quite happily using the news DTD in combination with the memo DTD, as shown in Figure 21-5.

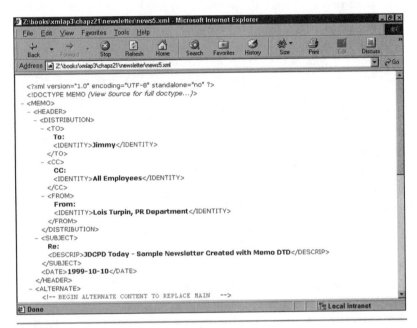

Figure 21-5 *The newsletter, parsed*

Using this model, other divisions can create their own ALTERNATE content models. The designers, for example, can develop a design brief that includes NOTATION elements enabling them to include all kinds of drawings and additional information. The public relations department can do the same to include its extra logos and perhaps even create an electronic version of the company letterhead. Although the memo model won't be able to cope with everything, XML gives it a chance to expand into new fields without becoming completely overloaded.

This is by no means the only way to add options. Instead of using an ALTERNATE element to enable expansion, it might be more useful to move the entire MAIN element definition out of the main DTD and into another file. The memo's core functionality is primarily the header and its distribution mechanism, so this might make sense. In this case, because approximately 90 percent of the documents created with this DTD are simple memos, and because the newsletter DTD reuses parts of the DTD under the MAIN element (for example, PARAGRAPH), it seems simplest to keep the DTD for a simple memo in the memo DTD. Yet another option would be to move the distribution information out of the memo DTD, making the memo DTD easier to reuse with other DTDs. Choosing from among these options is frequently difficult and your choice is very dependent upon the particular needs of your document structures and management systems.

Even though the document-management system won't care directly about the style sheets, it can keep track of which style sheet was used where. After all, style sheets are just another link. Placing your style information into a document-management tool makes it easy to foresee the impact of significant changes because the tool can let designers know which documents are about to receive the new style. Best of all, the document-management system may to able to support some kind of versioning. Older documents can stay with their older style sheet, whereas newer documents receive a facelift. The capabilities of the management system, of course, may vary.

It's probably best to create a separate style sheet for each DTD, even if you combine DTDs on a regular basis. In that way, the user's machine doesn't waste cycles parsing style information it won't be using, and developers don't waste time searching through an enormous collection of styles. Choose a naming convention and stick with it. I tend to name my DTD files *name*.dtd and the corresponding CSS files *name*.css. You can keep them in separate directories if you like, but try to maintain as much parallelism as possible between the two structures so that parts don't disappear. When it's time to modify a DTD, create a new DTD file (and associated CSS or other style sheet file) so that older documents don't suddenly become invalid. Document-management systems require humans to behave systematically — changing a DTD significantly could leave the document system stranded with files of documents it can't parse.

Although writing conversion programs is possible, it is rarely fun, and changing a significant library of documents by hand is even more tedious.

Building Histories: A DTD for Corporate Memory

History is rarely a favorite corporate subject. The future is always in sharp focus: companies strive to make the next quarter, the next year, or even the next decade their best one yet. Yesterday's sales figures may have paid for a new car or cost a promised bonus, but today's holdings and tomorrow's profits are of greater concern. As a result, companies often let their history slide. Memos and reports may accumulate in file cabinets, but periodically they are emptied or shipped to far-off storage, and key employees leave the company or retire. As employees have become more mobile, the odds of losing the person "who knows where all the bodies are buried" greatly increase. Most companies lack strategies for debriefing employees and organizing the information, which means wasted hours spent trying to determine what happened if a legal battle or a customer inquiry ever requires a reexamination of past activity.

The document structures you build in this example are designed expressly to keep some of that history alive and available at the end of a project or when an employee changes positions. Combined with a document management system, the information stored in that structure will make producing quick, comprehensive answers to questions about past projects easier. Large corporations that write proposals for large projects are often required to present past performance references; the information contained in this system will make it far easier for companies to describe their previous work, saving expensive resources for use on developing the forward-looking parts of the proposal.

This project and its associated DTDs could grow to be gigantic, especially if it were to expand from project history into project management. This discussion explores only some of the basic needs of the project and develops some of the core document types.

Undertaking this project means doing a considerable amount of political work before DTD design can even begin. Structured documents are useless if they aren't applied consistently. Even though it's easy to require that a particular element appear in a document, it's difficult to require that people who are on their way out the door fill out a few acres of paperwork. Building this document database successfully requires adding it to the process as a standard business procedure. The needs of that process will probably have direct effects on the nature of the DTD and the level of flexibility required. If this system is likely to be used regularly, it might even be worthwhile to build a custom interview application to collect the information.

Each project will probably have a set of data associated with it, representing interviews and other documents collected over the life of the project. Projects that last for years could end up with sizable quantities of information under a single header. Even though it's conceivable for all of this information to be assembled in a single document, large projects will quickly amass too much information even for a document-management system. Although a single-document approach makes great sense for small projects, a larger set of documents will function more smoothly if information is broken into more manageable chunks. Even though the use of elements makes finding relevant information easier, documents with thousands or hundreds of thousands of elements have probably outgrown a single-document file structure. This example reflects the need for larger structures by building several document types, each of which can connect to a central project record.

This project requires a set of DTDs, not just a single all-encompassing DTD. Because it is possible that all the DTDs will be combined in a single document, designers must take care not to use the same element name twice. You begin by creating a set of common elements that may be used throughout all the documents in the set. The IDENTITY element is even more important in this situation than it was in the previous example because the project's participants and their positions must be clearly defined. IDENTITY in this case will carry an attribute value linking it to a centralized directory of employees, and also provide space for the person's name, current title, and position, as follows:

```
<!ELEMENT IDENTITY (NAME,TITLE?,POSITION?)>
<!ATTLIST IDENTITY
     IDLINK CDATA #REQUIRED>
<!ELEMENT NAME (#PCDATA)>
<!ELEMENT TITLE (#PCDATA)>
<!ELEMENT POSITION (#PCDATA)>
```

Even though breaking the NAME element into first name and last name might be useful, it isn't really necessary because of the required IDLINK attribute of the IDENTITY element. IDLINK will connect the identity to a directory, which will include a full set of information. IDENTITY isn't restricted to individuals; it can also refer to departments or even companies. The link to the directory will produce some extra overhead because all people and groups referred to through IDENTITY must be entered in the directory. Not all organizations store customer information in their directories, although it's become more popular as the computer encroaches further and further on the turf of the Rolodex.

XML doesn't provide you with a way to check the value of the IDLINK. It can require that the IDLINK appear, but the parser will not itself check the value of IDLINK against the directory. That kind of logic must be placed in the application that processes the information returned by the parser. (The application can be the document-management system or another application preparing the information for display.) It should also be implemented in the program used to create the documents. Ideally, a simple lookup procedure enables authors to select IDENTITY values from a list of names provided by the directory.

LOCATION elements are similar to IDENTITY elements: they refer to individual units and can be looked up in a directory server, probably the same server that stores identities. However, because companies may briefly use locations all over the world, it doesn't seem as worthwhile to require that all LOCATION elements have a link in the directory. Key locations, such as company offices and workplaces, should definitely be listed, but hotels are probably not as important.

```
<!ELEMENT LOCATION (#PCDATA)>
<!ATTLIST LOCATION
    IDLINK CDATA #IMPLIED>
```

The next key element is the date. The documents themselves will be marked with the date on which they were written, and using a standard format for the date will make searching for information inside other elements much easier. The DATE element will be the same as the DATE element I use earlier in this chapter in the memo application, using ISO 8601 notation:

```
<!ELEMENT DATE (#PCDATA)>
```

This DTD will undoubtedly increase in size with additional elements for formatting and notation, but you can start simple. The four elements you include for content are EMPHASIS, RUMOR, QUOTE, and PARAGRAPH. EMPHASIS will enable authors to hit certain points harder; RUMOR will enable authors to include content that isn't certain, but that may be useful (and which probably should not be repeated); and QUOTE enables them to include material from customers and others. PARAGRAPH just provides a basic grammatical structure. These elements may all contain mixed content, which is represented by the parameter entity %TEXTELEMENTS;, as follows:

```
<!ENTITY % TEXTELEMENTS "(#PCDATA | EMPHASIS | RUMOR |
QUOTE | IDENTITY | LOCATION | DATE)*">
<!ELEMENT EMPHASIS (%TEXTELEMENTS;)>
<!ELEMENT RUMOR (%TEXTELEMENTS;)>
<!ELEMENT QUOTE (%TEXTELEMENTS;)>
<!ELEMENT PARAGRAPH (%TEXTELEMENTS;)>
```

Now that you have a set of elements you can use within the text, you can define some document-level structures. The information in this dataset will be stored in several different kinds of documents. Project managers will report different information from field technicians or accountants, and this will be reflected by a wide range of different document structures. For this example you use a project completion report, which is a general report by the project manager on a project that has just been finished. The root element is FINALREPORT, which contains elements identifying the project, the author, the date of the report, and the classification of the document. It also provides elements in which the author can add an overview of the project, financial information, schedule information, and detailed information regarding completed work, and list any commendations from the customer.

```
<!ELEMENT FINALREPORT (PROJECT, IDENTITY, DATE,
CLASSIFICATION, OVERVIEW, FINANCIALS, SCHEDULE, DETAIL,
COMMENDATIONS?)>
```

The PROJECT element, like the IDENTITY and LOCATION elements, links to other sources of information. This saves the author the effort of describing once again the project, the customer, the type of contract, and other stable information such as the start date of the project. (Start dates are not always stable, but they should be pretty firm by the time the project is completed.) As a result, the PROJECT element can remain simple, storing the name of the project in #PCDATA and linking to more detailed information through the PROJLINK attribute:

```
<!ELEMENT PROJECT (#PCDATA)>
<!ATTLIST PROJECT
     PROJLINK CDATA #REQUIRED>
```

The IDENTITY and DATE elements that follow the project indicate the author of this document and the date on which it was written, respectively. Their position in the PROJECT element is the only thing that identifies them as such; developers who want to make these elements more explicit (for example, to help out weaker search tools) could create wrappers for them:

```
<!ELEMENT AUTHOR (IDENTITY)>
<!ELEMENT REPORTDATE (DATE)>
```

Doing this would require a small change in the FINALREPORT element:

```
<!ELEMENT FINALREPORT (PROJECT, AUTHOR, REPORTDATE,
CLASSIFICATION, OVERVIEW, FINANCIALS,SCHEDULE, DETAIL,
COMMENDATIONS?)>
```

CLASSIFICATION is designed to help the document-management system control access to the document. Some documents may be OPEN (available to the public without restriction; handy for the public relations office), others may be PROPRIETARY (for use only within the company), some may even be SECRET (which limits access to particular readers within the company), and others may be SPECIAL. SPECIAL can be a classification above SECRET, or a general classification that requires the application to check the identity of the reader against a list someplace else.

No matter how this element is created, remember that the application, not the parser, must enforce security. XML has no built-in tools for providing security; document-management systems and other tools must take this responsibility, locking users out of documents until their identities and permissions have been validated.

Implementing this kind of element requires making some choices. The easiest way to implement this kind of element is to make CLASSIFICATION an element that uses #PCDATA as its data type. That way you can add new types easily; however, the parser won't check the types. An adventurous author could add GOOFY as a security classification.

```
<!ELEMENT CLASSIFICATION (#PCDATA)>
```

Another way to implement this element would be to make CLASSIFICATION an empty element with attributes that indicate the level of security:

```
<!ELEMENT CLASSIFICATION EMPTY>
<!ATTLIST CLASSIFICATION
    SECLEVEL (OPEN | PROPRIETARY | SECRET | SPECIAL)
"SPECIAL"
    SECLINK CDATA #IMPLIED>
```

SECLEVEL indicates the level of security, whereas SECLINK makes linking to an outside security directory for SPECIAL situations easy. (Depending on the type of application, you might want to set the default to a different value, or simply to #REQUIRED.)

You've finally reached the meat of the document: what was actually accomplished on this project, how much it cost, and how long it took. Because this document is a summary document, all this information can be easily stored. Heavy-duty accounting and schedule information can be stored in other documents (or even databases) and connected to the project by a centralized system, in much the same way that the PROJECT element is connected to the project by the PROJLINK attribute. The FINALREPORT document is here for quick reference, not to serve as a line-by-line account of every widget bought and sold. The overview section begins the summary:

```
<!ELEMENT OVERVIEW (PARAGRAPH+)>
```

The FINANCIALS element is broken down a little further but still presents only a general explanation of the project's costs:

```
<!ELEMENT FINANCIALS (ORIGINALQUOTE, FINALCOST,
EXPLANATION?)>
<!ELEMENT ORIGINALQUOTE (#PCDATA)>
<!ELEMENT FINALCOST (#PCDATA)>
<!ELEMENT EXPLANATION (PARAGRAPH+)>
```

The SCHEDULE element provides a similar broad description of the project schedule and uses the EXPLANATION element created for FINANCIALS:

```
<!ELEMENT SCHEDULE (ORIGINALSCHEDULE,ACTUALSCHEDULE,
EXPLANATION?)>
```

```
<!ELEMENT ORIGINALSCHEDULE (STARTDATE, ENDDATE?)>
<!ELEMENT ACTUALSCHEDULE (STARTDATE, ENDDATE?)>
<!ELEMENT STARTDATE (DATE)>
<!ELEMENT ENDDATE (DATE)>
```

In many cases you can simplify DTDs by using elements in more than one context, but doing so can create problems for simple processing applications. If someone wants a list of all the explanations for financial transactions, he or she needs a processor smart enough to separate EXPLANATION elements nested inside FINANCIALS elements from those nested inside SCHEDULE elements. Developers should find out the limitations of the planned processing application early. That way, creating separate FINEXPLANATION and SCHEDEXPLANATION elements is easy.

Despite its name, the DETAIL element receives a very simple XML declaration. DETAIL is the area in which the project manager enters detailed information, but from the perspective of the parser, all that information uses PARAGRAPH elements, which can contain all the elements listed in the %TEXTELEMENTS; parameter entity. The COMMENDATIONS element is likewise a container for text elements:

```
<!ELEMENT DETAIL (PARAGRAPH+)>
<!ELEMENT COMMENDATIONS (PARAGRAPH+)>
```

Now that you have all the parts defined, it's time to combine them into DTDs. The first DTD contains all the text elements needed in documents in this system, providing basic textual types:

```
<!---TEXT CONTENT ELEMENT INFORMATION -->
<!---IDENTITY INFORMATION -->
<!ELEMENT IDENTITY (NAME,TITLE?,POSITION?)>
<!ATTLIST IDENTITY
     IDLINK CDATA #REQUIRED>
<!ELEMENT NAME (#PCDATA)>
<!ELEMENT TITLE (#PCDATA)>
<!ELEMENT POSITION (#PCDATA)>
<!---LOCATION INFORMATION -->
```

```
<!ELEMENT LOCATION (#PCDATA)>
<!ATTLIST LOCATION
     IDLINK CDATA #IMPLIED>
<!---DATE INFORMATION -->
<!ELEMENT DATE (#PCDATA)>
<!---OTHER TEXT CONTENT -->
<!ELEMENT EMPHASIS (%TEXTELEMENTS;)>
<!ELEMENT RUMOR (%TEXTELEMENTS;)>
<!ELEMENT QUOTE (%TEXTELEMENTS;)>
<!ELEMENT PARAGRAPH (%TEXTELEMENTS;)>
<!ENTITY % TEXTELEMENTS "(#PCDATA | EMPHASIS | RUMOR |
QUOTE | IDENTITY | LOCATION | DATE)*">
```

The second piece, which actually defines your project report, includes the preceding DTD using a parameter entity:

```
<!---DTD for Final Project Reports -->
<!ELEMENT FINALREPORT (PROJECT, AUTHOR, REPORTDATE,
CLASSIFICATION, OVERVIEW, FINANCIALS,SCHEDULE, DETAIL,
COMMENDATIONS?)>
<!---Link to text content declarations -->
<!ENTITY % TEXTDECLARATION SYSTEM "textelem.dtd">
%TEXTDECLARATION;
<!---Project Identification -->
<!ELEMENT PROJECT (#PCDATA)>
<!ATTLIST PROJECT
     PROJLINK CDATA #REQUIRED>
<!---AUTHOR AND REPORT DATE WRAPPERS, FOR EASIER
SEARCHING -->
<!ELEMENT AUTHOR (IDENTITY)>
<!ELEMENT REPORTDATE (DATE)>
<!---CLASSIFICATION. ENFORCED BY DOCUMENT MANAGEMENT
SYSTEM -->
<!ELEMENT CLASSIFICATION EMPTY>
<!ATTLIST CLASSIFICATION
```

Continued

```
         SECLEVEL (OPEN | PROPRIETARY | SECRET | SPECIAL)
"SPECIAL"
         SECLINK CDATA #IMPLIED>
<!---REPORT ELEMENTS -->
<!ELEMENT OVERVIEW (PARAGRAPH+)>
<!ELEMENT FINANCIALS (ORIGINALQUOTE, FINALCOST,
EXPLANATION?)>
<!ELEMENT ORIGINALQUOTE (#PCDATA)>
<!ELEMENT FINALCOST (#PCDATA)>
<!ELEMENT EXPLANATION (PARAGRAPH+)>
<!ELEMENT SCHEDULE (ORIGINALSCHEDULE,ACTUALSCHEDULE,
EXPLANATION?)>
<!ELEMENT ORIGINALSCHEDULE (STARTDATE, ENDDATE?)>
<!ELEMENT ACTUALSCHEDULE (STARTDATE, ENDDATE?)>
<!ELEMENT STARTDATE (DATE)>
<!ELEMENT ENDDATE (DATE)>
<!ELEMENT DETAIL (PARAGRAPH+)>
<!ELEMENT COMMENDATIONS (PARAGRAPH+)>
```

This DTD is only one possible beginning for a much larger and more elaborate structure. With a well-built document management system you can construct multiple document types around a database of PROJECT information. You could keep document types for drawings, detailed reports of tasks carried out, customer orders, time spent on projects, status reports, and even project management information in the same system, which would give you secure but easy access and the ability to cross-reference. These systems have yet to appear, and most of them will undoubtedly need a considerable amount of customization, but they will probably be the most efficient keepers of XML information. With any luck, document management systems will replace the file cabinets and file systems of today, keeping track of large numbers of documents and their components and making them readily accessible.

Approaches to Document Distribution

Although it's easy to send XML documents over HTTP, the Web browser model of users entering URLs or clicking links to find information isn't the only option in town. Developers have created ways to use XML itself to establish communications between different kinds of systems to send information on a scheduled, as-needed, or even syndicated basis. Creating and storing XML documents is only part of the solution for many implementers; getting them to an appropriate audience is the other side of the coin. "Push" may seem dead as a consumer technology, but there are still plenty of tools available that use similar approaches to let content providers share information.

Syndicating documents with ICE

Information and Content Exchange is a difficult protocol to categorize. In some ways it manages document content, including XML, but primarily it uses XML to build a set of tools for managing business relationships, setting up a subscriber-syndicator model for content exchange. It doesn't handle secure transactions or financial obligations by itself; it relies instead on HTTP, SSL, and other supporting structures to handle those issues. ICE focuses on managing the subscriber-syndicator relationship, simplifying the task of letting Web sites share their information through the application of clearly defined, previously agreed-upon, and stable rules within a management framework supporting business needs. If a relationship goes sour, the syndicator can pull the plug on a subscriber, or a subscriber can stop making requests, without having to go to a lot of trouble. ICE is intended to move information sharing and reuse well beyond the HTML framing that has appeared on the Web, reducing the costs of distributing information and at the same time making it more manageable and potentially billable.

Tip

To read the ICE Protocol, visit `http://www.w3.org/TR/NOTE-ice`. For more information on the latest developments, visit `http://www.icestandard.org/`. Robin Cover's bibliography page on ICE, at `http://www.oasis-open.org/cover/ice.html`, also brings together a number of resources.

Using RSS to make headlines

RSS (RDF Site Summary, or Rich Site Summary, depending on which version and whom you ask) is a widely supported format for exchanging brief summaries of information, typically headlines. RSS began at Netscape as a tool for exchanging information between Web servers and the MyNetscape feature (`http://my.netscape.com/publish/help/mnn20/quickstart.html`) built into Netscape 4.0, but has grown into a general tool for exchanging headlines and summaries. Sites that integrate multiple RSS (and other) tools for delivery, search, and archiving, such as Moreover (`http://w.moreover.com/dev/index.html`) and Meerkat (`http://www.oreillynet.com/meerkat/`), however, give users new options beyond a stream of information from a single source. Web sites use the flows as well — XML.com, for instance, uses RSS feeds from several other XML-oriented Web sites to display updated headlines on its front page.

RSS documents begin by identifying the channel and basic metadata about the channel, like copyright status and maintainer, along with an image to represent the channel. After the metadata information is complete, items appear. Titles and link URIs are required, but descriptions are optional. RSS also has some features, such as text input, that aren't widely used outside of MyNetscape. A sample RSS file from `xmlhack.com` might look like this:

```
<?xml version="1.0" encoding="ISO-8859-1"?>
<!DOCTYPE rss PUBLIC "-//Netscape Communications//DTD RSS
0.91//EN" "http://my.netscape.com/publish/formats/rss-
0.91.dtd">
<rss version="0.91">
 <channel>
  <title>xmlhack</title>
  <link>http://xmlhack.com</link>
  <description>Developer news from the XML
community</description>
  <language>en-us</language>
  <copyright>Copyright 1999, xmlhack team.</copyright>
  <managingEditor>editor@xmlhack.com</managingEditor>
  <webMaster>webmaster@xmlhack.com</webMaster>
  <image>
    <title>xmlhack</title>
    <url>http://xmlhack.com/images/mynetscape88.gif</url>
    <link>http://xmlhack.com</link>
    <width>88</width>
    <height>31</height>
    <description>News, opinions, tips and issues
concerning XML development</description>
  </image>

<item>
<title>RELAX Namespace discussion, implementation</title>
<link>http://xmlhack.com/read.php?item=970</link>
<description>Although a formal specification is still in
the future, Murata Makoto has posted a design memo and
two examples (1 2) of RELAX Namespace, and Asami Tomoharu
announced support in an alpha version of
Relaxer.</description>
</item>
<item>
```

Continued

```
<title>SAX2 bugfix pre-release</title>
<link>http://xmlhack.com/read.php?item=969</link>
<description>David Megginson has put together a pre-
release of bug fixes for SAX2. A final release is
expected some time in January.</description>
</item>
<item>
<title>Talk back to XMLhack</title>
<link>http://xmlhack.com/read.php?item=968</link>
<description>We've added a commenting facility to
xmlhack, so now you can add extra information and
questions to the bottom of each article.</description>
</item>
<item>
<title>Love-hate relationships with XML</title>
<link>http://xmlhack.com/read.php?item=967</link>
<description>Two sites that both embrace XML and
criticize its flaws have appeared in the last few weeks:
xmlsuck.com and xmlbastard.com.</description>
</item>
<item>
<title>W3C releases new draft of XML Infoset</title>
<link>http://xmlhack.com/read.php?item=966</link>
<description>Although having previously reached Last Call
stage a year ago, the XML Core Working group has decided
to publish another Working Draft of the XML Infoset, due
to extensive reworking after feedback from the Last Call
draft.</description>
</item>
<item>
<title>New versions of Perl RDF tools RDF::Service and
RDFStore</title>
<link>http://xmlhack.com/read.php?item=965</link>
```

```
<description>RDF::Service 0.4, part of the Wraf Perl RDF
application framework, and RDFStore 0.31, a Perl API for
RDF Storage, have been released.</description>
</item>
 </channel>
</rss>
```

This file is updated every time a new story is posted to xmlhack. com, and new ones are available from http://xmlhack.com/ rss.php.

RSS is in something of a transition right now. Netscape has been focusing on other projects, and UserLand has been hosting the RSS specification (see http://backend.userland.com/rss091). RSS has been very useful, but developers are finding it more and more important to extend it, and some want to return to its roots in RDF, the Resource Description Framework, for a more concrete though somewhat more complex model. That work is proceeding on an eGroups list at http://www.egroups.com/group/rss-dev. The shift back to RDF — in fact any change whatsoever — has proven somewhat controversial, and the specification may fork. For the latest on RSS, you may want to check the UserLand RSS site, the RSS-DEV eGroups list, and xmlhack.com.

Using Channel Definition Format

CDF is the first XML-based standard to receive anything resembling widespread use. Microsoft submitted the proposal to the W3C in March 1997, but CDF has largely remained a Microsoft standard, though aggregators like moreover.com also support it. CDF contains a standard set of tags for defining channels for push content, sending information to users without requiring their intervention. Channels automate the flow of data from Web server to Web browser, providing the browser with a schedule for downloading new content from the channel's server and labeling that content with a button and some brief descriptions. CDF documents, like the following one, display information pointing the browser to the source of the information, descriptive information (such as the logo, an abstract, and a title), and a schedule for regular downloads. When users want to visit the channel, the information is already loaded for them. This system does away with waiting for downloads and makes it easy for users to reference Web information offline.

```
<CHANNEL HREF="http://www.simonstl.com/index.html">
<TITLE>Simon St.Laurent's Ravings</TITLE>
<ABSTRACT>Collected essays, projects, and book
information for Simon St.Laurent</ABSTRACT>

<LOGO HREF="http://www.simonstl.com/craneico.gif"
STYLE="ICON"/>
<LOGO HREF="http://www.simonstl.com/logo.gif"
STYLE="IMAGE"/>

<SCHEDULE>
<INTERVALTIME DAY="14">
</SCHEDULE>

<ITEM HREF="http://www.simonstl.com/articles/index.html">
<TITLE>Articles</TITLE>
<ABSTRACT>Articles on XML</ABSTRACT>
</ITEM>

<ITEM HREF="http://www.simonstl.com/projects/index.html">
<TITLE>Projects</TITLE>
<ABSTRACT>Projects, including open-source software
development</ABSTRACT>
</ITEM>

<ITEM HREF="http://www.simonstl.com/xmllinks.html">
<TITLE>XML Links</TITLE>
<ABSTRACT>Links to XML Resources, from specifications to
news sites to mailing lists.</ABSTRACT>
```

```
</ITEM>
```

```
</CHANNEL>
```

Channel content is still in HTML, not XML. XML just provides a framework that enables the browser to find and describe the content. Users can explore that content through the channel bar, even (to the extent that the browser has collected it) when not connected. The schedule can have odd effects on computers that use dial-up connections; since most schedules are designed to download data at off-peak times (midnight to 4 a.m.), Internet Explorer users may wake up in the middle of the night to the cheerful sound of their modems dialing out to their Internet service providers.

 Cross-Reference

You can access CDF information from several sources. View the submission to the W3C, which includes a full description of the DTD, at `http://www.w3.org/TR/NOTE-CDFsubmit.html`. Microsoft has white papers and other information available at its MSDN (`http://msdn.microsoft.com/`) and Internet Explorer (`http://www.microsoft.com/ie`) Web sites. For more information on CDF and push technologies in general, see Ethan Cerami's *Delivering Push* (McGraw-Hill, 1998).

Chapter 22

XML for Data-Driven Applications

The documents in the preceding chapters often correspond to real paper documents, the kind of documents that people can pick up (or load in a Web browser) and read. XML isn't limited to this kind of information; indeed, many of its earliest applications have supplied information in forms not readily presentable to humans. The field in which XML may make the greatest strides is the field of communication between computers and between computers and other devices. Machine-to-machine communications has proven difficult in the past. The DTDs and examples in this chapter provide solutions for what I call nontraditional documents — data structures for which XML is very appropriate but that humans wouldn't normally read. Instead of presenting information to people, these documents present information to programs, which in turn use that information to determine their behavior, not just to present information on a screen or a page.

Cross-Reference

This chapter presents an introduction to data-focused XML documents and their uses, including some applications that you might construe as programming. But it isn't a guide to XML processing in general. See Chapter 23 for more information on models and tools for processing XML.

Data for Interchange

The simplest (though in some ways most complicated) use of XML is as an interchange format for transmission between unlike systems. The concepts involved are fairly simple, though they offer infinite variations. (Some of those variations tie into the commercial dreams explored in Chapter 20.) As Chapter 4 briefly shows, XML can serve as a container for nearly any text-based information, simplifying the task of shipping information from one application to another, even if the application designers know nothing about the other's products and know only the rules for the file format. The tabular data commonly transferred among relational databases may not seem like a natural fit for XML's hierarchical structures, but XML can handle tables without a hitch, and database vendors are adding XML parsers and interfaces to their existing products. Nearly any application, not just databases, that needs to transfer information among formats can put XML to use as a commonly understood layer.

Making this work requires more than dumping information out of one application and pouring it into another verbatim. Both applications need to include components capable of parsing XML and relating the file contents to their internal data structures and/or taking their internal data structures and exporting them to XML files. Figure 22-1 demonstrates this process.

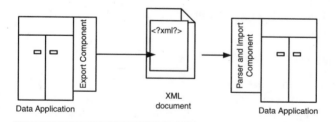

Figure 22-1 *Importing and exporting using an XML file for interchange*

Presently, database vendors are announcing tools that should make this process easier, but most current implementations involve an XML parser that uses SQL (through JDBC or ODBC, typically) to add information to a database, or Common Gateway Interface (CGI)–style programming to export database information into a template. Non-database applications typically require some custom programming, much like the tools used to import and export plain text and delimited text versions of information. Though the techniques appear primitive (and currently tend to produce fairly verbose output), XML's structures are well matched to raw-data interchange. Its use of Unicode as a foundation for text processing simplifies many of the chores involved in exchanging information among sources that use different character sets. Its structures promise more reliability and more manageability than the current delimited formats that provide baseline interchange services.

Data for Control

Many applications perform a limited number of tasks and need only a set of data to send them on their way. Programming a consumer VCR, for instance, means giving it start and stop times for recording, a channel, and possibly information (such as tape speed) about the way in which the information is recorded. In no case (unless there are some very unusual VCRs out there) does a user have to write the code that actually tells the VCR to check the time and compare it to a table, select the channel, move the mechanisms to start the recording process, and check the time until the stop time is reached.

Running a house

The first example in this chapter applies XML to a rather different computing field: device control. Given a system that responds to a small set of inputs without requiring processing of return values, you can write a "program" purely in data. For starters, you'll build a DTD able to control a set of light switches (or other electrical devices). Light switches are an extremely simple example, but many situations require the control of hundreds or thousands of lights. This example begins with the lighting in a typical house, but you could apply it to display lights or even stage lights.

My parents used to receive a catalog from DAK (a direct marketer selling electronics of all sorts) every few months; it was crammed with odd and unusual stereo equipment and gadgetry. One of the weirdest items DAK carried was the X-10 system, which enabled you to control electrical devices by remote control. Originally it came with a controller unit and modules that plugged in between the electrical socket and the plug of a lamp or other electrical device. The controller unit sent signals over the electrical wires to the individual boxes (up to 256 of them) telling them to turn on or off or to dim to a particular level. Eventually the controller unit sprouted a serial computer interface, which made it easy to program devices to turn on and off at various times of day — a more expensive, but more accurate, device timer than the boxes with dials on them. By now the X-10 system has grown considerably more elaborate (see `http://www.x10.com` for details). Remote controls that can run a house rather than a TV make it easy for the ultimate couch potatoes to do a lot without getting up.

Defining a document interface to light switches with a DTD

Although the DTD you develop in this chapter isn't designed expressly for the X-10 interface, you can easily build an interface that converts the data in these documents into the signals controlling electrical devices. The X-10 system actually uses a limited set of commands to control its devices, but your DTD doesn't need to worry about specific commands. It will just define particular states that the control system should achieve. A processing application would take the information returned by the parser and determine the necessary commands to achieve the state you want. Rather than give the controller a sequence of steps, your document will give it a desired result and enable the controller to figure out how best to achieve it.

You will control two different categories of equipment: lights and appliances. Lights can turn on or off and dim, whereas appliances can only turn on and off. (If users want to extend this DTD to control appliances, not just their power sources, via remote controls, it shouldn't be too difficult.) Lights and appliances are identified by addresses that effectively represent hexadecimal numbers. The address begins with a house code, A-P. Generally, users set up an entire system on one letter, which limits them to 16 devices but enables them to avoid conflicts with neighbors. Users without gadget-minded neighbors can use more than one house code. The unit code identifies the controlling module. It's a number from 1 to 16. Device modules can be set to the same address; all device modules with the same address will respond simultaneously to commands. A set of three lamps on address B10 will all turn on or off or dim as requested in response to commands sent to B10.

Your DTD will enable users to create documents to give orders to this system. A computer will process all these documents, but you can keep them human-readable for easy editing. To help with this, you may choose to include a description of all the modules on the system, followed by the states desired and the conditions that set them off, in your documents.

```
<!ELEMENT CONTROLSCHEDULE (MODULE*, STATE*, TRIGGER*)>
```

Your modules need several identifiers. For now, stick with the system that X-10 uses to build an address, adding two pieces that provide additional information to the processing application and human editors:

```
<!ELEMENT MODULE (ADDRESS, TYPE?, DESCRIPTION?)>
<!ELEMENT ADDRESS (HOUSE, UNIT)>
<!ELEMENT HOUSE (#PCDATA)>
```

Continued

```
<!ELEMENT UNIT (#PCDATA)>
<!ELEMENT TYPE (#PCDATA)>
<!ELEMENT DESCRIPTION (#PCDATA)>
```

You give the MODULE element a little extra flexibility by enabling it to contain ADDRESS and TYPE elements. You can require the user or the program creating these files to determine whether the module at a particular address is a light module or an appliance module and to identify the modules purely through addresses. Adding TYPE increases flexibility and makes these documents more portable. A processing application that doesn't care about TYPE can strip it out, whereas a new application set up for the first time might use the TYPE element to import more complete information about the control modules. TYPE also adds a bit of flexibility in case new varieties of a module appear, because commands may vary depending on the kind of module receiving them. (At present the X-10 system doesn't, but a more advanced future system might.) DESCRIPTION gives the humans programming these devices a description of the device and its location.

The ADDRESS element enables us to identify modules uniquely (or in sets, as described previously). A developer impatient with the A-P, 1-16 identifiers of the X-10 system could convert them to their hex equivalents easily and represent them in the DTD as follows:

```
<!ELEMENT ADDRESS (HEXADDRESS | (HOUSE, UNIT))>
<!ELEMENT HEXADDRESS (#PCDATA)>
```

For now, you can stick to using the HOUSE and UNIT identifiers.

Even though the MODULE element includes ADDRESS elements, it won't be very useful for issuing commands because multiple modules can share a single address. ADDRESS will be the key element for issuing commands. After a document's initial MODULE declarations, a series of STATE declarations may follow. STATE declarations define a final position rather than a means of getting there. You'll provide names for your STATEs, as well as a description and list of component parts:

```
<!ELEMENT STATE (NAME, DESCRIPTION?, COMPONENT+)>
```

The NAME element provides a reference your programs will use to find and implement this STATE. The DESCRIPTION element, the same one you used earlier in this chapter for modules, provides descriptions to human users. The COMPONENT element defines the final position for the devices on modules at a single address:

```
<!ELEMENT NAME (#PCDATA)>
<!ELEMENT COMPONENT (DESCRIPTION?, ADDRESS, POSITION)>
<!ELEMENT POSITION (#PCDATA)>
```

ADDRESS elements are the same elements I define earlier in the chapter for identifying modules. POSITION holds the data defining the position to which you should set the module. For appliance modules it can be ON or OFF; for the lamp module it can be ON, OFF, or a dimmer position defined by a percentage. If new modules came on the market the POSITION element could hold new values as necessary, because only the processing application interprets the meaning of this element.

Telling the system to move to one of these states is more complicated because a user might want to select a particular state for several different reasons. Timers control many of the home-automation uses for these modules. Lights can turn on and off depending on the time of day. This can make a house appear occupied while the owners are away, or it can just make sure that the lights are on when people come home from work. Users may also want the ability to select a state by flipping a (specially wired) light switch. Motion detectors and remote consoles can also select a state. This requirement makes constructing the TRIGGER element a little tricky.

```
<!ELEMENT TRIGGER (STATENAME, TIMED*, SWITCH*)>
<!ELEMENT STATENAME (#PCDATA)>
```

STATENAME is just a reference to a previously defined STATE element. TIME elements define a time for implementing the chosen STATE. Because users may need a variety of timing mechanisms, several options are available for daily events, weekly events, and events taking place on a particular day:

```
<!ELEMENT TIMED ((DAILY | WEEKLY | DATE), TIME)>
<!ELEMENT DAILY EMPTY>
<!ELEMENT WEEKLY (WEEKDAY*)>
<!ELEMENT WEEKDAY (#PCDATA)>
<!ELEMENT DATE (DAY,MONTH, YEAR)>
<!ELEMENT DAY (#PCDATA)>
<!ELEMENT MONTH (#PCDATA)>
<!ELEMENT YEAR (#PCDATA)>
<!ELEMENT TIME (HOUR, MINUTE, SECOND?)>
<!ELEMENT HOUR (#PCDATA)>
<!ELEMENT MINUTE (#PCDATA)>
<!ELEMENT SECOND (#PCDATA)>
```

As I mention in the previous chapter, many available date formats don't require that you atomize the day, month, year, and so on. For an application like this one, you might prefer those formats, but atomizing things can make it easier to create interfaces for them.

The SWITCH element contains a description — a name or address understood by the processing application — of the switch triggering the implementation of the state:

```
<!ELEMENT SWITCH (#PCDATA)>
```

The processing application for this document must parse the document and set up an internal timer as well as the serial connection to the modules and switches. When any of the trigger conditions are met it will send out the appropriate commands to the control modules, setting the lights and other devices to their appropriate positions.

Most wall and remote switches in these systems are hard-coded to particular modules. Users who need to connect only one switch to one device can still use direct calls to the module and bypass this processing system directly. The system that makes a later call to a module will simply override previous commands. Of course, if someone turns a light off or leaves it unplugged, nothing will visibly happen.

Assembling your DTD produces the following:

```
<!ELEMENT CONTROLSCHEDULE (MODULE*, STATE*, TRIGGER*)>
<!ELEMENT MODULE (ADDRESS, TYPE?, DESCRIPTION?)>
<!ELEMENT ADDRESS (HOUSE, UNIT)>
<!ELEMENT HOUSE (#PCDATA)>
<!ELEMENT UNIT (#PCDATA)>
<!ELEMENT TYPE (#PCDATA)>
<!ELEMENT DESCRIPTION (#PCDATA)>
<!ELEMENT STATE (NAME, DESCRIPTION?, COMPONENT+)>
<!ELEMENT NAME (#PCDATA)>
<!ELEMENT COMPONENT (DESCRIPTION?,ADDRESS, POSITION)>
<!ELEMENT POSITION (#PCDATA)>
<!ELEMENT TRIGGER (STATENAME, TIMED*, SWITCH*)>
<!ELEMENT STATENAME (#PCDATA)>
<!ELEMENT TIMED ((DAILY | WEEKLY | DATE), TIME)>
<!ELEMENT DAILY EMPTY>
<!ELEMENT WEEKLY (WEEKDAY*)>
<!ELEMENT WEEKDAY (#PCDATA)>
<!ELEMENT DATE (DAY,MONTH, YEAR)>
<!ELEMENT DAY (#PCDATA)>
<!ELEMENT MONTH (#PCDATA)>
<!ELEMENT YEAR (#PCDATA)>
<!ELEMENT TIME (HOUR, MINUTE, SECOND?)>
<!ELEMENT HOUR (#PCDATA)>
<!ELEMENT MINUTE (#PCDATA)>
<!ELEMENT SECOND (#PCDATA)>
<!ELEMENT SWITCH (#PCDATA)>
```

You can use this DTD to create files that a processing application uses to control a small set of lamps and a radio:

```
<?xml version="1.0" encoding="UTF-8"?>
<!DOCTYPE CONTROLSCHEDULE SYSTEM "controller.dtd">
<CONTROLSCHEDULE>
<MODULE>
```

Continued

```
<ADDRESS><HOUSE>B</HOUSE><UNIT>2</UNIT></ADDRESS>
<TYPE>APPLIANCE</TYPE>
<DESCRIPTION>Radio in livingroom</DESCRIPTION>
</MODULE>
<MODULE>
<ADDRESS><HOUSE>B</HOUSE><UNIT>10</UNIT></ADDRESS>
<TYPE>LAMP</TYPE>
<DESCRIPTION>Lamp in entryway</DESCRIPTION>
</MODULE>
<MODULE>
<ADDRESS><HOUSE>B</HOUSE><UNIT>10</UNIT></ADDRESS>
<TYPE>LAMP</TYPE>
<DESCRIPTION>Light outside front door</DESCRIPTION>
</MODULE>
<MODULE>
<ADDRESS><HOUSE>B</HOUSE><UNIT>11</UNIT></ADDRESS>
<TYPE>LAMP</TYPE>
<DESCRIPTION>Lamp in livingroom</DESCRIPTION>
</MODULE>
<STATE>
<NAME>AFTWORK</NAME><DESCRIPTION>Come home to a friendly
house.</DESCRIPTION>
<COMPONENT>
<DESCRIPTION>Turn the radio on</DESCRIPTION>
<ADDRESS><HOUSE>B</HOUSE><UNIT>2</UNIT></ADDRESS>
<POSITION>ON</POSITION>
</COMPONENT>
<COMPONENT>
<DESCRIPTION>Turn on the living room light</DESCRIPTION>
<ADDRESS><HOUSE>B</HOUSE><UNIT>11</UNIT></ADDRESS>
<POSITION>ON</POSITION>
</COMPONENT>
</STATE>
<STATE>
```

```
<NAME>AFTDINNER</NAME><DESCRIPTION>turn on front light,
dim lights</DESCRIPTION>
<COMPONENT>
<DESCRIPTION>Turn on porch, front lights</DESCRIPTION>
<ADDRESS><HOUSE>B</HOUSE><UNIT>10</UNIT></ADDRESS>
<POSITION>ON</POSITION>
</COMPONENT>
<COMPONENT>
<DESCRIPTION>Dim livingroom</DESCRIPTION>
<ADDRESS><HOUSE>B</HOUSE><UNIT>10</UNIT></ADDRESS>
<POSITION>80%</POSITION>
</COMPONENT>
</STATE>
<STATE>
<NAME>POWERSAVE</NAME><DESCRIPTION>Dim front
lights</DESCRIPTION>
<ADDRESS><HOUSE>B</HOUSE><UNIT>10</UNIT></ADDRESS>
<POSITION>40%</POSITION>
</STATE>
<STATE>
<NAME>MORNING</NAME><DESCRIPTION>Turn off front
lights</DESCRIPTION>
<ADDRESS><HOUSE>B</HOUSE><UNIT>10</UNIT></ADDRESS>
<POSITION>OFF</POSITION>
</STATE>
<TRIGGER>
<STATENAME>AFTWORK</STATENAME>
<TIMED>
<WEEKLY><WEEKDAY>MON</WEEKDAY><WEEKDAY>TUES</WEEKDAY><WEE
KDAY>WED</WEEKDAY><WEEKDAY>THURS</WEEKDAY><WEEKDAY>FRI</W
EEKDAY></WEEKLY>
<TIME><HOUR>17</HOUR><MINUTE>00</MINUTE></TIME>
</TIMED>
</TRIGGER>
```

Continued

```
<TRIGGER>
<STATENAME>AFTDINNER</STATENAME>
<TIMED>
<DAILY/><TIME><HOUR>20</HOUR><MINUTE>00</MINUTE></TIME>
</TIMED>
</TRIGGER>
<TRIGGER>
<STATENAME>POWERSAVE</STATENAME>
<TIMED>
<DAILY/><TIME><HOUR>23</HOUR><MINUTE>00</MINUTE></TIME>
</TIMED>
</TRIGGER>
<TRIGGER>
<STATENAME>MORNING</STATENAME>
<TIMED>
<DAILY/><TIME><HOUR>7</HOUR><MINUTE>00</MINUTE></TIME>
</TIMED>
</TRIGGER>
<TRIGGER>
<STATENAME>AFTWORK</STATENAME>
<SWITCH>RMT01 - ON</SWITCH><!-Remote Control in case we
get home early ->
</TRIGGER>
<TRIGGER>
<STATENAME>MORNING</STATENAME>
<SWITCH>LT01 - OFF</SWITCH><!-If you don't want to leave
lights on all night ->
</TRIGGER>
</CONTROLSCHEDULE>
```

   This document tells the controller of the existence of several modules controlling some lights and a radio. At 5 p.m., or when someone pushes a remote control button, the living room lights up and the radio turns on. At 8 p.m., the living room lights dim a bit (for better television viewing, perhaps) and the front porch light turns on to welcome visitors or frighten away thieves. At 11 p.m., the front lights dim to save a few dollars on power. In the morning (or when someone flips a switch off), the porch lights go off.

This is a fairly elaborate exercise for rather small results. The real power of this example, however, comes in situations involving more widespread automation. Although writing XML directly like this is tedious and error-prone, it could serve well as a file format for control data produced by a friendlier GUI application. File formats like this make it easier to exchange data written for a particular control program to a different program without losing all the logic. Because the information is presented as a series of states rather than direct commands, it doesn't matter what mechanism underlies those states. These files could work with an X-10 system, a different system that uses radio frequencies, a manual system that prints out instruction cards for lamplighters, or a much larger system controlling hundreds or thousands of lights. XML's easy-to-parse structure makes it a reliable tool for exchanging information among systems of every size.

Use DTDs like this one for simple control situations where the expected results are easily defined and it doesn't matter very much if something fails. XML is obviously not a programming language, but rather a delivery vehicle for data. This application of XML is ideal for situations where the flow of data is essentially one-way, but more complex situations that produce exceptions or errors demand a much richer set of commands delivered in a more interactive fashion. XML can transmit data between processing applications on different nodes on a network, where all nodes can send and receive XML responses, but the core logic must remain in the processing application. XML just provides a structured way of storing and communicating data.

Rebuilding the control structure with XML Schemas

Because XML Schemas provides more control over times and dates through its data-typing facilities, you can simplify a lot of the structures used to represent dates and times. The DATE element may now contain an ISO 8601 date format instead of multiple elements, as may the TIME element. Because you can define constraints for element types, you can supply extra rules for the WEEKDAY element as well. The following XML Schema is equivalent to the preceding XML 1.0 DTD except where it has been marked in bold.

```
<xsd:schema
xmlns:xsd="http://www.w3.org/2000/10/XMLSchema">
  <xsd:element name="CONTROLSCHEDULE">
    <xsd:complexType>
      <xsd:sequence>
        <xsd:element ref="MODULE" minOccurs="0"
maxOccurs="unbounded"/>
        <xsd:element ref="STATE" minOccurs="0"
maxOccurs="unbounded"/>
        <xsd:element ref="TRIGGER" minOccurs="0"
maxOccurs="unbounded"/>
      </xsd:sequence>
    </xsd:complexType>
  </xsd:element>
  <xsd:element name="MODULE">
    <xsd:complexType>
      <xsd:sequence>
        <xsd:element ref="ADDRESS"/>
        <xsd:element ref="TYPE" minOccurs="0"/>
        <xsd:element ref="DESCRIPTION" minOccurs="0"/>
      </xsd:sequence>
    </xsd:complexType>
  </xsd:element>
  <xsd:element name="ADDRESS">
    <xsd:complexType>
      <xsd:sequence>
        <xsd:element ref="HOUSE"/>
        <xsd:element ref="UNIT"/>
      </xsd:sequence>
```

```
    </xsd:complexType>
  </xsd:element>
  <xsd:element name="HOUSE" type="xsd:string"/>
  <xsd:element name="UNIT" type="xsd:integer"/>
  <xsd:element name="TYPE" type="xsd:string"/>
  <xsd:element name="DESCRIPTION" type="xsd:string"/>
  <xsd:element name="STATE">
    <xsd:complexType>
      <xsd:sequence>
        <xsd:element ref="NAME"/>
        <xsd:element ref="DESCRIPTION" minOccurs="0"/>
        <xsd:element ref="COMPONENT"
maxOccurs="unbounded"/>
      </xsd:sequence>
    </xsd:complexType>
  </xsd:element>
  <xsd:element name="COMPONENT">
    <xsd:complexType>
      <xsd:sequence>
        <xsd:element ref="DESCRIPTION" minOccurs="0"/>
        <xsd:element ref="ADDRESS"/>
        <xsd:element ref="POSITION"/>
      </xsd:sequence>
    </xsd:complexType>
  </xsd:element>
  <xsd:element name="POSITION" type="xsd:string"/>
  <xsd:element name="TRIGGER">
    <xsd:complexType>
      <xsd:sequence>
        <xsd:element ref="STATENAME"/>
        <xsd:element ref="TIMED" minOccurs="0"
maxOccurs="unbounded"/>
        <xsd:element ref="SWITCH" minOccurs="0"
maxOccurs="unbounded"/>
```

Continued

```
      </xsd:sequence>
    </xsd:complexType>
  </xsd:element>
  <xsd:element name="STATENAME" type="xsd:string"/>
  <xsd:element name="TIMED">
    <xsd:complexType>
      <xsd:sequence>
        <xsd:choice>
          <xsd:element ref="DAILY"/>
          <xsd:element ref="WEEKLY"/>
          <xsd:element ref="DATE"/>
        </xsd:choice>
        <xsd:element ref="TIME"/>
      </xsd:sequence>
    </xsd:complexType>
  </xsd:element>


  <xsd:element name="DAILY">
    <xsd:complexType>
      <xsd:sequence/> <!-- Empty element -->?
    </xsd:complexType>
  </xsd:element>
  <xsd:element name="WEEKLY">
    <xsd:complexType>
      <xsd:sequence>
        <xsd:element ref="WEEKDAY" minOccurs="0"
maxOccurs="7"/> <!--Limited to 7 days -->
      </xsd:sequence>
    </xsd:complexType>
  </xsd:element>
  <xsd:element name="WEEKDAY">
    <xsd:simpleType>
      <xsd:restriction base = "xsd:string">
        <xsd:enumeration value = "MON"/>
        <xsd:enumeration value = "TUES"/>
```

```
                    <xsd:enumeration value = "WED"/>
                    <xsd:enumeration value = "THURS"/>
                    <xsd:enumeration value = "FRI"/>
                    <xsd:enumeration value = "SAT"/>
                    <xsd:enumeration value = "SUN"/>
                </xsd:restriction>
            </xsd:simpleType>
        </xsd:element>
        <xsd:element name="DATE" type="xsd:recurringDate"/>
        <xsd:element name="TIME" type="xsd:time"/>
        <xsd:element name="SWITCH" type="xsd:string"/>
        <xsd:element name="NAME" type="xsd:string"/>
</xsd:schema>
```

Because of these type changes, you need to modify your files or they won't be valid any longer. The following new version contains changes that are highlighted in bold:

```
<?xml version="1.0" encoding="UTF-8"?>
<!DOCTYPE CONTROLSCHEDULE SYSTEM "controller.dtd">
<CONTROLSCHEDULE>
<MODULE>
<ADDRESS><HOUSE>B</HOUSE><UNIT>2</UNIT></ADDRESS>
<TYPE>APPLIANCE</TYPE>
<DESCRIPTION>Radio in livingroom</DESCRIPTION>
</MODULE>
<MODULE>
<ADDRESS><HOUSE>B</HOUSE><UNIT>10</UNIT></ADDRESS>
<TYPE>LAMP</TYPE>
<DESCRIPTION>Lamp in entryway</DESCRIPTION>
</MODULE>
<MODULE>
<ADDRESS><HOUSE>B</HOUSE><UNIT>10</UNIT></ADDRESS>
<TYPE>LAMP</TYPE>
<DESCRIPTION>Light outside front door</DESCRIPTION>
```

Continued

```
</MODULE>
<MODULE>
<ADDRESS><HOUSE>B</HOUSE><UNIT>11</UNIT></ADDRESS>
<TYPE>LAMP</TYPE>
<DESCRIPTION>Lamp in livingroom</DESCRIPTION>
</MODULE>
<STATE>
<NAME>AFTWORK</NAME><DESCRIPTION>Come home to a friendly
house.</DESCRIPTION>
<COMPONENT>
<DESCRIPTION>Turn the radio on</DESCRIPTION>
<ADDRESS><HOUSE>B</HOUSE><UNIT>2</UNIT></ADDRESS>
<POSITION>ON</POSITION>
</COMPONENT>
<COMPONENT>
<DESCRIPTION>Turn on the living room light</DESCRIPTION>
<ADDRESS><HOUSE>B</HOUSE><UNIT>11</UNIT></ADDRESS>
<POSITION>ON</POSITION>
</COMPONENT>
</STATE>
<STATE>
<NAME>AFTDINNER</NAME><DESCRIPTION>turn on front light,
dim lights</DESCRIPTION>
<COMPONENT>
<DESCRIPTION>Turn on porch, front lights</DESCRIPTION>
<ADDRESS><HOUSE>B</HOUSE><UNIT>10</UNIT></ADDRESS>
<POSITION>ON</POSITION>
</COMPONENT>
<COMPONENT>
<DESCRIPTION>Dim livingroom</DESCRIPTION>
<ADDRESS><HOUSE>B</HOUSE><UNIT>10</UNIT></ADDRESS>
<POSITION>80%</POSITION>
</COMPONENT>
</STATE>
<STATE>
```

```
<NAME>POWERSAVE</NAME><DESCRIPTION>Dim front
lights</DESCRIPTION>
<ADDRESS><HOUSE>B</HOUSE><UNIT>10</UNIT></ADDRESS>
<POSITION>40%</POSITION>
</STATE>
<STATE>
<NAME>MORNING</NAME><DESCRIPTION>Turn off front
lights</DESCRIPTION>
<ADDRESS><HOUSE>B</HOUSE><UNIT>10</UNIT></ADDRESS>
<POSITION>OFF</POSITION>
</STATE>
<TRIGGER>
<STATENAME>AFTWORK</STATENAME>
<TIMED>
<WEEKLY><WEEKDAY>MON</WEEKDAY><WEEKDAY>TUES</WEEKDAY><WEE
KDAY>WED</WEEKDAY><WEEKDAY>THURS</WEEKDAY><WEEKDAY>FRI</W
EEKDAY></WEEKLY> <!--Despite type change, WEEKDAY retains
the same content-->
<TIME>17:00</TIME>
</TIMED>
</TRIGGER>
<TRIGGER>
<STATENAME>AFTDINNER</STATENAME>
<TIMED>
<DAILY/><TIME>20:00</TIME>
</TIMED>
</TRIGGER>
<TRIGGER>
<STATENAME>POWERSAVE</STATENAME>
<TIMED>
<DAILY/><TIME>23:00</TIME>
</TIMED>
</TRIGGER>
<TRIGGER>
```

Continued

```
<STATENAME>MORNING</STATENAME>
<TIMED>
<DAILY/><TIME>7:00</TIME>
</TIMED>
</TRIGGER>
<TRIGGER>
<STATENAME>AFTWORK</STATENAME>
<SWITCH>RMT01 - ON</SWITCH><!--Remote Control in case we
get home early -->
</TRIGGER>
<TRIGGER>
<STATENAME>MORNING</STATENAME>
<SWITCH>LT01 - OFF</SWITCH><!--If you don't want to leave
lights on all night -->
</TRIGGER>
</CONTROLSCHEDULE>
```

Schemas make it easier to build this application, providing more built-in validation options while avoiding complex multipart representations for dates and times. Engineering a transformation from the old format to the new might take a little bit of work, but it isn't very complicated.

Instrument Control with Instrument Markup Language

Instrument Markup Language (IML) and an implementation of IML, Astronomical Instrument Markup Language (AIML), are both projects under development by NASA's Goddard Space Flight Center and Century Computing, a division of AppNet, Inc. These two markup languages take the basic concepts I described in the previous section's example and apply them to more difficult (and more useful) situations. Astronomers regularly deal with equipment kept in remote and inhospitable locations, from telescopes located far from urban light pollution to metering stations in uninhabited areas to satellites and spacecraft. AIML and IML use XML as a container for descriptions of instruments and commands to control them, giving astronomers and the engineers supporting them ready access to remote control for instruments anywhere. AIML's first project will provide support for instruments on the SOFIA (Stratospheric Observatory for Infrared Astronomy) project, which uses a Boeing 747 modified to carry a 2.5 meter reflecting telescope to make observations.

Cross-Reference

Both AIML and IML are still in development. For the latest on AIML, visit `http://pioneer.gsfc.nasa.gov/public/aiml/`. For the latest on IML, visit `http://pioneer.gsfc.nasa.gov/public/iml/`.

IML is a very general markup language for describing and controlling instruments, whereas AIML is an implementation of that language that a programmer may customize for astronomical needs. IML and AIML documents are parsed and fed into Java applications, which then present an interface to the controls and send information and orders to and from the controls. Hardware designers can create AIML documents that describe their instruments, and the software will configure its display and controls to reflect that description, greatly simplifying the task of integrating hardware and software. The general software that understands the AIML vocabulary can present detailed information about an instrument without being directly tied to code specific to that instrument. The following fragment, which describes a refrigeration component of the High Resolution Airborne Wideband Camera (HAWC), uses XML syntax to provide information about two ports (one for outgoing commands, one for incoming data) on the instrument.

```
<Instrument id="ADR"> <!- subsystem ->
   <Port name="ADR" function="command" number="2201"
type="ASCII" serverPort="false" >
```

Continued

```
    <Command name="HouseKeeping" >
        <Argument name="tag"        type="java.lang.String"
required="true" hidden="true" />
        <Argument name="Command" type="java.lang.String"
required="true" hidden="true" />
        <Argument name="RATE"
type="java.lang.Integer" required="true" >
            <ValidRange low="0" high="120000" />
        </Argument>
    </Command>


        <!- Note the special XML decimal-like encoding
for NEWLINE terminator ->
<RecordFormat name="HouseKeeping" size="-1"
ordered="true" terminator="&#10;" attributeSeparator=" ">
        <Format name="tag"        format="%s" size="16"
ordered="true" />
        <Format name="Command" format="HOUSEKEEPING"
size="-1" />
        <Format name="RATE"        format="%s"
ordered="false" header="RATE=" />
    </RecordFormat>
  </Port>
  <Port function="data" name="ADR" number="2200"
type="BINARY" serverPort="false" >


        <Telemetry name="Status" >
        <Field name="tag" type="java.lang.String"
required="true" />
        <Field name="Time" type="java.lang.Integer"
required="true" />
        <ArrayField name="Temperatures" required="true"
dimensions="10">
            <Field name="dataElement"
type="java.lang.Float" required="true" />
```

```
      </ArrayField>
      <Field name="Heat Switch"
type="java.lang.Integer" required="true" />
      </Telemetry>

      <RecordFormat name="Status" size="64"
ordered="true" >
         <Format name="tag"      format="%s" size="16"
ordered="true" />
         <Format name="Time"     format="%d" size="4"
ordered="true" />
         <ArrayFormat name="Temperatures" size="40"
ordered="true" >
            <Format name="dataElement" format="%f"
size="4" ordered="true" />
         </ArrayFormat>
         <Format name="Heat Switch" format="%d" size="4"
ordered="true" />
      </RecordFormat>
   </Port>
   </Instrument>
```

Tip

Note the use of Java types to identify the format of the information going to and returning from the instruments. XML Schemas may provide a cleaner way to formalize this convention, but the naming conventions may still prove useful for developers integrating XML with environments that use their own type systems.

This information will configure the software used to control the instrument. If the instrument gets another port, or if more commands become available for controlling the instrument, the hardware engineer simply adds that information to the interface by modifying this file. The next time the updated file loads into a Java program that presents an interface to the instruments, the interface will reflect the new information. Making small changes quickly makes it much easier to run projects on an iterative basis, starting with a foundation and moving forward in small steps, than would laying out the complete vision at the start of a project and making drastic changes throughout should that vision prove faulty.

Object Documents

XML's nested structure bears a strong resemblance to the hierarchies of data that appear in object-oriented programming's data structures. XML and object-oriented programming work together well because both systems typically store datasets within datasets within datasets. Storing the information contained in object structures has traditionally been difficult, because the linear and tabular file types previously used for documents don't work well for this kind of hierarchical structure. This section of the chapter doesn't produce any specific DTDs, because they vary radically from program to program. Instead, you examine a few general examples of projects that may help developers create complementary objects and file structures.

Bean Markup Language (BeanML)

The Bean Markup Language, a development of IBM's AlphaWorks (http://www.alphaWorks.ibm.com/formula/bml) reads very much like a command language, using a simple set of tags and attributes to instantiate Java Beans and add properties and event handling to them. BeanML doesn't really create new objects — it just enables you to describe the properties of Java Beans and connect them using a simple XML syntax. BeanML documents use a Bean element as their root element and then use child add, args, bean, call-method, cast, event-binding, field, property, and string elements to properly instantiate the Bean and connect it to other objects.

A very simple BeanML document might look like this:

```
<?xml version="1.0" encoding="UTF-8"?>
<bean class="java.awt.Panel" id="mainPanel">
   <add>
        <bean class="java.awt.Label">
          <property name="text" value="This is a
label"/>
        </bean>
   </add>
</bean>
```

This document creates a `Panel` using the Java AWT libraries, containing a `Label` announcing that "This is a label." You can use BeanML with any Java Beans, providing an XML vocabulary for building complex applications out of Beans without the need to write extended and repetitive Java code. You can even compile BeanML documents, thus eliminating the delay caused by parsing XML when the program starts.

Caution

BeanML is still a work in progress, like most things at alphaWorks. The material presented in this section is subject to change. Check the alphaWorks site (`http://www.alphaWorks.ibm.com/`) for the latest details.

Quick and QARE

Quick and QARE are two Java-based open-source projects that help developers process XML and make it immediately useful to Java developers as a means of serializing Java objects. Quick is a set of tools for feeding the data stored in XML documents into Java objects and back out again, whereas QARE is a server-based environment for using such objects and connecting them. Both use XML documents as a tool for controlling (indeed, creating) Java applications, freeing developers from the code-compile-debug cycle in many cases in which such coding is repetitive.

Developers can specify how Quick should process XML documents using Quick Data Markup Language (QDML), which can then be transformed into Quick Java Markup Language (QJML), which provides specific bindings to Java objects. When a program uses Quick it passes it a QJML document, which tells it how to set up the processing tree. A simple QJML document might look like this:

```
<qjml root="list">
  <element name="list">
    <targetClass>java.util.ArrayList</targetClass>
      <child element="item"
             optional="True"
             repeating="True"
             class="com.jxml.quick.access.QListAccess"/>
  </element>
  <element name="item"
           content="string"/>
</qjml>
```

Quick uses these binding documents to specify how Java classes should connect with XML document content. The processor loads the binding document, and then loads an XML document and connects the information in that document to Java objects as appropriate. This is useful in a lot of programming cases, from XML document processing (for which each element needs particular processing) to Java graphical interface development (for which even Sun's newest and friendliest interface tools still require a considerable amount of redundant code). Quick provides a set of tools that work for developers building XML processing applications, and (perhaps more important) provides a framework for building Java programs with XML documents.

Cross-Reference

For more information on Quick and QARE, visit http://www.jxml.com.

XML-RPC

XML-RPC uses XML syntax to describe remote procedure calls between computers over a network, transporting the calls and the responses to those calls over the ubiquitous HTTP protocol. Calls are made as XML documents, which are sent using POST HTTP requests. The header tells the receiving Web server where to direct the RPC call. For example, an XML-RPC request might look like this:

```
POST /rpchandler  HTTP/1.0
User-Agent: MyClient/1.0 (WinNT)
Host: mycomputer.simonstl.com
Content-Type: text/xml
Content-length:169


<?xml version="1.0" encoding="UTF-8"?>
<methodCall>
   <methodName>test.returnId</methodName>
   <params>
        <param>
              <value><string>ASCII</string></value>
        </param>
   <params>
</methodCall>
```

The Web server receives this request and passes it to /rpchandler, which could be a servlet, a CGI script, or a program set up to answer at that URL. It receives the XML, calls the method named test.returnId with the string parameter "UTF-8", and then responds with its own XML-RPC document, possibly the one that follows:

```
HTTP/1.1 200 OK
Server: JavaWebServer/1.1
Content-Length:
Content-Type: text/xml
```

Continued

```
Date: Fri, 12 Feb 1999 19:01:32 GMT
<?xml version="1.0?>
<methodResponse>
   <params>
        <param>
             <value><string>Server
12345</string></value>
        </param>
   </params>
</methodResponse>
```

It's a long route to travel to get a server identification (or a Hello World), but XML-RPC has a lot to offer, especially in cross-platform coordination. Unix servers, Windows 95 desktops, Macintoshes, System/390 mainframes, and any other networked system or environment can connect using this system, sharing processing over the network transparently. It doesn't matter what kind of computer it is, or what kind of operating system it's running — as long as it has an HTTP connection and the capacity to process XML, it can connect to a larger network of XML-RPC–enabled computers.

Developers used to the more complicated approaches of CORBA and COM may find this a useful alternative for simple solutions, though it doesn't yet have the level of support of those more established technologies. In the long run, XML's easy interchange and hierarchical structures may pose a significant challenge to the two current kings of the object world.

Cross-Reference

For more information on XML-RPC (including information on error messages, data types, and many other issues), visit http://www.xmlrpc.com.

SOAP

The Simple Object Access Protocol, SOAP, uses a framework like that of XML-RPC but extends it far beyond simple method request-response. In addition to passing parameters, SOAP environments pass representations of objects in XML. As a result SOAP is far more extensible than XML-RPC, providing a generic environment for transferring XML information between applications on different systems.

Although SOAP has the backing of Microsoft (its primary sponsor), IBM, and Sun, its future isn't entirely clear. The W3C has started an XML protocol activity to explore SOAP and similar options, and the IETF's Blocks activity (also called BXXP) provides yet another alternative, one that isn't layered on top of HTTP. The ideas in SOAP seem likely to survive, but it's not yet clear whether SOAP itself will survive.

Tip

For the SOAP 1.1 specification, visit http://www.w3.org/ TR/SOAP/. For more on the W3C's XML Protocols activity, visit http://www.w3.org/2000/xp/. The Blocks activity is described at http://www.bxxp.org. xmlhack.com also has a protocols category for the latest news at http://xmlhack.com/list.php?cat=25.

Metadata: Describing Resources Using XML

The information inside documents is important, but knowing which document to search can make that information more accessible. Metadata — data about data — can make information more accessible. Even before XML was finalized, a number of proposed standards that used it for metadata appeared. Microsoft's Channel Definition Format (CDF) was one of the first XML implementations to achieve widespread use, through the Channel Bar that has been a part of the Internet Explorer browser since version 4. More tools for describing documents, such as the W3C's Resource Description Framework (RDF) and the Dublin Core Metadata Initiative's Element Set, are on the way, attempting to provide a common vocabulary for describing the incredible quantity of resources available on the Internet and elsewhere. XSA, a completely separate initiative, is a simple but very useful specification that developers can use to describe the latest versions of their software.

XML Software Autoupdate (XSA)

XSA enables software designers to create description files for their software, making it possible for sites to poll those files and keep track of updates. XSA was created by Lars Marius Garshol, keeper of a list of XML tools (at `http://www.stud.ifi.uio.no/~larsga/linker/XMLtools.html`), with help from James Tauber (keeper of `http://www.xmlsoftware.com`) and Robin Cover (keeper of `http://www.oasis-open.org/cover/`). An explosion of free (and not-so-free) software tools in various stages of development marks XML's early development period. The "release early and often" strategy typical of open-source development makes it difficult for keepers of XML sites to keep up with the constant changes, and XSA's purpose is to lessen their difficulties while helping developers announce new software.

XSA files are pretty simple. An XSA document wizard remains in development, but creating XSA files by hand is fairly easy. The XSA element contains a vendor and multiple products. The vendor element contains name, e-mail, and URL information, and each product contains an ID, version information, the date of last release, an info URL for the product, and information about changes since the last version. (XSA makes no provision for describing multiple versions of a product, though multiple XSA files can represent multiple products.) For example, the XSA file describing the author's XLinkFilter might look like this:

```
<?xml version="1.0" encoding="UTF-8"?>
<xsa>
   <vendor>
          <name>Simon St.Laurent</name>
          <email>simontl@simonstl.com</email>
          <url>http://www.simonstl.com</url>
   </vendor>
   <product id="xlinkfilter">
          <version>0.20</version>
          <last-release>19981227</last-release>
          <info-url>
http://purl.oclc.org/NET/xlinkfilter</info-url>
          <changes>XLinkFilter 0.20 includes an image map
demo, more documentation, and support for generating
XPointers through a LocationFilter.</changes>
   </product>
</xsa>
```

The XSA file must then be placed someplace public — probably
on the vendor's Web site — and register with sites, which will then
check back periodically to see whether anything has changed and to
update their own information.

Cross-Reference

For more information on XSA, including a DTD, documentation, and examples, see `http://birk105.studby.uio.`
`no/www_work/xsa/`.

Resource Description Framework (RDF)

The W3C's Resource Description Framework (RDF) started at
about the same time as XML and solves many similar problems in a
different way. RDF is an extremely general tool for representing
metadata. RDF provides tools for describing entities and relationships between them, whereas XML's just represents document
structures. RDF uses XML as its "serialization syntax" but doesn't

use an XML DTD. From RDF's perspective, attributes are the same as subelements with text (but not subelement) content, and this different perspective results in a very different approach to information. You can, in theory, use RDF with nearly any kind of information presented as a directed graph or set of graphs, from simple information about a resource to complex relationships describing a matrix of content—even, perhaps, a document. Nonetheless, XML is the document syntax (it's both more convenient for many document applications and much more familiar) while RDF is supposed to be used for metadata, providing descriptions for those documents.

RDF performs as a key component in many of the W3C's plans, including the Digital Signature Initiative (DSIG), the Platform for Internet Content Selection (PICS), and the Platform for Privacy Preferences (P3P). RDF provides its own tools (schemas) for specifying the structure and content of RDF material. RDF by itself is fairly useless—sort of like XML by itself, before someone creates a vocabulary—and RDF's formal structures look more complicated than XML's, largely because of the more flexible syntax. I include an RDF example in the following section on Dublin Core, using a predefined vocabulary, but RDF, with all its implications, really deserves its own book—or three or four. The interactions between RDF processing and XML processing will undoubtedly grow more numerous, but currently (while RDF is still in working drafts), the applications haven't sprouted widely.

Cross-Reference

For a good tutorial on the graph theory underlying RDF, see http://www.utm.edu/departments/math/graph/. For an excellent (free) tool that will help you create RDF documents, try Reggie at http://metadata.net/dstc/. The W3C has an RDF validation service available at http://jigsaw. w3.org:8000/description, with a Java graphical viewer you will have fun exploring.

Dublin Core

The Dublin Core Metadata Initiative began long before either XML or RDF appeared on the W3C's radar screen, and provides a vocabulary for describing Web (and other) resources. The Dublin Core vocabulary is based on the information that has long been stored in library card catalogs, helping readers find the information they need. The Dublin Core Metadata Element Set, recently released as RFC 2413, and more descriptive tools will surely come from this project. The Dublin Core Metadata Element Set is only a vocabulary, with no dependencies on either XML or RDF. The RFC doesn't include either a DTD or an RDF schema (though an appendix of the RDF schema draft includes a schema for Dublin Core). Nonetheless, the Dublin Core information perfectly complements RDF, giving it a vocabulary you can instantly apply to a wide variety of Web documents.

Dublin Core uses the elements `Title`, `Subject`, `Description`, `Type`, `Source`, `Relation`, `Creator`, `Publisher`, `Contributor`, `Rights`, `Date`, `Format`, `Identifier`, and `Language`. Not all the elements will be needed for every document, though the more specific the information, the more useful it will be. If these headings seem like the information on a library card catalog card, that's because the Dublin Core group is composed primarily of librarians and their successors in information management. Making good use of Dublin Core helps to create catalogs that can find information more reliably than today's full-text search engines explored on the basis of much more tightly defined criteria. A sample Dublin Core document that describes the author's Web site follows:

```
<?xml version = "1.0"?>
<rdf:RDF xmlns:rdf = "http://www.w3.org/TR/WD-rdf-syntax"
    xmlns:DC = "http://info.internet.isi.edu/in-
notes/rfc/files/rfc2413.txt">

<rdf:Description xml:lang="en"
```

Continued

```
about="http://www.simonstl.com">
  <DC:Title>
    Simon St.Laurent's Web Site - Articles, Projects, and
Books
  </DC:Title>
  <DC:Creator>
    Simon St.Laurent
  </DC:Creator>
  <DC:Description>
    This Web site contains pointers to XML information,
as well as articles by Simon St.Laurent and links to
books he has written.
  </DC:Description>
  <DC:Subject>
    XML XLink XLinkFilter DDML XSchema CSS
  </DC:Subject>
  <DC:Publisher>
    simonstl.com
  </DC:Publisher>
  <DC:Identifier DC:Scheme="URI">
    http://www.simonstl.com
  </DC:Identifier>
  <DC:Rights>
    Copyright 1998-9 by Simon St.Laurent
  </DC:Rights>
</rdf:Description>
</rdf:RDF>
```

I hope that standard vocabularies for the Subject area will arrive soon, though that seems a much larger task in some ways than determining the broad categories, and is always open to new interpretations. With luck, however, the Dublin Core project and its vocabularies will make the Web a more searchable and hence a more useful place.

Cross-Reference

For more information on the Dublin Core Metadata Initiative, see http://purl.org/DC/. For RFC 2413, describing the Dublin Core Metadata Element Set, visit http://info. internet.isi.edu/in-notes/rfc/files/rfc2413.txt.

Futures

XML's popularity for data applications will depend heavily on how much use developers find for its combination of structure, flexibility, machine-readability, and human-readability. Unlike most documents in the previous chapters, the applications in this chapter aren't intended for direct consumption by human users. Readability is maintained to make documents easier to examine and debug, but few of the documents will ever see a style sheet or directly reach human readers. Even though XML does incur more overhead than traditional binary files, its verbosity and emphasis on nested structures give programmers new tools for communications between computers and applications. As use of XML spreads we may see more programs based on shared architectures, all using a common set of file formats for wildly different projects.

Cross-Reference

Though document-oriented, many of the tools for exchanging documents that I describe at the end of Chapter 21 operate on the principles that I discuss in this chapter.

Chapter 23

Storing, Managing, and Processing XML

Even though this book focuses primarily on how to write XML documents and create XML vocabularies, creating documents and vocabularies is only a part of XML. Documents without applications may be useful for learning syntax, but aren't very appealing otherwise. A full-scale treatment of architectures built on XML would take another book (or, more likely, a set of books), but a basic understanding of how these applications work is critical to creating usable XML. Many of the teams working on XML development will have separate groups building document types and creating processor applications because the two kinds of work demand different sets of skills. Still, both groups need to share a common vocabulary. In this chapter I examine the tools available for creating, storing, processing, and consuming XML, and how they may fit different situations.

Creating XML

Although most document formats in the past have seen substantial levels of human involvement in document creation, XML's flexibility has made it a useful tool for computer-to-computer communications. Humans are important document generators, but direct creation of XML documents is only one of many possible approaches. More and more programs are storing their information in XML formats, largely because of the conveniences XML offers programmers. Other developers are creating new means of sharing their information by retrofitting XML interfaces to existing data structures, and building new infrastructures that generate XML as part of their regular activity.

Editing XML

Creating a generic XML editor that meets user expectations of word processors is a greater challenge in many ways than creating an XML-aware browser. Creating an XML editor that can compete with the dominant WYSIWYG (what-you-see-is-what-you-get) word processors on the word processors' terms is a difficult proposition, requiring the creation of an interactive window on information that gives users the tools they need to create document structures, not just formatted text. Managing the creation of structures while presenting information in forms that users are accustomed to is a complicated job, and keeping the interface to such a tool simple will be a difficult task. Building such an editor as a generic tool, rather than as one focused on a particular XML vocabulary, is especially difficult. Perhaps because of these difficulties, developers have taken a number of very different approaches to creating XML editors.

One approach to creating XML documents, though not necessarily the best way to edit them, is through an interview model. An application can take an XML DTD, or schema, when it becomes available, and present it to the user as a set of possibilities, starting at the root element. DTDs don't identify which elements may be used as root elements, so the application will need to have some additional information to present the user with an intelligent set of possibilities. The user can make choices based on the DTD, as presented by the editor. The editor can enforce constraints and keep users from creating invalid documents, letting them move forward only when the current element is acceptable. For many situations, such as the project manager debriefing I discuss in Chapter 21, this approach is appropriate and enables the authors to dump all their information at one sitting. More complex documents may need a pause function for stopping in the middle, and full-scale editors will need to go far beyond this. Interviews are a good approach for information that can be entered in a single pass, but aren't very helpful for navigating previously entered information and making changes quickly.

Cross Reference

If you need to put together a editor for a particular XML DTD quickly, take a look at IBM's alphaWorks XML Editormaker (`http://www.alphaworks.ibm.com/aw.nsf/techmain/xmleditormaker`). It takes a DTD and creates a small editor based on that DTD.

Some XML editors give users access to the entire XML document, presenting it using the tree structure built into the document. Users insert and delete elements (and element content) as appropriate. For many documents, especially simple and highly structured documents, this approach works well, but for large documents or documents where users tend to confuse formatting and structure, these editors can become unwieldy. These tools can provide developers with a great deal of supporting information about context and document structure, as XML Spy is shown doing in Figure 23-1.

Altova offers XML Spy at `http://www.xmlspy.com`. XML Pro, aimed at developers, is available from Vervet Logic at `http://www.vervet.com`. Microsoft offers a very lightweight (and free) XML Notepad at `http://msdn.microsoft.com/xml/notepad/intro.asp`.

Although hierarchical editors do a good job of presenting a close-up view of XML documents, many users would prefer a more familiar, less hierarchical approach to the documents they use every day. Depending on how they prefer to see their information, users can either work directly in the markup or through an editor that hides the markup but presents the structure through formatting.

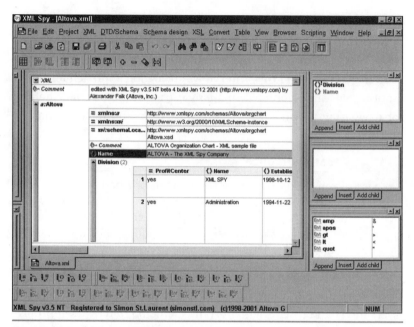

Figure 23-1 *Editing an XML document in Altova's XML Spy 3.5*

For those who want to work directly in the markup, plenty of options exist. Many developers (including this author) use plain old text editors for their XML editing. Emacs is a popular and customizable tool. A few text editors also are available that provide extra support for XML development. BBEdit (http://www.barebones.com), a popular text editor for the Macintosh, now provides syntax coloring and error checking for XML documents. Architag International, a provider of XML training, offers XRay (http://architag.com/xray/), a Windows-based XML editor. Developers work directly in the XML, but receive validation and well-formedness feedback while they type and can see their documents formatted with XSLT style sheets simultaneously.

There haven't been very many word processor-like editors for XML so far, and many editing environments are remarkably expensive, designed for use in highly customized corporate environments. SoftQuad, creator of the HoTMetaL HTML editor, has created an

XML editor that you can use off the shelf or with additional customization to integrate it with a particular vocabulary and environment. XMetal 2.0 offers multiple views of XML documents, from a pure text-editing view (shown in Figure 23-2), to a CSS styling and markup combination (shown in Figure 23-3), to a purely style-based approach that looks much like an ordinary word processor (shown in Figure 23-4.)

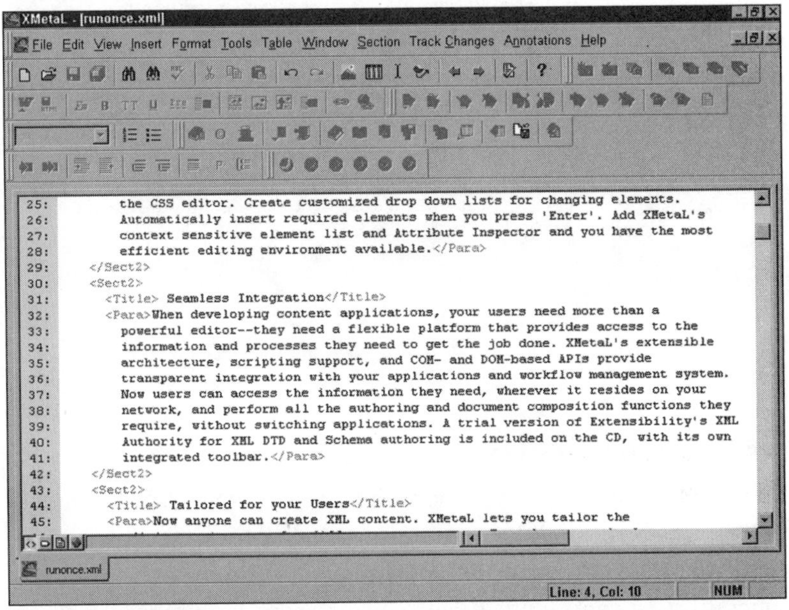

Figure 23-2 *Editing XML content directly in XMetal 2.0*

XMetal information and pricing is available at `http://www.softquad.com/products/xmetal/content_xmetal_intro.html`.

The possibilities for new editors and approaches are still wide open for developers with new ideas. The advent of XML may prove to be an opportunity for developers, spawning a new community of tool-builders the way HTML did.

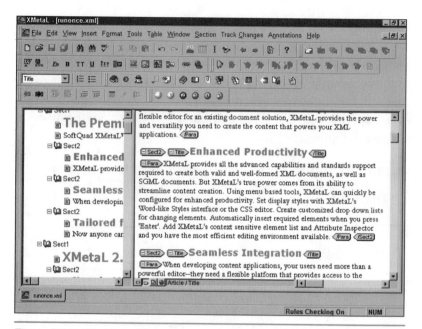

Figure 23-3 *Working with structure and style simultaneously in XMetal 2.0*

Generating XML

Editors give users and developers direct control over XML content, but the majority of XML currently traveling over the Internet is generated by programs communicating with other programs. XML generation is commonly performed at several different levels of abstraction: some programs simply export text, with little real understanding that they are working with XML, while others generate DOM trees or SAX event streams that are then written out as XML, and yet others rely on abstraction layers that perform tasks such as object-to-XML conversion.

The simplest approach, text generation, is used in a variety of different situations. Some developers just need to dump content from legacy systems, and pretty much every system out there can write to a text file in some form or another. This approach also works well for developers familiar with CGI, Active Server Pages, Servlets, and Cold Fusion, which can all generate XML as text. It's a change of format from the HTML they were created for, so you definitely have to pay some extra attention to syntax, but the transition doesn't have to be painful.

Developers working in environments in which DOM or SAX facilities are available have a few additional options that make it easier to build and manipulate documents without the same level of attention to syntactic detail. Generating SAX events provides a light layer of abstraction, because the developer still has to make sure that structures start and stop in the right places. Working with DOM trees provides a greater level of abstraction and provides the added benefit of being able to change content that has already been generated at any time up to the point at which the DOM is converted to an XML document and sent out.

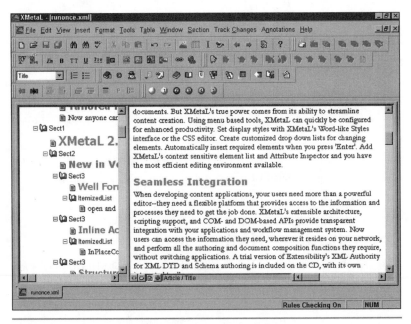

Figure 23-4 *The style-only approach in XMetal 2.0*

Note

For tutorials on building XML through text generation and the DOM in Microsoft's Active Server Pages environment, see `http://www.simonstl.com/articles/scripting/index.htm`.

Higher-level abstractions enable developers to pass data to a processor without any knowledge whatsoever of XML, DOM, or SAX. Many XML-RPC and SOAP interfaces are designed so that developers don't even need to be aware of the XML generation process, and more and more of these abstractions are in development. JXML's Quick processors enable developers to define relations between objects and XML document representations using XML, but once those relationships and interfaces have been established the Quick processor, not the developer, works directly upon the XML.

Using Intermediaries

Whereas some XML documents exist only on the wire, as a sequence of bytes transmitted directly from creator to consumer, other XML documents have a more complex lifespan. Some XML documents move into storage, where they may be archived or kept permanently accessible, and some XML documents must undergo transformations before reaching their final consumer. XML's structures open new possibilities in both of these fields for generic tools that work well with any XML vocabulary or structures.

Repositories – XML storage

Most of the information held in computers is stored in one of two kinds of architectures: databases or file systems. Both of these data stores have made the transition to the Web, providing foundations for application architectures still being used for XML. Typically, databases are connected to the Web through a program that accepts user's requests, makes a query against a server, and returns results formatted using HTML. Files have an easier path: The Web server translates the URL it received from the client into a path to a file and sends the client the information it finds in that file. There are times when databases lurk behind file-like URLs and times when files are actually stored in databases (usually as Binary Large Objects, or BLOBs), but generally the distinction between the two forms is fairly clear. Putting files into databases is rarely more efficient than putting them into file systems, and putting database information into files is almost always a losing proposition. Many relational database vendors have added support for XML importing and exporting from table structures, but it can be difficult to efficiently store loosely structured XML documents in relational databases.

XML threatens to add stress to the file-request structure by making much heavier demands of files in order to fulfill its validation and linking requirements. Although the extra transmission costs of DTDs and style sheets may not hit the ceiling of the current capabilities of file-based Web servers (DTDs and style sheets can be easily cached and used for multiple documents in most cases), the new linking features may. XLink's embed functionality and XInclude will encourage developers to create documents that include parts of other documents. XPointers make describing fragments of documents easy. If all the XPointer processing takes place on the client, servers will spend considerable amounts of effort sending files to clients that the clients can use only in part. Documents that link to multiple other documents this way could increase the load dramatically — especially if the processing applications are other programs voraciously seeking out important bits of information. While extended link groups may provide delightful functionality to the client by creating true multidirectional links, they also promise an enormous traffic jam at the server, especially if developers keep their links distributed across multiple files rather than consolidating them in centralized link-clearinghouse files. The prospect of XML query systems makes the need for efficient fragment processing more urgent.

XML also promises to blur the formerly clear distinction between file systems and databases because its sharply hierarchical structures are good candidates for storage inside databases and good carriers of information typically stored within databases. XML stored as a serial file can present a good representation of a table or even a set of tables, though the significant processing costs involved in parsing such a file continue to give relational databases a significant edge. Although XML files are great for interchange between databases and for archival storage of database information, using an XML file as a database itself is probably not the best idea when large amounts of information are involved. At the same time, complex XML documents can seriously tax the resources of a relational database that maps XML's hierarchical structures to its own internal tabular structures, making the storage of XML in a relational repository an equally chancy proposition, loaded with extra processing costs. (Many newer relational databases, object-relational databases, provide additional facilities that help with these issues.) Database information can flow smoothly into an XML document, but treating XML documents as databases or putting XML information into a relational database may not be the best idea.

Still, there are many cases in which a more flexible approach to XML document storages would have significant benefits. Cases in which the client only needs a fragment of a document (specified through an XPointer or other XML query approaches), or in which the document must be parsed and transformed before being sent to a client application, are both something of a hassle if XML documents are stored as long chains of bytes in serial order. Putting XML documents into a repository that can reflect (without breaking) their internal hierarchical structures is one answer that promises both efficient handling of XML document information and ready access to whatever pieces of information are needed at a given moment. Two kinds of databases, object stores and hierarchical databases, promise to streamline this process. (Neither of them is as efficient as a relational database at manipulating tabular data, so relational databases will definitely continue to fill that niche.)

Object stores, like those available from POET Software (`http://www.poet.com`) and Excelon (`http://www.excelon.com`) store objects like those created in Java, C++, and other object-oriented languages in a hierarchical format that is readily fed back to the programs that created them. Hierarchical databases (which provide the foundation for Tamino, at `http://www.softwareag.com`) are older, early competitors of relational databases, but are optimized to store hierarchically structured data such as XML documents. The details vary among the various database environments, but the general effect for XML processing is that a pre-parsed version of the documents is available, reducing or removing the overhead of serializing and parsing XML. Instead of loading a document, parsing it, and extracting the needed pieces, a Web server could just execute a query against the database, which would then return the needed pieces — as XML fragments, or possibly as a complete document. Knitting the pieces together is usually less costly than taking them apart.

Building efficient repositories out of this system is going to take considerable work: ideally, the interfaces would be much like those on a Web server, with a file system-like structure for organizing documents and a query language (XPointer and/or something else) to retrieve specific information when the entire document is not needed. Adding information to these systems will require a little more than today's file systembased File Transfer Protocol (FTP) tools can handle, but with luck, successors (such as the IETF's Web Distributed Authoring and Versioning, or WebDAV) can fill in the gaps and make using these systems both transparent and efficient. Plenty of document management vendors are moving into this space, and products are constantly evolving to meet corporate and Web development needs.

Note

For an exploration of some of the possibilities XML presents for document management, see my article, "Building the File System into the File," at `http://www.simonstl.com/articles/filesys.htm`.

Middleware

All but the most basic of Web servers perform some processing on the documents they serve. Some processing on the Web is done on servers, providing users access to repositories that store information in non-HTML formats. The servers can manage security, collect information, and perform other tasks. Other processing is done in Web browsers and other applications, using scripts, applets, and other objects, such as browser plug-ins. As support for XML grows, some of this processing will grow easier. In any case, more of it will become distributable, capable of moving from the repository server to a middleware server to the client, blurring the meanings of client, server, and middleware. The basic paradigm of Web servers storing information and passing it to Web clients (browsers) that display that information is in for a change.

Unlike HTML documents, XML documents are easy to tear apart and reassemble, and transformation and processing can both take place while the document is torn apart. In the HTML world, a flexible application that uses both client and server processing might involve a script that builds an HTML document, which is then transmitted to a browser, which uses a different script to animate the document according to the user's needs. In the XML world, a processing module can assemble an XML document from a relational database and pass that document to another module for reassembly as a table in a document. When the processing module reaches the user, another processing module a mouse-click away could transform that same information into a graph, a form letter, or an entry in a local database.

This flexibility is part of what makes XML so powerful as an interchange format, but it demands a change in the way we view documents. An XML document is not just a series of bytes (though it definitely is a series of bytes). Rather, it is a set of structures that can be presented, modified, manipulated, and extracted from. The style of markup will definitely have an impact on how much processing flexibility is available, but the processors can build on the structures inside the documents, transform those structures, and represent the new structures as new XML documents. Middleware tools that apply generic processing to particular documents based on their structure and content make it possible to build very specialized applications using generic components. The shared structures of XML documents enable developers to create tools that work across vocabularies.

XSLT is a good example of a generic application that has been built with processing on both the client and the server in mind. Browsers that support XSLT can perform its transformations and formatting at the client, but the server can perform the needed transformations (typically, to HTML) for clients that can't process XSLT themselves. This flexibility provides site designers with a good way to take advantage of the capabilities of the newer browsers, while still supporting (at a fairly low cost) legacy browsers that have no understanding of XML, much less XSLT. XSLT transformations can even be stacked — the results of an XML transformation are XML, which can then e processed for another round.

Interacting with Consumers (Browsers and Other Applications)

Getting information into and out of these repositories and processors requires another kind of application, one that interacts with the outside world. This gateway can be a browser, transforming an XML document into a set of pixels on a user's screen, an editor, enabling users to create new XML documents and modify old ones directly, or a gateway to another system, such as an instrument controlled by commands contained in an XML document. Input and output make storage and processing worthwhile. Like the other areas, this remains a field where the technology is in development, and no best solution to XML processing has yet emerged.

Typically, gateways are built on a parser that passes the information in the XML document to the application. The application then shows that information to the world in some non-XML format (possibly after some additional processing like the processing I describe in the previous section.) In some cases (such as with editors), that information can be mapped back to an XML document and shipped back to the repository; in others, it takes a one-way road from the gateway application to a user's screen or some code controlling a device, for instance. Some gateways just collect information that isn't in an XML format and convert it to XML, providing a one-way road for input. The next two sections take a close look at two important applications for everyday human interaction with information stored in XML, browsers, and editors.

Browsers: Anatomy and futures

Although XML hasn't exactly taken the traditional Web by storm, it is opening up new possibilities in Web browser architectures both for the established vendors — Microsoft, Netscape, and Opera — and for smaller players building more specialized tools. Building browsers remains a difficult task, but XML may both open new possibilities for specialist browsers and make the more traditional browsers more amenable to extensions. The old structure, shown in Figure 23-5, may be in for some reconfiguration.

In addition to opening up these possibilities for the major browser vendors, these developments open up larger possibilities for a wider audience of developers. While recreating the capabilities of Netscape Navigator or Microsoft Internet Explorer is well beyond the capacity (or interest) of most programmers and companies, XML opens up new possibilities for small browsers targeted at particular niches. Perhaps the first true XML browser was Jumbo (http://www.xml-cml.org/jumbo3/index.html), which Peter Murray-Rust built to demonstrate the possibilities of Chemical Markup Language (CML). Jumbo is a Java application that combines a parser, the Java Swing classes, and some custom code to display XML both generically, as a tree, with further information available in a right-hand pane (as shown in Figure 23-6), and as an application object, to do things such as draw molecule structures in a panel (as shown in Figure 23-7).

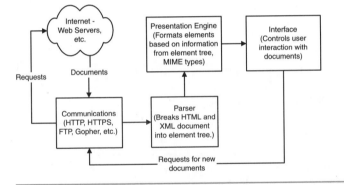

Figure 23-5 *The structure of a simple browser*

Jumbo is an experimental browser, not a commercial tool, but its foundations have significant promise. Jumbo's architecture strongly suggests ways that XML could be used with current architectures to supplement or replace the existing plug-in and object mechanisms for displaying content. Right now, all content that doesn't consist of images or markup must be declared with special tags: EMBED, APPLET, or OBJECT. Adding plug-ins to a browser isn't as easy as it should be. These tags (with the possible exception of applets) expose users to the risk of damage from poorly written or malicious code.

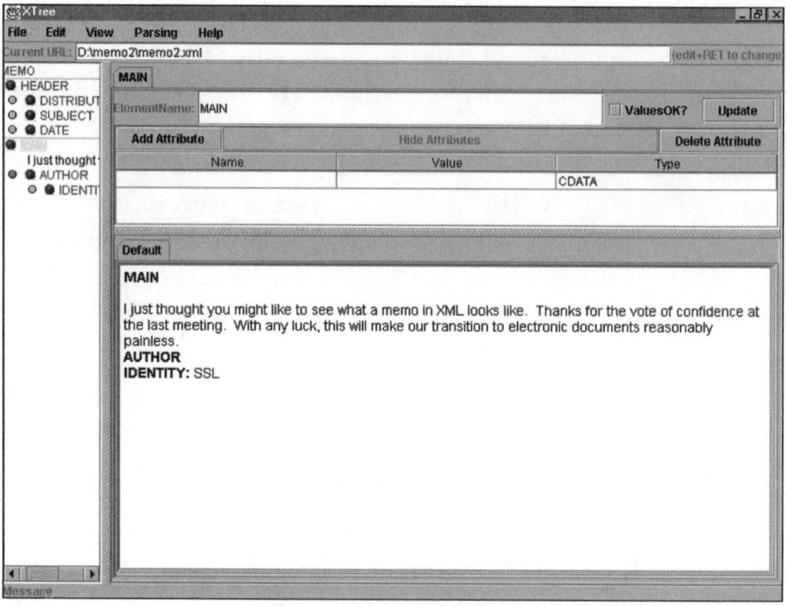

Figure 23-6 *Browsing generic XML in Jumbo*

Note

Although Jumbo illustrated new possibilities in browser architecture, the latest version (Jumbo 3) is becoming more like traditional browsers, using scripts and an SVG plug-in in contrast to its previous standalone approach. The earlier experiments remain emblems of the creative possibilities XML presents, but the change in approach may signal the difficulty of building any new browser architecture from scratch.

A more flexible architecture might enable users or documents to associate applets (or similar programs) with XML elements, providing element-specific processing either in the browser window or in separate pop-up windows. In this way, elements that contain only text can be displayed with the tools available for handling markup, whereas elements meant for further processing can receive it using tools they specify, as shown in Figure 23-8.

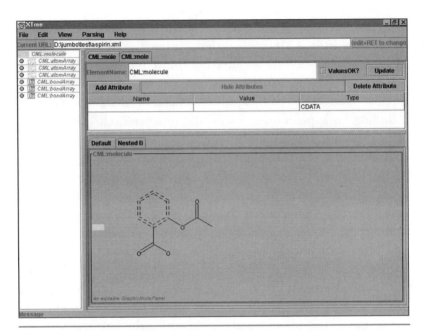

Figure 23-7 *Specific processing for particular elements in Jumbo*

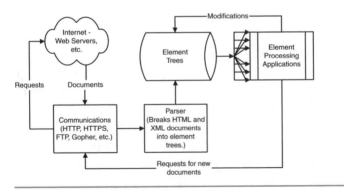

Figure 23-8 *The open browser enables elements to be processed by multiple tools*

Implementing this architecture in the current browsers will undoubtedly create yet another arena in which the competing browser developers can build incompatible standards, such as APIs that refuse to interoperate, and code that works only with a particular browser. Still, XML itself includes a few features that could be useful for parts of this architecture, most probably namespaces. Selective processing based on namespaces may allow browsers to support distinctive pathways for different XML vocabularies, including both processing within the browser itself and handing content off to external applications.

Adding this kind of support for processors handling particular XML elements may have an unexpected side effect on the browser. Opening the browser to external, in-line applications like this is a much more dramatic move than the earlier additions of plug-in architectures, or even applets. The browser could become much less integrated, reversing the trend of piling more and more applications into the same browser space. In this scenario, the browser is reduced to a communications engine and a parser, along with a framework that enables different applications to communicate and modify the element tree. The browser could still provide the interface services, if needed, and a basic set of tools for displaying text, but even those might be outsourced to other applications. Branding this browser and selling it would be much harder than marketing the current batch of integrated browsers, but this minimal structure may be the logical final destination of browser development.

In this possible browser future, the presentation and interface aspects of the browser would be taken over by other applications (even mini-applications) that process elements. These applications would have their own presentation and interface structures, which the browser might continue to coordinate. Much of the functionality that used to be in the browser would be distributed across applications devoted to the processing of particular elements. They could all share a parser, a communications engine, and perhaps the same element tree, but the browser as a unit will have become unnecessary. The parser, engines, and element-tree interface would become browser services rather than distinct units.

At this level, the much-discussed integration of operating system and browser would be possible, although both would disintegrate to a certain extent. An operating system is still needed to provide an environment for running these services, and several parts of the browser would become even more important than they had been previously, but the element processing applications and the services for keeping them in sync would provide a new area for applications and API development. The applications could be Java applets, ActiveX controls, or even COBOL programs—it wouldn't really matter, as long as they could communicate with the element trees and with each other. The processing applications could use Java's Abstract Windowing Toolkit or the Java Foundation Classes, Microsoft's Win32, or the Mac OS Toolbox. The model could work as well in any of those systems, or even in an entirely new system, provided it allowed for the communication and coordination among the growing number of parts.

Why would anyone want this Hydra-headed replacement for the friendly browser? It would offer a number of advantages. First, although it would actually be built out of a lot of different parts, it wouldn't need to look any different to the user. A single browser window would still be able to coordinate all of these parts (and provide a nice home for a company logo). Second, it would provide parsing services to many potential processing applications without requiring every application to include its own parser. It would provide a single interface for parsing services, enabling developers to build to a browser services API (Applications Programming Interface) rather than choose a parser, license it, and write code that fits it.

These developments may muddy the operating systems/graphical user interface/browser waters even more than Microsoft already has, but Microsoft's systems work on a somewhat different model. At present, Windows programs can use Internet Explorer as an ActiveX control, and Internet Explorer can provide a home for ActiveX controls and their data. This model could, if developed further by Microsoft, develop into the shared browser services model I described a few paragraphs ago, but for now Internet Explorer remains, in practice, a collection of programs that communicate with each other as pieces, but communicate to external programs as a unit. Microsoft certainly seems intent on piling as much of its browser into the operating system as possible, so this situation may change rapidly. Microsoft's Web clients grow ever larger, demanding more resources by the year.

The Mozilla project and Netscape are also moving toward making the browser an application-development platform, though they rebuilt the entire system along the way. The Mozilla project rebuilt the browser on top of XML, CSS, and the DOM, and uses these technologies to build and extend the browser itself. The old plug-in architecture lives on, but many Mozilla developers are reaching for more tightly integrated projects, using Mozilla as a cross-platform solution to the problem of user interaction with data. XML provides much of this extensibility, giving developers the flexibility they need to rebuild the browser logic to meet their needs.

Browsers have plenty of competition, however. As Jon Bosak of Sun Microsystems has stated in his white paper, "XML, Java, and the Future of the Web" (available at `http://sunsite.unc.edu/ pub/sun-info/standards/xml/why/xmlapps.htm`), "XML gives Java something to do." Java is already built on a standard set of class libraries, complete with network interfaces that already provide the functionality of the communications engine shown previously. The JavaBeans standard that arrived with Java Developer's Kit 1.1 provides mechanisms for applications and applets to communicate, providing direct channels of communication among large numbers of objects.

Portals and other gateways

Whereas browsers are changing slowly, other parts of the computing world are sprouting new features quickly. The middleware I describe earlier in this chapter for converting XML among different XML structures is critical, but feeding XML into non-XML systems is perhaps the leading integration task on which developers and vendors are focusing today. An information portal can be as simple as a network connection and a parser attached to a program, or as complex as an application of its own operating as a switchboard and directing XML traffic into the right formats and the right systems.

XML is able to slip into the Web-browser world pretty easily because it uses the same infrastructures as HTML. In the world of machine-to-machine communications, the infrastructures are often very different, with proprietary data formats, a wide variety of protocols, and a culture much less tolerant of variations in style. Adding XML to large-scale flows of information often requires rebuilding existing infrastructure and translating XML into the languages legacy systems expect to hear. Feeding information back into systems is often more difficult than extracting it, demanding more care to avoid corrupting data and disrupting information flows.

Many vendors are selling tools that handle some of this processing, including DataChannel (`http://www.datachannel.com`), Bluestone (`http://www.bluestone.com`), Excelon (`http://www.excelon.com`), and many others. Some come from XML; others come from other fields of application integration. If there's a gold rush in the XML community today, this is probably where it's happening. Establishing connections between internal data structures and XML documents is difficult work, especially when it must be done on a large scale. As more and more tools come to speak XML natively, some of this work may become easier (and less expensive), but the transition will probably take some time.

Integrating XML with Other Technologies

Plenty of parts are available for using XML, some still in development and others fully grown. Making these parts work together — especially those that were originally designed for XML's predecessor technologies, SGML and HTML — can be a challenge. If necessary, integrators can always build their own glue and their own parts, as I describe in the next section, but for now I explore less drastic options that use existing technologies. In the simplest, most Web-like case, shown in Figure 23-9, a browser that can present XML (using CSS or XSL) connects to a Web server, which retrieves an XML file and style sheet and sends them on to the browser. Files are added to the Web server using traditional file server and FTP mechanisms.

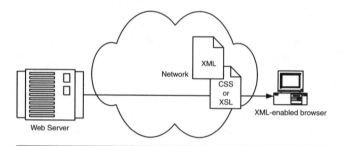

Figure 23-9 *Viewing XML documents over the Web*

Note

Although a browser is the client of this XML transmission, any gateway – a recipient database, a set of instruments, an e-mail system, or something completely new – could be at the end of the connection. Browsers are by no means the only XML clients. (Browsers do, however, provide a familiar set of mechanisms that simplify a discussion of the features.)

In another case likely to be typical of XML document distribution over the Web, a processor on the Web server translates the XML into HTML for presentation, as shown in Figure 23-10.

Caution

If you use server-side processing (with XSL or another tool) to convert your XML to HTML, be sure to have some kind of caching mechanism so that you don't have to perform the conversion every time a document is downloaded. Site performance may be drastically impaired unless you take steps to enhance efficiency.

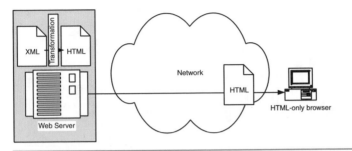

Figure 23-10 *Using server-side processing to convert XML documents into HTML for transmission over the Web*

Server-side processing may not be about transforming XML into another format; it may simply involve converting information stored in a non-XML format (a database, for example) to an XML document. You could perform this translation with traditional CGI processing, servlets, Active Server Pages, or whatever seems appropriate, as shown in Figure 23-11.

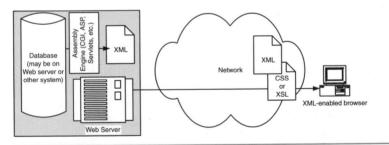

Figure 23-11 *Using server-side processing to assemble XML documents*

Additional processing (security management, caching, further transformations, and so on) can take place at any point between the repository and the viewer/editor. If this happens repeatedly, as shown in Figure 23-12, it may be time to find a more efficient approach than HTTP (which is pretty inefficient) for transmitting XML, a least to the point at which (if necessary) HTTP carries the information to the client computer.

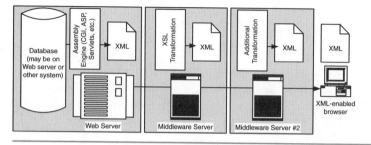

Figure 23-12 *Processing XML between the repository and the consumer*

Because of XML's readily processed structures, a variety of solutions for simplifying these complex models is available. If the processing is taking place within a single environment, you can often skip the laborious task of parsing and re-assembling. Processing, especially generic processing, like XSL transformations, can be done at the server, at the client, or anywhere in between, as appropriate. (It also depends on the environments used to support that processing, of course.) The same set of processes shown in Figure 23-12 could be handled by a smaller set of systems, as shown in Figure 23-13.

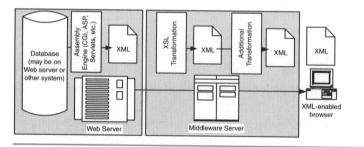

Figure 23-13 *Combining XML processing to reduce the number of parses and transmissions needed to process XML*

XML's flexibility creates perhaps as many questions as it answers, but the ease of XML processing makes it an excellent tool for integration, in whatever processing sequence you find most efficient and most appropriate to your needs.

Building Custom Applications for XML

Although you've taken as much advantage as possible of XML's ability to keep documents human-readable, the real reasons XML is exciting have to do with machine-readability. Markup is designed to be easy to program, using a nested structure that works well with both recursive functions and object-oriented programming. Although parsing valid XML documents is not a light task, neither does it present the enormous challenges faced by programs that must parse other formats. The developers of the XML specification made creating XML applications much easier by tightening the rules for XML document structure syntax, while simultaneously reducing the need for a lot of processing by adding the well-formedness option. XML's firm requirement that all elements have complete start and end tags, or indicate that they are empty by closing the tag with />, makes it far easier to write a parser. Both SGML and HTML allowed elements to skip end tags, which required significant processing to determine where exactly the end of an element was supposed to be. (Converting from these formats to XML is a hit-or-miss proposition as a result.) SGML also allowed abbreviated element names, adding an extra level of lookup to the parsing process. XML's basic structures, expressed in the criteria for well-formed documents, ensure that parsers can be reasonably simple programs that won't add incredible amounts of processing overhead to document processing.

Note

Although XML has made it much easier to write a parser, it's still a lot of work, especially as schemas, XInclude, XML Base, and other features get involved. Most applications rely on parser modules built by other developers, rather than building their own parsers.

Validating XML documents, as opposed to checking them for well-formedness, remains something of a challenge, thanks to parameter entities and the need to check element structures against the DTD. DTDs can be incredibly complex documents to interpret, especially DTDs that extend back through several files because of multiple parameter entities and DOCTYPE declarations (not to mention IGNORE and INCLUDE sections). Applying large DTDs to small files can waste processor cycles while the parser interprets extra information it will never apply and adds overhead to every element lookup. Still, validating documents is a critical part of much XML processing, and simplifies the processing that is left to applications. Validation may occur at several different points in the lifetime of a document, from its initial construction to its final presentation. Schema validation may occur in addition to or in place of DTD validation.

Many XML applications are probably going to end up using parts of XML rather than all of it, working with parsers that straddle the distinctions between well-formed and valid. Applications that can handle XML linking will probably need to do some validating, unless document creators want to present the attributes needed to create links in every single element instance. A document that uses entities extensively might not need a DTD that defines its elements and attributes, but it does need a parser that can expand its entity references. How far practice will diverge from the twin standards of valid and well-formed remains to be seen, but more levels are likely to appear. There are many situations for which full DTDs may not be appropriate. Combining the extreme flexibility of well-formed documents with the powerful tools available in valid documents and the new complexities of namespace processing will likely cause some problems for developers. Managing the flow of information between systems that need maximum efficiency and those that need maximum reliability will be a challenge for a while.

Cross Reference

The XML-Dev mailing list is a key forum for developers creating XML applications. The archives for the list and information on joining are available at `http://lists.xml.org/archives/xml-dev/`. When communicating on this list, keep in mind that it is a mailing list concerned with high-level development, not XML tutorials. Three other lists of particular note to developers are xml-app, java-xml-interest, and Perl-xml. A handy form for subscribing to these (and many other) mailing lists is available at Elliotte Rusty Harold's Cafe Con Leche site, `http://ibiblio.org/xml/mailinglists.html`.

Choosing Tools for Programming XML

XML is not a programming language; nothing in XML limits the development of XML-centric applications to a simple development environment or language. Although the W3C's Document Object Model (DOM) specifies bindings for Java and JavaScript (as well as a CORBA IDL binding), plenty of other environments, from C++ to Perl to Delphi to Visual Basic to Lisp, may be appropriate for your needs, depending on the experience you (or your organization) have. There's even been some development work in COBOL and XML. XML can be used as the glue between multiple applications written in completely different environments, enabling them all to trade data back and forth without having to build interfaces between specific components. As long as they can all process XML, they can use it as a common data format.

At this point, the leading contender for XML development appears to be Java. Java has a significant advantage over other languages and development tools for a very simple reason: like XML, it was built for Unicode from the ground up. The requirement that parsers be able to handle the full two-byte Unicode canonical encoding causes problems for C and C++ (although there are many ways around it), older versions of Perl (where parts of the language have received significant upgrades and extensions), and all other development tools that expect characters to occupy a single byte. As a result, much of the work currently underway in XML development is being done in Java. Java's hierarchical structures, are also a good match for XML. Java also provides easy interfaces between classes and objects, making it very simple to add a generic parser to a data-processing application. Even though Java's facilities for handling text are not the most advanced, they are more than a match for the level of processing required by XML parsing. Java applets also fit well with several of the Web-based possibilities for XML. Java applets provide a convenient mechanism for presenting XML content in browsers that don't themselves understand XML. Java offers several other significant advantages, including a community that is actively developing frameworks. The Java versions of SAX and DOM (described in Chapter 11) provide a standard foundation for many XML tools.

C++ is also a very viable environment for XML development. Like Java, its object structures can embrace nested element structures quite easily. Even though adding classes to a C++ project is somewhat more complex than it is with Java, there is no lack of powerful C++ tools. C++ is already in use for a wide variety of data processing projects, including markup processing, and libraries are available. Unfortunately, most of the C++ world still expects to see single-byte characters, making it fairly difficult to work with Unicode. Documents encoded in UTF-8 (and that use its ASCII subset) should work well with most standard flavors of C++, and more tools for C++ Unicode development are appearing.

Note

Does Unicode matter, anyway? The answer depends on your needs and the platforms you work with. Unicode has been slow to take off because of limited application support. However, both XML and Java provide support for processing Unicode characters (though not necessarily displaying them, which is more a matter of the operating system and the available font sets) at their foundations. Unicode has begun picking up steam, however, with native support available in both the Microsoft Windows NT and Sun Solaris 2.6 operating systems. Java and XML are two key components for the future of document processing, so expect to see more action in the Unicode field.

Perl has been the text hacker's choice for years, helping developers blast through seemingly impossible barriers with a few lines of code. Perl's rich support for regular expressions has helped thousands of programmers create CGI scripts, write HTML and interpret the data sent back by forms. At the same time, Perl has helped developers implement changes across entire sites, addressing challenges such as changing all the legal notices on a site overnight with elegance and ease. Perl use is hardly limited to HTML; SGML developers have used Perl to find problems in their documents and fix them as automatically as possible. Perl relies on external parsers to feed it XML information. The original Perl module for XML parsing, XML::Parser, was written by Larry Wall (Perl's creator) and Clark Cooper, and uses James Clark's C-based Expat parser. It has been available since October 1998. New modules are constantly under development, connecting Perl to more aspects of XML processing. For the latest, check the CPAN archives at `http://www.perl.org`.

Python, another scripting language with roots in Unix, has long been a popular tool for XML scripting. Resources including a Python parser (xmlproc), an implementation of SAX, and various other tools are available at `http://www.stud.ifi.uio.no/~larsga/download/python/xml/index.html`. Python is the language of choice for a significant number of developers working on XML and even within the XML working groups, so the number of tools available for Python is growing rapidly. XML is becoming more and more a part of the XML core, as documented at `http://www.python.org/topics/xml/`.

Cross Reference

Need to find some tools for working with XML in your favorite development environment? Visit `http://www.stud.ifi.uio.no/~larsga/linker/XMLtools.html` for a frequently updated list of free tools, or `http://xmlsoftware.com` for a list of tools that includes commercial products.

Chapter 24

Ever-Expanding Webs of XML

Even though the adoption of XML will clearly require some significant changes to the basic infrastructure of the Web, its impact on the structures of sites remains less clear. So far, XML has mostly seen use as a standard to define other standards, which in turn define other files, and not as a general document format. The W3C's positioning of XML in the Architecture Domain leaves many questions about what XML is really for: the W3C's move to rebuild HTML as a set of XML modules represents one possibility, while continuing development of XML-based network protocols is another. Concluding this exploration of XML's potential, I survey its implications for traditional Web sites and other fields now taking advantage of technologies built for the Web.

XML and the Traditional Web

When the Web first appeared sites had extremely simple structures, modeled after the hierarchical models of the Web's predecessors, FTP and Gopher. All requests for files referred to actual files, stored in the file system of the server. URLs corresponded to a subset of the file structure on the server, and answering requests was a matter of finding the right file, adding an appropriate header, and sending it back to the browser that requested it. Hyperlinks contained the URL information, enabling developers to create crazy quilts of HTML without having to create crazy-quilt file structures. Directory structures were the most commonly used organizational tool in the early days, which enabled developers to create somewhat structured sites.

As the demand for more up-to-date information has exploded across the Web, many sites have turned to database-driven sites. Tools like CGI, Cold Fusion, Java servlets, and Active Server Pages (ASP) put attractive front ends on information stored in relational database systems and even legacy mainframes. Database-generated pages make sites like the FedEx tracking page possible, but are also used for many pages that seem like ordinary HTML to users. Visitors to the Microsoft site, for example, will encounter many pages created with ASP. Microsoft uses a database system in the background to manage data used on many of its pages, enabling it to make changes quickly.

Database-driven sites power many intranets as well, enabling employees to tap into data sources once locked in cold rooms guarded by protective MIS staff. Groupware and communications software have metamorphosed into Web applications. Lotus Domino's transition from Notes server to Web server was a notable change, providing instant translation of Notes-formatted documents into Web pages. The complex data structures behind Notes have applications on the public as well as the private Web, and Domino has moved out from behind the corporate firewall to power a few Internet servers.

There are several problems with database-driven sites, however. First, they tend to require more horsepower to overcome the overhead of connecting to a database; or the database server may need more horsepower to handle the increased demand placed on it. Second, database-driven sites are rarely search engine–friendly; most of them in fact put up "Do not enter" signs with the robots.txt file. Although the information contained in the database is probably well structured and easily searchable, there's no easy way for a search engine to connect to a database and collect structured data. (It would probably indicate an enormous security hole as well.) Finally, complex database-driven sites usually require a fairly dedicated team of developers to build applications that can manage the database in addition to the usual team of HTML developers, adding considerable expense to a Web project.

The slow spread of Cascading Style Sheets and dynamic HTML has also had an impact on site architecture. It's becoming more common for certain aspects of Web design to become centralized. Centrally controlled style sheets make it easier for a company to provide a basic look for its sites that it can then modify. Dynamic HTML interfaces can be stored as JavaScript code files or as Microsoft's new scriptlets, which combine scripting with HTML to create reusable interface controls. HTML documents today are far more than text with markup. Currently, the roster of items that can appear in Web pages includes the following:

- HTML
- Images (GIF, JPEG, PNG, XBM, and so on)
- Sounds (AIFF, AU, WAV, and so on)
- Video (QuickTime, MPEG, AVI, and so on)
- Specialized Plug-in Content (Splash, Shockwave, Acrobat, and so on)
- JavaScript
- VBScript (Internet Explorer only)
- Java applets
- ActiveX controls (Internet Explorer only)

The Web is already a rich programming environment, with constantly improving tools for programming and presentation. Many people, including Web developers, would argue that the Web is complex enough as it is without another layer of complication. Adding XML (and all its associated standards) to the Web may be, from this perspective, unnecessary.

Upgrading HTML: Moving to XML syntax

Even though most of this book has focused on creating new XML vocabularies that have little to do with HTML, the W3C is moving HTML itself to a new XML foundation. Moving HTML to an XML vocabulary involves much more than just achieving syntactical consistency within the W3C. Over the years HTML has grown from a simple set of elements with a few attributes to a gigantic collection of elements and attributes using an SGML DTD. The sheer bulk of HTML makes it hard to create new HTML browsers — supporting the entire standard requires a lot of coding, and designers have enough trouble building documents for the few browsers that dominate the market without having to worry about new subsets appearing in newly developed browsers. Non-PC devices, such as cell phones and personal digital assistants, don't have the displays or the processing facilities needed to implement a "full" version of HTML or to successfully process the wide variety of syntaxes used in current HTML development. Full-sized PC browsers don't mind missing end tags or unquoted attributes, but extra processing cycles are required to compensate. To address these needs, the W3C HTML Activity is developing the next generation of HTML, called Extensible Hypertext Markup Language (XHTML).

Rather than adding new features, as in past versions, the Working Group is converting HTML to an XML syntax (done in version 1.0, now a Recommendation), and breaking the HTML vocabulary into a group of smaller modules (in *Modularization of XHTML*, and used in *XHTML 1.1*). The *Composite Capabilities/Preference Profiles* (CC/PP) specification will make these modules more useful by allowing devices to identify their capabilities to servers, which will make it possible for servers to customize content to meet the capabilities of a given device, which will in turn make the modules more useful.

Note

Material in this section is subject to change as the XHTML family of specifications develops. For the latest top-level view of what the W3C is doing with HTML, visit http://www.w3.org/MarkUp/Activity.html.

The XHTML 1.0 Recommendation describes the syntactical changes HTML developers will need to learn to acclimate to the new XML-based model. This book has covered all of them, with the significant exception of the fact that HTML element and attribute names are all going to be in lower case from now on. Documents will need to be well-formed, meaning that script and style elements must either resort to CDATA sections (if they include <, >, or & characters) or use external scripts. Empty elements must use the /> syntax, though the specification recommends using a space before the slash (as in br />) for compatibility with older browsers. Some elements (notably title and base) will need to appear in a particular sequence to conform to the XHTML DTDs. XHTML uses XML namespaces to inform processors of which vocabulary is in use, relying mostly on the default namespace, which doesn't require a prefix, to maintain compatibility with older browsers. XHTML, which uses style sheets for much of its formatting, should be usable in both HTML browsers and generic XML processors. As far as vocabulary is concerned, XHTML adheres to the HTML 4.01 rules.

The next phase of development moves on to the larger project of breaking the HTML vocabulary into smaller chunks, making it possible to use subsets of HTML or to integrate HTML vocabulary with XML. The current Candidate Recommendation of *Modularization of XHTML* identifies 29 modules, listed in Table 24-1.

Table 24-1 *XHTML Modules*

Module	Module Contents
Attribute Collections	Attributes used by other modules
Core Structure	html, head, title, body
Core Text	abbr, acronym, address, blockquote, br, cite, code, dfn, div, em, h1, h2, h3, h4, h5, h6, kbd, p, pre, q, samp, span, strong, var
Core Hypertext	a
Core List	dl, dt, dd, ol, ul, li
Applets	applet, param (contents deprecated)
Text Extensions – Presentation	b, big, hr, i, small, sub, sup, tt
Text Extensions – Edit	del, ins
Text Extensions – Bi-directional text	bdo
Basic Forms	form, input, label, select, option, textarea
Forms	form, input, label, select, option, textarea, button, fieldset, label, legend, optgroup
Basic Tables	caption, table, td, th, tr
Tables	caption, table, td, th, tr, col, colgroup, tbody, thead, tfoot
Image	img
Client-side Image Map	a, area, img, map, object (adds attributes to a, img, and object)
Server-side Image Map	img (adds ismap attribute)
Object	object, param
Frames	frameset, frame, noframes
Target	Adds the target attribute to a, area, base, link, and form
Iframe	iframe
Intrinsic Events	Adds onblur, onfocus, onreset, onsubmit, onload, onunload, and onchange attributes as appropriate to the a, area, form, body, label, input, select, textarea, and button elements.

Module	Module Contents
Metainformation	`meta`
Scripting	`noscript, script`
Stylesheets	`style` element
Style Attribute	`style` attribute
Links	`link`
Base	`base`
Name Identification	Adds the `name` attribute to `a, applet, form, frame, iframe, img,` and `map` (contents deprecated)
Legacy	`basefont, center, font, s, strike, u,` and a variety of formatting-oriented attributes (contents deprecated)

Note

This list is subject to change as XHTML modules develop. For the latest see `http://www.w3.org/TR/xhtml-modularization/abstract_modules.html`.

XHTML 1.1 is built out of these modules, as is XHTML Basic, a smaller subset of XHTML intended for use on cell phones, PDAs, and other devices without the capability to run a full-scale browser.

Tip

For more information on XHTML, you may want to explore *XHTML: Moving Toward XML* by Simon St.Laurent and B. K. DeLong (IDG Books, 2000). There's also a mailing list for XHTML issues. Information on the mailing list is available at `http://www.yahoogroups.com/group/XHTML-L`.

Using XML on the traditional Web

Adding XML to the existing Web architecture isn't especially difficult, as I mention in Chapter 23. Existing Web servers and the HTTP protocol can handle XML just as they handled HTML, without needing to know about the files they are transferring. Much of the application architecture surrounding HTML can be reused for XML, requiring closer attention to the syntax and vocabulary of the documents produced, but not many other changes. Although this scenario sounds fairly rosy, some problems remain. Browsers have been slow to support XML and still have inconsistent implementations of Cascading Style Sheets. Making the transition from HTML to XML requires that some component in the process learn about XML — either the browser presenting the information, or the server sending it.

Both Netscape and Microsoft are revising their browsers to accommodate XML. As of this writing, both companies have released software capable of displaying XML documents using Cascading Style Sheets, though with different levels of support. Netscape's Gecko preview release focuses on presenting HTML and XML information with the assistance of Cascading Style Sheets. Microsoft's Internet Explorer 5.0 includes an implementation of XSLT in addition to limited Cascading Style Sheet support for XML, plus a rendering engine for vector graphics stored in its XML-based Vector Markup Language (VML). The third graphical browser vendor, Opera, has added substantial XML+CSS support in versions 4.0 and later of its browser. Links between XML documents remain something of a problem — Netscape supports simple XLinks, Opera can support simple XLinks through CSS extensions, and Internet Explorer only supports HTML linking.

Note

For more on details on how to use XML in these browsers, and workarounds for their varying degrees of support, see my "Cross-Browser XML" presentation at http://www.simonstl.com/articles/xbrowse/index.html, along with a series of articles on XML.com at http://www.xml.com/pub/a/2000/05/03/browserchart/index.html.

Even as these browsers are released, users will take a number of years to upgrade (if, indeed, they ever do). It may take several years before developers can assume that most of their audience is using tools that can cope with information in an XML format. In the meantime, developers who want to move forward into XML for reasons beyond the desire to present data to Web users (such as the desire for efficient management and storage) will have to provide tools for presenting information stored in XML formats to users whose software lacks XML support. The transition architecture will probably be the one shown in Figure 23-8 (shown in Chapter 23), in which a processor on the server examines the information a browser sent with the request that identifies its capabilities, and transforms the XML document into an HTML equivalent when necessary. In addition to the extra processing cycles this architecture can consume, it means that developers and designers are going to need to create a map between XML elements and their HTML equivalents. This can be done with XSLT or it can be done with a custom software tool, but in either case it means extra information about the documents that needs to be created.

Designers who've worked with HTML for years have seen this pattern before, wherein sites have had to have multiple faces for different browser versions. Every new technology added to the Web left behind users who didn't upgrade until the costs of not having support for that technology become sizable enough to drive them to the effort of downloading (or getting a new computer). Frames, scripts, applets, and even tables all caused problems at one time or another. XML offers the advantage over these older technologies that it is easily processed, which enables developers to automate the process of presenting two faces (new XML and old HTML) — but there will still, as always, be some transition costs.

Whether or not Web browsers and Web servers undergo the dramatic transition I suggest in the previous chapter, the advent of XML document presentation in the browser will likely change the underlying architectures of many sites. The XML syntax itself and the XLink specification will drive these changes in architecture and design, although in different ways. XML syntax promises to engender a Web where content, presentation, and scripts are separated from each other more distinctly than they have been in HTML, while XLink will distinguish itself by providing richer interfaces and a fragment model for document retrieval.

XML continues the trend of separating content from formatting, which already gained some momentum in the HTML world with the appearance of the Cascading Style Sheets recommendation and the important role it plays in both Netscape's and Microsoft's implementations of dynamic HTML features. The most appealing aspect of Cascading Style Sheets to many designers is its ability to centralize style information, which does away with much of the repetitive work once involved in creating and updating HTML pages. Style sheets are an automated version of the graphic designer's spec book, providing a smooth path for formatting to flow into documents without constant hand-tweaking. CSS also provides advantages for application development, providing a basic structure for formatting that can be applied to elements without much concern for what kind of element the target of an operation is.

Note

An interesting counterpoint to this "separation of structure and formatting" argument is the case for using XML for markup that purely indicates formatting, such as XSL Formatting Objects, or Scalable Vector Graphics (SVG). The ease with which XML documents can be transformed from structured documents to these formatting documents, however, still makes for a strong argument for using formats that reflect the content structure of a document as base formats. These structures can then be annotated with styles (with CSS) or transformed into a formatting-oriented markup language.

CSS2, the newest finished version of Cascading Style Sheets, brings HTML developers used to working with its predecessor (CSS1) much more power, including support for tables, positioning, and other layout tasks. CSS2 provides a tutorial for using it with XML, not just HTML, and promises to be the primary tool for lightweight styling on the Web. XSL (which claims not to be a competitor with CSS, just a different way of doing things) is much more complicated, but offers much more power, especially in transforming documents between formats. XSL's rule-based transformations open up entirely new horizons for browsers, enabling authors to create different sets of rules for different situations and make better use (and reuse) of the information stored in XML documents.

The relationship of XML to scripting is more complex. SGML purists seem puzzled, and occasionally offended, by the common mixture of scripts and markup that is common practice in the HTML world. Because of its use as an interface as well as a document presentation format, HTML has needed stronger, more flexible tools than are commonly used in SGML environments. The introduction of the SCRIPT tag in Netscape 2.0 opened the floodgates for millions of documents that combine some amount of scripting with document information. The appearance of dynamic HTML has led to the creation of documents that contain complete interface structures (for example, a program to handle opening and closing headings on an outline) as well as the content they display. More and more of these documents, in fact, are becoming incomprehensible without the scripts needed to make them work. Because of the often close relationship between a script and the structure of a particular document (and the odd problems that can happen when transmission difficulties prevent the scripting file from loading properly), HTML scripters have tended to combine as much information as possible in a single file. Scripts are sometimes stored in separate files (using the SRC attribute or server-side includes), but usually this degree of separation is reserved for scripts that are used by multiple documents. Library files containing code used by multiple HTML documents are easier to manage than duplicate copies of code stored in 50 different files.

XML's advent will probably push many developers to begin separating code from content. XML's syntax is not friendly to SCRIPT elements, requiring CDATA-marked sections for any code that includes markup characters. Even if developers can cope with these requirements, XML's status as a potential universal file format may further promote the separation of code from content. Probably not all processing applications will be script-enabled, and some will need to ignore scripting content anyway. Separating script from content will reduce the load on these applications. Changing from HTML's integrated model to XML's modularized architecture will cause some problems at first, although HTML developers have certainly had to learn to keep track of all the images, applets, controls, and other content material linked into documents. The change will require close examination of documents and their structures to determine what can profitably be shared across multiple documents. In an ideal case, a set of HTML documents that was stored as shown in Figure 24-1 could be reorganized with XML's tools, as shown in Figure 24-2.

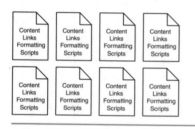

Figure 24-1 *HTML's original integrated model tends to keep content, links, formatting, and scripting in the same document.*

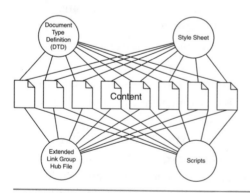

Figure 24-2 *XML's linking structures and encouragement of modularity can break documents down into content and a set of shared components.*

Keeping track of these relationships and making them work efficiently will require another generation of tools. At present, the available Web-building tools can keep up with HTML documents, graphics, and a few components, but few of them can manage scripts or style sheets this way, and extended linking groups have added an entirely new dimension to the task. Until the tools catch up, it's likely that developers will continue to mix and match content, format, script, and links, if only because that way they won't need a librarian to keep track of all the parts. Java applets and ActiveX controls can still play roles similar to the ones they play now, although they may be activated quite differently, as you see in Chapter 23. Images, sounds, and other data files will also remain separate. The need for site organizers is, as always, on the rise.

XLink's long-term impact on site architectures will probably be even greater. XLink makes it possible to split and combine documents in ways that get developers past the limitations of conventional file structures. Although taking full advantage of these abilities will require the repository developments outlined in Chapter 23, fragments (identified with XPointers) and linking offer developers a new way of thinking about their documents that makes the file-based systems of HTML seem as quaint as the terminal interfaces of yesteryear. Because of their grounding in file systems, HTML documents have had to appear as complete units. Half an HTML file might occasionally be readable (as long as it isn't a table), but there's no way to download portions of files. As a result, most developers have leaned toward creating sets of smaller documents, which load more quickly but can become difficult to manage. Anyone who has had to print out documentation that was spread out over hundreds of HTML pages has encountered the limitations of this method firsthand.

Fragments and linking make it possible to refer to parts of documents and embed them in other documents to create new documents. Fragments and linking have the potential to unseat some of the database-driven applications currently available by making it easy for developers to reuse data and include it in multiple documents without needing to write custom applications. A catalog, for example, could store all its information in an enormous document that does nothing but keep track of items. The "pages" of the catalog could reference that catalog with XPointers to retrieve chunks based on attributes and content. As a result, templates could link to all the items on sale, all sporting goods, a particular deck of cards requested by a customer, or even all the items in the catalog by making the appropriate request. If the server was capable of handling fragments efficiently, all of this information could be transferred appropriately, with only the needed items being sent.

Making fragmenting and linking work to full effect requires a whole set of enabling technologies: servers that can process XPointers efficiently to return appropriate fragments, browsers that can cope with the XLink specification to enable embedding of linked content, and authoring tools that will help site managers keep track of the data stored in these new document structures. The revolution this can make possible is probably a few years off, if the speed at which HTML tools have been developed up to this point is any indication.

Even though Web browsers have rapidly grown into a popular interface, they haven't yet been able to offer the kinds of services that users expect of their computers. The latest rounds of improvements to Web browsers and servers have beefed up the Web's claim of being a universal interface for all kinds of data. Although Java arrived several years ago, Java development is only now reaching the point where applets and Java applications are capable of competing with full-blown operating system-specific applications. Dynamic HTML and the Document Object Model (DOM) have made it possible to create polished interfaces inside a Web browser that offer considerably more functionality than form fields, drop-down boxes, and clickable buttons and images. The scripting languages, particularly JavaScript, have grown up, acquiring object-oriented extensions and other improvements in the course of their development from form validators to interface managers. In the midst of this explosive growth, XML has appeared to clean up the messes created by six years of rapid development and provide a firm foundation for all of these technologies.

XML does have its limits, however. It is not likely to make the browser a better interface for creating graphics editors or video games. XML is not the solution for every problem by any means. Long strings of binary data, such as those for sound, bitmapped graphics, and video, are very bad candidates for XML formats. (Base64, an encoding that could be used to slip binary information into XML files, is much more verbose than the data it represents.) Still, XML is a useful solution for projects handling structured information from CAD/CAM (where it enables users to exchange information across platforms and companies) to document management to presentations to possibly even the worlds of word processing, spreadsheets, and (to a certain extent, taking full advantage of repository technologies) databases. XML's structures are flexible enough to store hierarchies, tables, spreadsheet information, and complex documents. Developing interfaces that will make writing XML documents as easy as reading them will take years of development and improvements in other standards. Changing the Web from a presentation engine to a workhorse will require many more steps, and probably years of development. XML may find a "killer app" that moves it quickly to the fore, or years of quiet infiltration may be necessary.

XML and the Creation of a New Kind of Web

XML offers the Web real potential to become a tool both for exchanging information and for managing documents — not just in the familiar context of Web sites, but also in the realms of Electronic Data Interchange (EDI) for business-to-business communications, and the possible replacement of the familiar file system with new systems better able to share documents with multiple users, keep track of versioning, and manage the connections among documents. In both cases, some definite gains are to be had for the Web users and the EDI, and document-management-systems users. For the Web, these changes would signal that the patchwork system connecting megabytes of information had matured into a powerful family of standardized and reliable protocols, giving vendors with Web experience new opportunities to enter additional markets. For EDI and document management, it would mark a dramatic shift from custom-built (and often proprietary) systems to a world of commodity components, where building these systems becomes a matter of connecting readily available tools rather than hand-coding complex applications. The architectures I describe in Chapter 23 — repositories, processors, and gateways — have applications that extend well beyond the traditional Web space into all forms of distributed computing. These architectures are appropriate foundations for an enormous number of different applications.

XML's billing as "SGML for the Web" has played out in a way that extends the Web into machine-to-machine communications. Application developers can now use Web technologies independent of Web browsers, and the transformation of Web servers into "application servers" has gotten a boost from XML's ability to carry structured information over infrastructures originally built with HTML in mind. In this case, XML competes not with HTML, but with architectures like CORBA, COM, and Enterprise Java Beans (EJB). XML itself isn't a direct competitor with these architectures, but it does offer a toolkit that developers can use to build alternatives, connecting a variety of different types of systems in ways the developer can control directly.

XML and Web infrastructures have a few critical problems that will likely keep the markets for CORBA, COM, and EJB flourishing, though XML's low cost and relative convenience give it significant advantages over its competition. Serializing information into XML and then parsing it out inflicts significant performance costs, and XML is pretty verbose as well. Using HTTP as a transfer protocol inflicts further performance costs, and the design of HTTP was definitely optimized for retrieving documents from Web sites and not efficient two-way conversation between computers. Developers also have to map XML document structures to internal application structures, and often face trade-offs between generic designs and custom creations that take much longer to develop.

On the other hand, XML has definite potential for developers who need to get simple things done simply. Writing code that exports information to text files with XML syntax is usually reasonably easy, even in systems that have no understanding of XML. Reading XML takes more work, though XML parsers are available for a very wide array of different kinds of computing environments. Integrating XML with an application involves writing import and export mechanisms, which is often less of a task than creating an API that meets the requirements of other interoperability tasks. XML's clean fit with HTTP makes reusing existing HTTP toolkits easy, and this simplifies the transmission process. XML's generic nature seems to be encouraging developers to build similarly generic toolkits that provide extra layers of functionality.

XML's basic structures are also capable of representing existing interchange formats, even if no XML document is ever created. A number of developers are building tools that read in non-XML formats but report them to applications as a series of SAX events or as DOM trees, insulating developers from having to work with multiple underlying formats differently. The Open Healthcare Group (`http://openhealth.org/`), a group of developers building open-source solutions for health-care information interchange, has used this approach to bridge X12 EDI information flows and XML processing. XML's generic approach to structured information can make it a useful tool for integrating information in many different forms, giving applications a common view of a variety of different pieces.

Note

For a more detailed look at some of the side effects XML and these new uses for Web technologies are having on Internet infrastructures, you might take a look at my article, "XML: A Disruptive Technology," at `http://www.xml.com/pub/a/2000/06/21/disruption/index.html`.

Webs and Webs and More Webs

The scenarios I suggest here are only a few of many possibilities. Even though many HTML developers might prefer that XML stay in a separate world of Web services — if only to prevent yet another learning curve — and although some of the XML community seems hostile to the tools used on the Web today, it seems as if new possibilities are emerging rapidly and will be here for a while. XML, built for the Web, may now transform that Web. Web developers will still be able to create beautiful presentations, but with an added layer of information about the content. Client-server developers who have struggled with complex tools but haven't been able to make the Web do what they need it to may see XML and the accompanying document object model as their best option. Developers who just want to make computers talk with each other have a new set of cheap tools with which to build and manage data flows. With any luck XML will drive changes in the tools we use to read, write, process, and share those data as well.

Despite the challenges it faces, XML seems likely to succeed. The SGML community provided an initial base of applications (including open-source components and software) and support, and the interest of major players like Microsoft, Netscape, and Sun betokens a bright future. So far the W3C has provided XML with a strong center, a place where these competitors can participate in discussions leading to common standards and prepare to implement those standards. If XML continues to develop as it has, it should quickly find favor as the architecture that enables the Web to finally deliver on its promises of convenient, friendly, cheap, and interactive information access.

Note

If you want to keep up with the latest and greatest in XML you may want explore two key sites. xmlhack, at `http://xmlhack.com`, is a constantly updated site with brief updates on happenings in XML. `XML.com` (at `http://xml.com`) provides longer articles, updated weekly, on specific subjects, as well as a resource guide.

Glossary

Active Server Pages
A server-side tool, created by Microsoft, that combines scripting and objects with markup, and is used to create dynamic Web sites.

ancestor
An element that contains another element, even when other container elements are in between. The root element, for example, is the ancestor of all of the elements in an XML document. In `<FIRST><SECOND><THIRD/></SECOND></FIRST>`, the `FIRST` element is the ancestor of both the `SECOND` and `THIRD` elements.

application
Either a program that does something (views, formats, sorts, imports, and so on) with XML, or a set of markup tags created with XML. HTML, for example, is an application of SGML, defined with an SGML DTD, whereas XHTML is an application of XML defined with an XML DTD (and schemas eventually).

application programming interface (API)
A specification that programmers can use to create interoperable software.

arc
In XLink, a connection between two resources in an extended link.

ASP
See Active Server Pages.

attribute
A source of additional information about an element. Attribute values may be fixed in the DTD or listed as name-value pairs (`name="value"`) in the start-tag of an element.

attribute declaration
A declaration within the document type definition that identifies that a particular attribute may be used with a particular element, which may also identify its type, provide default (or fixed) values, and limit its permitted values.

Blocks
A generic "protocol for protocols" that uses XML on top of TCP/IP to create custom protocols.

C++
An object-oriented language commonly used to build high-performance software.

Cascading Style Sheets (CSS)
A standard that describes how XML document structures should be presented. Less powerful than XSL, it nonetheless appears to have a bright short-term future as the only style mechanism already recommended by the W3C and (partially) implemented in major browsers, and a longer-term future in projects where XSL would be overkill.

case sensitive
Case sensitivity means that the case of characters must match exactly in all instances of a word or phrase. An application is said to be case sensitive if it differentiates between uppercase and lowercase letters. Non-case-sensitive applications typically transform lowercase and uppercase characters into a single case, and treat "THIS" and "this" as identical. XML is almost entirely case sensitive (except for `xml:lang` attribute values).

CDATA
See character data.

CDF
See Channel Definition Format.

CGI
See Common Gateway Interface.

Channel Definition Format (CDF)
An XML-based "push" standard that describes documents containing URL information along with descriptions, icons, and information on when the material should be automatically retrieved.

character data (CDATA)

CDATA has two very different meanings in XML. First, CDATA is used in attribute declarations to indicate that an attribute may contain character (non-enumerated text) content, including entities that should be expanded. Second, CDATA sections use markers (<![CDATA[and]]>) to indicate text within documents that is *purely* character data, containing no elements or entities. CDATA sections provide an "escape" mechanism for authors whose documents contain characters (typically <, >, and &) that would otherwise interfere with normal processing.

child element

An element nested inside another element. In <FIRST><SECOND/></FIRST>, the SECOND element is the child element of the FIRST element.

Common Gateway Interface (CGI)

An interface commonly used by Web servers to connect user requests to programs running on the server for processing.

content

The text and markup within an element or attribute.

content model

A set of rules describing the content that may appear inside an element, typically specified by element declarations.

CSS

See Cascading Style Sheets.

DCD

See Document Content Description.

DDML

See Document Description Markup Language.

descendant

An element that is contained by another element, even when other container elements are in between. All the elements in an XML document are descendants of the root element, for example. In <FIRST><SECOND><THIRD/></SECOND></FIRST>, the THIRD element is the descendant of both the SECOND and FIRST elements.

document

A "textual object." In HTML, documents (or "pages") are single files containing HTML. In XML, documents may contain content from several files (or other sources) and should include markup structures that make the document valid or well-formed.

Document Content Description

A schema language proposed by IBM and Microsoft that combined some ideas from XML-Data Reduced with syntax from RDF.

Document Description Markup Language

A simple schema language developed by the XML-Dev mailing list. Effectively, it permitted developers to created DTDs using XML syntax.

Document Object Model (DOM)

A means of addressing elements and attributes in a document from a processing application or script. The W3C Document Object Model Working Group is developing a standard model for HTML and XML documents. Level One and most of Level Two are W3C Recommendations, while Level Three is in development.

Document Style Semantics and Specification Language (DSSSL)

A transformation and style language for the processing and formatting of SGML documents. A predecessor to XSL.

document type declaration

In valid documents, the declaration that connects a document to its document type definition. The declaration may connect to an external file or include the definition within itself.

document type definition (DTD)

A set of rules for document construction that lies at the heart of SGML development and all valid XML document construction. Processing applications and authoring tools rely on DTDs to inform them of the parts required by a particular document type. A document with a DTD may be validated against the definition.

DOM

See Document Object Model.

EBNF

See Extended Backus-Naur Form.

ECMAScript

The standard for JavaScript syntax, as laid down by the European Computer Manufacturers Association in ECMA-262.

element

The fundamental logical unit of an XML document. XML documents contain a few opening declarations (the XML declaration and prolog) followed by a root element, which may in turn contain other elements and content.

element declaration

A declaration (appearing in the document type definition) identifying an element's name and describing its content model.

empty element

An element that has no textual content. An empty element may be indicated by a start tag and end tag placed next to each other (`<EMPTY></EMPTY>`) or by a start tag that ends with `/>` (`<EMPTY />`). Empty elements may contain attributes only.

encoding declaration

The encoding declaration is part of the XML declaration at the start of an XML document, and specifies which mapping of numerical values to characters is used for that document.

end tag

A tag that closes an element. An end tag follows the syntax `</Name>`, in which *Name* matches the element name declared in the start tag.

entity

A reference to other data that often acts as an abbreviation or a shortcut. By declaring entities, developers can avoid entering the same information in a document or DTD repeatedly.

event-based model

A model for processing XML documents in which the content of the document is expressed as a series of method calls whose type and content describe the document. Event-based models are lightweight and easily chained, making it easy to create filters and small applications. Many parsers provide event-based interfaces, and SAX is the most common standardized event-based interface.

Extended Backus-Naur Form (EBNF)

The formal notation used in the XML 1.0 specification to represent XML grammar. EBNF is also used to describe standards where XML DTD notation is inappropriate, such as the Resource Description Framework.

extended link

A link that contains locator elements rather than a simple HREF attribute to identify the targets of the link.

Extensible Markup Language (XML)

A standard created by the W3C that provides a much simpler set of rules for markup than SGML, while offering considerably more flexibility than HTML.

Extensible Style Language (XSL)

A style-sheet standard under development at the W3C. XSL enables developers to specify formatting far more precisely than do Cascading Style Sheets. XSL uses a transformation-based approach built on XPath, XSLT, and formatting objects.

external DTD subset

The portion of a document type definition stored outside the document. External DTDs are convenient for storing document type definitions that will be used by multiple documents, enabling the document type definitions to share a centrally managed definition.

external entity

An entity whose declaration contains a reference to an external resource rather than the content of the entity itself.

fatal error

A violation of the well-formedness constraints. Parsers should stop processing the document and report an error to the application. (Note that a fatal error for the parser is not necessarily a fatal error for the application.)

filter

A small piece of software, typically used with event-based interfaces, that processes or transforms document events before passing them to the application.

formatting object

In XSL, the set of tools used to describe presentation. A source XML document is transformed into a set of formatting objects, which are then displayed or otherwise processed.

fragment

A portion of a document identified by an XPointer or other query mechanism. A fragment may refer to one element and all its content (including subelements), a group of elements, or even a selection based on content. The W3C XML Activity has a working group focusing on fragment handing.

general entity

An entity for use in document content. When used in documents, the name of a general entity must be preceded by an ampersand (&) and must be followed by a semicolon (;).

Generalized Markup Language (GML)

The predecessor to SGML, developed in 1969 by IBM in efforts led by Charles Goldfarb. GML represents the origin of the use of <, >, and / for markup and is still in use for document applications.

group element

An XLink element containing a set of additional XML files that are considered potential candidates for multidirectional linking.

hedge

In RELAX, a reusable description of element content. Hedges are processed using hedge automata, the mathematical underpinning of RELAX.

Hypermedia/Time-based Structuring Language (HyTime)

A set of multimedia and linking extensions to SGML, formalized as ISO/IEC 10744-1992. HyTime is one of the foundations of XML-LINK.

HyperText Markup Language (HTML)

An application of SGML and the most popular markup language in use today. HTML is one of the foundations of Web development, providing formatting and basic structures to documents for presentation via browser applications.

HyperText Transfer Protocol (HTTP)

The protocol that governs communications between clients and servers on the World Wide Web. HTTP enables clients to send requests to servers, which reply with an appropriate document or an error message.

instance

The actual use of an element or document type in a document, as opposed to its definition. An instance may also refer to an entire document; a document may be an instance of a DTD if it can be validated under that DTD.

internal DTD subset

The portion of a document type definition that appears inside the document to which it applies. Internal DTD subsets can be hard to manage but provide developers with an easy way to test out new features or develop DTDs without disrupting other documents.

internal entity

An entity whose declaration contains its content rather than a reference to an external resource.

Internet Engineering Task Force (IETF)

A community of developers who create open standards for the Internet, including TCP/IP and HTTP. Visit `http://www.ietf.org` for more information.

ISO

The International Organization for Standardization, which sets industrial standards relating to everything from measurement to character sets to shipping containers to quality processes to SGML.

Java

An object-oriented language optimized for use over the Internet.

JavaScript

A scripting language typically used in Web browsers, though it can also be used on the server as part of Active Server Pages or other development environments. Apart from some surface similarities, JavaScript is definitely not Java, or even a "lite" version of Java. JavaScript is standardized as ECMAScript.

linkbase
A document containing links to help establish two-way links without requiring the links' declaration in every document.

location set
A description of locations in an XPath expression — generally one step in the "path" from an entire document to the part needed for processing.

markup
Structural information stored in the same file as the content. Traditionally, structural information is separated from the content and isolated in elements (defined with tags) and entities.

markup declaration
The contents of document type declarations, which define the elements, attributes, entities, and notations. They specify the kinds of markup that will be legal in a given document.

Mathematical Markup Language (MathML)
An XML application developed by the W3C for the presentation and communication of mathematical structures, particularly equations.

Meta-Content Framework (MCF)
A standard developed by Apple and continued by Netscape that represented metadata as a multidimensional space for user navigation. MCF is one of the many inputs to the Resource Description Format (RDF).

mixed content
Content within an element that includes text, possibly including other child elements. Mixed content models have limited options for constraints in XML; once an element contains text, additional elements declared within that content model may appear as few or as many times as the author likes, in any order.

name characters
Letters, digits, hyphens, underscores, colons, and full stops. (Full stops in Latin character sets are periods.) Colons are reserved for use with namespaces by the *Namespaces in XML* recommendation, so don't use them unless you're supporting namespaces.

name

A label used in an XML document or DTD. A name must begin with a letter and may only contain name characters.

namespace

An additional layer of naming information that uses Uniform Resource Identifiers to provide unique names for elements. Useful for combining information defined in multiple DTDs or schemas.

name token

Any string composed of name characters.

notation

An XML structure that identifies the type of content contained by an element by providing an identifier for the content type.

open source

Typically used to refer to software released with source code and a license that permits modification of that source code. Licenses vary with regard to the constraints they place on modification and redistribution.

parameter entity

An entity used to represent information within the context of a document type definition. Parameter entities may be used to link the content of additional DTD files to a DTD, or as an abbreviation for frequently repeated declarations. Parameter entities are distinguished from general entities by their use of a percent sign (%) rather than an ampersand (&).

parent element

An element in which another element is nested. In `<FIRST>` `<SECOND/></FIRST>`, the `FIRST` element is the parent element of the `SECOND` element.

parsed character data (#PCDATA)

Parsed character data is text that will be examined by the parser for entities and markup. Parsed character data should not contain any &, <, or > characters; these must be represented by the `&amp;`, `&lt;`, and `&gt;` entities, respectively.

parser

An application that converts a serial stream of markup (an XML file, for example) into an output structure accessible by a program. Parsers may perform validation or well-formedness checking on the markup as they process it.

Perl

A scripting language, first developed for Unix by Larry Wall, that has become a vital part of many CGI applications as well as a general-purpose text-processing utility language.

processing application

An application that takes the output generated by a parser (it may include a parser, or be a parser itself) and does something with it. That something may include presentation, calculation, or anything else that seems appropriate.

processing instruction

Directions that enable XML authors to send instructions directly to a processing application that may be outside the native capacities of XML. A processing instruction is differentiated from normal element markup by question marks after the opening < and before the closing > (i.e. `<?instruction ?>`). The XML declaration looks like a processing instruction but is technically not one.

processor

In the XML 1.0 specification, another term for the software commonly referred to as a parser.

prolog

The opening part of a document, containing the XML declaration and any document type declarations or markup declarations needed to process the document.

Python

A scripting language popularly used for XML applications.

recursion

A programming technique in which a function may call itself. Recursive programming is especially well suited to parsing nested markup structures.

RELAX

Regular Language Expressions, a schema language created by the Japanese standards organization and in the process of becoming an ISO technical report.

Resource Description Framework (RDF)

A standard for storing metadata (information about information) under development by the W3C that uses several XML syntaxes.

root element

The first element in a document. The root element is not contained by any other elements (though the prolog may come before it) and forms the base of the tree structure created by parsing the nested elements.

SAX

See Simple API for XML.

Schema for Object-Oriented XML

A schema language proposed by CommerceOne which describes XML documents using a vocabulary based on object-oriented development.

servlet

A server-side Java component, typically used to generate markup for transmission over the Web.

sibling

An element with the same parent element as another element. In `<A><B/><C/></A>`, the B and C elements are siblings because they are both children of the A element.

Simple API for XML (SAX)

An event-based API for connecting Java parsers to applications, also used to create filters between the parser and the application. Most Java parsers provide SAX support.

simple link

A link that directly includes its target locator in an `href` attribute.

Simple Object Access Protocol (SOAP)

A protocol built on top of HTTP, used to exchange information about application objects using an XML vocabulary.

SMIL

See Synchronized Multimedia Integration Language.

SOAP

See Simple Object Access Protocol.

SOX

See Schema for Object-Oriented XML

standalone

A declaration that indicates whether a document references external resources.

Standard Generalized Markup Language (SGML)

The parent language of HTML and XML. SGML provides a complex set of rules for defining document structures. HTML uses structures defined under that set of rules; XML provides a subset of the rules for defining document structures. SGML is formally standardized as ISO/IEC 8879-1986, although a series of later amendments have continued its development.

start tag

The opening tag that begins an element. The general syntax for a start tag is `<Name attributes>`, where `Name` is the name of the element being defined, and `attributes` is a set of name-value pairs. All start tags in XML must either have end tags or use the empty-element syntax, `<Name attributes/>`.

Structured Vector Graphics

A W3C standard under development that uses an XML vocabulary TO describe easily scaled and processed vector graphics.

style sheet

A formatting description for a document. Style sheets may be stored in separate files from the documents they describe.

SVG

See Structured Vector Graphics.

Synchronized Multimedia Integration Language

A W3C recommendation providing an XML vocabulary that provides references to resources and organizes them into presentations based on both spatial and time-based layout.

tag

A component of markup used to delineate element beginnings and endings. In `<A><B />`</A>`, `<A>` is the start tag for the element A, `</A>` is the end tag for the element A, and `<B />` is an empty tag representing the element B.

tree-based model

A model for processing XML documents in which an object tree representing the document is constructed and then processed. Once the tree is built, the entire document content is available at any time. The Document Object Model (DOM) is a common tree-based document model.

TREX

Tree Regular Expressions, a schema language created by James Clark and currently hosted at OASIS-Open.

UCS-2

The standard encoding for Unicode characters, presenting the complete two-byte representation for every character.

Unicode

A standard for international character encoding. Unicode supports characters that are two bytes wide rather than the one byte currently supported by most systems, enabling it to include 65,536 characters rather than the 256 available to one-byte systems. Visit http://www.unicode.org for more information.

Uniform Resource Identifier (URI)

An identifier for a resource that may contain either a Uniform Resource Locator or a Uniform Resource Number.

Uniform Resource Locator (URL)

An identifier for a resource that provides a pathway for retrieving the resource. A complete URL identifies a protocol, a computer to contact, and the location of the resource on that computer.

Uniform Resource Number (URN)

A number that an application may resolve to refer to a resource. Because of their lack of cataloging systems, URNs have received much less use than URLs.

unparsed entity

An entity that refers to an external resource (typically a binary file). Unparsed entities are passed to the application, which may then process the entity however it likes.

URI

See Uniform Resource Identifier.

URL

See Uniform Resource Locator.

URN

See Uniform Resource Number.

UTF-8

An encoding that provides access to the Unicode character set but uses an algorithm to enable the presentation of characters with values of less than 128 in a single byte (very useful for English), while requiring two or three bytes for characters with values greater than 128.

valid

Of a document, conforming to a declared document type definition (DTD) and meeting the conditions for well-formedness. All elements, attributes, and entities must be declared in the DTD, and all data types must match their definition's requirements.

validity constraint

A rule that only validating parsers are required to enforce. Violations typically indicate that a document doesn't match up to the rules set forth in its document type definition (DTD).

VBScript

A scripting language created by Microsoft, based on its Visual Basic language. VBScript works in the Internet Explorer browser, Active Server Pages, and some other Microsoft applications.

well-formed

Of a document, beginning with an XML declaration and containing properly nested and marked-up elements. A well-formed document may or may not have a DTD.

well-formedness constraint

A rule that all XML parsers are required to enforce. If a document doesn't meet the well-formedness constraints (which lay out basic document syntax), the parser is required to stop and present the application with a fatal error.

World Wide Web Consortium (W3C)

The standards body responsible for many of the standards underlying the World Wide Web, including HTML, XML, and Cascading Style Sheets. The W3C site includes the latest public versions of its standards as well as other information about the Web and standards processes. Visit http://www.w3.org for more information.

W3C XML Schemas

The schemas project currently underway at the World Wide Web Consortium. Written in two separate documents, W3C XML Schemas defines Structures and Datatypes.

XDR

See XML-Data Reduced.

XHTML

The W3C HTML Activity's project to describe HTML as a set of XML modules.

XLink

The W3C's set of rules for establishing links among XML documents.

XML

See Extensible Markup Language.

XML-Data Reduced

A schema language proposed by Microsoft, DataChannel, and Inso, and implemented in Microsoft's Internet Explorer browsers and MSXML parsers.

XML declaration

The processing instruction at the top of an XML document. It begins with
<?xml, includes a version identifier, encoding identifier (optional) and
standalone declaration (optional), and closes with ?>. (The XML declaration is case-sensitive. Although the standard is referred to as XML, the
XML declaration must open with <?xml.)

XML-RPC

An XML standard for making Remote Procedure Calls (RPC) among
computers on a network.

XPath

A set of rules for identifying portions of XML documents used by XSLT,
XPointer, and some DOM processing. XPath itself does not use an XML
syntax, as it is intended for use in attributes.

XPointer

A reference to a fragment of a XML document. XPointers use a syntax
derived from XPath, modified to take into account the needs of the HTTP
protocol for encoding URLs. Also used to describe the W3C's set of rules
for creating XPointers.

XSchema

See DDML for the project originally called XSchema; see W3C XML
Schemas for the current W3C work on schemas.

XSL

See Extensible Style Language.

XSLT

The transformation language used by Extensible Stylesheet Language
(XSL) to convert input documents to output documents. Originally
intended to create output documents containing XSL formatting objects,
but is commonly used to generate other kinds of XML output.

Index

Continued